Confessing the Faith
Yesterday and *Today*

Confessing the Faith
Yesterday and *Today*

Essays Reformed, Dissenting, and Catholic

ALAN P. F. SELL

⌘PICKWICK *Publications* • Eugene, Oregon

CONFESSING THE FAITH YESTERDAY AND TODAY
Essays Reformed, Dissenting, and Catholic

Copyright © 2013 Alan P. F. Sell. All rights reserved. Except for brief quotations in critical publications or reviews, no part of this book may be reproduced in any manner without prior written permission from the publisher. Write: Permissions, Wipf and Stock Publishers, 199 W. 8th Ave., Suite 3, Eugene, OR 97401.

Pickwick Publications
An Imprint of Wipf and Stock Publishers
199 W. 8th Ave., Suite 3
Eugene, OR 97401

www.wipfandstock.com

ISBN 13: 978-1-62032-594-0

Cataloguing-in-Publication data:

Sell, Alan P. F.

Confessing the faith yesterday and today : essays reformed, dissenting, and catholic / Alan P. F. Sell.

xii + 306 pp. ; 23 cm. Includes bibliographical references and indexes.

ISBN 13: 978-1-62032-594-0

1. Reformed Church—Creeds. 2. Christian union—History. 3. Dissenters—Religious. I. Title.

BX8969.5 S45 2013

Manufactured in the U.S.A.

To Martin Fitzpatrick
Enlightenment scholar and enlightened man

"Belief in God as our Father, and in Christ as the Saviour of the world, is Christian faith. Whatever obscures this is leaven of the Scribes and Pharisees."

Robert Mackintosh (1858–1933)
Essays Towards a New Theology, 1889, 475.

Contents

Preface · ix

PART ONE: Confessing the Faith in Context

Introduction to Part One · 3

1. Confessing the Faith and Confessions of Faith · 5
2. Varieties of English Separatist and Dissenting Writings, 1558–1689 · 23
3. Separatists and Dissenters amidst the Arguments For and Against Toleration: Some Soundings, 1550–1689 · 51
4. Christianity, Secularism, and Toleration: Liberal Values and Illiberal Attitudes · 80
5. The Use, Abuse, and Relevance of Religion: Some Reflections upon Abraham van de Beek's Proposal · 105
6. Confessing the Faith in the Intellectual Context · 118

PART TWO: Confessing the Faith Ecclesially and Hopefully

Introduction to Part Two · 143

7. Calvin's Challenges to the Twenty-First-Century Church: Reflections on the 500th Anniversary of Calvin's Birth · 147
8. Rectifying Calvin's Ecclesiology: The Doctrinal and Ecumenical Importance of Separatist Catholicity · 176
9. Receiving from Other Christian Traditions and Overcoming the Hindrances Thereto: Some Reformed Reflections · 207

Contents

10 Eschatology: Historical Fluctuations and Perennial, Practical Importance · 233

11 Confessing the Faith in Systematic Theology? The locus and Authority of Revelation *vis à vis* Systematic Method: An Epilogue Light-hearted in Style, Serious in Intention · 268

Index of Persons · 293

Index of Subjects · 301

Preface

IN THIS BOOK ARE gathered some of the papers I have written during the past seven years. The overall theme is the confession of the Christian faith: its inspiration, content, and context. I take soundings from the past both by way of exposing some of the roots of a confession which I deem to be Reformed, Dissenting, and Catholic, and with a view to illuminating the present. The essays are arranged in two parts: Confessing the Faith in Context, and Confessing the Faith Ecclesially and Hopefully. In a few places I have updated notes and removed purely local references. Since my objectives are sufficiently explained in the Introductions to each Part, I shall here confine myself to thanking those who have granted permission to reprint papers that have already been published in widely-scattered places, and those connected with the publication of this book.

Three of the papers (chapters 7, 9, and 11) are published here in English for the first time.

Chapters 1, 5, and 6 were written at the invitation of the editor, Professor Eduardus Van der Borght for occasions and publications connected with the International Reformed Theological Institute. Chapter 1, "Confessing the Faith and Confessions of Faith," and chapter 6, "Confessing the Faith in the Intellectual Context," were first delivered at the Institute's Conference held in Seoul, South Korea, in July 2005. The former subsequently appeared among the conference papers published in *Christian Identity* (2008), the latter, in which I responded to a request to outline the position taken in my trilogy on Christian apologetic method, in *The Journal of Reformed Theology* 1.2 (2007). In November 2005, at the kind invitation of Dr. Lee Barrett, I read a version of chapter 2 at Lancaster Theological Seminary, Pennsylvania, and in the following year I lectured on the topic at a conference of Polish Reformed ministers held in Warsaw, where Pastor Roman Lipinski was his usual hospitable self. Chapter 6, on "The Use, Abuse, and Relevance of Religion" is found in

Preface

Religion Without Ulterior Motive (2006), the volume published to mark the first decade of the International Reformed Theological Institute's life, and the contribution to its nurture of Professor Abraham van de Beek. The three papers were published by Brill Academic Press, to whom I am grateful for permission to reprint them here.

Chapter 2, on "Varieties of English Separatist and Dissenting Writings," was written at the invitation of my brother, Roger D. Sell, the H. W. Donner Professor of Literary Communication at Åbo Akademie University, Finland. The memorable conference of 2006, held in that delightful city, marked the first occasion on which he and I had shared in a project. The paper was published by Ashgate in *Writing and Religion in England 1558–1689: Studies in Community-Making and Cultural Memory* (2009), edited by my brother and his colleague Anthony W. Johnson, and it appears here by kind permission of the publisher. A version of the paper was delivered at the University of Łodz in October 2009, at the invitation of Professor Jarosław Płuciennik who, with his family, entertained me most kindly.

Chapter 3, "Separatists and Dissenters Amidst the Arguments for and Against Toleration," was delivered in May 2011 at a colloquium held at Dr. Williams's Library, London, under the auspices of the Centre for Dissenting Studies, to mark the thirtieth anniversary of the journal *Enlightenment and Dissent*. The editor of the journal, Dr. Martin Fitzpatrick, has published the paper in number 28 (2012), and I thank him for his willingness to allow it a fresh lease of life here.

Chapter 4, "Christianity, Secularism, and Toleration," was originally written for a colloquium convened by Professor Nigel Biggar at Trinity College, Dublin in June 2006. The paper was presented again in May 2007, at a conference at the University of Łodz organized by Professor Płuciennik, the proceedings of which appeared first in Grzegorz Gazdam, Irena Hübner, and Jarosław Płuciennik, editors, *Literatura Kultura Tolerancja*, Karków: Universitas, 2008, and then in Andrew R. Murphy, Charles Russell, Jarosław Płuciennik, and Irena Hübner, editors, *Literature, Culture, and Tolerance*, Frankfurt am Main: Peter Lang, 2009. I am grateful for the permission of the publishers to reprint it here.

Chapter 7 represents my addition to the torrent of publications prompted by the 500th anniversary, in 2009, of Calvin's birth. I had the pleasure of delivering my paper at a conference at the University of Exeter convened by Dr. David Cornick and others; at the ecumenical Christian Theological Academy in Warsaw; and at the Reformed theological

Preface

faculties in Budapest, Sárospatak and Debrecen, with which institutions I have had most cordial relations for some thirty years. The paper was published in Polish in *Rocznik Teologiczny* 51 (2009), and in Hungarian and English in *Sárospataki Füzetek* (2010).

Chapter 8, on Calvin's ecclesiology, was written at the invitation of Dr. Gerard Mannion, and it appeared in a collection he edited with Eduardus Van der Borght, entitled, *John Calvin's Ecclesiology: Ecumenical Perspectives* (2011). The paper is reprinted by kind permission of the publisher, T. & T. Clark.

Chapter 9 was written at the request of Professor Paul Murray of the University of Durham, and an abbreviated version of it was delivered at a stimulating and well-attended conference on "Receptive Ecumenism" which was held at Ushaw College in January 2009. I am most grateful for Professor Murray's gracious invitation and generous hospitality.

I come finally to chapter 10. I was pleased to be invited by Professor Van der Borght to contribute to a *Festschrift* for Professor Abraham van de Beek. The suggestion was that I might write on eschatology, and this I did. However, so great was the clamour of scholars to be included in this volume that we were all required to limit our papers to 5,000 words. An abbreviated version of my paper thus appeared in E. Van der Borght and P. van Geest, *Strangers and Pilgrims on Earth: Essays in Honour of Abraham van de Beek*, Leiden: Brill, 2012. The full version is published here for the first time, with the blessing of Brill.

In attempting to ensure a degree of thematic coherence in a collection of papers written on different occasions one runs the risk of repetition—especially the repetition of quotations. I confess that the same words of two or three writers appear more than once in this book. Among them is a quotation from Thomas Helwys's book, *The Mistery of Iniquity*, which appears in longer or shorter form in chapters 2, 3, and 4. I hope that readers will agree that his words are of sufficient importance to bear repetition—especially in a collection of papers prepared during 2012, the year in which the quatercentenary of the publication of Helwys's book is being commemorated.

In the footnotes ODNB stands for *Oxford Dictionary of National Biography*, edited by Colin Matthew and Brian Harrison, Oxford: OUP, 2004.

Once again it has been a great pleasure to work with Dr. K. C. Hanson, Dr. Robin Parry, and their obliging and efficient colleagues at the

Preface

enterprising and ever-expanding publishing company, Wipf and Stock. My thanks to them all.

Two living Dissenters remain to be mentioned. The first is Karen, my wife, whose love and support continue unabated, and this means more to me than I can say. The second is Dr. Martin Fitzpatrick, with whom I first had contact through the *Price-Priestley Newsletter*, which he and the late D. O. Thomas founded in 1977, and which blossomed into *Enlightenment and Dissent* in 1982. Dr. Fitzpatrick is a careful and stimulating scholar of the Enlightenment, and through his university teaching and the journal he has encouraged many other scholars. Above all, he is a good friend, and I have much pleasure in dedicating this book to him.

Alan P. F. Sell
University of Wales Trinity Saint David, U.K.

PART ONE

Confessing the Faith in Context

The sum of the Gospel is that our Lord Jesus Christ, the true Son of God, has made known to us the will of His heavenly Father, and by His innocence has redeemed us from death and reconciled us to God.

ULRICH ZWINGLI (1484–1531)

Introduction to Part One

To say that the Christian faith has been communicated in a variety of contexts over the preceding two millennia is to utter a truism. But what is it to confess the faith and, more particularly, what is the status of the classical Reformed confessions? These questions are discussed in the following chapter. In chapter 2 we meet some Puritans. The Puritans, as their name implies, sought further reform of the Church and purity of worship according to the Word of God. Of those who thought that these objectives were achievable within an established Church some favoured episcopal government, others presbyterian. The more radical Puritans, however, wishing to uphold the sole Lordship of Christ over his church, could not conceive how adequate reformation could be achieved under the auspices of a state church. Accordingly, they declined to opt into, or subsequently repudiated, the Anglican Settlement. They believed that the saints should be separate from the ungodly world, and that through lack of church discipline the parish churches were tainted by that world. Named "Separatists" from their invocation of the biblical verse, "come out from among them, and be ye separate" (2 Corinthians 6: 17), they were the harbingers of the Congregational and Baptist strands of later Dissent. I shall present examples of the variety of writings which flowed from the pens of early Separatists and Dissenters as they sought to confess the faith in their severely restricted socio-political contexts

Not surprisingly, a prominent concern of the Dissenters was their plea for religious toleration under the law, and the ways in which that case was made is the subject of chapter 3. In chapter 4 we jump across the centuries and come to our own time, where we find that issues concerning toleration and tolerance are still very much alive, albeit our context is very different from that of the Separatists and early Dissenters. It is a context in which the relevance of religion is denied by many—an issue discussed in chapter 5. This scepticism regarding religion is in some cases allied to the widespread realisation that the classical arguments for the existence of God, and the alleged "evidences" of miracle and the fulfilment of prophecy can no longer serve Christian believers as once they might have done. In this context what is required is a fresh approach to Christian apologetic method—as I make bold to argue in chapter 6.

CHAPTER ONE

Confessing the Faith and Confessions of Faith

To the puzzlement (real or pretended) of some of our dialogue partners of other ecclesiastical traditions, the Reformed family has spawned not one but many confessions of faith. More than sixty such documents were devised during the sixteenth century, and the high degree of mutual consistency between them is a tribute to those theologians who energetically commuted between the Reformed centres of Europe, and corresponded with one another in Latin, the language common to scholars of the time. The Reformed are not alone in having produced numerous confessions of faith: the Baptists, for example, were not dilatory in this matter.[1] It is more than likely, however, that more such documents have emerged from Reformed circles during the past century than from any other quarter.[2]

Confessions of faith embody doctrinal propositions which their authors hold to be true. At their best they achieve clarity, and there is much to be said for this. They are, moreover, corporate affirmations; they announce the things "commonly believed among us." Again, they are, in the language of J. L. Austin, performative statements, for confessing is something that we *do*. Thus sentences beginning, "I/We believe . . ." are in the same category as sentences beginning, "I/We promise . . ." Confessions of faith also serve as doctrinal boundary-markers both explicitly, as when they counter the claims of Rome, for example, and implicitly,

---

1. See Lumpkin, *Baptist Confessions of Faith*.
2. Some of these are to be found in Vischer, *Reformed Witness Today*.

as when they do not affirm universalism or Arminianism. We might say that, like the Chalcedonian Formula of 451 with its four famous adverbs denying Arianism, docetism, and the like, confessions of faith erect doctrinal road blocks against untoward doctrines. As P. T. Forsyth observed, "There must surely be in every positive religion some point where it may so change as to lose its identity and become another religion."[3] At the same time, Forsyth elsewhere reminds us that "Revelation did not come in a statement, but in a person"; but he immediately adds, "Faith ... must be capable of statement, else it could not be spread; for it is not an ineffable, incommunicable mysticism."[4] In all of this we see both the importance of doctrinal affirmation, and are cautioned against elevating our confessional statements which, at most, are subordinate standards, above the One to whom they bear witness. If we forget that confessions of faith are subordinate we are on the way to idolatry; if we forget that they are standards, heresy may beckon.

Before proceeding further I wish to state something which is so obvious that only the most hard-line and blinkered of confessional purists would overlook it: formal confessions of faith are not the only means by which the Reformed have made, and continue to make, corporate confessional affirmations. For example, I have argued that the English Congregational branch of the Reformed family probably developed more ways of corporately confessing the faith than any other strand of that tradition.[5] In addition to their *Savoy Declaration of Faith and Order* (1658) and subsequent documents,[6] they sang their faith in the words of their pioneer hymns writers, Isaac Watts, Philip Doddridge, and others; they identified with the corporate confession when "giving in" their experience at their local Church Meeting prior to their reception as communicant members; they heard rehearsals of the orthodox faith in the personal

---

3. Forsyth, *The Principle of Authority*, 219. Forsyth (1848–1921) served five pastorates over a period of twenty-five years, and was Principal of Hackney [Congregational] College from 1901 until his death. Strongly emphasizing the centrality of the cross, he was, in my opinion, the most stimulating British theologian of the twentieth century. See further, Sell, *Testimony and* Tradition, chs. 7 and 8; Sell, *Nonconformist Theology in the Twentieth Century*.

4. Forsyth, *The Person and Place of Jesus Christ*, 15. Cf. Forsyth, *Faith, Freedom and the Future*, 239.

5. Sell, *Dissenting Thought*, ch. 1.

6. For which see Walker, *The Creeds and Platforms of Congregationalism*; Vischer, *Reformed Witness Today*, 109–61.

confessions their ministers were required to produce at ordination and induction services; and they signed the locally devised covenant.

The phrase "locally devised" reminds us that these covenants were frequently contextually influenced. For example, that of Angel Street Congregational Church, Worcester, the scene of my second pastorate, was written in 1687, and it is unusually strongly trinitarian in doctrine.[7] Why? Because already in that district some of the Presbyterian brethren were flirting with "Arianism." A moral question, rather than a doctrinal one, was of concern to the saints at the seaside town of Ramsgate. In 1767 they wished to call the Reverend David Bradberry to be their minister. He had been converted under the preaching of George Whitefield, and he said that he would accept the pastorate only if a strictly Calvinistic covenant were devised. The Church Meeting promptly set about agreeing such a statement. It comprised nine clauses, of which the first eight were Calvinistic, while the ninth, clearly contextually-inspired, denounced "the infamous practice of smuggling" as contrary to civil law and God's word. Following Bradberry's departure some years later, the Church Meeting gathered again to rescind clause nine because it had served only to encourage deception and hypocrisy![8] Again, in 1786 the villagers of Bluntisham, relying upon God's grace, covenanted, among other things, "not to countenance the works of darkness such as Adultery, Fornication, Uncleanness, Murder, Drunkenness and such like. And not to frequent public places of amusement such as Horse-racing, Playhouses, Dancing, Cardplaying, Gaming, nor to frequent Ale-houses . . ." but rather to "come out from amongst them, and have no fellowship with the unfruitful works of darkness, but reprove them."[9]

But if such local covenants were, to a greater or lesser degree, contextually-inspired and diverse as to their contents, so were more widely-owned Reformed confessions. This is precisely what we should expect, given that in the first instance confessions of faith are not texts for later students to ponder, they are acts of confessing by Christian communities in particular times and places. We hear the gospel and confess the faith where God has placed us, or not at all. But this means that confessional documents are necessarily time-bound, and this can raise problems for

---

7. See Noake, *Worcester* Sects, 111–14.
8. See Hurd, *These Three Hundred Years*, 4.
9. See Dixon, *A Century of Village Nonconformity*, 157.

PART ONE: Confessing the Faith in Context

subsequent confessors.[10] There are the related issues of method, content and use. I shall examine each of these in turn.

I

As to method, we may reflect upon the starting-points of a selection of Reformed confessions. Thus, for example, the authors of the *First Confession of Basel* (1534) set out from a strong statement of belief in the Holy Trinity, as do *The Confession of the English Congregation in Geneva* (1556) and the *Scots Confession* (1560). By contrast, the *Second Basel Confession*, published in 1536, only two years after the first, begins with Holy Scripture and, when it finally comes, in its sixth clause, to God, it omits reference to the Holy Spirit. The *Geneva Confession* (1536) opens with a brief paragraph on the Bible, proceeds to God as our only Saviour, comes in paragraphs six and seven to Jesus, and in paragraph eight to the Holy Spirit as regenerator (only). All of which is to say that there is not a strong trinitarian claim here; rather, the trinitarian position is reached by a process of induction. The *French Confession* (1559) opens with a list of God's communicable and incommunicable attributes, but there follow four further paragraphs before we reach the Trinity, and a similar pattern is adopted in the *Belgic Confession* (1561, revised 1619). The *Second Helvetic Confession* (1566) does not begin from God as such, but from a confession of belief in the Scriptures as his Word, and comes to the Trinity in chapter three.[11] This procedure is followed in the *Westminster Confession* (1647) in which, as I have elsewhere pointed out,[12] we have to wait for the eight lines on the triune God until we have waded through ten paragraphs on the Bible, including a list of all the biblical books, and two paragraphs on the attributes of God. Clearly, the methods adopted by the authors of a number of classical Reformed confessions were influenced by medieval discussions of the divine attributes and/or by their Reformation context in which the openness to God's authoritative Word took precedence over any ecclesiastical authoritarianisms.

---

10. See further Sell, *Aspects of Christian Integrity*, 88–92; Sell, *Confessing and Commending the Faith*, 27–29.

11. For the confessions so far mentioned in this paragraph see Cochrane. *Reformed Confessions*.

12. Sell, *Enlightenment, Ecumenism,* Evangel, 163–64. This *Confession* has been reprinted numerous times.

Confessing the Faith and Confessions of Faith

We may nevertheless ask whether we should necessarily remain content with a pattern in which scholastic lists of attributes, or convictions concerning the Book precede convictions concerning the triune God's grace. The underlying issue is the degree to which the classical confessions are intended as testimonies of faith (*fiducia*) or as mini-systematic treatises to which we are invited to give assent (*assensus*). Are they to be construed experimentally or cerebrally? It seems to be the case that some at least of the documents referred to have mixed objectives. I shall return to this point in due course. In the meantime, I would simply note with Forsyth that "The Bible . . . never demands faith in itself as a preliminary of faith in Christ,"[13] and that "The triune God . . . is what makes Christianity Christian."[14]

Turning now to later Reformed confessions we find even greater methodological variety. The *Articles of Faith of the Presbyterian Church of England* (1890)[15] set out from the triune God and deal with the Bible in the nineteenth of twenty-four paragraphs. The Presbyterian Church of Canada's confession (1984)[16] likewise opens in a strongly trinitarian way, as do those of the United Church of Christ (1959)[17] and the Cumberland and Second Cumberland Presbyterian Churches.[18] On the other hand, the creed of the United Church of Canada (1968, revised 1980) begins and ends with the anthropocentric assertion that "We are not alone . . ."[19] Can this be a product of a tendency in an affluent society towards "feel-good" religion? Be that as it may, Forsyth's cautionary words merit attention: "[A] creed which starts from the glory of God has more power for man's welfare than one that is founded on the welfare of man alone."[20]

Before leaving the question of method, the hermeneutics of those who devised the classical confessions must be noted. I have already said

---

13. Forsyth, "Revelation and the person of Christ," in *Faith and Criticism*, 135.

14. Forsyth, *Faith, Freedom and the Future*, 263.

15. The Presbyterian Church of England was constituted in 1876 on the union of the Presbyterian Church *in* England (1842), which included Church of Scotland immigrants and the remnant of old English Presbyterianism which had not gone Congregationalist or Unitarian by the end of the eighteenth century, with the English Synod of the United Presbyterian Church of Scotland (1863).

16. Anon., *Living Faith*.

17. Vischer, *Reformed Witness Today*, 197–218.

18. Anon., *Confession of Faith and Government*.

19. *Reformed Witness Today*, 193–96.

20. Forsyth, *The Justification of God*, 83.

that their appeal was to Scripture as authoritative, but we must also take account of the fact that the authors were working on the far side of modern biblical criticism from ourselves. They made assumptions about the content, dating and authorship of the biblical books that we no longer can; and they did not balk at proof-texting in a way which has become impossible for us. For them, the Bible replaced the ecclesiastical apparatus of Rome, but in their hands it was a quarry to be plundered in order to devise doctrinal systems deemed orthodox, in which the glue was supplied by the Aristotelian logic in which they had been schooled. I do not say that they could have done anything else as children of their times, but I do not think that we can approach the Bible in exactly the way they did.

Robert Mackintosh, the self-styled "refugee" from the high Calvinism of the Free Church of Scotland, who found a home in the broader streams of Congregationalism, published a provocative tract in 1889 entitled, *The Obsoleteness of the Westminster Confession of Faith*. In this he teased the Westminster authors for the way in which they had responded to Parliament's request that they add biblical proof texts following the completion of their text. With characteristic irony he writes,

> That an oath cannot oblige to sin is proved by the example (?) of David in his relations with Nabal and Abigail. The "contingency of second causes" is proved by a man "drawing a bow at a venture", or by the occurrence of a fatal accident when an axehead "lights" on a bystander. Difficult questions on the doctrine of Providence are settled by the story of David and the men of Keilah. Finally—and I specially recommend this to the admirers of the Establishment principle—the proof that the civil magistrate may lawfully summon religious synods is found in the fact that Herod consulted the chief priests in order to plot more successfully how to murder the infant Jesus. Comment on these citations could be nothing but a feeble anti-climax. Let us treasure them up in our hearts.[21]

II

I turn next to the problems raised by the content of earlier confessional statements. It would be surprising, given the church's obligation to confess the faith afresh in every age, if we could simply regurgitate the

---

21. R. Mackintosh, *The Obsoleteness of the Westminster Confession*, 48.

contextually-influenced confessions of the past. On the one hand, some of them anathematize the Anabaptists and brand the Pope Antichrist, and we need no longer indulge in such obsolete polemics. Again, we may with some justification feel that church practice, family life, and moral duties, to which the *Second Helvetic Confession* devotes considerable attention, properly belong to the category of ecclesiastical advice and moral guidance, and that when placed in a confession such matters yield overload. This practice also seems to elevate polity and ethics as then understood to the same level as the major doctrinal testimonies. More seriously, it can be argued that in the *Westminster Confession* God's eternal decrees take precedence over his grace.[22] In these ways and others we can see how questions arise for subsequent confessors by what their forebears wrote.

But questions arise equally because of what they omitted. While we can readily understand why they made so much of justification by grace through faith, their affirmations concerning creation, for example, are minimal. For my part, I should be hard put to understand a Reformed church that was drafting a confessional statement today which did not include a substantial paragraph on creation. Quite apart from the Bible's witness on the matter, with ecologists all around us we cannot be unaware of the seriousness of the challenges regarding our stewardship of the created order. Again, in face of the poor, the needy and the oppressed we today are bound to heed the call for justice; and when we ponder the life and death issues of abortion, euthanasia and genetic engineering, we should, surely wish to say more in doctrinal terms than our forebears did about the sanctity of human life and the *imago dei*, whilst refraining from delving into the intricacies of Christian social ethics. In a word, classical confessions can provoke unease both by what they say and by what they fail to say.

This point was fully appreciated by Forsyth: "The life is in the body, not in the system. It must be a dogma, revisible from time to time to keep pace with the Church's growth as a living body in a living world."[23] Hence, for example, the nineteenth-century debates in Scotland over God's universal love *vis à vis* election and predestination, which yielded the Declaratory Acts of the United Presbyterians in 1879 and the Free Church in 1892, which bodies united in 1900; these Acts in turn flowed into the Church of Scotland at the union of that Church with the United

---

22. See, for example, J. B. Torrance, "Strengths and Weaknesses of the Westminster Theology," 46.

23. Forsyth, *The Person and Place of Jesus Christ*, 213.

PART ONE: Confessing the Faith in Context

Free Church in 1929. The Acts permitted liberty of opinion on matters that did not concern "the substance of the faith," though, whether in a mood of political realism or godly amnesia, they did not stay to define that substance.[24] Clearly, conscientious difficulties with the content of confessional documents raises the question of their status and the use to which they are put. To this issue I now turn.

III

Confessional documents have been, and are, used in a variety of ways within the Reformed family. On the one hand, we find Fred H. Klooster of the Christian Reformed Church upholding "the binding character of confessions", and endorsing the Formula of Subscription of his Church.[25] Over against this position is that of the Congregationalist strand of the Reformed family, to whom the formal act of confessional subscription is anathema. It is important to understand that this stance is not adopted on grounds of doctrinal laxity but, once again, as a faithful response in a particular socio-political context in England. My forebears, in peril of their lives, refused to subscribe to the words of men, especially when those words were legally enforced by governmental authorities bent on securing ecclesiastical comprehension as an aid to national cohesion in face of enemies. They upheld the church's right and duty to submit to the Word of God alone; hence the martyrs of 1593 and surrounding dates.[26] They also had a profound sense of the continuing guidance of the Holy Spirit, and felt that to elevate, or fossilize, a specific form of words might in time constrain their response to the Spirit's contemporary address to them through the Word—the very reason for the Scottish Declaratory Acts to which I referred. As I have already indicated, none of this prevented the Congregationalists from confessing the faith in a variety of ways, not least in declarations of faith. Indeed, they participated in the Westminster Assembly, and the doctrinal sections of their *Savoy Declaration of Faith and Order* (1658) largely follows *Westminster*. Such documents were regarded by the Congregationalists not as tests of faith but as acts of confessing, as constituting testimony, not as having the binding force of law.[27]

24. See further Ross, "The Union of 1900."
25. See Klooster, "Theology, Confession and the Church."
26. See further Sell, Commemorations, ch. 4.
27. See further Sell, *Dissenting Thought*, 57–58; Nuttall, *Congregationalists and Creeds*.

Where confessional documents are elevated into tests of faith or criteria of church membership, a number of undesirable consequences can follow. First, we may subtly substitute cerebralism for faith, *assensus* for *fiducia*. It should never be forgotten that "Christianity spread not as a religion of truth, but of power, help, healing, resurrection, redemption."[28] We may feel that Forsyth here overstates his point, for the apostles had no doubt that Jesus Christ was the way, the truth and the life. But his point is that the apostles did not turn Christianity into a matter of a check-list of doctrines to be subscribed to. The emphasis of their activity was in the experimental direction. To them Jesus was Saviour before he was teacher; he had done something redemptive, not simply peddled teachings: "Christ did not come chiefly to teach truth, but to bring the reality and power of eternal life."[29] After all, "We do not review God's claims and then admit Him as we are satisfied."[30] None of this is to deny that a Church may well wish to affirm more than the individual church member feels able to do, but the latter, sincerely believing in Jesus as Lord and Saviour, is not to be excommunicated because some doctrines—the pre-existence of Christ, for example—are beyond his or her grasp at present. As John Owen wisely wrote in the Preface to the *Savoy Declaration*,

> The *Spirit of Christ* is in himself too *free*, great and generous a Spirit, to suffer himself to be used by any humane arm, to whip men into belief; he drives not, but *gently leads into all truth*, and *persuades* men to *dwell in the tents* of like precious Faith; which would lose its preciousness and value, if that sparkle of freeness shone not in it.[31]

Furthermore,

> A Christian church is not a private society, whose regulations can be modified by its members at their pleasure, but a society founded by Christ Himself. . . . Nothing, therefore, should be required of any applicant for membership but personal faith in Christ. . . . Men come into the Christian church not because they have already mastered the contents of the Christian revelation, but to be taught them. . . . [E]rror and ignorance which do not

---

28. Forsyth, *Missions in State and Church*, 11.
29. Forsyth, "Unity and theology," 74.
30. Forsyth, *The Principle of Authority*, 146; cf. Forsyth, "Revelation and the Person of Christ," 109.
31. Matthews, *The Savoy Declaration*, 53.

separate a man from Christ should not separate him from the church.[32]

Secondly, the use of confessions as tests of faith may foster the myth of the saving *system*. At their best the drafters of the classical confessions knew that people are saved by grace, not by doctrinal systems. The authors of the *Scots Confession* fully understood that their work was liable to imperfection and was hence revisable:

> [I]f any man will note in our Confession any chapter or sentence contrary to God's Holy Word, that it would please him of his gentleness and for Christian charity's sake to inform us of it in writing; and we, upon our honour, do promise him that by God's grace we shall give him satisfaction from the mouth of God, that is, from Holy Scripture, or else we shall alter whatever he can prove to be wrong.[33]

There is no confessional "fundamentalism" here. Over against the idea of the saving system, "the sole content of Revelation, the power and gift in it, is the love, will, presence and purpose of God for our redemption."[34]

Thirdly, the elevation of system plays into the hands of ecclesiastical agents of a controlling disposition, who may be inclined to, and may actually, brandish the system over the heads of those whom they suspect of being what our present-day politicians call "off message." Even the Congregationalists, who should have known better, fell into this trap from time to time, as when the Puritan John Goodwin was cut off because of his Arminianism. The Church is a fellowship of believers, called by grace, before it is a corporation bound by trust deeds. James Moffatt once noted that the idea of the Church as "the company of those who uphold and profess saving doctrine" first appears in the Socinian Racovian Catechism of 1604.[35] By contrast the Congregational scholar, F. J. Powicke, declared that

> [I]f the constitutive principle of a church, what makes it a church, what forms it and holds it together, is the abiding presence in and among its members of a living Spirit, whose holy task is so to inspire the love of truth and so to cleanse the inner eye as that knowledge of Christ and the things of Christ shall

32. Dale, *A Manual of Congregational Principles*. 186, 187.
33. Cochrane, *Reformed Confessions*, 165.
34. Forsyth, "Revelation and the person of Christ," 102.
35. So Nuttall, *Congregationalists and Creeds*, 10–11.

be growing perpetually clearer and fuller, then for a church to fancy it even possible that the sum of Christian truth has been compressed into the phrases of an ancient creed, or that its present apprehension and statement of the truth can be more than partial, is self-destructive and even sin against the Holy Ghost.[36]

It cannot, however, be denied that the Reformed have sometimes found it hard to hold themselves to this high ideal. Descents into confessional legalism are not unknown in our history,[37] as if there were saving truths in the sense of truths which save. To hold this is to dethrone Christ. Hence the protests of the Arian Presbyterian divines of the eighteenth century, who charged their orthodox brethren with "Protestant popery" because of their elevation of confessional standards into tests of faith at the expense, as they thought, of the clear teaching of Scripture. To take but one of many examples, Samuel Bourn (1689–1754) declared that to impose a trinitarian test was "to give up *Scripture-sufficiency*, it is to return back into the Tenets of Popery. . . . If we pay that Regard to any Body of men, tho' the most learned Assembly in the World, which is due to *Christ* only; we make a *Christ* of these Men; they are our Rabbi."[38]

Fourthly, sectarianism is the offspring of authoritarian, legalistic ecclesiasticism, and our Reformed family is replete with examples of it. If over the past eighty years it is possible that we have entered into more transconfessional unions than any other tradition, we can almost certainly outdo everyone else in the number of inner-family secessions we have spawned through the centuries. Quite frequently, though not always, these have resulted from the flexing of confessional muscles in unduly rigorist ways. Confessions have been used to justify withdrawal from the faithful rather than to confess the faith.

Underlying the four points just made is a fifth: the Reformed have sometimes managed to persuade themselves that confessional documents guard the faith (rather in the way that bishops—though presumably not

---

36. Powicke, "Historic Congregationalism in Britain," 268. See further, Sell, *Saints: Visible, Orderly and Catholic*.

37. I do not imply that confessional documents alone have on occasion been abused in such a way as to threaten the gospel. Forsyth declared that the gospel's "three great products—the Church, the Ministry, the Bible—have all threatened its life at some time and in some way." See *The Church, The Gospel and Society*, 89.

38. Bourn, *The True Christian Way*, 23. At his ordination Bourn refused to assent to the *Westminster Confession*, for which reason some Presbyterian ministers boycotted the occasion. See further Sell. *Dissenting Thought*, ch. 7; Sell, *Enlightenment, Ecumenism, Evangel*, ch. 3.

heretical ones—are said to do in some other Christian communions). But the Reformed should think more that twice before subscribing to this view, for our own history bears witness to the fact that notwithstanding the *Westminster Confession*, the majority of old English Presbyterians who did not become Congregationalist during the eighteenth century, became Unitarian by the end of that century or early in the next.[39] This clearly demonstrates that confessions of faith can but witness to the faith if it is there. They do not create it, and it would be a usurpation of the role of God the Holy Spirit, *the* guardian of the faith, to suppose that were particular confessions to fall the gospel would fall with them. Hence the Puritan Thomas Goodwin's words, "If Christian judgments be well and thoroughly grounded in the doctrine of God's free grace and eternal love and redemption through Jesus Christ alone, and in the most spiritual inward operations of God's Spirit, that will fence them against all errors."[40]

Standing staunchly in this line, my late college principal, Gordon Robinson, wrote,

> [A] genuine trust in the operation of the Holy Spirit, held humbly, prayerfully and expectantly by ministers and people in their private devotion and in their gathering at worship and in the Church Meeting is not only our ultimate safeguard in matters of faith. Even to call it a safeguard is to speak on too mean a level. It is of the essence of our existence.[41]

Herein lies a caution against any confessional antiquarianism which would take our eye off our supreme task of discerning the mind of Christ by the Spirit in the here and now. However inconvenient it may sometimes be for professional ecclesiastics, God's gift of the Spirit, addressing his people through the Word may be found "quite as much with the intellectual babes whom the wise and prudent of John Robinson's day nicknamed Symon the Sadler, Tomkin the Taylor, Billy the Bellows-mender, as with the wise and prudent themselves."[42] Nor should we forget the biblical rebuke addressed to those who mouthed all the right things—"the temple of the Lord, the temple of the Lord"[43]—and failed to realize that their actual practice completely undermined their verbal confession.

---

39. For this complicated story see Sell, *Dissenting Thought*, ch. 5.
40. Quoted by Forsyth in *Faith, Freedom and the Future*, 119.
41. W. G. Robinson, "Congregationalism and the historic Faith," 213.
42. Powicke, "The Congregational Churches," 118.
43. Jeremiah 7:4.

IV

The upshot is that none of our confessional documents can be the guarantor of our identity as Reformed, still less as Christians. A free-wheeling, free-thinking liberalism is not, however, the only alternative to the undue elevation of such statements. Against all who thought it was, Forsyth thundered, "Too many are occupied in throwing over precious cargo; they are lightening the ship even of its fuel."[44] But if hard-line confessionalism and free-wheeling liberalism will not suffice, what does constitute our identity and hold us in fellowship with Christians through the ages?

In my opinion, the only possible answer to that question, is, "The grace of God in the gospel." By God's grace we are granted forgiveness and new life, given our new identity as adopted sons or daughters in Christ, and engrafted into the fellowship of the Church as branches of the Vine. In other words, our final authority is not our little accounts of what the mighty God has done, but God's saving act at the cross. While the Incarnation of Jesus Christ is temporally prior to Calvary, and while his person is logically prior to his work, for he cannot do what he does unless he is who he is, it is at the cross, not in the cradle, that the saving act is accomplished.[45] "It is from the experience of Christ's salvation", insisted Forsyth, "that the Church proceeds to the interpretation of the Saviour's person."[46] This was the historical order: this is what Jesus Christ has done; then who must he be? As Forsyth more fully explained:

> Christ came not to *say* something, but to *do* something. His revelation was action more than instruction. . . . The thing He did was not simply to make us aware of God's disposition in an impressive way. It was not to *declare* forgiveness. And it was

---

44. Forsyth, *The Principle of Authority*, 261.

45. Forsyth never ceased to insist upon this point. It is at the very heart of his teaching. See, for further examples, *The Justification of God*, 89–90; *The Church, The Gospel and Society*, 120; *The Cruciality of the Cross*, 39, 50 n.; *Positive Preaching and the Modern Mind*, 216; *The Person and Place of Jesus Christ*, 10; *God the Holy Father*, 40, 41. He deeply regretted that the Church's early "ecumenical symbols not only do not start from the real source of authority in Christianity, but scarcely allude to it. I mean, of course, redeeming grace. . . . There is far too much said, even among ourselves, about the creeds and their simplicity and the way they keep to the Christian facts. Yes, and all but ignore the one fact on which Christianity rests—the fact of redemption by grace alone through faith." See *The Church, The Gospel and Society*, 124. For further expositon of the idea that "the rationale of the incarnation is in the atonement," see Denney, *The Christian Doctrine of Reconciliation*, 65; Sell *Aspects of Christian Integrity*, ch. 2.

46. Forsyth, *The Person and Place of Jesus Christ*, 332.

not even to *bestow* forgiveness. It was certainly not to *explain* forgiveness. It was to *effect* forgiveness, to set up the relation of forgiveness both in God and man.[47]

To God's saving deed the Bible actually bears witness. The compilers of the United Presbyterian Church in the U.S.A.'s *Confession of 1967* rightly declared that "The Bible is to be interpreted in the light of its witness to God's work of reconciliation in Christ."[48] Our confessional documents inadequately testify to the same thing; and the consciences of the Lord's individual saints, his adopted sons and daughters, concur as they are enabled by the Holy Spirit. "In a word," wrote Forsyth, "that is over the Bible which is over the Church and the Creeds. It is the Gospel of Grace, which produced Bible, Creed and Church alike."[49] Zwingli said it much earlier: "The sum of the Gospel is that our Lord Jesus Christ, the true Son of God, has made known to us the will of His heavenly Father, and by his innocence has redeemed us from death and reconciled us to God."[50]

In view of this, it seems to me that the ideal Reformed confession of faith would set out from an assertion of the good news that by the victory of the cross God the Father's holiness is satisfied, Christ the Son's Saviourhood confirmed, and God the Holy Spirit's work of engrafting believers into the Church as branches of the Vine is under way, and will continue until he come. Such an assertion sets out from God's saving act; it is deliberately couched in trinitarian terms; it includes an ecclesiological element over against any individualism whether "evangelical" or "liberal"; and the reference to the Spirit's continuing work covers the eschatological dimension. Such a confession stimulates the brain; but above all it stands as the joyous testimony of the heart on the part of those who have been saved by grace through faith. The first paragraph of the 1967 *Confession* of the United Presbyterian Church U.S.A. comes as close as any such document to what I have in mind:

---

47. Forsyth, *God the Holy Father*, 19.
48. *Reformed Witness Today*, 210.
49. Forsyth, *The Church, The Gospel and Society*, 67. Cf. Forsyth, *The Principle of Authority*, 53. Interestingly, the Baptist Union Declaration of Principle of 1904 reads, "The basis of this Union is that our Lord and Saviour Jesus Christ, God manifest in the flesh, is the sole and absolute authority in all matters pertaining to faith and practice as revealed in the Holy Scriptures . . ." Quoted by Hayden, "The Particular Baptist Confession," 407.
50. *Zwingli's Sixty-Seven Articles of* 1523. In Cochrane, editor, *Reformed* Confessions, 36.

> In Jesus Christ God was reconciling the world to himself. Jesus Christ is God with man. He is the eternal Son of the Father, who became man and lived among us to fulfill the work of reconciliation. He is present in the church by the power of the Holy Spirit to continue and complete his mission. This work of God, the Father, Son and Holy Spirit, is the foundation of all confessional statements about God, man, and the world. Therefore the church calls men to be reconciled to God and to one another.

No doubt any Reformed church would wish to say more than this. My concern is that they do not say less. Such a primary confession can be filled out in many ways for purposes of exposition, teaching and the like. It can have polity clauses appended and ethical guidance attached. But no confessional document, however long, will be adequate if it is not rooted in the primary testimony to God's good news.

V

The implications of such a starting-point are manifold. The first is that the truth is underscored that the Church is God's creation by the Holy Spirit on the ground of the Son's finished work. It is not a human invention. Secondly, the ecumenical point follows that any doctrine or practice which would exclude those called by grace from fellowship at the Lord's table is inherently sectarian, and a denial of the Spirit's work.[51] For "The unity of the Church rests on the evangelical succession and not on the canonical . . . which ties up the Church more than it unites it."[52] Thirdly, this primary act of confessing has implications for our worship. It stands as a corrective to any anthropocentric coddling of the saints; it does not permit a subjective, sentimental, wallowing in God's love, because it understands that "Faith . . . is more concerned with the nature of the object than with the mood of the subject,"[53] that God's love is holy love, and that "love is not holy without judgment."[54] Centring as it does in the cross, it forbids the kind of incarnationalism which becomes indistinguishable from benign, ahistorical, immanentist process.[55] Above all, it encourages

---

51. See further Sell, *Enlightenment, Ecumenism, Evangel*, ch. 11.

52. Forsyth, "Unity and theology," 77. Cf. Forsyth, *Congregationalism and Reunion*, 21–22.

53. Ibid., 60.

54. Forsyth, *The Work of Christ*, 84.

55. See further Sell, *Philosophical Idealism and Christian Belief*, ch. 5; Sell, *Confessing and Commending the Faith*, ch. 5.

heartfelt rejoicing in God's *act* of redeeming grace, apart from which we should have no forgiveness, no new life in Christ, no identity in him, no communion of saints. Such a confession will revive our preaching, for we shall not merit the stricture which Forsyth levelled against some of the preaching of his day: "It wrestles with many problems between man and man, class and class, nation and nation; but it does not face the moral problem between the guilty soul and God."[56] Neither shall we fall for precisely the kind of crowd-pulling antics which Jesus steadfastly repudiated during his temptations in the wilderness: "[W]e must not empty the Gospel in order quickly to fill the Church."[57] Rather, our outreach will be informed by the manner of him who is the good news, and our ethics will be motivated by gratitude for all that God has done for us and for the world.

But some would raise the question, "Can we any longer confess in the terms presented above?" I have heard some theologians say that we could not nowadays write an account of the things commonly agreed among us because we do not share enough of a common language. There are those who do not wish to use Fatherhood language of God; there are those who wish to substitute functional terms for trinitarian persons;[58] and within the Reformed family worldwide there is a wide diversity of belief. In such a situation the only recourse, I believe, is to return to the cross, which puts all our ideologies and sectarianisms in perspective, and gives us a gospel that it should be our greatest joy to proclaim. Has God saved? Has God brought us into his one Church? If we own a common Saviour we shall think more than twice before unchurching one another over differences of linguistic expression. "I am sure", wrote Forsyth, "that, if we had a theology brought entirely up to date in regard to current thought, we should not then have the great condition for the kingdom of God. It is the wills of men, and not their views, that are the great obstacle to the Gospel, and the things most intractable."[59] Hence the cross. Thence the gospel.

---

56. Forsyth, *The Person and Place of Jesus Christ*, 24. Cf. Forsyth, *Positive Preaching and the Modern Mind*, 5, 89: "We must all preach *to* our age, but woe to us if it is our age we preach, and only hold up the mirror to the time. . . . We must, of course, go some way to meet the world, but when we do meet we must do more than greet."

57. Forsyth, *Theology in Church and State*, 25.

58. See further Sell, *Enlightenment, Ecumenism, Evangel*, 365–75.

59. Forsyth, *Positive Preaching and the Modern Mind*, 197.

BIBLIOGRAPHY

Anon. *Articles of Faith of the Presbyterian Church of England.* London, 1890.
———. *Confession of Faith and Government.* Memphis: Frontier, 1984.
———. *Living Faith: A Statement of Christian Belief.* Winfield, BC: Wood Lake, 1984.
———. *The Subordinate Standards of the Free Church of Scotland.* Edinburgh: Free Church of Scotland, 1933.
Bourn, Samuel. *The True Christian Way of Striving for the Faith of the Gospel.* London, 1738.
Cochrane, Arthur C. *Reformed Confessions of the 16th Century.* Philadelphia: Westminster, 1966.
Denney, James. *The Christian Doctrine of Reconciliation.* London: Hodder and Stoughton, 1917.
Dale, R. W. *A Manual of Congregational Principles.* London: Hodder and Stoughton, 1884.
Dixon, R. W. *A Century of Village Nonconformity . . . 1787 to 1887.* London: Samuel Harris, 1887.
Forsyth, P. T. *The Church, the Gospel and Society.* London: Independent, 1962.
———. *Congregationalism and Reunion.* London: Independent, 1952.
———. *The Cruciality of the Cross.* 1909. Reprint. London: Independent, 1948.
———. *Faith, Freedom and the Future.* 1912. Reprint. London: Independent, 1955.
———. *God the Holy Father.* London: Independent, 1957.
———. *The Justification of God: Lectures for War-time on a Christian Theodicy.* 1917. Reprint. London: Independent, 1957.
———. *Missions in State and Church: Sermons and Addresses.* London: Hodder and Stoughton, 1908.
———. *The Person and Place of Jesus Christ.* 1909. Reprint. London: Independent, 1961.
———. *Positive Preaching and the Modern Mind.* 1907. Reprint. London: Independent, 1949.
———. *The Principle of Authority in Relation to Certainty, Sancity and Society.* 1913. Reprint. London: Independent, 1952.
———. "Revelation and the Person of Christ." In *Faith and Criticism: Essays by Congregationalists.* London: Sampson, Low Marston, 1893.
———. *Theology in Church and State.* London: Hodder and Stoughton, 1915.
———. "Unity and Theology." In *Towards Reunion: Being Contributions to Mutual Understanding by Church of England and Free Church Writers,* 51–81. London: Macmillan, 1919.
———. *The Work of Christ.* 1910. Reprint. London: Independent, 1938.
Hayden, Roger. "The Particular Baptist Confession of 1689 and Baptists Today." *The Baptist Quarterly* 32 (1988) 403–19.
Hurd, Alan G. *These Three Hundred Years: The Story of Ramsgate Congregational Church, 1662–1962.* Ramsgate: n.p., 1962.
Klooster, F. H. "Theology, Confession and the Church." In *Church and Theology in the Contemporary World,* 28–33. Grand Rapids: Reformed Ecumenical Synod, 1977.
Lumpkin, William L. *Baptist Confessions of Faith.* 2nd rev. ed. Valley Forge, PA: Judson, 1969. (3rd expanded ed., edited by Bill J. Leonard, 2011.)

PART ONE: Confessing the Faith in Context

Mackintosh, Robert. *The Obsoleteness of the Westminster Confession of Faith*, bound with his *Essays Towards a New Theology*. Glasgow: Maclehose, 1889.

Matthews, A. G. *The Savoy Declaration of Faith and Order*. London: Independent, 1959.

Noake, John. *Worcester Sects; or A History of the Roman Catholics & Dissenters of Worcester*. London: Longman, 1861.

Nuttall, Geoffrey F. *Congregationalists and Creeds*. London: Epworth, 1966.

Powicke, F. J. "The Congregational Churches." In *Evangelical Christianity: Its History and Witness*, edited by W. B. Selbie, 81–130. London: Hodder and Stoughton, 1911.

———. "Historic Congregationalism in Britain." In *Proceedings of the Third International Congregational Council*, 260–69. London: Congregational Union of England and Wales, 1908.

Robinson, W. Gordon. "Congregationalism and the Historic Faith." *The Congregational Quarterly* 29 (1951) 202–13.

Ross, Kenneth R. "The Union of 1900 and the Relation of Church and Creed in Scotland. *Scottish Church History Records* 23 (1988) 241–53.

Sell, Alan P. F. *Aspects of Christian Integrity* (1990). Eugene, OR: Wipf & Stock, 1998.

———. *Commemorations: Studies in Christian Thought and History*. 1993. Reprint. Eugene, OR: Wipf & Stock, 1998.

———. *Confessing and Commending the Faith: Historic Witness and Apologetic Method*. 2002. Reprint. Eugene, OR: Wipf & Stock, 2006.

———. *Dissenting Thought and the Life of the Churches: Studies in an English Tradition*. Lewiston, NY: Mellen, 1990.

———. *Enlightenment, Ecumenism, Evangel: Theological Themes and Thinkers 1550–2000*. Carlisle, UK: Paternoster, 2005.

———. *Nonconformist Theology in the Twentieth Century*. Milton Keynes, UK: Paternoster, 2006. Reprint. Eugene, OR: Wipf & Stock, 2012.

———. *Philosophical Idealism and Christian Belief*. 1995. Reprint. Eugene, OR: Wipf & Stock, 2006.

———. *Saints: Visible, Orderly and Catholic: The Congregational Idea of the Church*. Allison Park, PA: Pickwick, 1986.

———. *Testimony and Tradition: Studies in Reformed and Dissenting Thought*. Aldershot, UK: Ashgate, 2005.

Torrance, James B. "Strengths and Weaknesses of the Westminster Theology." In *The Westminster Confession in the Church Today*, edited by Alasdair I. C. Heron. , 40–54. Edinburgh: Saint Andrew, 1982.

Vischer, Lukas. *Reformed Witness Today: A Collection of Confessions and Statements of Faith issued by Reformed Churches*. Bern: Evangelische Arbeitsstelle Oekumene Schweiz, 1982.

Walker, Williston. *The Creeds and Platforms of Congregationalism*. 1893. Reprint. Boston: Pilgrim, 1960.

CHAPTER TWO

Varieties of English Separatist and Dissenting Writings, 1558–1689

THIS CONFERENCE PAPER IS contributed by a theological-*cum*-philosophical lamb who finds himself surrounded by literary wolves. I am concerned with what all can agree are writings, but I shall not presume to annex the literary scholar's hobby of arguing over whether any or all of them constitute "literature." Turning from lambs and wolves to rabbits, I invoke the old adage and say that where the communication of theological ideas designed to encourage and nurture Christian communities is concerned, there is more than one way to skin a rabbit. This is what I shall hope to demonstrate by reference to the considerable variety of types of writing produced by English Separatists and Dissenters between 1558 and the Toleration Act of 1689.

Were I attempting this task in the company of a certain type of social historian, I should risk rough handling; for their statistical methods, though valuable as aids to understanding the context of thought and action, can never adequately accommodate things spiritual, and these were what sustained the clandestine and sometimes persecuted groups with whom we are here concerned. The law, the force of numbers, the Established Church—all of these were against them. Deprived of that freedom of worship which we nowadays take for granted, what they had were their pens. I agree with Neil Keeble that "communication and writing were essential to the continuance of nonconformity."[1] The Separatists

---

1. Keeble, *The Literary Culture*, 82.

PART ONE: Confessing the Faith in Context

and Dissenters wrote in order to sustain their fellowships, to rebuke their intellectual foes, to express their faith and, above all, to propagate the gospel.[2] Since community-making is a prominent theme of this consultation, I shall concentrate upon writings which were available during the period under review—a point to which I shall return in my conclusion.

I

The 140 years during which the writings to be considered were produced may be divided into four periods. In the first, from the 1550s to the end of the sixteenth century, we are concerned predominantly with the Separatists. These comprised the radical wing of Puritanism. To them it was not enough to have broken with Rome and to have modified the liturgy. Scripture, they were convinced, made it incumbent upon Christians to press for a more "root and branch" reformation which would make it clear that Christ alone is Head of the Church (not Christ plus the monarch/Parliament), and that the Church comprises the saints—those called by grace (not the entire population of the land). To them this entailed separation from the Church "by law established." In the same period we meet the Puritan Thomas Cartwright (1535–1603), the most important advocate of a religious establishment on presbyterian, rather than episcopalian, lines.

The second period may be dated from King James I's remark of 1604, directed against the Separatists: "let them conform themselves and that shortly, or they shall hear of it."[3] By 1604 a number of Separatist works had been published in Holland and smuggled into England; by 1605 a community of exiled Separatists was already forming in the Netherlands. Such were the constraints upon those who remained in England that we know of only two Separatist congregations in London which maintained a continuous existence from 1600 to 1640. By the latter date exiles who had not gone to the New World as Pilgrims in 1620, were returning home in anticipation of political change.

The third period, 1640–60, covers the Civil War, the killing of Charles I in 1649, and the Cromwellian Protectorate, during which those of an orthodox Dissenting type enjoyed a liberty previously denied to

---

2. In addition to their pens, the Separatists and Dissenters had their publishers; see Keeble, *The Literary Culture*, chs. 2–4; Ian Green, *Print and Protestantism*.
3. Barlow, *The Summe and Substance*, 102.

them, but found it necessary to distinguish themselves from a variety of Commonwealth sectaries ranging from Seekers quietly awaiting a word from the Lord to Thomas Venner's fanatical Fifth Monarchy Men who fomented uprisings designed to usher in the millennial reign of Christ with his saints, but whose leaders lost their heads before their objective was attained.

The final period runs from the Restoration of the Monarchy in 1660 to the Toleration Act of 1689. In his Declaration of Breda of 4 April 1660, Charles II had promised "a liberty to tender consciences . . . in matters of religion which do not disturb the peace of the Kingdom." To this extent he was in Cromwell's line. Unfortunately, however, this policy was overturned when, in January 1661, the Fifth Monarchy Men launched their second uprising. The immediate effect of this was a severe clampdown not only upon the perpetrators, but upon others deemed suspicious—Baptists and Quakers among them. Indeed, 4,230 Quakers were imprisoned, including their prominent members, John Whitehead and Isaac Penington, and some of these were not released until 11 May 1664. Meanwhile a series of laws was in the process of being enacted, designed to enforce religious conformity with a view to national cohesion—a return, in other words, to the medieval church-state ideal. Of these laws the most important was the Act of Uniformity of 1662, which required all ministers of religion and schoolmasters to give their "unfeigned assent and consent" to the *Book of Common Prayer*, and to use it, and it alone, in services of worship; otherwise they were to be ejected from their livings. Ministers who had been ordained during the Protectorate were required now to be episcopally ordained, and the Solemn League and Covenant between Scotland and England of 1643 was to be abjured. A particularly nasty twist in the legislation was that assent and consent had to be given by Bartholomew's Day, 24 August 1662. Since the annual tithes were due shortly after that date, those who were ejected would lose not only their ministries and their homes, but their previous year's income as well. Nevertheless approximately two thousand ministers (one fifth of the clergy of the Church of England) left their posts between 1660 and 1662. Of these about 172 were Congregationalists, about 1,700 were Presbyterians, and seven or eight only were Baptists—because the Baptists, being voluntarists, had not for the most part taken ministerial positions which entitled them to the receipt of tithes. While many of the ejected had scruples concerning the contents of the *Book of Common Prayer*, their main complaint was that since Christ alone is Head of the Church, it was not for the monarch or parliament to prescribe the Church's worship. To this conviction the Presbyterians added their displeasure at the clause requiring them to abjure the Solemn League and Covenant. From now on it became possible to speak of the "three denominations" of Old Dissent, with the proviso that we must not think so much in terms of national structures, which are creatures of the nineteenth century, as of tendencies marked by a degree of fluidity such that, for example, ministers trained in a Baptist environment might minister to Congregationalists, and Presbyterians might do likewise. This fourth period, and this paper, ends with the so-called Toleration Act of 1689—"so-called" because the term "toleration" occurs neither in its title nor in its contents. It legalized Nonconformist worship for the first time in England, whilst at the same time ensuring that Nonconformists would be second-class citizens from the point of view of social and political life. In a word it inaugurated and legitimated the Church/Chapel distinction. It was also a beautifully English piece of legislation, because none of the anti-nonconformist legislation was repealed; it was simply declared that its provisions would not be applied to orthodox Protestant Dissenters (that is, it did not encompass Unitarians and Roman Catholics, who had to wait until the nineteenth century for legal toleration and full emancipation respectively).[4]

Differences of opinion and degrees of fluidity among the Separatists and Dissenters notwithstanding, we may nevertheless agree with Bernard Lord Manning's remark concerning the Congregationalists, Presbyterians and Baptists:

> We of the Three Dissenting Bodies never "left the Church." From the moment when, at the Reformation, the mediaeval Church began to split up, there were churchmen who stood in this country for a Church after the Calvinist pattern, and hoped to make such a Church the Church of England. . . . From the beginning of modern history we have put up an alternative notion of what the Church is and what churchmanship is . . .[5]

Against the background thus very briefly sketched we may now ask, What types of writings formed and sustained the Separatists and Dissenters during the turbulent years from the 1550s to 1689?

---

4. See further on the matters raised in this paragraph and the previous three, Sell, *Commemorations*, ch. 5; and for a fuller account see M. R. Watts, *The Dissenters*. See also Sell, *The Great Ejectment of 1662*, ch. 4.

5. Manning, *Essays in Orthodox Dissent*, 132–33.

II

Local Covenants

I offer three examples of local covenants which bound Separatists and Dissenters together and gave them their identity as churches. The Separatist conventicles, being clandestine, lived a shadowy existence. We do, however, have the 1567 covenant of Richard Fitz's "privie church", which reads as follows:

> Beyng throughly perswaded in my conscience, by the working and by the worde of the almightie, that these reliques of Antichriste be abominable before the Lorde our God.
>
> And also for that by the power and mercie, strength and goodnes of the Lorde my God onelie, I am escaped from ye filthynes & pollution of these detestable traditions, through the knowledge of our Lorde and sauiour Jesus Christ:
>
> And last of all, in asmuch as by the workyng of the Lord Iesus his holy spirite, I hauve ioyned in prayer, and hearyng Gods worde, with those that haue not yelded to ths idolatrouse trash, notwithstandyng the danger for not commyng to my parysh church. &c,
>
> Thefore I come not backe agayn to the preachynges. &c. of them that hauve receauved these markes of the Romysh beast.

There follow nine further paragraphs in justification of their separation. They particularly denounce the wearing of ecclesiastical vestments ("Popish garments"). The covenant concludes thus "God geue vs strength styl to stryue in suffryng vndre the crosse, that the blessed worde of our God may onely rule, and haue the highest place, to cast down strong holdes, to destroy or ouerthrow policies or imaginations, and euery high thyng that is exalted agains the knowledge of God, and to bryng in to captiuitie or subiection, euery thought to the obedience of Christ . . ."[6]

This is a clear statement, positively and negatively, of the position of Richard Fitz's church. Its members are opposed to what they see as the abuses of Rome that are perpetuated in the Church of England; positively, they believe that the church comprises saints separated from the world, and from a Church which the "world" has invaded.

In writing their covenant of 1660, the Congregationalists of Axminster made the theologically important point that the local covenanting

---

6. See Burrage, *The Early English Dissenters*, II, 13–15.

of the saints with one another was itself a response to God's initiating a covenant with his people:[7]

> The Lord having called us into fellowship with His Son, and convinced us of the necessity of church fellowship we do solemnly profess in the strength of Christ, the accepting of the Lord for our God, and the giving up ourselves to Him to walk, through the strength of Christ, together in His holy commandments and ordinances according to the rule of His word. And we do likewise give up ourselves to one another in the Lord, to walk together in the exercise of all those graces and discharging all those duties that are required of us as a church of Christ.[8]

For our final example we may turn to the covenant of Angel Street Congregational Church, Worcester:

> 1687. The record of a particular Church of Christ at Worcester, consisting of Pastor and people united in the Christian profession and covenant following.
>
> We do believe that there is one only God; the Father, Infinite in being, wisdom, goodness and power; the maker, preserver and disposer of all things, and the most just and merciful Lord of all. We believe that mankind being fallen by sin from God and happiness ... God ... gave his only Son to be their Redeemer.... We believe that God the Holy Ghost ... was sent from the Father by the Son, to inspire and guide the prophets and Apostles that they might fully reveal the doctrine of Christ.... We do heartily take this one God for our only God and our chief good, and this Jesus Christ for our only Lord, Redeemer and Saviour, and this Holy Ghost for our Sanctifier.... And repenting unfeignedly of our sins, we do resolve through the Grace of God sincerely to obey Him, both in holiness to God and righteousness to men, and in special love of the Saints, and communion with them, against all the temptations of the Devil, the world, and our own flesh, and this to the death.[9]

---

7. One implication of which is that the membership comprises people who may have very little in common—status, wealth, interests, age, etc.—except the conviction that God has called them together.

8. Howard, *The Axminster Ecclesiastica*, 29. The same theological emphasis is found in the covenant of Hitchin Baptist Church of 1681. See Ivimey, *A History of the English Baptists*, II, 195–96.

9. See Noake, *Worcester Sects*, 111–14; William Urwick, *Nonconformity in Worcester*, 75–82.

By virtue of its strong trinitarian emphasis, this local covenant assumes the form of a strongly contextual theological statement. The subtext is that already some Presbyterians are tending in an Arian direction, and the Worcester saints have no intention of following them! Within four years of the date of the Worcester covenant, the proposed Happy Union of Congregationalists and Presbyterians foundered in London largely because the former regarded the latter as doctrinally lax, the latter regarded the former as doctrinal antinomians.[10]

III

Polemical Tracts

The following highly selective but representative set of examples will sufficiently indicate the ecclesiological position of the Separatists which underlay their local covenants.[11] That the church comprised the gathered saints, not of all the residents of a parish, was crystal clear to Robert Browne (c.1550–1633), Henry Barrow (c.1550–93) and John Greenwood (d.1593). In *A True and Short Declaration*, probably written before he left Middelburg in 1583, Browne, dismayed by what he perceived as the spiritual bondage of the parish churches, declared that "the kingdom of God Was not to be begun by whole parishes, but rather of the worthiest, Were thei never so feuve."[12] Elsewhere, in one of his most famous passages, he writes,

> The Church planted or gathered, is a companie or number of Christians or beleeuers, which by a willing couenant made with their God, are vnder the gouerment of god and Christ, and kepe his lawes in one holie communion: because Christ hath redeemed them vnto holiness & happines for euer, from which they were fallen by the sinne of Adam. The Church gouernment, is the Lordshipp of Christ in the communion of his offices: whereby his people obey to his will, and haue mutual vse of their graces and callings, to further their godliness and welfare.[13]

---

10. For a fuller discussion of Congregational covenants see Sell, *Dissenting Thought*, ch. 1. For Baptist covenants see Deweese, *Baptist Church Covenants*.

11. For a fuller account which brings the story down to our own time, see Sell, *Saints: Visible, Orderly and Catholic*.

12. Browne, *A True and Short Declaration*, 404.

13. Browne, *A Booke which Sheweth*, 253.

PART ONE: Confessing the Faith in Context

Browne summed up his underlying voluntarism in the phrase, "the Lord's people is of the willing sort."[14]

In a work of 1588 entitled *The True Church and the False Church*, which may have been jointly written by Barrow and Greenwood, the Separatist understanding of the true Church according to Scripture is neatly summarized:

> The true planted and rightlie established church of Christ is a companie of faithfull people; separated from the unbelievers and heathen of the land; gathered in the name of Christ, whom they truly worship, and redily obey as thier only king, priest, and prophet; joyned together as members of one bodie; ordered and governed by such officers and lawes as Christ in his last will and testament hath thereunto ordayned . . .[15]

That is to say, the true Church comprises believers whom God has called out of "the (ungodly) world" (which "world" has, sadly, invaded the Church of England) and gathered together in fellowship. Clearly the Separatists could not live their daily lives utterly divorced from their neighbours, but they were challenged to live among them as those leading a "godly walk," and their more formal religious activities were unavoidably clandestine. Barrow and Greenwood were hanged at Tyburn for their convictions on 6 April 1593, and they were not the only Separatist martyrs.[16]

Turning from the polity of the gathered Church, which the Separatists urged against Anglicans and Presbyterians alike, we may note two important statements which make it plain that while they denied the right of the monarch to prescribe the worship of the Church, what one might call "main line" Separatists and Dissenters were not for the most part republicans. Thus, an unknown Separatist of 1567 declared with reference to Queen Elizabeth I, "Our bodies, goods and lives be at her commandment, and she shall have them as of true subjects. But the soul of man for religion is bound to none but unto God and His Holy Word."[17] It remained for the Baptist, Thomas Helwys, the founder of the first Baptist church on English soil, to claim the honour of drawing the conclusion regarding religious toleration; and this he did as early as 1612:

---

14. Browne, *A Treatise of Reformation*, 162.
15. H. Barrow or J. Greenwood, or both, *The True Church and the False Church*, 98.
16. See Peel, *The Noble Army of Congregational Martyrs*.
17. Peel, *The Seconde Parte of a Register*, 158.

"men's religion to God is betwixt God and themselves: the King shall not answer for it, neither may the King be judge betwene God and Man. Let them be heretikes, Turcks, Jewes, or whatsoever, it apperteynes not to the earthly power to punish them in the least measure."[18]

For some concluding examples of polemical literature we may turn to the Quakers, who offer us a veritable feast of it. The Quakers devised more ways of getting across the authorities than the members of the Three Denominations. They refused to pay tithes to "hierling priests"; they would not doff their cap to their betters; when hauled before the court they refused on scriptural grounds to take the oath. In addition, they constantly tackled the perceived errors of Baptists, Congregationalists and Presbyterians, not to mention the Church of England. In pursuit of such quarries the Quakers "Fox, Nayler, Burrough, Penington, Penn, and Samuel Fisher each published nearly a thousand pages of such material, and dozens of other men were involved."[19] Among the Quaker targets was Richard Baxter who, in his word "To the Reader" prefixed to *The Quaker's Catechism* (1655), branded the Friends a wild generation, and said (which was saying something), "I had far rather that men continued Separatists and Anabaptists than turned Quakers . . ."[20] James Nayler replied to Baxter, and Fox followed up with *The Great Mistery of the Great Whore Unfolded* (1659). At the heart of the dispute was the Quakers' assertion, and the Dissenters' denial, of direct illumination by the Holy Spirit. In the wake of the Civil War and the antics of the Commonwealth sectaries, many orthodox Dissenters and Anglicans alike, were highly suspicious of "enthusiasm". They feared that the Quakers would lose their anchorage in Scripture and claim revelations of an idiosyncratic, possibly even of a dangerous, kind. Thus, in his blow-by-blow rebuttal of Baxter, Fox writes:

> Pr. He saith, "The scripture is God's law, and a sufficient rule for doctrine and worship itself . . ."
> Ans. Now many may have the scriptures, and if they have not the Spirit that gave them forth, they do not worship God in the Spirit. And they who have the scriptures and do not do the will of Christ, they know not his doctrine. And the law is light.[21]

---

18. Helwys, *A Short Declaration of the Mistery of Iniquity*, 69.
19. So Barbour and Roberts, *Early Quaker Writings*, 262.
20. Baxter, *The Quaker's Catechism*, 265.
21. Fox. *The Great Mistery of the Great Whore Unfolded*, 293.

It is by no means fanciful to suppose that many an unlettered Separatist, Dissenter, and Quaker, though not personally competent to contribute to the written cut and thrust of debate, would nevertheless be aware of the main issues at stake (it would have been difficult to have been within earshot of Fox and others, and to have remained unaware of them), not least because those who thus contended were prepared to suffer for their faith, and none more so than the Quakers; which brings us to our next type of writing.

IV

Letters

Letters on all manner of subjects have come down to us from Separatists and Dissenters. Thus, in a surviving fragment of 1584 the Separatist Robert Harrison laments that "M. B[rowne] hath cast vs off, and that with the open manifesting of so many and so notable treacheries, as I abhorre to tell, and if I should declare them, you could not beleeue me."[22] The issue seems to have been Harrison's inclination, against that of Browne, to grant that there were some godly ministers of the Church of England, whose services it was not improper to attend. In a letter to Harrison, written at about the same time, the Presbyterian Thomas Cartwright concurred, granting that

> Where therefore there is no ministerie of the worde there it is playne that there are no visible and apparent churches. . . . Wheresoeuer therefore there is no obedience of the people giuen to the ministers that in the Lordes name preach vnto them, there also can be no churche of christ, but where these two be, although other points wante . . . yet doe they for the reason abouesaide retaine the right of the churches of God.[23]

Cromwell was an inveterate letter-writer, traversing as he does affairs of state, religious matters and international concerns.[24] Out of pastoral concern the young Presbyterian minister, Philip Henry, writes to his former Oxford tutor, the Congregationalist John Owen in 1655, concerning the vacant pastorate at Holt, Denbighshire, "but I think a

---

22. Peel and Carlson, *The Writings of Robert Harrison and Robert Browne*, 149.
23. Peel and Carlson, *Cartwrightiana*, 54.
24. See *Oliver Cromwell's Letters & Speeches*.

man may throw a stone out of it into Cheshire." The proposed stipend is £45 per annum, though it may increase to £65; and the plea is, "Sir, if God, the Lord of the harvest, shall make use of you in his providence, as an instrument of thrusting forth a faithful labourer into this corner of his vineyard, I in no way doubt but you will be often mentioned by some of them with rejoicing at the throne of grace . . ."[25]

As the records of Broadmead Baptist Church make plain, local churches were often in written communication with their members, and with other local churches.[26] By means of letters fellowship was fostered, but never more so, perhaps, than when, in turbulent times, respected leaders wrote to their co-religionists from gaol.

It was almost certainly in 1587 that Henry Barrow wrote to fellow-Separatists from prison in the Gatehouse. He informs them of his situation; he urges them to be faithful, for "The Lord above all things abhoreth a dubell minded man"; and the tone of the whole is set by the prayer with which he opens:

> The Lord hime self of all comfort and truthe replenish our harts with the knowledge and knowledging of his truth; that wee may both see and taste the heavenly word and salver of our sowles in the world to come. Amen.[27]

In 1652/3 the Quaker James Nayler wrote to Friends from Appleby Gaol in these terms:

> It is my joy to do or suffer the will of my father. . . . Oh dear Friends, rejoice with me, for I see that to be taken out of all created things is perfect freedom. . . . Dear hearts, you make your own troubles, by being unwilling and disobedient to that which would lead you. . . . If [God] seem to smile, follow him in fear and love; and if he seem to frown, follow him, and fall into his will, and you shall see he is yours still.[28]

When we come to the prison experience of the Dissenters following the Restoration, a certain caution is required. Just as the punitive laws were not applied with full force in every part of the land, so some magistrates and gaolers were more lenient than others. Thus, although John

---

25. Williams, *The Life of Philip Henry, A.M.*, 28.

26. See, for example, *The Records of a Church of Christ Meeting in Broadmead, Bristol*, 99–101, 117–20.

27. Carlson, *The Writings of Henry Barrow*, 108.

28. Nayler, Swarthmore MSS, 3. 66.

PART ONE: Confessing the Faith in Context

Bunyan served his sentence in Bedford Gaol from 1660 to 1672, he was allowed out to attend church meetings in 1661, 1668, 1669, and 1670.[29] As well as writing his autobiography and beginning *The Pilgrim's Progress*, he also had time to make a flute out of a chair leg. Another who turned his sojourn in gaol to literary use was the twenty-four-year-old Quaker William Penn, incarcerated for the alleged blasphemy of his work, *The Sandy Foundation Shaken* (1668). Penn states his objective in writing *No Cross, No Crown* (1669) in no uncertain terms:

> Come, Reader, hearken to me awhile; I seek thy salvation; that is my plot; thou wilt forgive me. A refiner is come near thee, his grace hath appeared unto thee: it shows thee the world's lusts, and teaches thee to deny them. Receive his leaven, and it will change thee. . . . What rests to us, then, that we must do, to be thus witnesses to his power and love? . . . Christ's Cross is Christ's way to Christ's Crown. This is the subject of the following Discourse . . .[30]

The path to glory is the path of self-denial, of heeding biblical precepts, and of living the Quaker way of simplicity of life. Among things to be shunned is attachment to sartorial finery: "But there is another part of luxury that has great place with vain man and woman, and that is the gorgeousness of apparel, one of the most foolish, because most costly, empty, and unprofitable excesses people can well be guilty of."[31] This example typifies much more in the same vein.

Of the few months during which Richard Baxter was incarcerated in 1670 for keeping a conventicle he later wrote, "My imprisonment was no great suffering to me, for I had an honest jailor, who showed me all the kindness he could; I had a large room, and the liberty of walking in a fair garden; and my wife was never so cheerful a companion to me as in prison, and was very much against my seeking to be released."

The delightful ambiguity of those last remarks is capped only by the experience of the Reformed pastor *par excellence*, that too much pastoral care could be tiresome: "the number of visitors by day did put me out of hope of studying, or doing anything but entertain them."[32]

---

29. See Brown, *John Bunyan*, ch. 8; Whitley, "Bunyan's imprisonment"; Godber, "The imprisonments of John Bunyan."

30. Penn, *No Cross, No Crown*, iv–v.

31. Ibid., 189.

32. R. Baxter, *The Autobiography*, 207–8.

Although it has been estimated that during the reign of Charles II some 15,000 Quakers were fined, imprisoned, or transported, and of these 450 died,[33] a certain licence was on occasion extended even to them. For example, John Gratton was imprisoned for five and a half years in Derby Gaol. One of his gaolers was strict, but another was more lenient. Indeed on one occasion the latter allowed him to visit his dying son; on another Gratton travelled to London with the gaoler's son with a view to securing employment for the lad with the Quaker George Watts. In 1683 Gratton wrote a prison letter to the London Yearly Meeting, in which he salutes the Friends, exhorts them to allow nothing to hinder the increase of God's kingdom, and continues thus:

> Oh! how largely hath the Lord our God made it manifest, that this your meeting is well-pleasing unto him, by giving you his presence in church in such a powerful and glorious manner, as is beyond my ability to declare, and hath sealed it in my heart, and I am sure in your hearts, that it is a right, good, and honourable thing; and declares us to all the world, that though we be of several counties of this nation, yea, and of several nations, yet we are one body, in one spirit and mind . . .[34]

He next prays God's blessing upon them, and asks that they may have wisdom to "set true judgment on the head of transgression and transgressors, wherever it is found, and so clear truth . . . that God may be glorified . . ."[35] He concludes by assuring them that he is with them in spirit, and ends with an ascription of praise: "Everlasting praises be given to our God for ever!"[36]

V

Spiritual Autobiography and Allegory

If we wished to persuade anyone that letters, homilies and autobiographical reminiscences do not comprise the whole of prison writings by Separatists and Dissenters, we should not need to look further than John

---

33. Braithwaite, *The Second Period of Quakerism*, 115.

34. *A Journal of the Life of . . . John Gratton*, 169. For Gratton (c.1641–1712) see further Sell, *Enlightenment, Ecumenism, Evangel*, ch. 2.

35. Gratton, *Journal*, 170.

36. Ibid., 171.

PART ONE: Confessing the Faith in Context

Bunyan. He was by no means the first to write a spiritual autobiography, but *Grace Abounding to the Chief of Sinners* (1666) was written in prison, while *The Pilgrim's Progress* (1678) was begun there. It would be a case of carrying coals to Newcastle to rehearse the contents of these two books to readers of this volume. It is more tempting to offer a critique of some recent writers on Bunyan who offer psychological interpretations of him which major on his anxiety, and derive this from Calvinism.[37] It cannot be denied that Calvinism did spawn in some people an introspective attitude which could verge upon the morbid as people constantly took their spiritual temperature to see whether they manifested the signs of grace and possessed the feeling of assurance. But no theological position deserves to be defined in terms of its excesses. I shall shortly cite Thomas Watson on Christian joyfulness—and when the burden of sin was loosed from his back, did not Bunyan's Christian have a "merry heart," give "three leaps for joy" and go on singing?[38] Indeed, I should be prepared to argue that Bunyan's two books supply an antidote to such a distorted view of Bunyan's psyche. To the readers of his autobiography he writes,

> In this discourse of mine you may see much; much, I say, of the grace of God towards me. I thank God I can count it much, for it was above my sins and Satan's temptations too. I can remember my fears, and doubts, and sad months with comfort; they are as the head of Goliath in my hand. . . . My dear children, the milk and honey is beyond this wilderness, God be merciful to you, and grant that you be not slothful to go in to possess the land.[39]

The final sentence just quoted makes it clear that Bunyan is offering words of encouragement from a saint in prison to saints outside; and this applies both to the autobiography and to *The Pilgrim's Progress*. As Hugh Martin rightly claimed, "*Pilgrim's Progress* is only *Grace Abounding* translated and dramatized."[40] Bunyan wishes his friends to understand that despite all sins and difficulties, sovereign grace prevails. This is the note of authentic Calvinism: indeed of the gospel itself. *Grace Abounding* is

---

37. See Stachniewski, *The Persecutory Imagination*; Beth Lynch, *John Bunyan*. Similarly mistaking the part for the whole, Sim has declared that "it is anxiety, more than any specific point of doctrine, that is the distinguishing characteristic of Calvinism." See his review of Bouwsma, *John Calvin: A Sixteenth-Century Portrait*, 79.

38. Bunyan, *The Pilgrim's Progress*, 46.

39. Bunyan, *Grace Abounding to the Chief of Sinners*, 13, 15.

40. Martin, "Foreword" to Bunyan, *Grace Abounding*, 7.

no more a blow-by-blow account of Bunyan's life[41] than the four Gospels are of the life of Jesus. The message, rather than the biographical details, is paramount in Bunyan's mind. And if Bunyan (like others) does emphasize the depth of sin and his private fears as a way of magnifying the gulf between himself as once-born and twice-born, this does not excuse partisan literary critics for overlooking the fact that as an older Bunyan interpreter wrote, "The man with the burden on his back is the most clear-sighted man in the City of Destruction. His neighbours are free from the load resting upon him, not because they are braver or better, but because they are blinder than he."[42] (I resist the unsanctified, Puritan-style, speculation that perhaps some literary critics who psychologize Bunyan and make him irredeemably morbid are among the "neighbours.")

That these and other works of Bunyan struck a chord in his own time is clear from the fact that no fewer than ten English editions of *The Pilgrim's Progress* were published between the first, in 1678, and Bunyan's death ten years later. Of these, one appeared in Boston (1681). Five Dutch editions were published by Johannes Boekholt between 1682 and 1687. *Grace Abounding to the Chief of Sinners* passed through six editions during Bunyan's life-time. It may be that not the least reason for their widespread appeal both when they first appeared and since is that persecuted Christians have been reassured that their hope, and their conscientious stand, are not in vain (at which point a comparison with John the Seer's Revelation comes to mind); while those who have not been physically persecuted or otherwise restricted have been reminded that they are called to participate in spiritual warfare which "is not against human foes, but against . . . the authorities and potentates of this dark age . . ." (Eph 6: 12).[43]

---

41. A point well made by Michael Mullett, *John Bunyan in Context*, 26–27.

42. Stevenson, *Exposition of the Pilgrim's Progress*, 11.

43. The literature on Bunyan is vast; for a selection see ODNB. There remains much of value in Brown, *John Bunyan*. See also Sharrock, *John Bunyan*; Greaves, *John Bunyan and English Nonconformity*.

PART ONE: Confessing the Faith in Context

VI

Aids to Bible Study

It is hardly surprising, given their concern to live by God's Word, that Separatists and Dissenters should produce aids to Bible study. The Separatist Henry Ainsworth (1569–1622) earnestly believed that careful examination of the Hebrew text of the Bible enabled one more readily to discern the mysteries of godliness contained therein. To this end he published a series of *Annotations*. The first of these, on the Psalms, appeared in 1612, and others followed, until a composite volume was published in 1627. Its title sufficiently indicates its scope: *Annotations upon the Five Bookes of Moses, the Booke of the Psalmes, and the Song of Songs, or Canticles. Wherein the Hebrew words and sentences, are compared with, and explained by the ancient Greeke and Chaldee versions, and other Records and Monuments of the Hebrewes: But chiefly by conference with the holy Scriptures, Moses his words, lawes and ordinances, the Sacrifices, and other Legall ceremonies heretofore commanded by God to the Church of Israel, are explained. With an Advertisement touching some objections made against the sincerity of the Hebrew Text, and allegation of the Rabbines in these Annotations. As also tables directing unto such principall things as are observed in the annotations upon each severall booke.* To his annotations of the Psalms, Ainsworth added a psalter, which was used by exiles in Amsterdam and Pilgrims in the Plymouth colony.

Samuel Clark (1626–1700/01), Rector of Grendon Underwood, Buckinghamshire, was ejected from his living on 28 July 1662. In 1683 he published his *Annotations* on the New Testament, which was highly commended by Richard Baxter, John Owen, and others; and in 1690 there followed *The Holy Bible, containing the Old Testament and the New: with Annotations and Parallel Scriptures. To which is Annex'd the Harmony of the Gospels: as also the Reduction of the Jewish Weights, Coins and Measures, to our English Standards. And a Table of the Promises in Scripture.* In his Preface Clark explains that he has striven for brevity, and that he has sought to "unriddle and unfold the Scriptural Significance" of the ceremonial laws in the Pentateuch. While he does refer to the literal sense of prophecies, since prophecies are quoted in the New Testament and given a typological sense by "the Spirit of God himself," Clark follows suit. Running throughout his work is a strong sense that those who are committed to the Christian faith are those most readily able to discern the Bible's message. As he says, only those who have "some experience in their own Souls of the work of that Grace which [Paul] does so exactly describe" can satisfactorily interpret the Pauline letters. Towards the end of his Preface he poignantly remarks that this work has occupied him for many years, "and indeed, in a manner, ever since I was reduced to a state of *Silence*, and into a sort of *private Capacity*, as to the publick Exercise of my Ministry." Clark's *A Survey of the Bible*—a synopsis of every chapter—appeared in 1693, followed by a concordance in 1696.

VII

Sermons

Where sermons are concerned, selection is made difficult by the considerable quantity of examples which have survived. The importance of sermons, thousands of which were printed, in educating church members, encouraging godly living, urging the importance of private devotion—in which connection Oliver Heywood's *Closet Prayer a Christian Duty* (1671) comes to mind—cannot be over-estimated. Of particular interest are funeral sermons in which a text is expounded, the deceased honoured, and the hearers exhorted to consider their own end and prepare themselves for it. Ordination and induction charges, too, were of some importance in community-making, since they clearly prescribed the duties of both ministers and people. If some Dissenting preachers went over the heads of their hearers, others pierced their hearts. The best of them expounded the Bible in an orderly way, with reference both to exegesis, exposition and application. They knew that if they on occasion were called upon to challenge the flock, the homiletic task itself was a challenge to themselves. If they forgot this, Richard Baxter would remind them. Referring to the skills required in the work of the ministry he writes,

> To preach a sermon, I think, is not the hardest part; and yet what skill is necessary to make the truth plain—to convince the hearers—to let irresistible light in to their consciences, and to keep it there, and drive all home—to screw the truth into their minds, and work Christ into their affections—to meet every objection, and clearly to resolve it—to drive sinners to a stand, and make them see that there is no hope; but that they must unavoidably either be converted or condemned,—and to do all

this, in respect of language and manner, as beseems our work, and yet as is most suitable to the capacities of our hearers.[44]

From the many preachers of the period I select for brief reference John Flavel (1628–91),[45] who was ordained by the Presbyterians at Salisbury in 1650, but from 1656 travelled under the Congregational label. He was ejected from his living as lecturer at St. Saviour's, Dartmouth in 1662, but retained connections there until, in 1682, circumstances became so dangerous that he had to flee to London. An edition of six volumes of his sermons was published in 1820, and this was reprinted in 1968. The set includes thirty-five sermons on "The method of grace in the gospel of redemption," and no fewer than forty-two on "The fountain of life: a display of Christ in his essential and mediatorial glory." From the latter I select at random sermon twelve in order to illustrate Flavel's method and manner.

The sermon is entitled, "Of the Excellency of our High-Priest's Oblation, being the first Act or Part of his Priestly Office."[46] The text is Hebrews 10:14: "For by one offering, he hath perfected for ever them that are sanctified." Flavel begins by expounding the idea of Christ's once-for-all oblation. It is never to be repeated, and it is efficacious. It is also extensive: "not being restrained to a few, but applicable to all the saints, in all the ages and places of the world: for this indefinite, *them that are sanctified*, is equivalent to an universal . . ." Finally, it is eternally efficacious. The theme introduced, Flavel proceeds to draw out the doctrinal implications of it. He observes that the one oblation was made by our high priest, Jesus Christ, God-man; that he did not offer the blood of animals, but his own blood. This implies that the offering is infinitely precious, and that "the virtue of this sacrifice . . . reacheth backward as far as Adam, and reacheth forward to the last person of the elect springing from him." For this reason "it must needs be a most grateful oblation to the Lord, highly pleasing and delightful in his eyes." Christ is the surety, God the creditor incensed by human sin. Hence "To this incensed Majesty, Christ our High-priest approached, as to a devouring fire, with the sacrifice." He offered himself in the place of God's elect, "neither more nor less." General offers of the gospel may be made to all, since preachers do not know who the elect are, but the elect alone will reap its benefits. The purpose of the

---

44. Baxter, *The Reformed Pastor*, 114.
45. For Flavel see ODNB; Matthews, *Calamy Revised* (1934).
46. See Flavel, *Works*, I, 154–65.

oblation was to atone, "by giving [God] a full and adequate compensation or satisfaction for the sins of these his elect."

From this Flavel says that he will draw five inferences, but three only are set out:

1. "That actual believers are fully freed from the guilt of their sins, and shall nevermore come under condemnation."
2. That God's justice is of "inflexible severity," for it "could be no other way diverted from us, and appeased, but by the blood of Christ."
3. That since Christ has offered himself as a sacrifice to God for us, "let us improve, in every condition, this sacrifice, and labour to get hearts duly affected with such a sight as faith can give us of it."

There follow four paragraphs of application. Those who are despondent under their own guilt may be comforted by Christ's full satisfaction for all sin. Those who are suspicious of God's promises will see that they are "all ratified and established in the blood of the cross." Those who fret and are disquieted and impatient under trials will see "how quietly Christ your sacrifice came to the altar", and they will be silenced, convinced and shamed:

> In a word, here you will see so much of the grace of God, and love of Christ, in providing and becoming a sacrifice for you: you will see God taking vengeance against sin, but sparing the sinner . . . that whatever corruption burdens, this, in the believing application, will support; whatever grace is defective, this will revive it. *Blessed be God for Jesus Christ.*

VIII

Confessions and Catechisms

It is not too much to say that the period with which we are concerned was replete with confessions of faith and catechisms. Some of them were composed by individuals. John Smyth, the fountain-head of the General Baptists, wrote a confession of faith comprising twenty paragraphs in Latin in 1609/10.[47] As for catechisms, quite apart from a number of anonymous ones, Carlson is able to name fifteen Puritans who prepared these

---

47. See Burrage, *The Early English Dissenters*. II, 179-80.

between 1580 and 1593.⁴⁸ The Presbyterian, Cartwright, wrote *A Short Catechisme*, which appeared in various forms, and which in modern type runs to fourteen pages.⁴⁹ The first known Congregational catechism is that of Henry Jacob (whose London church turned believer baptist in 1633, hence the Particular Baptists). It was written in 1604 or 1605. As we might expect, Jacob is very clear as to the nature of the Church: "A true Visible or Ministeriall Church of Christ is a particular Congregation being a spirituall perfect Corporation of Believers, & having power in it selfe immediately from Christ to administer all Religious meanes of faith to the members thereof."⁵⁰

But the most important confessions and catechisms are those devised by what one might call the seventeenth century's "committee theologians." Of the confessions, the *Westminster* (1647) is probably the most important because of it global influence throughout the Presbyterian world, and because it was largely followed by the Congregational *Savoy Declaration* (1658) and the Particular Baptist *Second London Confession* (1677). It will, indeed, be remembered that while the majority of those participating in the Westminster Assembly were Presbyterians, the prominent Congregationalists, Thomas Goodwin, Philip Nye, Sidrach Simpson, Jeremiah Burroughes, and William Bridge were also present. Notwithstanding this, the Congregationalists amended *Westminster* at certain points when preparing *Savoy*. They also added paragraphs on the extent of the grace of the gospel and on the Church, and appended thirty clauses under the heading, *Savoy Declaration of the Institution of Churches, and the Order appointed in them by Jesus Christ*. The Particular Baptists adopted *Savoy*'s chapter on the extent of the grace of the gospel and, as we might expect, declared the only proper baptism to be that of believers by immersion. In their *Standard Confession* of 1660 the General Baptists both advocated the baptism of believers only and castigated paedobaptists as followers of the works of darkness.⁵¹

48. See Carlson, *Cartwrightiana*, 157.
49. Ibid., 159–73.
50. See Burrage, *The Early English Dissenters*, II, 157.
51. For *Westminster* see numerous editions; for *Savoy* see Matthews, *The Savoy Declaration of Faith and Order 1658*; Walker, *The Creeds and Platforms of Congregationalism*; Sell, *Saints: Visible, Orderly and Catholic*, ch. 3; Sell, *Dissenting Thought*, ch. 1. For the Baptist confessions see Lumpkin. *Baptist Confessions of Faith*. Sell, *Testimony and Tradition*, ch. 4. For the Westminster Assembly see Paul, *The Assembly of the Lord*. The so far unpublished Minutes of the Assembly, held at Dr. Williams's Library, London, are currently being worked on by Chad van Dixhoorn.

Without question, the most prominent "committee" catechisms of the seventeenth century were the *Westminster Shorter* and *Larger* ones.[52] Richard Baxter, for example, was one among many who believed that the Church's preaching ministry presupposed catechetical instruction, and in a systematic way he ensured that this was given in the homes of his Kidderminster flock. His advice was, "Learn first your catechism at home, and the great essential points of religion, contained in the creed, the Lord's prayer, and the ten commandments.... You can scarce bestow too much care and pains in learning these great essential points."[53]

Alongside the catechisms there grew up a veritable industry of written expositions of them. One example must suffice: Thomas Watson's *A Body of Practical Divinity* (1692). Watson, an ejected minister who died in 1686, was a notable preacher and a prolific author.[54] In his *Body* he expounds the *Westminster Shorter Catechism*, as well as the Beatitudes, the Lord's Prayer and the Ten Commandments. That he is firmly in the Calvinist camp is clear from his exposition of the federal theology. But what is of particular interest is Watson's memorable turn of phrase. Of all Puritans, he is surely the pithiest. In his Preliminary Discourse he advocates firm roots in Christian teaching: "As feathers will be blown every way, so will feathery Christians"; and that he was in entire accord with Baxter is clear from his declaration that "To preach and not to catechise is to build without foundation." Elaborating upon "man's chief end" he reminds his readers that "It is not profession, but fruit that glorifies God." Against any (not least some latter day literary critics?) who may be inclined to suppose that Calvinism is necessarily gloomy, he writes, "The people of God have ground for cheerfulness. They are justified and adopted, and this creates inward peace." Watson is adept at illustration:

> As the silkworm, when she weaves her curious work, hides herself under the silk, and is not seen; so when we have done anything praiseworthy, we must hide ourselves under the veil of humility, and transfer the glory of all we have done to God. As Constantine used to write the name of Christ over his door, so should we write the name of Christ over our duties. Let him wear the garland of praise.

---

52. For these see Torrance, *The School of Faith*. For the entire subject see Green, *The Christian's ABC*.

53. Baxter, *Christian Directory*, in his *Works*, IV, 253. See further Sell, *Testimony and Tradition*, ch. 3.

54. For Watson see ODNB; Matthews, *Calamy Revised*.

More generally, "You that have been monuments of God's mercy, should be trumpets of praise."

On the thorny question of providence, Watson confidently declares that, "The wheels in a clock seem to move contrary to one another, but they help forward the motion of the clock, and make the larum strike: so the providences of God seem to be cross wheels; but for all that, they shall carry on the good of the elect." Concerning sin and Christ's saving work, he points out that "The evil of sin is not so much seen in that one thousand are damned for it, as that Christ died for it." Indeed, "Jesus Christ is the sum and quintessence of the gospel; the wonder of angels; the joy and triumph of saints. The name of Christ is sweet, it is as music in the ear, honey in the mouth, and a cordial at the heart." In pastoral vein he reassures his readers that "We must distinguish between weakness of faith and no faith. A weak faith is true. The bruised reed is but weak, yet it is such as Christ will not break. Though thy faith be weak, be not discouraged." Again, "The crown is set at the end of the race; and if we win the race, we shall wear the crown."[55]

IX

Theological Treatises

As if we have not already seen enough types of writings used by Separatists and Dissenters to communicate their theological ideas and encourage their communities, there remain formal theological treatises. Of these there were many—not least that of the Quaker, Robert Barclay.[56] However, it would be difficult to dispute the claim that the seventeenth-century Dissenting theologian *par excellence* was John Owen (1616–83), or to disagree with J. M. Rigg that "he ranks with Baxter and Howe among the most eminent of puritan divines."[57] Originally a Presbyterian, he became a Congregationalist by conviction. In 1651 Oliver Cromwell appointed him Dean of Christ Church, Oxford, and in the following year

---

55. Watson, *A Body of Divinity*, 1, 5, 12, 14, 17, 98, 125, 135, 161, 220, 289.

56. Barclay, *An Apology for the True Christian Divinity*. See also Sell, *Commemorations*, ch. 6.

57. Rigg in DNB. For a summary of the controversies in which Owen engaged and an indication of his influence at home and abroad see Greaves, "John Owen" in ODNB.

Vice-Chancellor of the University. He retained the latter post until 1658, and was deprived of the former in 1660.[58]

It is not possible even to list the contents of the sixteen reprinted volumes of Owen's *Works* here,[59] still less to discuss them. Suffice it to say that they contain controversial writings against Arminians, and against those who deny the substitutionary death of Christ; pastoral writings on sin and temptation; extended discourses on the person of Christ, the Holy Spirit, and justification by faith; and, in *The True Nature of a Gospel Church*, staunch advocacy of the Congregational Way, though with the clarification that as well as the gathered church there may also be synods; this with a view to "the edification of the *church catholic*."[60] The power of synods is said to be threefold: "The first is *declarative*, consisting of an authoritative teaching and declaring of the mind of God in the Scripture; the second is *constitutive*, appointing and ordaining things to be believed, or done and observed, by and upon its own authority; and, thirdly, *executive*, in acts of jurisdiction towards persons and churches."[61] The deliverances of synods "are to be received, owned and observed on the evidence of the mind of the Holy Ghost in them, and on the ministerial authority of the synod itself."[62] One could write the subsequent history of Congregational polity in terms of its affinities with, and departures from, Owen's position as here set down.

X

I fully recognize that in the space available to me I have done little more than produce a list. I hope, however, that it is an informative list which shows the many ways in which Separatists and Dissenters, variously deprived, sought to communicate their ideas and sustain their communities.[63] I am conscious of the fact that although I have quoted from the autobiographies of John Gratton and Richard Baxter, I have not outlined their contents, and have not mentioned George Fox's *Journal* at

---

58. See Matthews, *Calamy Revised*.
59. *The Works of John Owen*, edited by William H. Goold.
60. Ibid., XVI, 196
61. Ibid., 205.
62. Ibid., 208.
63. It goes without saying that within the confines of this chapter I have not been able to discuss the many who took up their pens against the Separatists and Dissenters.

PART ONE: Confessing the Faith in Context

all. This is because (to resume the point I made at the outset) all three were published after the 1689 terminus of this paper: in 1720, 1698, and 1694 respectively, and therefore they could not be said to have fostered community-building among Separatists and Dissenters during the period under review. The same may be said of a number of personal diaries, such as that of Oliver Heywood. He kept a diary from the time of his removal under the Five Mile Act from his Coley, Halifax, pulpit in 1666 until his death in 1702. It was not published, however, until the nineteenth century.

There remains the question of hymns. During the period with which we are concerned a number of writers wrote verse which has subsequently found its way into hymn books. For example, Baxter's widely-known hymn, "Lord, it belongs not to my care Whether I die or live," is extracted from his poem, "The covenant and confidence of faith." Better known still is Bunyan's hymn of the Christian pilgrimage, "Who would true valour see . . ." It is also the case that some were trying their hands at original hymns as such. Of these the most prolific was Benjamin Keach (1640–1704), none of whose three hundred hymns continue in use. But it was one thing for hymns to be written, another for them to be sung during public worship. Whereas in General (Arminian) Baptist circles music and song of any kind were ruled out, the Particular (Calvinist) Baptists, Vavasor Powell and Hanserd Knollys among them, were more open to hymn singing in worship. Keach, who had begun as a General Baptist, transferred his allegiance to the Particulars on adopting Calvinistic views, and in 1673, now pastor in Southwark, he introduced a hymn at the close of the Lord's Supper. For this the justification was that Jesus and his disciples had sung a hymn at the close of the *Last* Supper (Matt 26:30; Mark 14:26). Almost twenty years later, in 1691, the Church Meeting resolved to have hymns at every service. However, a significant minority objected and seceded to found the cause at Maze Pond.[64] For their part, the Presbyterians and Congregationalists adhered strictly to the exclusive use of metrical Psalms on the ground that scriptural words only should be employed in worship.[65] Writers who thought otherwise (especially, perhaps, if they were ministers who could be at the mercy of disgruntled Church Meetings) had to proceed cautiously. We thus find Isaac Watts

---

64. See further Haykin, *Kiffin, Knollys and Keach*, ch. 8; Walker, *The Excellent Benjamin Keach*.

65. The same ground was offered for the refusal to recite creeds, "the words of men," in services of worship.

(1674–1748), who began to write hymns in 1694, explaining—as late as 1718—that in giving the metrical Psalms a Christian hue, "I have kept my grand design in view, and that is, to teach my author [that is, David (*sic*)] to speak like a Christian."[66] This may be understood as a halfway house between strict metrical psalms and original Christian hymns. Indeed, Watts entitles the Psalms section of his collection, *The Psalms of David, Imitated in the Language of the New Testament, and Applied to the Christian State and Worship*. His original hymns comprise the second part of the collection (and cover nineteen more pages than "David's"). The upshot is that while during the period 1550–1689 there were writers of hymn-like stanzas as well as some writers of actual hymns, there was widespread and often determined resistance to the use of hymns in public worship. It was only in the eighteenth century that hymns could really begin play their impressive community-cementing role in English Dissent.

That the several categories of writings to which I have drawn attention have subsequently been influential goes without saying. Even down to our own time those in the line of the Separatists and Dissenters who have not fallen victim to historical amnesia can still find themselves instructed by their forebears in the faith. Over the years I have sought to communicate some of their ecclesiological ideas through print and in ecumenical dialogue: notably the convictions that Christ alone is Head of the Church, that the Church comprises Christians, and that the only way to be a member of the Church catholic is to be a locally-anchored saint. I hope that I should be willing to die for the principle of the "crown rights of the Redeemer in his Church." I hope, with equal fervour, that it will not come to that.

---

66. Preface to *The Psalms and Hymns of the Rev. Isaac Watts, D.D.*, v.

PART ONE: Confessing the Faith in Context

BIBLIOGRAPHY

Ainsworth, Henry. *Annotations upon the Five Bookes of Moses, the Booke of Psalms, and the Song of Songs, or Canticles. Wherein the Hebrew words and sentences, are compared with, and explained by the ancient Greeke and Chaldee versions, and other Records and Monuments of the Hebrewes: But chiefly by conference with the holy Scriptures, Moses his words, lawes and ordinances, the Sacrifices, and other Legall ceremonies heretofore commanded by God to the Church of Israel, are explained. With an Advertisement touching some objections made against the sincerity of the Hebrew Text, and allegation of the Rabbines in these Annotations. As also tables directing unto such principall things as are observed in the annotations upon each severall booke.* London: Flesher and Haviland, 1627.

Anon. *The Book of Common Prayer.* Cambridge: Baskerville, 1662.

———. *Records of a Church of Christ Meeting in Broadmead, Bristol, 1640–1687.* London: J. Haddon, 1847.

Barclay, Robert. *An Apology for the True Christian Divinity, as the same is Held Forth and Preached by the People, in Scorn, called Quakers* (1678). Glasgow: Barclay Murdoch, 1886.

Barlow, William. *The Summe and Substance of the Conference . . . at Hampton Court, January 14, 1603.* London: John Windet for Matthew Law, 1604.

Barrow, Henry or John Greenwood, or both. *The True Church and the False Church.* In Leland H. Carlson, *The Writings of John Greenwood 1587–1590 together with the Joint Writings of Henry Barrow and John Greenwood.* London: Allen and Unwin, 1962.

Baxter, Richard. *The Autobiography of Richard Baxter being the Reliquiae Baxterianae abridged from the folio.* 1696. Reprint. London: Dent, 1931.

———. *The Quaker's Catechism*, 1655. In *Early Quaker Writings, 1650–1700*, edited by Hugh Barbour and Arthur O. Roberts, 262–89. Grand Rapids: Eerdmans, 1973.

———. *The Practical Works of the Rev. Richard Baxter with a Life of the Author and a Critical Examination of his Writings* (by William Orme). London: Duncan, 1830.

———. *The Reformed Pastor.* Revised and abridged by William Brown. Glasgow: Collins, 1835.

Braithwaite, W. C. *The Second Period of Quakerism.* 2nd ed. Edited by Henry J. Cadbury. Cambridge: Cambridge University Press, 1961.

Brown, John. *John Bunyan, His Life, Times and Work.* London: Isbister, 1885.

Browne, Robert. *A Booke which Sheweth the Life and Manner of all True Christians*, Middleburg, 1582. *A Treatise of Reformation without Tarrying for Anie*, Middleburg, 1582. *A True and Short Declaration, both of the Gathering and Joining Together of Certain Persons: and also of the Lamentable Breach and Division which Fell Amongst Them*, 1583. In *The Writings of Robert Harrison and Robert Browne*, edited by Albert Peel and Leland H. Carlson, 221–395, 150–70, 396–429. London: Allen and Unwin, 1953.

Burrage, Champlin. *The Early English Dissenters in the Light of Recent Research (1550–1641).* 2 vols. Cambridge: Cambridge University Press, 1912.

Bunyan, John. *Grace Abounding to the Chief of Sinners.* London: Larkin, 1666.

———. *The Pilgrim's Progress.* London: Ponder, 1678.

Cartwright, Thomas. *A Methodicall Short Catechisme: containing briefly all the Principall Grounds of Christian Religion.* London: Alsop, 1623.

Varieties of English Separatist and Dissenting Writings, 1558-1689

Clark, Samuel. *A Survey of the Bible: or, an Analytical account of the holy Scriptures.* London, 1693.

———. *The Holy Bible, containing the Old Testament and the New: with Annotations and Parallel Scriptures. To which is Annex'd the Harmony of the Gospels: as also the Reduction of the Jewish Weights, Coins and Measures, to our English Standards. And a Table of the Promises in Scripture.* London: Rawlins, 1690.

Cromwell, Oliver. *Oliver Cromwell's Letters & Speeches with Elucidations by Thomas Carlyle.* 3 vols. London: Dent, 1908.

Deweese, Charles W. *Baptist Church Covenants.* Nashville: Broadman, 1990.

Flavel, John. *The Works of John Flavel.* 1820. Reprint. London: Banner of Truth, 1968.

Fox, George. *The Great Mystery of the Great Whore Unfolded.* In *Early Quaker Writings 1650-1700*, edited by Hugh Barbour and Arthur O. Roberts, 289-94. Grand Rapids: Eerdmans, 1973.

Godber, Joyce. "The Imprisonments of John Bunyan." *Congregational Historical Society Transactions* 16 (1949) 23-32.

Gratton, John. *A Journal of the Life of that Ancient Servant of Christ, John Gratton* (1720). Stanford, NY: Hull, 1805.

Greaves, Richard L. *John Bunyan and English Nonconformity.* London: Hambledon, 1992.

———. "John Owen." In *The Oxford Dictionary of National Biography.* Oxford: Oxford University Press, 2004.

Green, Ian. *The Christian's ABC: Catechisms and Catechizing in England c. 1530-c.1740.* Oxford: Clarendon, 1996.

———. *Print and Protestantism in Early Modern England.* Oxford: Oxford University Press, 2000.

Haykin, Michael A. G. *Kiffin, Knollys and Keach.* Leeds, UK: Reformation Today Trust, 1996.

Helwys, Thomas. *A Short Declaration of the Mistery of Iniquity.* London: Kingsgate, 1612.

Heywood, Oliver. *Closet Prayer a Christian Duty.* London: Parkhurst, 1671.

Howard, K. W. H. *The Axminster Ecclesiastica.* Sheffield, UK: Gospel Tidings, 1976.

Ivimey, Joseph. *A History of the English Baptists*, vol. 2. London: printed for the author, 1814.

Keeble, Neil H. *The Literary Culture of Nonconformity in Later Seventeenth-Century England.* Leicester, UK: Leicester University Press, 1987.

Lumpkin, William L., *Baptist Confessions of Faith.* Valley Forge, PA: Judson, 1969.

Lynch, Beth. *John Bunyan and the Language of Conviction.* Cambridge: Brewer, 2004.

Manning, Bernard Lord. *Essays in Orthodox Dissent.* 1939. Reprint. London: Independent, 1953.

Martin, Hugh. "Foreword" to J. Bunyan, *Grace Abounding to the Chief of Sinners* London: SCM, 1955.

Matthews, A. G. *Calamy Revised.* 1934. Reprint. Oxford: Clarendon, 1988.

———. *The Savoy Declaration of Faith and Order 1658.* London: Independent, 1959.

Mullett, Michael. *John Bunyan in Context.* Keele, UK: Keele University Press, 1996.

Nayler, John. Swarthmore MSS, Friends House Library, London.

Noake, John. *Worcester Sects; or A History of the Roman Catholics and Dissenters of Worcester.* London: Longman, 1861.

PART ONE: Confessing the Faith in Context

Owen, John. *The Works of John Owen* (1850–1853). Edited by William H. Goold. London: Banner of Truth, 1957.

Paul, Robert S. *The Assembly of the Lord. Politics and Religion in the Westminster Assembly and the "Grand Debate."* Edinburgh: T. & T. Clark, 1985.

Peel, Albert. *The Noble Army of Congregational Martyrs*. London: Independent, 1948.

———. *The Seconde Parte of a Register*. Cambridge: Cambridge University Press, 1915.

———. Peel, Albert, and Leland H. Carlson. *Cartwrightiana*. London: Allen & Unwin, 1951.

Penn, William. *No Cross, No Crown*. 1669. 26th ed. Reprint. London: Office of the Society of Friends, 1896.

———. *The Sandy Foundation Shaken*. London, 1668.

Rigg, J. M. "John Owen." In *The Dictionary of National Biography*, vol. 42, edited by Leslie Stephen, 424–28. London: Smith, Elder, 1896.

———. *The Sandy Foundation Shaken*. London: n.p., 1668.

Sell, Alan P. F. *Commemorations: Studies in Christian Thought and History*. 1993. Reprint. Eugene, OR: Wipf & Stock, 1998.

———. *Dissenting Thought and the Life of the Churches: Studies in an English Tradition*. Lewiston, NY: Mellen, 1990.

———. *Enlightenment, Ecumenism, Evangel: Theological Themes and Thinkers 1550–2000*. Carlisle, UK: Paternoster, 2005.

———. *The Great Ejectment of 1662: Its Antecedents, Aftermath, and Ecumenical Significance*. Eugene, OR: Pickwick, 2012.

———. *Saints: Visible, Orderly and Catholic: The Congregational Idea of the Church*. Allison Park, PA: Pickwick, 1986.

———. *Testimony and Tradition: Studies in Reformed and Dissenting Thought*. Aldershot, UK: Ashgate, 2005.

Sharrock, Roger. *John Bunyan*. London: Hutchinson, 1954.

Sim, Stuart. Review of William J. Bouwsma, *John Calvin: A Sixteenth-Century Portrait*. *Bunyan Studies* 1 (1989) 79.

Stachniewski, John. *The Persecutory Imagination: English Puritanism and the Literature of Religious Despair*. Oxford: Clarendon, 1991.

Stevenson, Robert. *Exposition of The Pilgrim's Progress*. London: A. & C. Black, 1914.

Torrance, Thomas F. *The School of Faith: The Catechisms of the Reformed Church*. London: Clarke, 1959.

Urwick, William. *Nonconformity in Worcester*. London: Simpkin, Marshall, Kent, 1897.

Walker, Austin. *The Excellent Benjamin Keach*. Guelph, ON: Joshua, 2004.

Walker, Williston. *The Creeds and Platforms of Congregationalism*. 1893. Reprint. Boston: Pilgrim, 1960.

Watson, Thomas. *A Body of Divinity*. London: Banner of Truth, 1965.

Watts, Isaac. *The Psalms and Hymns of the Rev. Isaac Watts, D.D. With copious Indexes, Tables of Contents; and Many Additional Hymns, selected from the Doctor's Works*. London: Caxton, n.d.

Watts, Michael R. *The Dissenters from the Reformation to the French Revolution*. Oxford: Clarendon, 1978.

Whitley, W. T. "Bunyan's Imprisonment: A Legal Study." *Transactions of the Baptist Historical Society* 6 (1918–19) 1–24.

Williams, J. B. *The Life of Philip Henry, A.M.* 1698. Reprint. London: Banner of Truth, 1974.

CHAPTER THREE

Separatists and Dissenters amidst the Arguments For and Against Toleration

Some Soundings, 1550–1689

The ramifications of the terms "tolerance" and "intolerance" are bewildering to the point of intolerable. In common parlance the attitude labelled "tolerance" is generally held to be "good" (though G. K. Chesterton wrote, disapprovingly, that "Tolerance is the virtue of the man without convictions"), whereas "intolerance" is deemed to signify an attitude of which the subject ought to feel ashamed. Further thought will, however, suggest that tolerance of wrong is often deemed to be "bad," while intolerance of cruelty is thought to be "good." Things become even more complicated when we realize that whereas "tolerance" is a term often annexed to liberalism—especially by liberals, while "intolerance" is regarded as the characteristic attitude of conservatives, it is perfectly possible for a liberal to be wrongly intolerant (of those outside the fashionable politico-cultural sect, for example),[1] and for a conservative to be mistakenly tolerant (as when gross financial inequalities as between citizens of the same country do not appal).

It might be thought that we can bracket all of these considerations by focusing our attention upon "toleration" in the sense of "the legal right

---

1. For further thoughts on this intriguing reality see ch. 4 below.

PART ONE: Confessing the Faith in Context

of *a*, *b* and *c* to do *x*, *y* and *z*." We shall swiftly discover, however, that while some have been tolerant of toleration in this sense, others have been noticeably intolerant of it. It will also become apparent that the question of toleration both in the sense of what is deemed to be legally tolerable in society and in relation to degrees of tolerance within the church is bound up with the question, how far are punishment or persecution appropriate when people appeal to liberty of conscience? By whom, and upon what grounds should they be administered? In a word, we are stepping into an argumentative hornet's nest.

In the hope of bringing some order to the matter, and fully recognizing the risk of falsification that I run in making the attempt, I shall classify the arguments for and against toleration under the headings, broadly philosophical, broadly political, broadly ecclesiastical, and broadly theological. I hide behind the adverb, "broadly," because I know that many arguments overlap my categories; I am simply trying to bring some semblance of intellectual coherence to the discussion of a variety of conflicting, and frequently mutually contradictory, arguments that I cannot expunge from the record because they are there. I by no means suggest that individual authors focused upon one type of argument to the exclusion of all others. On the contrary, the approach of many of them was eclectic, as is exemplified in the case of the Congregationalist politician, Charles Wolseley (1629/30–1714), a member of Oliver Cromwell's inner circle and a lifelong advocate of toleration, who published *Liberty of Conscience* in 1668. He adduces three types of argument in defence of the proposition "That no Prince, nor State, ought by force to compel men, to any part of the Doctrine, Worship, or Discipline of the Gospel." First, compulsion in this matter would violate natural law, and be opposed to "the common Light and Reason of mankind"; secondly, appealing now to the gospel, compulsion is "no means appointed by *Christ* to bring about any Gospel end"; and thirdly, now the pragmatist, he contends that error is not banished, nor the truth embraced, by force: it is "not adequate to the Malady,"[2] he declares. It is my hope that the recognition of the diversity of types of argument (none of which I can here discuss in detail, and some of which I shall not pursue[3]) will bring home to us something of the

---

2. Wolseley, *Liberty of Conscience*, 26, 28, 34. He proceeds to argue, *inter alia*, that gospel worship cannot be established by force (a) because it is spiritual; and (b) because it is voluntary. Hence, to force people in this matter is to make hypocrites of them and to commit sin.

3. For example, John Howe's proto-psychological argument that mental idiosyncrasies or, as we should call them, temperamental differences, may prompt differences

nature of the intellectual Babel in which the Separatists and Dissenters sought to make their voices heard.

I

Under the heading, "broadly philosophical", we may first note the epistemological argument that toleration is the child of scepticism. In general terms the upshot is that since we have no access to absolute truth it behoves us to adopt a tolerant attitude towards the beliefs, opinions and claims of others. When we view the matter more closely we see that scepticism is a stream that runs in many channels, and that thinkers as various as Platonists and naturalists have had recourse to it. In the opinion of the Platonist Nicholas of Cusa (1401–64) precise truth is unattainable because our minds cannot comprehend the "unqualifiedly Maximum."[4] By no means an absolute sceptic, Nicholas nevertheless holds that human knowledge of the truth is necessarily and unavoidably partial and approximate only. When he draws out the implications of his epistemology for religion, he concludes that diversities of religious belief and practice originate in, and reflect but do not replicate, the truth of God which none can attain; and that sincere believers, regardless of their particular rites and practices are worshipping the one God.[5] Ideas of this kind filtered down to Herbert of Cherbury (1582–1648), who in *De Veritate* (1624) argued on grounds of the limitations of human knowledge that tolerance of differing views was to be commended. Thereafter the stream bifurcates, flowing on the one hand to the Cambridge Platonists, and on the other to Locke.

The Cambridge Platonists, whose general approach is epitomized by the text, "The spirit of man is the candle of the Lord" (Prov 20:27), were well aware that this implied both that the human spirit reflected its Creator and thus to a degree had knowledge of him, and that it was a candle, not a searchlight. "All our Notions and Opinions can be but broken Things," declared Peter Sterry (1613?–72): "Truth is a Spiritual

---

of view which should be tolerated; and Thomas Pope Blount's view that forbearance was required because differences of opinion could be caused by dietary and climatic differences. See Howe. *A Sermon Concerning Union Among Protestants*; T. P. Blount, *Essays on Several Subjects*.

4. *De Docta Ignorantia*, I.2–3.

5. *De pace fidei*, ch. 19. Cf. Cudworth, *The True Intellectual System of the Universe*, I, 366. The idea flows down to our own time in the writings of John Hick.

Thing, and Divine; The Opinions and Notions in which we see it, are all Earthly Things, and Natural Things: And therefore it's impossible for any one Notion or Opinion to give you the full Truth; but we have that little Truth, which we have in a Thousand broken Notions."[6] In the participatory language characteristic of Platonism, Ralph Cudworth (1617–88) pointed out that "Truths are not multiplied by the diversity of minds that apprehend them; because they are all but ectypal participations of one and the same original or archetypal mind and truth. . . . [S]o when innumerable created minds have the same ideas of things, and understand the same truths, it is but one and the same eternal light that is reflected in them all . . . or the same voice of that one eternal Word, that is never silent, re-echoed by them."[7] The resulting pluralism of thought requires that when individuals see matters in differing ways, toleration is called for not only because of the epistemological deficiency which afflicts all human beings (a deficiency exacerbated in the opinion of some writers by a wilful blindness deriving from sin), but also because of differing cultural and life experiences. As Sterry put it, "Had my Education, my Acquaintance, the several Circumstances and Concurrences been the same to me, as to this person from whom I now Dissent, that which is now his sense and state, might have been mine."[8]

In 1661 Joseph Glanvill (1636–80) published *The Vanity of Dogmatizing*. This caused a flurry of pamphleteering, and in 1665 Glanvill brought out a revised edition under the title, *Scepsis Scientifica, or Confest Ignorance, the way to Science; in an Essay on The Vanity of Dogmatizing*. He here protested against scholastic philosophy, and staunchly advocated the experimental method. He brings the following considerations against dogmatizing: "(1) 'Tis the effect of ignorance. (2) It inhabits with untamed passions, and an ungoverned spirit. (3) It is the great disturber of the world. (4) It is ill manners, and immodesty. (5) It holds men captive in error. (6) It betrays a narrowness of spirit."[9] However, Glanvill sought a comprehensive, non-dogmatic Church of England within which a wide range of opinions might be tolerated, and hence he did not favour the toleration of Dissenters, his friendship with some of them—Baxter

---

6. Sterry, *The Appearance of God to Man in the Gospel*, 410.

7. Cudworth, *The True Intellectual System of the Universe*, III, 71.

8. Sterry, *A Discourse of the Freedom of the Will*, 4–5. Again, John Hick has remarked that had he been born elsewhere than in England he might well have been of another faith.

9. Glanvill, *Scepsis Scientifica*, 165–72.

among them—notwithstanding, because such toleration would defeat his primary objective. We are some way from the post-Toleration atmosphere of the 1730s when those opposed to Dissenters took continuing attempts to restrict them as evidence of the truth of their position, and more liberal members of the Church of England drew the sting of their more Erastian colleagues by arguing that a tolerant spirit demonstrated the purity of their Church.

In somewhat different tones from Glanvill, Locke likewise advanced an epistemological argument for toleration:

> Since, therefore, it is unavoidable to the greatest part of Men, if not all, to have several *Opinions*, without certain and indubitable Proofs of their Truths; and it carries too great an imputation of ignorance, lightness or folly, for Men to quit and renounce their former Tenets, presently upon the offer of an Argument, which they cannot immediately answer, and shew the insufficiency of: It would, methinks, become all Men to maintain *Peace*, and the common Offices of Humanity, and *Friendship, in the diversity of Opinions*, since we cannot reasonably expect, that any one should readily and obsequiously quit his own Opinion and embrace ours, with a blind resignation to an Authority, which the Understanding of Man acknowledges not. For however it may often mistake, it can own no other Guide but Reason, nor blindly submit to the Will and Dictates of another.[10]

At this point I jump forward to the nineteenth-century historian, Lecky, who, according to the theologian A. M. Fairbairn, "argued that toleration is the child of scepticism, possible only in an age when men have grown conscious of the difficulties that beset belief."[11] We have already seen that epistemological scepticism is prompted by factors other than difficulties regarding religious belief. But Fairbairn finds that Lecky errs in another way: "Toleration," he contends, "is not only possible, but necessary, the moment religion is made a matter for the conscience rather than the magistrate, but impossible the moment it becomes an affair of the magistrate rather than the conscience."[12] With this the morality is added to the philosophical mix and we plunge into a recent debate in Locke interpretation. Jeremy Waldron has argued against Locke, that if

---

10. Locke, *An Essay concerning Human Understanding*, IV, xvi.4.

11. Fairbairn, *Jubilee Lectures*, lx. Fairbairn quotes Lecky, *History of the Rise and Influence of the Spirit of Rationalism in Europe*, II, 56 ff.

12. Fairbairn, *Jubilee Lectures*, lx.

due account is not taken of the moral dimension and we are left only with epistemological scepticism, we shall be able to show that intolerance is irrational, but we shall have no grounds for withstanding coercion.[13] Susan Mendus's retort is justified: for Locke "the moral wrongness of intolerance consists precisely in its irrationality."[14] I myself have suggested that Waldron abstracts from Locke's overall position; indeed, he himself uses the phrase, "When stripped of its Christian premises (if indeed it can be so stripped . . .)"—a question that he begs and declines to pursue.[15] That it cannot be so stripped is made clear by Locke's own words. He argues that "The toleration of those that differ from others in matters of religion, is agreeable to the gospel of Jesus Christ," and that "we must not content ourselves with the narrow measures of bare justice: charity, bounty, and liberality must be added to it. This the Gospel enjoins, this reason directs, and this the natural fellowship we are born into requires of us."[16] Near the beginning of his paper Waldron quotes Locke to this effect, branding it an *ad hominem* address to the Christian authorities, but ruling it out as philosophically interesting, because what is required is an argument addressed to civil magistrates as wielders of state power not as church members. But here Waldron drives a wedge between what to Locke and most others were two sides of the same coin: the civil magistrates were God's appointees and were called to serve him, hence the Christian's *prima facie* obligation to respect and obey them. If our interest is in the thought of Locke, and not in abstracting general arguments for toleration we may not overlook these considerations.

With his phrase, "the natural fellowship we are born into," Locke balances his appeal to the gospel with one to natural law, and here we have a link between Locke, the Cambridge Platonists, and the later Rational Dissenters. Thus, Henry More (1614–87) asserts that "there is a Right in every Nation and Person to examine their Religion, to hear the Religion of Strangers, and to change their own, if they be convinced";[17]

---

13. Waldron. "Locke: Toleration and the Rationality of Persecution." In Mendus, *Justifying Toleration*, ch. 3; reprinted in Horton and Mendus, *John Locke, A Letter Concerning Toleration in Focus*, 98–124. I refer to this edition of Locke's *Letter* throughout.

14. Mendus, *Toleration and the Limits of Liberalism*, 41.

15. Waldron, "Locke: Toleration and the Rationality of Persecution," 149. See further, Sell, *John Locke*, 330.

16. Locke, *A Letter Concerning Toleration*, 16, 23.

17. More, *An Explanation of the grand Mystery of Godliness*, 521.

while on 22 May 1772 Richard Price (1723–91) wrote to the Earl of Chatham concerning still-delayed toleration. He thanks Chatham for what he had said in the House of Lords three days earlier, namely, "I am for this bill, my Lords, because I am for toleration, that sacred right of nature and bulwark of truth and most interesting of all objects to fallible man," and regrets that "no force of argument could secure success for us; and that we must still continue to owe to our governors a security to which we have, as we apprehend, a natural right."[18] Price's point is that the state should not interfere in religious matters at all except with a view to offering equal protection to all varieties of non-order-threatening beliefs. Strictly, the state was in no position to grant or withhold toleration, for religious and civil liberty "must be enjoyed as a right derived from the Author of nature only.... If there is any human power which is considered as *giving* it, on which it depends, and which can invade or recall it at pleasure, it changes its nature, and becomes a species of slavery."[19]

II

Something else that Chatham said in the House of Lords will lead us to some broadly ecclesiastical arguments for and against toleration. In answering Hay Drummond, the Archbishop of York, Chatham declared, "You talk of our English Church system; but we have no system: we have a Calvinistic creed, a Popish liturgy, and an Arminian clergy. The Dissenters you revile contend for a spiritual creed and spiritual worship."[20] This, although not an entirely accurate—nor, in the circumstances, the most diplomatic—judgment, does at least make the point that if doctrinal diversity could be tolerated within the Church of England, it ought to be possible to tolerate it elsewhere. Once again we may return to the Cambridge Platonists for a witness to charitable tolerance. "The Spirit of Religion," wrote Benjamin Whichcote (1609–83) during a time of religious upheaval, "is a Reconciling Spirit."[21] Locke concurred: "peace, equity, and friendship, are always mutually to be observed by particular churches, in the same manner as by private persons, without any

---

18. Thomas and Peach, *The Correspondence of Richard Price*, I, 131 and n.
19. Price, *Additional Observations*, 4.
20. Thomas and Peach, *The Correspondence of Richard Price*, I, 131.
21. Whichcote, Aphorism 712 in *Moral and Religious Aphorisms*.

pretence of superiority of jurisdiction over one another."²² Indeed, he was more specific than that, and drove to the sectarian root of the matter as he opposed those who "impose their own inventions and interpretations upon others, as if they were of divine authority; and . . . establish by ecclesiastical laws, as absolutely necessary to the profession of Christianity, such things as the holy Scriptures do either not mention, or at least not expressly command." He cannot understand "how that can be called a church of Christ, which is established upon laws that are not his, and which excludes such persons from its communion as he will one day receive into the kingdom of heaven."²³

Edward Stillingfleet (1635–99), at the time Dean of St. Paul's, unsurprisingly, took a different view. For his sermon entitled, *The Mischief of Separation*, preached in the Guildhall Chapel before the Lord Mayor, Robert Clayton, on 11 May 1660, he took Philippians 3:16 as his text: "Nevertheless, whereunto we have already attained, let us walk by the same rule, let us mind the same thing." The gist of his argument is that since the Nonconformists are able to affirm the doctrinal Articles of the Church of England; since they generally grant that the parochial churches are true churches; and since many have no objection to taking communion in those churches, he can see no justification for their continued separation, least of all at a time when the country is in great danger owing to the threat posed by Roman Catholicism.²⁴ John Owen (1616–83) was but the most prominent of a number of Dissenters who came out in hot pursuit of the Dean. While not denying that "the parochial churches, at least some of them, in this nation are true churches," he nevertheless levels the following charges against them: they need to be further reformed; they impose "many things . . . on the consciences and practices of men, which are not according to the mind of Christ"; they are lax in true church discipline, and are governed by courts that are "unknown to Scripture"; they deprive the people of the liberty of choosing their own pastors; and while failing to edify the people themselves they forbid them to seek edification elsewhere.²⁵ Stillingfleet returned to the fray with a *Discourse of the Unreasonableness of Separation*, to which Owen produced *An Answer* appended to *An Enquiry into the Original*,

---

22. Locke, *A Letter Concerning Toleration*, 24.
23. Ibid., 21–22.
24. Stillingfleet, *The Mischief of Separation*, 21–22, and cf. the Epistle Dedicatory.
25. Owen, *A Brief Vindication of the Non-Conformists*, 35–36.

Nature, Institution, Power, Order, and Communion of Evangelical Churches. In his note "To the reader" Owen rebuts Stillingfleet's charge that the Nonconformists' objective is "the furtherance and promotion of the designs of the Papists and interest of Popery," pointing out that "we should be the very first who should drink of the cup of [the Jesuits'] fury, could they ruin the protestant interest in England."[26]

Lest it be thought that no Church of England parson lifted a finger in support of Nonconformists, the minority view of Samuel Bold, who later defended Locke against his critics, may be noted. In 1682 Bold published *A Plea for Moderation towards Dissenters*, in which he concluded that "The overdoing of Conformity, that is, making more necessary to Conformity than the Laws of the Land have made necessary, is as great a fault as Nonconformity.... From the subtle and deceitful Craftiness, and the violent Rage and Force of [those who endorse such a policy] and of their Brethren and Companions the Papists, the merciful and good Lord deliver every Sincere and Hearty Protestant."[27] These sentiments earned Bold prosecution at the Sherborne assizes. He was fined and imprisoned for seven weeks, before being summoned before William Gulston, Bishop of Bristol, charged with libel and sedition. These proceedings were terminated on Gulston's unexpected death. More prominent than Bold, Gilbert Burnet (1643–1715) was similarly-minded.[28]

We have already begun to veer towards broadly political arguments for and against toleration, but before briefly reviewing these we must notice how in ecclesiastical circles arguments could readily cancel one another out. Tertullian had long ago argued that God would not welcome worship unwillingly offered,[29] and flowing down from the Renaissance was the conviction that enforced religion is harmful. This idea received stimulus from Castellio who in 1562, at a time of religious strife in France, rhetorically asked, "Do you urge your enemy to act against his conscience? If he does, it will be fatal to his soul."[30] Again, it was argued that compulsion in religious matters could lead to hypocrisy, to which the answer came, "I have a Lewd *Negro*, who was bred an Idolater, I must not compel him to go to Church, for fear I *only* make him a hypocrite. Oh

---

26. Owen, *An Enquiry*, unpag., but 1, 8.

27. Bold, *A Plea for Moderation towards Dissenters*, 42.

28. See Burnet, *The Case of Compulsion in Matters of Religion Stated*; Burnet, *An Exhortation to Peace and Unity*; and the first of Burnet's *Two Sermons*.

29. Tertullian, *Apologeticus*, XXIV.

30. Castellio's anonymous work, *Conseil à la France desolée*, (1562).

uncharitable!"³¹ Others maintained that punishment of error (error being, of course, determined by those inflicting the punishment) removes a troubling virus and thus protects others. From the other side the Separatist John Robinson (c.1575–1625) contended that while compulsive laws might yield hypocrisy they could never create the spirit "that received the word gladly."³² For his part the Baptist Samuel Richardson (fl. 1643–58) urged that "Corporal punishments cannot suppress errors, neither doth truth need any such help to maintain it."³³ This did not silence those who believed that while torture was not called for, other forms of coercion could encourage the erring to reconsider their position. In the view of Henry Dodwell (1641–1711) it was not true that "*coercion is not a probable means* of bringing even *good men* to a *conscientious* change of their Opinions. For . . . [i]t is of itself likely to allay that *tumour and rigour* of spirit, to which even *good men* are betrayed by *prosperity*, which does usually alienate them from all sober thoughts of *accommodation*, and even of sober and impartial *inquiry*."³⁴ I find that none in our period were quite as blunt as Augustine who, being cruel to be kind, declared that the Church "persecutes in the spirit of love, [the impious] in the spirit of wrath"³⁵—a distinction likely to have brought little solace to the persecuted.

By contrast it is cheering note the strenuous efforts exerted by those who in the seventeenth century worked tirelessly for tolerance and harmony among the churches. They frequently recalled the supreme command of Jesus Christ himself: "Love one another as I have loved you" (John 13:34), and transformed it into an affective ecclesiastical argument for toleration. In so doing they were not originators. The basis of the argument is found, for example, in the writings of John Foxe (1517–87) the martyrologist, who declared that

> The nearer each approaches to the sweet spirit of the Gospel, by so much farther he is from the hard decision of burning and torturing. It is tyrannical to constrain by faggots. Consciences love to be taught, and religion wants to teach. The most effective master of teaching is love. Where this is absent there is never anyone who can teach aright nor can anyone learn properly.³⁶

---

31. Anon., *Toleration and Liberty of Conscience Considered*, 23.
32. Robinson, *The Works of John Robinson*, II, 488.
33. Richardson, *The Necessity of Toleration*, 275.
34. Dodwell, *A Reply to Mr. Baxter's Pretended Confutation*, 200.
35. Augustine, *Epistle* 185, 11.
36. Quoted by Dickens, "Religious Toleration," 69.

Separatists and Dissenters amidst the Arguments For and Against Toleration

No one in the seventeenth century made more of this approach than that most pacific of Presbyterian Puritans, John Howe (1630–1705), in his *Sermon Concerning Union Among Protestants*. His text is Colossians 2:2, "That their hearts might be comforted, being knit together in love, and unto all riches of the full assurance of understanding." Howe's case is that truly to grasp the gospel with the understanding is to love the saints. Christian love, he declares, is not "a love to Christians of this or that party or denomination only. That were as much as to unduly straiten and confine it. . . . To limit our Christian love to a party of Christians . . . is so far from serving the purpose now to be aimed at, that it resists and defeats it; and instead of a preservative union, infers most destructive divisions. It scatters where it should collect and gather."[37] Howe did not only speak along these lines; he strove put his ideas into practice, working tirelessly for the Happy Union between Presbyterian and Congregational ministers. Indeed, he drafted the *Heads of Agreement* on which the Union was based. Sadly, the Union that was inaugurated with such promise in 1690 had collapsed owing largely to doctrinal strife by 1693.

III

The broadly political arguments advanced against toleration were, unsurprisingly, prompted by the perceived need to deal with the state's enemies of one kind and another. There was, as we shall see, genuine fear that Rome wished to undo the English Reformation, and hence that those who supported the alien power were tantamount to traitors; there was also, in the wake of the regicide of 1649, a powerful memory of the disruption that could be caused to civil society by unrestrained radical sectaries. Responses to this situation varied, and some arguments cancelled one another out, with some writers, pragmatically, contending that toleration makes for a tranquil society, others, equally pragmatically, countering that in fact it leads to ungovernable anarchy and must therefore be resisted. Thus, for example, on the one hand Anthony Collins (1676–1729) spoke—albeit in 1726—for those who believed that "*Toleration* or *Liberty of Conscience* in matters of mere Religion, was the way of Knowledge and *Truth*, the way of good Neighbourhood, and Peace, and Order, and the way of Wealth and strength in Society."[38] On the other

37. *The Works of the Rev. John Howe*, I, 475.
38. Collins, *A Letter to the Reverend Dr. Rogers*, 2.

hand, Samuel Parker expostulated that "*Indulgence and Toleration is the most absolute sort of* Anarchy."[39] In 1670, in the wake of the Ejectment of 1662, Parker (1640–88), the Erastian Bishop of Oxford, threw down the gauntlet in *A Discourse of Ecclesiastical Politie: wherein the Authority of the Civil Magistrate over the Consciences of Subjects in Matters of Religion is Asserted; the Mischiefs and Inconveniences of Toleration are Represented, and all Pretences Pleaded in Behalf of Liberty of Conscience are Fully Answered.* "Where a Religion is Establish'd by the Laws," he thunders, "whoever openly refuses Obedience plainly Rebels against the Government, Rebellion being properly nothing else but an open denial of Obedience to the Civil Power."[40] For his pains, Parker and others of his ilk were accused of Hobbism. For their part, Dissenters—and especially Quakers—were frequently, and hysterically, portrayed as disguised agents of Rome. It was against this background that in 1660 the Presbyterian, John Corbet, argued for uniformity in preference to toleration of difference, on the ground that "the dividing of Church communion is the dividing of hearts, and . . . we shall not live like brethren, till we agree to walk in one way."[41] The upshot was that those who stood on theological and conscientious grounds against the attempted imposition of uniformity of faith and practice were not only regarded as criminals deserving of punishment but as traitors. Moreover, if the Act of Uniformity of 1662 was directed against ministers of religion and schoolmasters, other acts impinged directly upon the lives of church members. Among these was the Conventicle Act of 1664, which provided that if five or more persons, other than those of the same household, met for religious purposes they were liable to a fine of £5 for the first offence, £10 or imprisonment for a second offence, and transportation—but not to Virginia and New England—for a period of seven years for the third offence. While it is true that the adverse laws were applied across the country with varying degrees of rigour, the intention was clear, and many in fact suffered under them.

But at the top of the list of suspected religious bodies was the Church of Rome. To this day Dissenters can be disquieted by Rome, but they are not generally afraid of it. It is therefore not easy for us to get into the mindset of those who regarded Rome and the territories under its sway

39. Parker, *A Discourse of Ecclesiastical Politie*, liv.

40. Ibid., 105. Even Jeremy Taylor had taken a similar anti-toleration line in a sermon preached at the opening of the Irish Parliament on 8 May 1661. See further Schochet. "Samuel Parker." In Lund, *The Margins of Orthodoxy*, ch. 5.

41. Corbet, *The Interest of England in the Matter of Religion*, 73–74.

as an "axis of evil", to purloin a certain cattle rancher's phrase. Many who were not thrown into hysteria at the thought of Rome nevertheless regarded English Roman Catholics as owing allegiance to a foreign power, and therefore as not to be tolerated. In 1680 John Owen, for example, asked a question to which he thought the answer was obvious: "Who knows not that the present danger of this nation is from *Popery*, and the endeavours that are used both to introduce it and enthrone it, or give it Power and Authority among us?"[42] At roughly the same time Locke referred to the popery "that so nearly surrounds and threatens us."[43]

But Rome was not the only bogeyman. There was atheism too. This was regarded as a threat to civil society because of the Psalmists's declaration that "The fool hath said in his heart, There is no God" (Ps 14:1)—and the Psalmist's "fool" is not the stupid or silly person, but the immoral person. God was regarded as the source of the moral law and to repudiate God was to repudiate morality as well. Atheists were thus deemed to be undermining the moral fabric of society, and it was not until well into the nineteenth century that it began to be widely conceded that one could be both an atheist and a person of high moral standards. It is therefore not surprising that with enemies without and within, toleration could be regarded as a dangerous objective and arguments for it could be deemed foolhardy and even subversive of good order in society.

The strength of these ideas is clearly seen in the case of Locke, who became a great apostle of toleration. I say "became," because it is well known that in the 1650s he was opposed to it in the interests of national stability; he later became persuaded that Dissenters should be tolerated, partly through conversations with Shaftesbury, and partly because of his favourable experience first in the Duchy of Cleves[44] and later in the Netherlands of a degree of religious tolerance that was unknown in England; partly through his friendship with the Remonstrant theologian Philippus van Limborch;[45] and partly on the ground that owing to epistemological deficiency magistrates were in no position to enforce conformity. This last position had been articulated by the General Baptist, Thomas Monck, and six of his colleagues in 1661: "That magistrates may err in spiritual and religious matters, woful experience hath taught the world in

---

42. Owen, *A Brief Vindication of the* Nonconformists, 1.

43. Unreferenced quotation in Marshall, *John Locke*, 28.

44. See Locke's letter of 12/22 December 1665 to Robert Boyle, in Goldie, *John Locke. Selected Correspondence*, 27.

45. For a helpful account of "The Dutch influence on English toleration" see Haley.

all ages."⁴⁶ But (however inconsistently) Locke did not extend his pro-toleration argument to accommodate Roman Catholics and atheists for, in his view, both, in their different ways, posed threats to civil order. While he did not inveigh against Roman Catholic doctrinal and sacramental beliefs in the way that some other Protestants did, Locke nevertheless held that because Roman Catholics "deliver themselves up to the protection and service of another prince," and atheists are guilty of "The taking away of God, [which] though but even in thought, dissolves all"⁴⁷ neither party was to be tolerated.⁴⁸

The so-called Toleration Act of 1689⁴⁹ provided that while all the legislation adverse to the Dissenters remained unrepealed on the statute book, its penalties would not be applied to orthodox Protestant Dissenters. In its own words, it was "An Act for exempting their Majesties' Protestant subjects dissenting from the Church of England, from the penalties of certain laws." Here was the blatant exclusion of Jews, and also of the Roman Catholics. Section XVII of the Act further excludes "any person that shall deny in his preaching or writing the doctrine of the blessed Trinity as it is declared in [the Thirty-nine Articles of the Church of England]." With this we are reminded that Socinians, were regarded by some, along with blasphemers, as disturbers of the civic peace—an accusation levelled from time to time least until the Priestley riots of 1791.

For more than a century the political motivation of those who designed successive Uniformity Acts had been to convert into policy the idea concisely expressed by Richard Hooker: "there is not any man of the Church of England but the same man is also a member of the commonwealth; nor any man a member of the commonwealth, which is not also of the Church of England"⁵⁰—and this in the interests of national unity. The Toleration Act of 1689 testifies to the impracticality of seeking

---

46. Monck and others. *Sion's Groans for the Distressed*. In Underhill, *Tracts on Liberty of Conscience*, 365.

47. Locke, *A Letter Concerning Toleration*, 46, 47. In the *Areopagitica* (1644) Milton had argued for a wide toleration—not excluding Socinians—on the ground that in a free society truth could take care of itself. However, he was content to except Roman Catholics from toleration on the ground that once in power they would deny toleration to others. We should note that although Locke completed his *Letter Concerning Toleration* in 1685, his mature views on the subject were not widely known until after the Toleration Act of 1689.

48. See further on the progress of Locke's view, Sell, *John Locke*, 151–57.

49. I William and Mary, sess. I, c.18.

50. Hooker, *Works*, III, 330.

national unity by the legalized imposition of religious uniformity. Some of the Dissenters had known from the outset that this was not only a policy doomed to fail in practice; it was mistaken from the outset because when the chips are down, God takes precedence over Caesar. With this we come to their broadly theological argument.

IV

It is first necessary to face up to the fact that where toleration was concerned the Dissenters were well versed in dissenting from one another. It will emerge that they were capable of arguing both for and against toleration. This implies that the theological argument for toleration, pioneered by Baptists and, with some exceptions, endorsed by Congregationalists was capable of being blunted by ecclesiological considerations. On all sides there were those who could find it easier and more proper to tolerate those of their own polity, presumed to have been ordained in Scripture.

Although, as we have seen, the Separatist John Robinson was opposed to enforced belief, he nevertheless, like most in his age, believed that godly magistrates were appointed by God and that their tasks were "by compulsion to repress public and notable idolatry, as also to provide that the truth of God in his ordinance be taught, and published in their dominions."[51] The problem here, of course, is that Robinson holds the magistrate responsible for enforcing Christ's rights, and Robinson knows what those rights are. This is why, concluded W. B. Selbie, "the early Independents could condemn persecution of themselves and at the same time tolerate, or even approve, persecution of others. They were ensnared by the usual sophism that, since their doctrine was the truth, it was just for them to be encouraged and for its adversaries to be put down."[52]

To this general rule the early General Baptists provided a notable exception. To them we must turn for pioneering advocacy of universal toleration on theological grounds. Shortly before his death John Smyth (c.1570–1612), exiled in the Netherlands, had prepared the draft of one hundred *Propositions and Conclusions*, and these were published in 1612. The eighty-fourth proposition is to the effect that "the magistrate is not by virtue of his office to meddle with religion, or matters of conscience, to force or compel men to this or that form of religion, or doctrine: but

51. Robinson, *Works*, III, 105.
52. Selbie, *Evangelical Christianity*, 112.

to leave Christian religion free, to every man's conscience, and to handle only civil transgressions . . . for Christ only is the king and lawgiver of the church and conscience."[53] Here we have the seeds of the anti-establishment argument, but it is important to understand that this is more than a straightforwardly political argument; it is an inference drawn from the prior fact that Christ alone is Lord of the conscience. It would be thoroughly anachronistic to read this as a secular-humanist argument for liberty of conscience, or freedom of the will. On the contrary the General Baptists believed that, owing to the pernicious effects of sin, the individual's will was bound until released by God's grace.[54] These General Baptists were not apostles of latter day human rights; they stood for the rights of God over conscience, church and world. The point is underlined by Thomas Helwys (c.1575–c.1616), who had returned from the Netherlands in 1611, who founded the first Baptist church on English soil, and who published *A Short Declaration of the Mistery of Iniquity* in 1612. Here, in the wake of a good deal of anti-Roman-and-Church of England polemics, he famously advocates universal religious toleration:

> Our lord the King is but an earthly King, and he hath no authority as a King but in earthly causes, and if the Kings people be obedient and true subjects, obeying all humane lawes made by the King, our lord the King can require no more: for mens religion to God is betwixt God and themselves; the King shall not answer for it, neither may the King be iugd between God and man. Let them be heretickes, Turcks, Jewes, or what soever, it apperteynes not to the earthly power to punish them in the least measure. This is made evident to our lord the King by the Scriptures.[55]

The theological point is reiterated in a personal note written by Helwys inside the cover of the copy of his book that he sent to James I: "The king," he declares, "is a mortal man and not God."[56] As Brian Haymes rightly says, "The crucial matter for Helwys is the sovereign right of Christ the King and the holy nature of the human conscience before God,"[57] and

---

53. Lumpkin, *Baptist Confessions of Faith*, 140.

54. For a full discussion of this and related points see Canipe, "'That most damnable heresie.'" Cf. Jordan, "The early Independents and the visible Church," 303–4.

55. Helwys, *A Short Declaration of the Mistery of Iniquity*, 69.

56. This book is at the Bodleian Library, Oxford. I owe the information to Brian Haymes, "On Religious Liberty."

57. Ibid., 201. I am pleased that Haymes and I are in accord: "It is crucial," he insists, "to recognize that Helwys' argument is theological." Ibid., 204.

Separatists and Dissenters amidst the Arguments For and Against Toleration

this, I would add, as declared in the Scriptures. Thus, when later Locke likewise esteemed it "above all things necessary to distinguish exactly the business of civil government from that of religion," and contended that "it appears not that God has ever given any such authority to one man over another, as to compel any one to his religion,"[58] he was so far in agreement with the General Baptist pioneers. For their part they were not harbingers of Locke's epistemological argument for toleration.

That Smyth and Helwys were not alone in advocating the pro-toleration case is clear from such publications as *Religion's Peace* (1614) by Leonard Busher; *Objections Answered* (1615) and *A Most Humble Supplication* (1620) by John Murton;[59] and *The Bloudy Tenent of Persecution* by Roger Williams (c.1606–83). Williams's book appeared in 1644, and in the same year seven Particular Baptist Churches in London published their *London Confession*, in which they agreed that "a civill Magistrate is an ordinance of God set up by God for the punishment of evill doers, and for the praise of them that doe well," but also affirmed that "wee desire to give unto God that which is Gods, and unto Caesar that which is Caesars."[60]

By now the Westminster Assembly was in session, and tensions among the Dissenters over toleration were exhibited both within and without the Assembly. I shall first note some of the external rumblings. In his work of 1644 Roger Williams, whose endorsement of Baptist views had earlier led to his banishment from Massachussetts to Rhode Island by the Congregationalists, adduced biblical texts "against the *Doctrine* of *Persecution* of the *cause* of *Conscience*." He set out to answer from Scripture the "objections produced by Mr. *Calvin*, Beza, Mr. *Cotton*, and the Ministers of the New English Churches, and others former and later, tending to prove the *Doctrine* of *Persecution* for cause of *Conscience*," and to show that that doctrine "is proved guilty of all the *blood* of the *Soules* crying for *vengeance* under the *Altar*."[61] Throughout, Williams emphasises the distinction between Church and state that is to be observed where religious matters are concerned, and he addressed his work to Parliament.

In the same year in which Williams's book appeared the John Cotton to whom he refers, published his book, *The Keyes of the Kingdom*.

---

58. Locke, *A Letter Concerning Toleration*, 17, 18.
59. Busher's and Murton's tracts appear in Underhill, *Tracts on Liberty of Conscience*.
60. Lumpkin, *Baptist Confessions of Faith*, 169–71.
61. Williams, *The Bloudy Tenent, of Persecution for cause of Conscience*, a2.

PART ONE: Confessing the Faith in Context

Cotton (1584–1652) had emigrated to the New World in 1633, and there he became a leading exponent of the Congregational Way. It was when he set out to rebut Cotton's arguments that John Owen was converted to Congregationalism.[62] To Cotton and others in New England, the Congregational Way was the only divinely sanctioned model of Church order, and they were not disposed to tolerate those who diverged from it. Many Congregationalists who remained in England cited their transatlantic co-religionists with approval. William Bartlet (1609/10–1682), minister at Wapping, was as bold as any in denying that the Congregationalists favoured the toleration of all doctrines and church practices. Indeed, he lamented that some did not join the Congregational Way precisely because they thought that in that fold "every man may do as he list", and that Arianism and Socinianism were rife in the churches. This, Bartlet thunders, "is a great *untruth*, and so nothing but a *slander*, and an evill report that some evill Spyes give out . . ."[63]

We do not have to look far to discover who these "evill Spyes" might be. Some Presbyterians were, without question, among them, supremely the virulent Thomas "Gangraena" Edwards (1599–1647). "A *Toleration*," he declares, "is the grand design of the Devil, his Masterpiece and the chief Engine he works by at this time to uphold his tottering Kingdom; it is the most compendious, ready, sure way to destroy all Religion. . . . As original sin is the most fundamental sin of all sin, having the seed and spawn of all in it; So a *Toleration* hath all errors in it, and all evills."[64] Edwards has the Congregationalists particularly within his sights. Indeed, he thinks that "as Independency is the mother and originall of other sects, so 'tis the nurse and patroness that nurses and safeguards them."[65] He accuses Independent ministers of having pleaded for the toleration of Anabaptists and others, and is convinced that if toleration were granted the result would be "Scepticism in Doctrine, and looseness of life, and afterwards all Atheisme."[66] Milton was not altogether without justification when, in 1646, the same year in which Edwards launched his torpedo,

---

62. For the ecclesiological background see Sell, *Saints: Visible, Orderly and Catholic*, ch. 3.

63. Bartlet, Ἰχνογραφια. *Or A Model of the Primitive Congregational Way*. 124.

64. Edwards, *Gangraena*, 153–54.

65. Ibid., 158. Edwards had first inveighed against the Independents in *Reasons against the Independent Government of particular Congregations; as also against the Toleration to be erected in this Kingdome*.

66. Edwards, *Gangraena*, 188.

he wrote his poem entitled, "On the new forcers of conscience under the Long Parliament", and declared that "New *Presbyter* is but old Priest writ large."

Exceptional in his antagonism Edwards may have been, but so balanced a person as the moderate episcopalian Richard Baxter nevertheless affirmed more than forty years later—indeed, in the very year that the Toleration Act reached the statute books, that "We are not for unlimited Toleration: But that the Rulers justly distinguish in Law and Licence; 1. The approved, whom they must own and maintain. 2. The tolerable, whom they must tolerate. 3. The intolerable, whom they must restrain from doing hurt."[67]

Among those who subscribed to the Particular Baptist *London Confession* was Samuel Richardson who, in 1647, published *The Necessity of Toleration in Matters of Religion*. In answer to the question why the Nonconformists cannot subscribe to the deliverances of the Westminster Assembly he explains that "You would all be tolerated, and would have none tolerated but yourselves; you would suffer none to live quietly, and comfortable, but those of your way." He exhorts them to love their enemies, "or else, how can we look upon you to be reformed, much less to be reformers."[68] With this we come to the tensions over toleration exhibited during the Westminster Assembly.

Largely Presbyterian in composition, the Westminster Assembly nevertheless had five significant Congregationalists: Thomas Goodwin, Philip Nye, Sidrach Simpson, Jeremiah Burroughes and William Bridge, and four or five others, among its number. In his 1882 paper on "The Westminster Assembly" John Stoughton said of these that "Their chief distinction, and it is a highly meritorious one, is that in an age when the current ran in the opposite direction, they contended for religious toleration."[69] This eulogy requires qualification. We have already seen that the Congregationalist William Bartlet was still opposing complete toleration in 1647, and he was not alone in so doing. The truth, as exposed by Robert Paul, would seem to be that the Congregationalists of the Westminster Assembly found their pro-toleration voice only when, during the sessions, it became clear that if the Presbyterians succeeded

---

67. Baxter, *The English Nonconformists as under King Charles II and King James II*, 15.

68. Richardson, *The Necessity of Toleration*. In Underhill, *Tracts on Toleration*, 284, 285.

69. Stoughton, "The Westminster Assembly." In *Jubilee Lectures*, I, 170.

PART ONE: Confessing the Faith in Context

in enforcing their polity across the country they themselves would be seriously disadvantaged. As Paul puts it,

> There is no reason to think that when they entered the Assembly the Independents would have been any more reluctant to see Congregationalism established in England than their colleagues had been to establish it in America. . . . Liberty of conscience, which had no place among the pre-war prejudices of New England Congregationalism, within a few years became the main plank in [the English Congregationalists'] platform within the Assembly and in their representations to Parliament.[70]

Something of the change of tone as between Presbyterians and Congregationalists will become clear from a comparison of some statements issuing from the Westminster Assembly with some drawn from the Congregationalists' *Savoy Declaration of Faith and Order* of 1658. In the first place we may note that according to the *Westminster Larger Catechism*, among the sins forbidden under the second of the Ten Commandments is that of "tolerating a false religion . . ."[71] There is nothing like this in Savoy. There is, however, a positive statement in the Preface, namely, that "amongst all Christian States and Churches, there ought to be vouchsafed a forbearance and mutual indulgence unto Saints of all perswasions, that keep unto, and hold fast the necessary foundations of faith and holiness, in all matters extrafundamental, whether of Faith or Order."[72] When the saints step out of line in matters of doctrine or worship, the *Westminster Confession* says that "they may lawfully be called to account, and proceeded against by the censures of the church, and by the power of the civil magistrate."[73] *Savoy* omits this section. Savoy's most significant amendment of *Westminster*[74] is in its deletion of the latter's chapter XXIII.iii, which affirms the civil magistrate's power to suppress blasphemies, heresies and corruptions and abuses in worship and discipline by the calling of synods if necessary, and its replacement by the following:

> Although the Magistrate is bound to incourage, promote, and protect the professors and profession of the Gospel, and to

---

70. Paul, *The Assembly of the Lord*, 31. Cf. ibid., 50, 103, 440, 477.
71. *The Larger Catechism*, Answer to Q, 109.
72. Matthews, *The Savoy Declaration*, 56.
73. *Westminster Confession of Faith*, XX.iv.
74. Apart from the introduction of a completely new chapter XX, "Of the Gospel, and of the extent of the Grace thereof."

> manage and order civil administrations in a due subserviency to the interest of Christ in the world.... Yet in such differences about the Doctrines of the Gospel, or ways of the worship of God, as may befall men exercising a good conscience . . . not disturbing others in their ways or worship that differ from them; there is no warrant for the Magistrate under the Gospel to abridge them of their liberty.[75]

That the point was by no means immediately, still less universally, taken is clear from the fact that in 1659, the year following the publication of *Savoy*, Milton addressed *A Treatise of Civil Power in Ecclesiastical Causes* to Richard Cromwell's first and only Parliament. On the basis of a number of biblical texts, and bolstered by the *argumentum ad hominem*, he affirms, "That Christ is the only lawgiver of his church . . . in religious matters, no well grounded Christian will deny."[76] He elaborated thus:

> Christ hath a government of his own, sufficient of it self to all his ends and purposes in governing his church; but much different from that of the civil magistrate; and the difference in this verie thing principally consists, that it governs not by outward force, and that for two reasons. First, because it deals only with the inward man and his actions, which are all spiritual and to outward force not liable: secondly, to shew us the divine excellence of his spiritual kingdom, able without worldly force to subdue all the powers and kingdoms of this world, which are upheld by outward force only.[77]

Milton draws the distinctions between matters spiritual and civil, and between the spiritual and worldly kingdom clearly enough, but he must surely have known that the saints lived in both kingdoms, and that the saints were sinners: otherwise why the Puritan concern for godly discipline in the Church? John Owen was among others who expatiated on the point.

Arguments of a somewhat different flavour emanated from those industrious pamphleteers, the Quakers. In 1663 William Smith (d. 1673), at the time imprisoned in Nottingham County Gaol, addressed a "tender Message of Love unto the King" entitled, *Liberty of Conscience Pleaded by several weighty Reasons on the Behalf of the People of God called Quakers*. His argument in a nutshell is that since Quakers have received "the Light

---

75. *The Savoy Declaration*, XXIV.iii.
76. Milton, *A Treatise of Civil Power in Ecclesiastical Causes*, 10.
77. Ibid., 37–38.

that comes from Jesus Christ, and walk in the same... they ought to have that Liberty granted them into which Christ hath restored them."[78] By no means all were persuaded that the Quakers had received the light of Christ, still less did they approve of the type of witnessing that Quakers undertook in consequence of their claimed divine illumination. For example, whereas other Dissenters were seeking freedom to worship without let or hindrance, the Quakers could justify disturbing the worship of others because they deemed it false. To Edward Burrough (1634–62) it was wrong that the Quaker practice of entering "steeple-houses" to reprove sin, to exhort people unto good, and to denounce deceitful hireling teachers, should be called "a disturbance of the peace, and an unlawful practice."[79] For his part, Isaac Penington (1616–79) argued that their persecution constituted evidence that the Quakers were born of God's Spirit and "new-created in Christ"; they are hated and persecuted because they do not follow the ways of the world. On the contrary, their Light condemns the world, and their persecutors are trying to bring them back to the world again. Penington exhorts the magistrates not to "suppress the plants of God," but to wield the sword against evil.[80] The implication of Penington's argument would seem to be that if the Quakers were to be tolerated, that could only be because either the whole world had seen the light, or because they had fallen from grace.

It is not without significance that John Owen was a primary architect of *Savoy*, or that he was primarily responsible for its temperate Preface. It is clear, however, that there was a significant gap between the degree of toleration—largely of worship and church order—advocated by even the most advanced Congregationalists, and the universal toleration for which Helwys and his fellow Baptists had appealed. This becomes clear in the pro-toleration writings of Owen, the most intensely theological,[81] if also on occasion the most prolix, author among the Congregationalists.

78. Smith, *Liberty of Conscience Pleaded*, 6.
79. Burrough, *A Message for Instruction to all the Rulers*, 13.
80. See Penington, *Concerning Persecution*.
81. Not, indeed, that he eschewed "that prime dictate of nature which none can pretend ignorance of, viz., 'Do not that to another which thou wouldst not have done unto thyself.'" *Works*, VIII, 195. This "do as you would be done by argument" was quite frequently advanced by Dissenters over a long period. Priestley, for example, invoked it in 1789 when welcoming Roman Catholics in the cause of religious liberty: "While we join in asserting our own rights, let us not be unmindful of the rights of others, especially the common rights of *humanity*..." *The Theological and Miscellaneous Works of Joseph Priestley*, XV, 403.

Thus on the question of compulsion he does not appeal to natural law, or to epistemological deficiency, or to the human conscience as such, but to God as Lord of the conscience. In his view, "The sole question is, Whether God has authorized and doth warrant any man . . . to compel others to worship and serve him contrary to the way and manner that they are in their consciences persuaded that he doth accept and approve. . . . [T]o affirm that he hath authorized men to proceed in the way before mentioned is to say that he hath set up an authority *against himself*."[82]

In all of this one is reminded of the opening pages of Locke's *Letter Concerning Toleration*, and it is tempting to think that Locke may have been influenced by Owen, who had been Dean of Christ Church, Oxford, during Locke's student days there. Clearly, immediate influence cannot be contended for because it took Locke a long time to reach his mature conclusions on toleration; and there is no positive evidence to suggest that when he wrote his *Letter* he was consciously recalling Owen's teaching. None of which need prevent our hearing of echoes. In his concern "to distinguish exactly the business of civil government from that of religion," Locke writes:

> [T]he care of souls is not committed to the civil magistrate, any more than to other men . . . because it appears not that God has ever given any such authority to one man over another, as to compel any one to his religion. . . . [N]o man can, if he would, conform his faith to the dictates of another. All the life and power of true religion consists in the inward and full persuasion of the mind; and faith is not faith without believing. . . . The care of souls cannot belong to the civil magistrate, because his power consists only in outward force. . . . And . . . the understanding . . . cannot be compelled to the belief of anything by outward force.[83]

Elsewhere Owen undertakes to discuss what "is commonly called, Toleration in Religion, or toleration of several religions,"[84] and his emphasis is upon the appropriateness or otherwise of forbearance in cases spiritual and civil. As to the former, he declares that "Personal forebearance of errors . . . is a moral toleration or approbation of them; so also is ecclesiastical."[85] Against such forebearance Owen inveighs with

82. Owen, *Works*, XIII, 530.
83. Locke, *A Letter Concerning Toleration*, 17, 18.
84. Owen, *Works*, VIII, 163.
85. Ibid., 170.

spine-chilling rhetoric: "Hath the sword of discipline no edge? . . . Are the hammer of the word and the sword of the Spirit, which in days of old broke the stubbornest mountains, and overcame the proudest nations, now quite useless? God forbid!"[86] On the question whether "persons enjoying civil authority over others . . . are invested with power from above, and commanded in the word of God, to coerce, restrain, punish, confine, imprison, banish, hang, or burn, such of those persons under their jurisdiction as shall not embrace, profess, believe, and practise, that truth and way of worship which is revealed to them by God," Owen is no less clear: "I desire it to be observed that the general issue and tendence of unlimited arbitrary persecution, or punishing for conscience' sake . . . hath been pernicious, fatal, and dreadful to the profession and professors of the gospel'—little or not at all serviceable to the truth."[87] Magistrates are to serve as under God; they must know God's mind and will regarding his honour and worship; they must ensure that the gospel is preached to every citizen; those who hold false opinions and disturb civil society must be dealt with; and "If any persons . . . shall offer violence or disturbance to the professors of the true worship of God . . . such persons are to fear that power which is the minister of God, and a revenger to them that do evil."[88] As to matters spiritual, magistrates are "not bound by any rule or precept to assist and maintain [persons] in the practice of those things wherein they dissent from the truth"; they are required "to protect them in peace and quietness in the enjoyment of all civil rights and liberties"; and they may not proceed against then "for their dissent in those things they cannot receive. Attempts for uniformity among saints . . . by external force, are purely antichristian."[89]

V

We have seen that between 1550 and 1689 arguments of diverse kinds and degrees of rigour were advanced in favour of, and against, religious toleration. Those more philosophically inclined adduced arguments which turned upon the imperfections of human knowledge, the deliverances of natural law and the rights of conscience. In ecclesiastical circles the case

86. Ibid., 171.
87. Ibid., 171, 178.
88. Ibid., 195.
89. Ibid., 205.

was made that while people cannot be coerced into uniformity of belief and practice, the love of one another that Christians are commanded by Christ to display should be the spur to mutual tolerance and even union. Among political arguments was one to the effect that toleration would make for societal tranquillity, and another which concluded that it would lead to anarchy. The realization slowly dawned that uniformity of belief and practice was not achievable by legislation, and that in certain matters Church and state must be considered as distinct from one another.

The theological argument for toleration turned upon the conviction that God was Lord of the conscience, and that where Caesar opposed him, Christians were to give God precedence. Within this general stance, however, differing degrees of toleration were advocated. Whereas the General Baptists of Helwys's generation, and later Roger Williams, were pioneer advocates of universal religious toleration—and even of the toleration of atheists, the Quakers felt entitled to toleration because they were children of the Light, and had a clear idea as to those who were not. For their part, the Presbyterians did not, and the Congregationalists did not at first, advocate toleration at all. Both parties, like the Separatist John Robinson before them, were inhibited by their view that the Bible, the Word of God, prescribed one church polity only, namely their own, and that to flout it was to disobey God and repudiate the Church's Lord, Jesus Christ. Those Congregationalists who had taken charge of parishes in Cromwellian times, and all of the Presbyterians, would not have baulked at an established Church provided that it were of their own sort. It was only when, during the Westminster Assembly, it appeared that the Presbyterians were likely to gain the upper hand that some Congregationalists, unlike their New England counterparts who were the power in their new land, began to urge toleration. But neither Congregationalists nor Presbyterians would have extended it to Roman Catholics. When toleration came in 1689, restricted and mean-spirited though the Act was,[90] it was not because Christians of differing stripes had come to mutual agreement. As Robert Paul said, it was "imposed on the theologians from without."[91] Much more water was to flow under

---

90. In that, while it accorded freedom of worship to Protestant orthodox Dissenters (that is, not to Roman Catholics, Socinians or Jews), the existing anti-Nonconformist legislation was not repealed, the Dissenters were reduced to the status of second-class citizens, and the divisive Church-chapel distinction was enshrined in English and Welsh life.

91. Paul, *The Assembly of the Lord*, 491.

the bridge before we come to the rueful judgment passed upon his own generation exactly a century ago by P. T. Forsyth: "The inviolable freedom of the individual takes the place once kept for his absolute dependence and obedience before God."[92]

---

92. Forsyth, *Faith, Freedom and the Future*, 129.

Separatists and Dissenters amidst the Arguments For and Against Toleration

BIBLIOGRAPHY

Act of Parliament. I William and Mary, session Ic.18.
Anon. *Toleration and Liberty of Conscience Considered, and Proved Impracticable.* London: printed for Thomas Dring, 1685.
———. *The Subordinate Standards and Other Authoritative Documents of the Free Church of Scotland.* Edinburgh: The Free Church of Scotland, 1933.
Augustine. *Letters 156-210.* New York: New City, 2004.
Bartlet, William. Ιχνογραφια. *Or a Model of the Primitive Congregational Way.* London: Overton, 1647.
Baxter, Richard. *The English Nonconformists as under King Charles II and King James II.* London: Parkhurst, 1689.
Blount, T. P. *Essays on Several Subjects.* London: Bentley, 1697.
Bold, Samuel. *A Plea for Moderation towards Dissenters; occasioned by the Grand-Juries presenting the Sermon against Persecution at the Assizes holden at Sherburn in Dorsetshire. To which is added, an Answer to the Objections commonly made against that Sermon.* London: Janeway, 1682.
Burnet, Gilbert. *The Case of Compulsion in Matters of Religion Stated.* London: T.S., 1688.
———. *An Exhortation to Peace and Unity.* London: Chiswell, 1689.
———. *Two Sermons Preached in the Cathedral Church of Salisbury.* London: Churchill, 1710.
Burrough, Edward. *A Message for Instruction to all the Rulers, Judges and Magistrates, to whom the Law is committed.* London: Symmons, 1658.
Busher, Leonard. *Religion's Peace, or A Reconciliation between Princes & Peoples, & Nations.* Amsterdam, 1614.
Canipe, Lee. "'That Most Damnable Heresie.' John Smyth, Thomas Helwys, and Baptist Ideas of Freedom." *The Baptist Quarterly* 40 (2004) 388–411.
Castellio, S. *Conseil à la France desolée.* Paris: n.p., 1562.
Collins, Anthony. *A Letter to the Reverend Dr. Rogers.* London: n.p., 1727.
Corbet, John. *The Interest of England in the Matter of Religion.* London: J.M., 1660.
Cudworth, Ralph. *The True Intellectual System of the Universe.* 3 vols. London: Tegg, 1845.
Dickens, A. G. "Religious Toleration." *Transactions of the Congregational Historical Society* 20 (1965) 58–73.
Dodwell, Henry. *A Reply to Mr. Baxter's Pretended Confutation of a Book entituled Separation from Churches with Episcopal Government . . . Schismatical.* London: Tooke, 1681.
Edwards, Thomas. *Gangraena: or A Catalogue and Discovery of many of the Errours, Blasphemies and Pernicious Practices of the Sectaries of this Time, etc.* London: Smith, 1646.
———. *Reasons against the Independent Government of particular Congregations; as also against the Toleration to be Erected in this Kingdome.* London, 1641.
Fairbairn, A. M. "Ecclesiastical Polity and the Religion of Christ." In *Jubilee Lectures . . . of the Congregational Union of England and Wales,* I, ix–lxvii. 2 vols in one, London: Hodder and Stoughton, 1882.
Forsyth, P. T. *Faith, Freedom and the Future.* 1912. Reprint. London: Independent, 1955.
Glanvill, Joseph. *Scepsis Scientifica.* London: E. Cotes for Henry Eversden, 1665.

PART ONE: Confessing the Faith in Context

Goldie, Mark. *John Locke: Selected Correspondence*. Oxford: Clarendon, 2002.
Haley, K. H. D. "The Dutch Influence on English Toleration." *The Journal of the United Reformed Church History Society* 4 (1989) 255–65.
Haymes, Brian. "On Religious Liberty: Re-reading *A Short Declaration of the Mistery of Iniquity* in London in 2005." *The Baptist Quarterly* 42 (2007) 197–217.
Herbert of Cherbury. *De Veritate* (1624). London: Routledge/Thoemmes, 1992.
Hooker, Richard. *The Works of that Learned and Judicious Divine, Mr. Richard Hooker*. 3 vols. 3rd ed. Oxford: Oxford University Press, 1845.
Horton, John, and Susan Mendus. *John Locke:* A Letter concerning Toleration *in Focus*. London: Routledge, 1991.
Howe, John. *A Sermon concerning Union among Protestants*. London, 1683.
———. *The Works of the Rev. John Howe, M.A., with Memoirs of his Life by Edmund Calamy*. 2 vols. New York: Haven, 1808.
Jordan, M. Dorothea. "The Early Independents and the Visible Church." *Transactions of the Congregational Historical Society* 8 (1922) 258–66, 296–305.
Lecky, W. E. H. *History of the Rise and Influence of the Spirit of Rationalism in Europe*. 2 vols. London, 1865.
Locke, John. *An Essay concerning Human Understanding*. Edited by Peter H. Nidditch. Oxford: Clarendon, 1975.
———. *A Letter concerning Toleration*. In *John Locke:* A Letter concerning Toleration *in Focus*, edited by John Horton and Susan Mendus. London: Routledge, 1991.
Marshall, John. *John Locke, Toleration and Early Enlightenment Culture*. Cambridge: Cambridge University Press, 2006.
Matthews. A. G. *The Savoy Declaration of Faith and Order 1658*. London: Independent, 1959.
Mendus, Susan. *Toleration and the Limits of Liberalism*. London: Macmillan, 1989.
Milton, John. *Areopagitica*. Cambridge: Cambridge University Press, 1918.
———. *A Treatise of Civil Power in Ecclesiastical causes, shewing that it is not Lawfull for any Power on Earth to Compel in Matters of Religion*. London: Newcombe, 1659.
More, Henry. *An Explanation of the Grand Mystery of Godliness*. London: Flesher, 1660.
Murton, John. *A most Humble Supplication of many of the King's . . . subjects, ready to testify all civil obedience, by the Oath of Allegiance*. Amsterdam(?): Thorp(?), 1620.
———. *Objections: Answered by way of a Dialogue, wherein it is Proved by the Law of God, by the Law of the Land . . . that no Man ought to be Persecuted for his Religion, so he testifie his allegiance by the Oath appointed by Law*. The Netherlands:, n.p., 1615.
Nicholas of Cusa. *De docta ignorantia*. Translated and appraised by Jasper Hopkins. Minneapolis: Benning, 1981.
———. *De pace fidei; cum epistula ad Ioannem de Segobia*. London: Aedibus Instituti Warburgiani, 1956.
Owen, John. *A Brief Vindication of the Non-conformists from the Charge of Schisme*. London: Ponder, 1680.
———. *An Enquiry into the Original, Nature, Institution, Power, Order, and Communion of Evangelical Churches . . . with an Answer to the Discourse of the Unreasonableness of Separation written by Edward Stillingfleet, Dean of Pauls, and in Defence and Vindication of Non-conformists from the Guilt of Schism*. London: J. Richardson for Nath. Ponder, 1681.

Separatists and Dissenters amidst the Arguments For and Against Toleration

Parker, Samuel. *A Discourse of Ecclesiastical Politie* (1659). London: Martyn, 1670.

Paul, Robert S. *The Assembly of the Lord: Politics and Religion in the Westminster Assembly and the "Grand Debate."* Edinburgh: T. & T. Clark, 1985.

Penington, Isaac. *Concerning Persecution, which is the Afflicting or Punishing that which is Good under the pretence of its being Evil.* London: Wilson, 1661.

Price, Richard. *Additional Observations on the Nature and Value of Civil Liberty and the War with America.* 3rd ed. London: n.p., 1777.

Priestley, Joseph. *The Theological and Miscellaneous Works of Joseph Priestley.* Edited by J. T. Rutt (1817–31). Reprint. Bristol: Thoemmes, 1999.

Richardson, Samuel. *The Necessity of Toleration in Matters of Religion.* London, 1647.

Robinson, John. *The Works of John Robinson.* Edited by R. Ashton. 3 vols. London: Snow, 1851.

Schochet, Gordon. "Samuel Parker, Religious Diversity, and the Ideology of Persecution." In *The Margins of Orthodoxy. Heterodox Writing and Cultural Response, 1660–1750*, edited by Roger D. Lund, 119–48. Cambridge: Cambridge University Press, 1995.

Selbie, W. B. *Evangelical Christianity: Its History and Witness.* London: Hodder & Stoughton, 1911.

Sell, Alan P. F. *John Locke and the Eighteenth-Century Divines.* 1997. Reprint. Eugene, OR: Wipf & Stock, 2006.

Smith, William. *Liberty of Conscience Pleaded by several weighty Reasons on the Behalf of the People of God called Quakers.* London, 1662.

Sterry, Peter. *The Appearance of God to Man in the Gospel.* London: n.p., 1710.

———. *A Discourse of the Freedom of the Will.* London: printed for John Starkey, 1675.

Stillingfleet, Edward. *A Discourse concerning the Unreasonableness of Separation.* London: Chiswell, 1680.

———. *The Mischief of Separation: A Sermon Preached at Guild-Hall Chappel.* London: Mortlock, 1680.

Stoughton, John. "The Westminster Assembly." In *Jubilee Lectures: A Historical Series delivered on the occasion of the Jubilee of the Congregational Union of England and Wales.* 2 vols in one, I, 139–72. London: Hodder and Stoughton, 1882.

Tertullian, Q. S. F. *Apologeticus.* Translated by Alexander Souter. Digital ed. Cambridge: Cambridge University Press, 2012.

Thomas, D. O., and Bernard Peach. *The Correspondence of Richard Price. Volume I: July 1748–March 1778.* Cardiff: University of Wales Press, 1983.

Underhill, Edward Bean. *Tracts on Liberty of Conscience and Persecution 1614–1661.* London: Haddon, 1846.

Waldron, Jeremy. "Locke: Toleration and the Rationality of Persecution." In *Justifying Toleration: Conceptual and Historical Perspectives*, edited by Susan Mendus, 61–86. Cambridge: Cambridge University Press, 1988.

Whichcote, Benjamin. *Aphorisms, Collected from the Manuscript Papers of the Reverend and Learned Doctor Whichcote republished by Samuel Salter.* London: Payne, 1753.

Williams, Roger. *The Bloudy Tenent, of Persecution for Cause of Conscience, Discussed in a Conference between Truth and Peace.* London, 1644.

Wolseley, C. *Liberty of Conscience, upon its True and Proper Grounds Asserted and Vindicated. Proving that no Prince nor State, ought by Force to Compel Men to any part of the Doctrine, Worship or Discipline of the Gospel. To which is added, The Second Part, viz. Liberty of Conscience, The Magistrate's Interest.* London, 1668.

CHAPTER FOUR

Christianity, Secularism, and Toleration

Liberal Values and Illiberal Attitudes

As sceptics, secularists, and others are the first to remind Christians, the socio-political record of the church at large is, to put it mildly, ambiguous. I suspect that none are more aware of this than thoughtful Christians, whose dismay—even, on occasion, disgust—at some of the antics of the Church is tempered only by that humility which recognizes that since the saints are also sinners, no Christian has entirely clean hands.

With this paper I invite reflection upon the concepts "toleration" and "tolerance," which are widely, and rightly, thought of as denoting, respectively, a legal position and a broad-minded attitude that are much favoured by those of a liberal disposition. By means of a few historical soundings I shall seek to show that in the Western world these concepts came to prominence in connection with the quest of religious freedom which set Christian against Christian and some Christians against the state; and I shall then adduce evidence to show that secular liberals who have inherited the benefits of toleration can adopt stances which, at least intellectually (that is, without the thumb screws), mirror the inquisitorial attitudes that they otherwise abominate. All of this will support my contention that a constellation of values—freedom, love, and truth among them—underlie talk of toleration and tolerance, and that the variously selective positions taken on these explain the attitudes adopted by secular

Christianity, Secularism, and Toleration

liberals and Christians alike. I shall conclude that the Christian faith affords guidance on these matters which the Church itself should heed if it wishes to witness in the real world as an earnest or foretaste of God's kingdom of righteousness and peace.

It will already be clear that by "toleration" I mean "toleration under the law." By "tolerance" I mean an attitude of openness (sometimes more, sometimes less, grudging) towards beliefs to which one is not personally committed and actions of which one does not approve. "Intolerance" will then denote positive opposition to beliefs and attitudes deemed unacceptable. Intolerance, nowadays generally regarded as a vice, has, in particular historical circumstances, been deemed a virtue, as it was by those who sought to quell Commonwealth sectaries in the interests of national security and cohesion. The terms "toleration" and "tolerance" collide in interesting ways when things which the law tolerates (Sunday shopping, going to war without just cause) are not tolerated by some citizens, and, conversely, when individuals tolerate activities (the growing of cannabis in gardens, the counterfeiting of bank notes) that are not tolerated under the law. Again, "tolerance" as used, for example, in mechanics, signifies the amount of stress which may be applied to a metal before it fractures.[1] By analogy, the question arises for both the church and for society at large, What are the permissible degrees of tolerance if fracture is to be avoided? With these considerations in mind we may proceed to the historical soundings.

I

Classical antecedents granted, in Reformation times it is to the Socinians, migrating from Italy to Geneva and thence to Transylvania, Poland, and Holland, that we owe early defences of toleration and the repudiation of persecution for religious beliefs. Whereas Socinus conceived of a state church broad enough to include those of differing opinions, the Dutch Arminians argued that the separation of church and state was the only biblical option: their objective was theocratic. The same was true of those English Puritans who went from exile in Holland, and also from England, to the New World in 1620. Thus the Independents were quite content with a religious establishment provided that it was of their polity; hence when Roger Williams adopted believer baptist principles and argued for

---

1. I need not refer to Johnny Mercer's application of this principle in his 1954 hit, "Something's gotta give."

PART ONE: Confessing the Faith in Context

church-state separation, he was banished to Rhode Island, where very soon both Christians of all stripes and Jews were tolerated under the law, while non-Christians only, though not banished, were denied political rights. The Quakers likewise suffered under the Independents of New England, but William Penn secured toleration for all in Pennsylvania in 1682.

It is from exiled General Baptists that we have the first clear statements from English citizens in favour of religious toleration. In 1612 the followers of John Smyth the *se*-Baptist published their *Propositions and Conclusions concerning True Christian Religion, containing a Confession of Faith of certain English people, living in Amsterdam*. Clause eighty-four reads as follows:

> the magistrate is not by virtue of his office to meddle with religion, or matters of conscience, or doctrine; but to leave Christian religion free, to every man's conscience, and to handle only civil transgressions (Rom. xiii), injuries and wrongs of man against man, in murder, adultery, theft, etc., for Christ only is the king and law-giver of the church and conscience (James iv: 12).[2]

In the same year Thomas Helwys returned to England, established the first General Baptist Church on English soil and published *A Short Declaration of the Mistery of Iniquity*, in which he famously declared that "men's religion to God is betwixt God and themselves: the King shall not answere for it, neither may the King be jugd betwene God and Man. Let them be heretikes, Turcks, Jewes, or whatsoever, it appertaynes not to the earthly power to punish them in the least measure."[3]

It was to be a long time before most Christians learned this lesson. For example, during the 1640s the majority Presbyterian party at the Westminster Assembly hoped that their confessional, catechetical, and liturgical products would comprise the foundation of an English church ordered along Presbyterian lines. I find it somewhat distressing to note that it was only when this outcome seemed likely that the minority of Congregationalist representatives, fearful for their own future position in society, began to argue for the principle of toleration.[4] In the event, when Presbyterian hopes were dashed at the Restoration of the Monarchy in 1660, none became stronger advocates of toleration than they. Of course,

2. See Lumpkin, *Baptist Confessions of Faith*, 140.
3. Helwys, *A Short Declaration of the Mistery of Iniquity*, 69.
4. See Paul, *The Assembly of the Lord*, *passim*.

this entailed that on this issue "respectable" orthodox Christians would find themselves with some occasionally uncomfortable bedfellows, notably the Quakers, one of whom, Edward Burrough, reminded the King that "it is not given of God to any *Earthly King* or *Ruler* whatsoever, to exercise *Lordship* over the *Consciences of People* in the Matters of *Faith* and *Worship*, and the things pertaining to *God's* Kingdom."[5] To this point of high theological principle, some General Baptists under the leadership of Thomas Monck added the pragmatic consideration that magistrates were fallible: "That magistrates may err in spiritual and religious matters, woful experience hath taught the world in all ages."[6]

Time would fail to tell of the series punitive laws (patchily enforced across the country) that were enacted against roughly two thousand ministers who, on the ground that it was not the function of the monarch or Parliament to prescribe the worship of the Church, refused to give their "unfeigned assent and consent" to the *Book of Common Prayer* as enjoined by the Act of Uniformity of 1662 and were ejected from their livings.[7] Suffice it to say that for a variety of reasons—not least the high calibre of many of the ejected ministers—it became increasingly difficult to entertain the medieval aspiration of a nation cemented into unity by a fully comprehensive Church. Toleration came more and more to be seen as the only viable option. Hence the so-called Act of Toleration of 1689, which for the first time legalized the worship and religious practice of orthodox Protestant Dissenters (that is, not Unitarians, Roman Catholics or Jews), whilst at the same time, since none of the civil disabilities enshrined in previous legislation was repealed, confining them to an underclass in society—a position from which they have now largely emerged.[8]

---

5. Burrough, *A Visitation of Love*, 14.

6. Monck and others, *Sion's Groans for her Distressed*, 1661. In Underhill, *Tracts on Liberty of Conscience*, 365.

7. For this see Sell, *Commemorations,* ch. 5. For a full account see Watts, *The Dissenters.* See also Sell, *The Great Ejectment of 1662.*

8. Not, indeed, that this implies that the Dissenting witness is redundant. The theological questions surrounding the sole Lordship of Christ in his Church and the "matter" of the Church remain to be adequately addressed, as, until recently, did the matter of the reconciliation of memories between the Church of England and historic Dissent. In 1995 I began to urge the need of a service of reconciliation, thinking that it might take place at the beginning of the new millennium. This did not come to pass, but on 7 February 2012, in the year of the 350th anniversary of the Great Ejectment, and the fortieth birthday of The United Reformed Church, such a service was finally held in Westminster Abbey. The Order of Worship was jointly prepared by Anglicans and members of The United Reformed Church. For the outstanding theological issues

PART ONE: Confessing the Faith in Context

II

The way in which support for the idea of religious toleration grew in the mind of a particular individual may be illustrated by reference to John Locke.[9] From his student days onwards Locke was alive to the issue of toleration. He had access to Socinian writings,[10] but there were more local influences upon him too. His tutor at Christ Church, Oxford, was the Independent, Thomas Cole; the Professor of History was the Huguenot, Lewis Du Moulin, who had published on liberty of conscience and toleration; and the Dean of the College and University Vice Chancellor was John Owen, a prime mover in the modification by Independents of the *Westminster Confession*. This revision, the *Savoy Declaration of Faith and Order* (1658), includes the following clause:

> God alone is Lord of the Conscience, and hath left it free from the Doctrines and Commandments of men which are in anything contrary to his Word, or not contained in it [*Westminster* has, "or beside it in matters of faith and worship"]; so that to believe such Doctrines, or to obey such Commands out of conscience, is to betray true Liberty of Conscience; and the requiring of an implicit faith, and an absolute and blinde obedience, is to destroy Liberty of Conscience, and Reason also.[11]

It is inconceivable that Locke could have been unaware of sentiments of this kind; indeed, he shared them, but they did not, for him, entail separation from the Church of England, in whose ranks he found congenial Latitudinarians such as Tillotson. It gradually dawned on him, however, that a full religious comprehension was unlikely to be achieved. This conviction was strengthened by his reading of Herbert of Cherbury who, in his *De Veritate* (1624) had argued for toleration on epistemological grounds, namely, that since human knowledge is limited, absolute certainty is impossible to attain; hence the propriety, indeed the necessity, of tolerating differing views. To this we may add Locke's dislike of

---

that remain to be resolved see, Sell, *Testimony and Tradition*, ch. 11, and *The Great Ejectment of* 1662, ch. 4.

9. For a fuller account see Sell, *John Locke*, 151–62. For an exhaustive study see Marshall, *John Locke*.

10. Locke was accused by some of being a Socinian. For this tangled web see Sell, *John Locke*, 212–29, 273–74.

11. Matthews, *The Savoy Declaration*, 103 (XXI.ii).

sectarian strife.¹² While not objecting to Roman Catholic *beliefs*, which did not adversely affect civil order, he disagreed with Henry Stubbe's advocacy of toleration for Roman Catholics on the ground that the latter owed allegiance to a foreign power.¹³ Positively, he urged loyalty to Charles II, whose accession to the throne he supported, not least because he thought it would bring stability to the land in the wake of Civil War and the antics of Commonwealth sects (he feared disruptive "enthusiasm" almost as much as he feared Rome); and he wrote *Two Tracts* in reply to Edward Bagshaw's pro-toleration pamphlets of 1660 and 1661.

However, by the time Locke wrote four drafts of *An Essay concerning Toleration* in 1667, he had experienced toleration in the Duchy of Cleves, and had become secretary to the tolerationist, Shaftesbury. He began to urge Charles II to take up the cause of toleration on conscientious and epistemological grounds; and it was not long before he progressed from saying that people had a right to their conscientious convictions, to saying that they had a duty to defend them if they were threatened.[14] He developed this position in his *Two Treatises on Government* and *A Letter concerning Toleration*. Further impetus to Locke's developing position came during his exile in Holland (1683–88) and his friendship with Philip Limborch, the Remonstrant, to whom he dedicated his *Epistola de Tolerantia* (1689). To his argument from conscience and epistemology, Locke now added one from the gospel itself:

> The toleration of those that differ from others in matters of religion, is so agreeable to the gospel of Jesus Christ, and to the genuine reason of mankind, that it seems monstrous for men to be so blind, as not to perceive the necessity and advantage of it, in so clear a light.... [W]e must not content ourselves with the narrow measures of bare justice: charity, bounty, and liberality must be added to it. This the Gospel enjoins, this reason directs, and this that natural fellowship we are born into requires of us.[15]

For all that, Locke could not open the door to Roman Catholics or atheists, being convinced that neither were, for different reasons, to be trusted.

Among pointers to our future discussion arising from this truncated account of Locke's position are the following: Locke was able to

---

12. See Locke, *Two Tracts on Government*, 119.
13. Letter of Locke to Stubbe in De Beer, *The Correspondence of John Locke*, I, 111.
14. See Locke, *A Letter from a Person of Quality to His Friend in the Country*, 1675.
15. Locke, *A Letter Concerning Toleration*, 393, 400.

tolerate certain Roman Catholic beliefs—for example, concerning transubstantiation—whilst not being willing to grant Roman Catholics toleration under the law; and, more generally, with Locke's adverting to liberty of conscience, human epistemological deficiencies, and the spirit of the gospel, my earlier claim that attitudes towards toleration, and the determining of what is tolerable, turn upon value judgments passed upon underlying issues is reinforced.

III

Throughout the eighteenth century there were those who wished to turn back the clock of toleration. The Sacheverell riots of 1715, during which Dissenting meeting houses were burned, and the Birmingham riots of 1791, which forced Joseph Priestley out of the town, stand as testimonies to the fact at either end of the century.[16] Again we see that toleration could not by itself secure tolerance. But the mention of Priestley directs us to his staunch advocacy of toleration for all. In July 1773 he wrote *A Letter of Advice to those Dissenters who Conduct the Application to Parliament for Relief from certain Penal Laws*. He was confident that his readers would agree that there was no need to be "so distrustful of the cause of Christianity, as to think that any thing is necessary for its security and flourishing state, besides its own proper, rational evidence." Therefore, "Let us then act upon this generous principle, and at the same time assert the honour of our country and the dignity of human nature, by petitioning for a bill by which *Unbelievers* shall be as much at liberty to attack, as ourselves to defend, either Christianity in general, or particular opinions concerning it."[17]

In his letters to Oxford and Cambridge students Priestley took the Anglican, Dr. Purkis, to task on the subject of toleration. He sets out from the observation that "If any subject had been well understood, I should have thought it had been that of toleration. But I perceive it is of very difficult comprehension to those who have it in their power to be intolerant." Purkis, he continues, will not tolerate disbelievers in the gospel on the ground that "the religion of Jesus manifestly excludes every other;

---

16. See further, for example, Sell, *Dissenting Thought*, ch. 11; Wykes, "'A finished monster of the true Birmingham breed,'" in Sell, *Protestant Nonconformists and the West Midlands of England*, ch. 3.

17. Priestley, *The Theological and Miscellaneous* Works, XXII, 442–43.

and that we must adhere to this exclusive principle, if we assert its divine authority." But, Priestley concludes, "if the civil governors of a country, *as such*, have a right to use their power in support of what they deem to be true religion, *Heathens* and *Mahometans* have the same right to persecute Christians. . . . If, therefore, we Christians would think it right that we should be tolerated among Heathens or Mahometans, we ought to tolerate them among us."[18]

In 1787 William Pitt the Younger spoke against the repeal of the Test and Corporation Acts, and this drew a lengthy response from Priestley. He begins rather patronisingly by advising the twenty-eight-year-old Pitt that "it is not disgraceful to any man, and least of all to a young man, to change his opinion, on farther reflecting upon a subject," and then takes Pitt to task for arguing that the present church establishment is necessary for the peace and happiness of the country. This is a fallacious argument, declares Priestley, for behind England as it is now known there is England the Catholic country and England the heathen Saxon country. If those in previous eras had pursued Pitt's "no change" policy, the established religion of the land would now be a pagan one with druid priests. Against one of Pitt's arguments he cites Ireland, Russia, Prussia, and Holland as lands in which "no danger has ever been apprehended from employing troops of all religions", and he concludes by urging the repeal of King William's law which makes it blasphemy to impugn the doctrine of the Trinity: "I think it my duty to attempt the utter overthrow of this doctrine, which I conceive to be a fundamental corruption of the religion which I profess, the greatest of those that mark the Church of Rome, and which was left untouched at the Reformation."[19]

Two years later Priestley returned to the issue in a sermon on *The Conduct to be observed by Dissenters in order to procure the Repeal of the Corporation and Test Acts*. He now welcomed Roman Catholics as allies in the cause of religion and liberty: indeed, "they ought to class with *English Dissenters*"; and he concludes with a yet broader vision:

> while we join in asserting our own rights, let us not be unmindful of the rights of others, especially the common rights of *humanity*, of which the poor negroes have long been deprived, being treated as brutes, and not as men. . . . Let us, with our prayers and good wishes at least, aid a neighbouring nation [France], and all who are now struggling for liberty, civil or

---

18. Ibid., XVIII, 359.
19. Ibid., XIX, 115, 119, 122.

> religious, throughout the world; that *the voice of the oppressor may every where cease to be heard;* that by this means we may see the nearer approach of those glorious and happy times, when *wars shall cease to the ends of the earth,* and when *the kingdoms of this world shall become the kingdoms of God and of his Christ.*[20]

Finally, on 1 January 1791 Priestley wrote to Edmund Burke, who was more than a little disquieted by the French Revolution, in terms which eulogized that Revolution and the previous American one: "Such events as these teach the doctrine of *liberty, civil* and *religious,* with infinitely greater clearness and force than a thousand treatises on the subject. They speak a language intelligible to all the world, and preach a doctrine congenial to every human heart." To Priestley it is a glorious prospect that people would enjoy "as many of their *natural rights* as possible", and that there would be "no more interfering with matters of religion, with men's notions concerning God and a future state, than with philosophy or medicine."[21]

To take stock thus far: while Locke and Priestley are at one in advocating liberty of conscience, Locke takes a more tolerant attitude towards beliefs he does not share—provided that they do not threaten the peace of society—than Priestley, who would have welcomed the reasoned overthrow of trinitarian doctrine. On the other hand, Priestley, unlike Locke, is for an universal toleration that encompasses not only Roman Catholics but unbelievers too. Unlike Locke, he does not advance an argument from human epistemic limitations for this, but appeals to natural rights and utilitarian considerations; nor does he invoke the spirit of the Gospel in the way Locke does. When we now turn to John Stuart Mill we shall find not only that his liberalism requires no recourse to the gospel, but that he hopes that, with the passage of time not just one doctrine, but Christianity as a whole, will be replaced by his desired Religion of Humanity. He is, we might say, in favour of religious toleration and tolerance *pro tem*—that is, until they are no longer needed because religion has been superseded.

---

20. Ibid., XV, 402, 403–4.
21. Ibid., XXII, 236, 237.

IV

Mill is extraordinarily difficult to pin down.[22] We should never forget that he was a social reformer and man of affairs, not simply a closeted philosopher. Thus when we find inconsistencies in his writings—and there are many of these—we should ponder the possibility that they may be the product of that prudential trimming in which those who wish to carry people of diverse views with them for political ends are sometimes prone to indulge. Nor were his objectives confined to the short term; we might almost call them eschatological. He writes:

> I looked forward, through the present age of loud disputes but generally weak convictions, to a future which shall unite the best qualities of the critical with the best qualities of the organic periods; unchecked liberty of thought, unbounded freedom of individual action in all modes not hurtful to others; but also, convictions as to what is right and wrong, useful and pernicious, deeply engraven on the feelings by early education and general unanimity of sentiment, and so firmly grounded in reason and in the true exigencies of life, that they shall not, like all former and present creeds, religious, ethical, and political, require to be periodically thrown off and replaced by others.[23]

Mill's disquiet at "loud disputes" is understandable, but overall his aspiration is unrealistic, and his method, turning as it does upon feelings "deeply engraven" by early education, comes oddly from one whose own early education at the hands of his father James, might be said to have left intellectual impediments and emotional wounds from which he never fully recovered.

Whatever the final outcome, Mill thinks the time has now come for all who believe that "current opinions are not only false but hurtful, to make their dissent known . . ." This "would put an end . . . to the vulgar prejudice, that what is called, very improperly, unbelief, is connected with any bad qualities either of mind or heart."[24] (Mill presumably intends "necessary connection" here, since wicked unbelievers are not unknown.) The context of this remark is the long-standing conviction of many that atheists cannot be other than wicked. This idea was a long

---

22. Hence the subtitle of my book, *Mill on God: The Pervasiveness and Elusiveness of Mill's Religious Thought*.

23. Mill, *Autobiography and Literary Essays*, 173.

24. Mill, *Autobiography*, CW, I, 47.

time dying: indeed speakers on certain religious television programmes espouse it to this day. Mill was right to press for tolerance over against this "vulgar prejudice," especially at a time when "an author who should openly admit to antireligious or even antichristian opinions, would compromise not only his social position, but also . . . his chance of being read."[25] Here is hint of the prudential trimming to which I alluded earlier.

In the interests of making common cause with people of good will, Mill declares that "Honesty, self-sacrifice, love of our fellow-creatures, & the desire to be of use in the world, constitute the true point of resemblance between those whose religion however overlaid with dogmas is genuine, & those who are genuinely religious without any dogmas at all."[26] Passing over the gentle swipe at dogmas, there is indeed socio-ethical common ground between Christians and other people of good will and it is indicative of Mill's tolerant spirit that he should seek this out. However, some of his critics were not slow to point out that there is also that common ground to which the doctrine of sin points, namely, that whereas human beings frequently know the good, they do not always will it. Elsewhere, their dogmas notwithstanding, Mill can even endorse the position of those Anglican clergymen who "elect to remain in the national church, so long as they are able to accept its articles and confessions in any sense or with any interpretation consistent with common honesty," on the ground that otherwise religious teaching and worship would devolve upon those with the narrowest minds.[27]

As a general principle, Mill believed in separating the wheat from the chaff in the several intellectual and religious systems which confronted him, as is clear from his response to the Anglo-Catholicism of E. B. Pusey and his friends:

> We not only esteem it a more healthful exercise of the mind to employ itself in learning from an enemy, than in inveighing against him; but, we believe, that the extirpation of what is erroneous in any system of belief is in no way so much promoted as by extricating from it, and incorporating into our own systems, whatever in it is true.[28]

---

25. Letter of Mill to Comte, 18 December 1841 In Haac, *The Correspondence of John Stuart Mill and Auguste Comte*, 42. Cf. Mill's "Law of Libel and Liberty of the Press," 1825. CW, XXI, 13–14.

26. Letter of Mill to Thomas Dycke Acland, 1 December 1868. CW, XVI, 1499.

27. Mill, "Inaugural Address delivered in the University of St. Andrews," 1867. CW, XXI, 251.

28. Mill, "Puseyism – 1," CW, XXIV, 812.

He reached a further stage when he concluded that "It is ... perfectly conceivable that religion may be morally useful without being intellectually sustainable."[29] This would seem to betoken the forlorn view that one may consistently tolerate the fruits of religion whilst being intolerant of its dogmatic roots. Hence the comment of the philosopher W. G. De Burgh:

> It was a fatal misapprehension that led John Stuart Mill, after declaring that self-respect was one of the noblest incentives to a life of virtue, to claim, almost in the same breath, that his Utilitarianism was wholly in accord with the teaching of the Founder of Christianity.... It is clear that the new motive, the love of God, involves a transvaluation that is radical and all-pervasive.[30]

We might also recall that in other places Mill levelled strong objections against Christian morality, as being predominantly concerned with "thou shalt nots," and as being a matter of the selfish quest of eternal reward.[31]

Lest there be any doubt of Mill's intolerance of doctrines he deemed objectionable, let us ponder his declaration to Comte: "I would be filled with hope if I believed that the time had come when we could frankly hoist the flag of positivism and succeed, shake off every shred of the doctrines of the past (except for their historical value) and refuse all the concessions, even tacit, to theories of the supernatural."[32]

But there is something disturbingly elitist, if not downright sinister, in Mill's agreement with Comte that the Humanity which is to be the object of veneration in the religion which will eventually replace all others, is not the aggregate of all human beings who have ever lived, but of the worthiest of them. He could even write that the unworthy "are

---

29. Mill, "Utility of Religion." CW, X, 405.

30. De Burgh, *From Morality to Religion*, 237, 239. For this neglected philosopher see Sell, *Four Philosophical Anglicans*.

31. See Mill, *On Liberty*. CW, XVIII, 255.

32. Letter of Mill to Comte, 27 January 1845. In Haac, *Correspondence*, 288. At a number of points in *Mill on God* (e.g., pp. 32, 37–38, 98–99, 175–77) I have adduced evidence to show that Mill (like many other agnostics and secularists) was not well versed in Christian thought. His early education was a-theistic, not in the sense that he was taught dogmatic atheism, but in the sense that God and religion were absent from the curriculum rigorously applied by his father. Though Mill later read the New Testament, he never made good this general theological deficiency. The result is that some of his anti-dogmatic intolerance is, literally, ignorant, or, at least it accords with popular views (ever with us) that represent Christianity in its worst light.

best dismissed from our habitual thoughts."³³ A significant dent this, one would think, in the armour of one who declared that "'tis of the nature of the human mind to be progressive."³⁴ For all his intolerance of Christian dogmas and unworthy persons, Mill nevertheless concurred with Locke in holding that "the sole end for which mankind are warranted, individually and collectively, in interfering with the liberty of action of any of their number, is self-protection."³⁵ But, unlike Locke, he does not ground upon human epistemic deficiencies and Gospel principles; unlike Priestley, his appeal is not to natural rights; it is to the principle of utility:

> I forego any advantage which could be derived to my argument from the idea of abstract right, as a thing independent of utility. I regard utility as the ultimate appeal on all ethical questions; but it must be utility in the largest sense, grounded on the permanent interests of man as a progressive being. Those interests, I contend, authorise the subjection of individual spontaneity to external control, only in respect to those actions of each, which concern the interest of other people.³⁶

In a word, as with Locke, so with Mill: liberty may be constrained if and when civil order is at risk.

I shall return to Mill shortly, but for the moment I leave him—a rather elusive mixture of liberal principles and illiberal attitudes, the latter frequently tempered by the political need to carry people with him along his reforming path. Over against both Locke and Priestley, Mill has no theoretical need of Christianity. With his liberal values of toleration under the law and tolerance between people and societies, he stands as a pioneering advocate of secular liberalism, albeit one for whom religion, on occasion at least, has its uses.

V

I now proceed to offer some reflections upon toleration, tolerance, and liberalism in the light of the foregoing historical soundings. The first thing to note is the apparent ease with which the liberal avowal of tolerance can

---

33. Mill, *Auguste Comte and Positivism*, CW, X, 334.

34. Mill, "The Church," CW, XXVI, 424.

35. Mill, *On Liberty*. CW, XVIII, 223. Letter of Mill to Comte, 27 January 1845. In Haac, *Correspondence*, 288.

36. Ibid., 224.

so readily transmute into, and even licence, intolerance. The stimulus to this paradoxical situation is frequently the determination by the intolerant to deploy their freedom in the interests of illiberal goals of which they are tolerant. Fiona Ross has, with some justification, pointed out that "Though the curtailment of freedoms on the basis of group identities has lessened over the centuries [the present position of English Dissenters exemplifies this], the same case could not be made with regard to freedom from government or its instruments of surveillance."[37] In this connection we might ponder legislation passed by the United States House of Representatives and, at the time of writing, under consideration by the Senate: the Broadcast Decency Enforcement Act. This would make broadcasters liable to a fine of $500,000 for disseminating obscene or indecent material. The humourist, Garrison Keillor, has observed that for major companies this would hold no fears, but small broadcasters would feel threatened. A Kentucky radio station cancelled one of Keillor's broadcasts because he read a perfectly respectable poem containing the word "breast." This prompted Keillor to wonder how people in Kentucky, of all places, order chicken?[38]

But there are commercial pressures as well as legal ones. E. J. Dionne has argued that "Liberals should feel no obligation to defend all aspects of commercial culture. When TV networks and Hollywood exploit sex to make money, shouldn't liberals ask why it is that the very free market so revered by the right wing promotes values that the very same right wing claims to despise?"[39]

All of this prompts the question, When should tolerance fracture, and on what grounds? Locke was clear that an important occasion would be the collapse of civil order, and Mill recognized that "All that makes existence valuable to anyone, depends on the enforcement of restraints upon the actions of other people. Some rules of conduct, therefore, must be imposed, by law in the first place, and by opinion on many things which are not fit subjects for the operation of law."[40] Again, in 1847 Mill published his *Principles of Political Economy*. In a chapter entitled, "The grounds and limits of the *laissez-faire* or non-interference principle,"

37. Ross, review of Hackett, *Liberty and Freedom. The Times Higher Education Supplement*, 17 June 2005, 26.

38. In this illustration I quote freely from a report in *The Christian Century*, 4 October 2005, 7.

39. Quoted in *The Christian Century*, 22 March 2005, 7.

40. Mill, *On Liberty*. CW, XVIII, 220.

he upholds the principle while at the same time listing exceptions such as the state's right to compel parents to send their children to school; moreover, his list of exceptions increased in length as new editions of the book appeared. In our present world the situation in respect of calling a halt to tolerance seems more complex than ever before. We have our modern democracies, organized Christian denominations, and a host of other bodies such as trades unions, which attempt to reach collective judgements on the permissible degrees of tolerance at a time when the individualism which flows down from Locke and Mill seems to legitimate personal autonomy as the supreme value and to make Cole Porter's song "Anything goes" sound like the anthem of a proto-postmodernist of the relativist sort. It seems clear to me that the only way to justify what might be termed liberal intolerance of what is destructive or wrong is by appealing to an underlying complex of values to which liberals are committed.

I shall return to this point, but first I wish to advert to a most important pitfall in the path of those for whom "Tolerance is only another name for indifference,"[41] and who are so *laissez faire* as to emulate the novelist Thorne Smith's character, Harris Stevens, whose "mind was so tolerant that he could have attended a lynching every day without becoming critical."[42] The pitfall is that of bracketing question of truth. This was the concern of Pierre Bayle when he declared immoral any requirement that people should believe things to which they could not conscientiously assent; he thought that truth would more readily be found by the open discussion of opposing views. In our own time the peril arises in the form of what I shall call selective tolerance. This comes in many guises, and operates in popular, academic and ecclesiastical circles.

One example will suffice to illustrate selective tolerance at the popular level. Many British citizens deplore what is called the drug culture, and are frequently intolerant of those who have succumbed to it. But they are selective. They generally have in mind cocaine, which killed 369 people in England and Wales between 1997 and 2001; ecstacy, which killed 145 in the same period; and opiates which killed 5,188. Many do not have in mind the "socially acceptable" drug, alcohol, which killed up to 200,000 in the same period, or nicotine, not as "socially acceptable" as once it was, which killed about 500,000.[43] Examples of popular selective

---

41. Maugham, *A Writer's Notebook*, 40.

42. Smith, *The Jovial Ghosts*, 85. Cf. the reference in Ward, *Robert Elsmere*, I, 324, to "This Laodicean cant of tolerance."

43. I reproduce these statistics from *The Observer*, 16 October 2005, 6.

tolerance could be multiplied, but I turn to academia, the alleged bastion of liberal values, and to the Church, which is called to be the foretaste of the kingdom of love, light, and peace. In the case of both I wish to draw attention to methodological and socio-political stances which yield intolerance—even sectarianism.

VI

Methodological intolerance is exemplified in the following quotation from Mill:

> It being granted then that the legitimate conclusions of science are entitled to prevail over all opinions, however widely held, which conflict with them, and that the canons of scientific evidence which the successes and failures of two thousand years have established, are applicable to all subjects on which knowledge is attainable, let us proceed to consider what place there is for religious beliefs on the platform of science; what evidences they can appeal to, and what foundation there is for the doctrines of religion, considered as scientific theorems.[44]

Even with Mill's honest recognition of the fact that a large part of the history of science is the story of its failures and of the replacement of the disproved by newer hypotheses which, when sufficiently demonstrated, are accepted *pro tem*, this remains a remarkable example of begging the question. That scientific conclusions should prevail over all other opinions is by no means granted by everyone; and it is not necessary to be a paid up philosophical idealist to protest that Mill has so marked out the playing field that religious claims (logically) cannot be properly scrutinized. For example, a Christian belief in the supernatural—not in the sense of Hollywood spookery, but in the sense of believing that saving grace does not originate in natural processes—is ruled out *a priori* and *ab initio* on Mill's principles; for there is no way in which such a claim can be squeezed within his parameters of acceptable evidence. Such doctrines are not, by those who hold them, "considered as scientific theorems."

In all of this Mill stands as a harbinger of secularists, positivists and others who have won their victory, such as it is, by marking out the pitch in such a way that they alone can play the game.[45] It is an inherently

---

44. Mill. "On Theism," CW, X, 430–31.
45. See further, Sell, *Confessing and Commending the Faith*, especially ch. 4 and 305–7.

PART ONE: Confessing the Faith in Context

intolerant stance which forecloses the question of truth. It is a stance of which, in the interests of a genuinely liberal higher education, I profess myself to be mildly intolerant.[46] Prominent among our contemporaries who adopt this method are those who espouse the faith of scientism. I call it a faith, because to posit scientistic reductionism is to advance a claim which is not itself amenable to scientific investigation, and is therefore self-refuting.[47] Some adherents of scientism, like Mill before them, are less than well versed in Christian doctrine, though they are adept at slaying caricatures of it. I sometimes find that the doctrinal Aunt Sallies which they set up with a view to knocking down concern claims to which it has never occurred to me to give assent. However advanced their science, in religious matters they frequently seem to be in a late-nineteenth-century time warp, except that, whilst trotting out the tired arguments of their secularist predecessors, they frequently do not display the literary wit of the best of them. They have forgotten, or simply deny, that "It is an unwarranted extension of the realm of science, when instead of describing the actual, it undertakes to determine the possible."[48] This amnesia or denial leads them to espouse that prejudice which cannot conceive how religion and science could ever walk hand in hand;[49] and with their narrow conception of "science", their constriction of the connotation of such terms as "fact," and their sectarian refusal seriously to consider alternative ideas (a strangely unscientific attitude), they are the mirror image of those Christian fundamentalists, whom they sometimes despise, who would unchurch those who do not set sail from their methodological

---

46. I note with interest that on this issue Alister McGrath outdoes me in intolerance: "Maybe it was once brave and intellectually sophisticated to dismiss those who believe in God as deluded, unthinking fools. Now it just seems outdated, arrogant and intolerant." See his "'God is Not Dead Yet." *The Times Higher Education Supplement*, 22 October 2004, 16. See also his book, *Dawkins' God*; and Keith Ward, *God, Chance and Necessity*. This is not the only way of foreclosing the quest of truth in higher education, of course. Secularists indebted for their convictions to the Enlightenment individualism flowing down from Locke and Mill, as well as Christians indebted to the Evangelical Revival with its emphasis upon personal salvation and the conversion of individuals, may persuade themselves that such personal matters are really private, and that it is not done to challenge them in polite society, for to do so is to appear to attack the person's deepest *feelings*.

47. I am well aware that here I write in shorthand. For full critique of scientism see Stenmark. *Scientism*.

48. Garvie, "The Limits of Doctrinal Restatement," 95.

49. See further Gouldstone, *The Rise and Decline of Anglican Idealism*, 109–10.

harbour of biblical inerrantism.[50] The force of P. T. Forsyth's words of 1913 has not diminished with the passage of the years. Writing of Christians, he warns, "We have been too susceptible to the imposing and monopolist claims of a science and a philosophy which have had enormous success with the world."[51] Perhaps some such idea was in Mrs. Humphrey Ward's mind when she wrote, "It had begun to be recognised, with a great burst of enthusiasm and astonishment, that, after all, Mill and Herbert Spencer had not said the last word on all things in heaven and earth."[52] It takes no great imaginative skill to conjure up names that we today might substitute for those of Mill and Spencer; nor, if Bonaventure is to be believed, were they the first of the secularizing kind:

> opposing the concelebration of divine praise, we have the spirit of presumption and curiosity, in the sense that the presumptuous does not glorify God but praises himself, while the curious is lacking in devotion. There are many men of this kind, empty of praise and devotion, although filled with the splendors of knowledge. They build wasp's nests without honeycombs, while the bees make honey . . .[53]

50. The swashbuckling Richard Dawkins is reported as declaring that creationists are "ignorant, stupid, insane or simply wicked" in a profile of him by Robin McKie, "Doctor Zoo," *The Observer*, 25 July 2004, 25. This is good knockabout fun, but faintly disturbing nonetheless. I should be the last to banish Dawkins from the academy, as some of his kind may wish to banish theologians therefrom; on the contrary, I much prefer having people of his persuasion where I can see them. My allusion to biblical inerrantists reminds us that within the Church there are methodological questions which demand tolerance and call forth intolerance. I can but allude to these here, but see further, Sell, *Theology in Turmoil*, especially chs. 5 and 6. I have it on good authority that there are departments of religious studies in the United States which, having gone all "scientific," would not dream of employing a Christian theologian or, indeed, a theologian of any other faith. So much, once again, for liberal values in higher education.

51. Forsyth, *The Principle of Authority*, 206. Cf. his remark in his essay, "Revelation and the Person of Christ," in *Faith and Criticism*, 99: "To make Nature the site of Revelation, to seek it in the Kosmos rather than in the Ethos, is the very genius of Paganism, and it is the source of the humanist and scientific Paganism of our own day." Cf. also John Baillie, *Natural Science and the Spiritual Life*, 43: "I can imagine nothing more convenient to my sloth, my selfishness, and my concupiscence than a philosophy which persuaded me, in the name of scientific outlook, to regard myself only as a part of nature and as subject to none but nature's laws; nor can I imagine anything that would be more destructive of the very foundations of my humanity—and therefore, in the end, of my very science itself."

52. Ward, *Robert Elsmere*. I, 122.

53. Bonaventure, *Hex* I.8., p. 4.

At the very least the irritation fostered in some Christians by those who espouse scientism can produce a degree of empathy with non-Christians who find some expressions of Christianity banal, distasteful, or downright immoral.

VII

I come, secondly, to socio-political stances which yield intolerance. As in the case of methodological intolerance, these may be found in both secular and churchly circles. As before, I begin with the academy. Professor Daphne Patai of the University of Massachusetts offers us an example of fluctuating intolerance of an hypocritical kind. She recalls a meeting at which some postmodernist academics, prone to debunking the values of liberal education, accomplished a sea-change of opinion when a philanthropist asked them why anyone should support their institution: "Instantly the group reconfigured its allegiances and, to my astonishment, a parade of entirely traditional justifications of the importance of the university as a site for impartial research and teaching was trotted out, replete with affirmations of commitment to precisely those liberal views that for the preceding two days had been roundly denounced."[54] She proceeds to recount the following atrocity:

> "feminist activism" is now indispensable to women's studies. Job postings reveal just how undisguised this agenda is. One Texas university is seeking someone with specialisations in "transnational or global feminism, women's health, feminist/womanist community activism and/or feminist disability studies," while a California university needs a specialist in "feminist activism, policy and social justice." Other schools seek evidence of progressive "dispositions" or "cultural competency"—codewords for political agendas [sic].[55]

As we might expect, there are points to be made on the other side; for example, that there is no equality of opportunity without some equality of circumstance, and that women have in many fields suffered oppression for too long. The question how far this justifies the transformation of the curriculum into a socio-political crusade (and I have no evidence to show how frequently this happens) requires seriously to be debated, not

---

54. Patai, "You say social justice, I say political censorship," 12.
55. Ibid.

least because of the sectarian implications of intolerance of the views of non-"paid-up"-women, not to mention the rest of the university community. It would not surprise me if some of those behind the advertisements cited above would be horrified if they found a department of theology in a public university advertising for "born again evangelists with an exemplary record of conversions," or for "scholars skilled in proselytizing in Orthodox lands." Not the least of the skills required by those with a sense of mission is knowing where they are at any given time: whether university teachers are Christian or not, the university classroom is not a mission hall; rather, it is a place for the cut and thrust of debate, and the wider the spread of views (atheists in theological classes, misogynist males in classes on feminism) the livelier it should be. Tolerance is diminished if it comes to be construed as maintaining silence rather than advancing a contrary view; but it is replaced by intolerance if the expression of alternative views is proscribed from the outset. When intolerance is accompanied by the questioning of the motives of those who advocate positions deemed unpalatable (as, for example, when an academic adduces arguments against the Iraq War and is then branded unpatriotic), we have implicit totalitarianism.

Political activism of the kind just discussed increasingly rears its head in church circles. In synods and assemblies where the stated objective is a common seeking of the mind of Christ on a particular issue the presence of activist groups, sometimes well funded, bent on securing their own objectives can result in "packing" the assembly in such a way that minority interests prevail. We then have the embarrassing situation in which what must be deemed to be the mind of Christ is repudiated by the majority of the Church's membership. Some such activist groups can be so aggressive and so sure of their ground that they even give the impression, and sometimes state the alleged fact, that those who are not on their platform are not *bona fide* Christians. This is the sectarian attitude once again. One has only to think of the agonies which many churches have endured, and continue to endure, over the question of homosexuality or the ordination of women to perceive that two significant questions are too frequently unaddressed: What are the degrees of tolerance within the church and on what criteria is this matter to be determined? And, How necessary is it that we should seek a common mind on certain issues? In most Christian traditions differences over political allegiance, pacifism and non-pacifism, or teetotalism and the drinking of alcohol have not been permitted to become church-dividing. It has been tolerantly assumed that Christians may legitimately adopt opposing views and practices on these issues. But where the ordination of women is concerned, one would assume that in the interests of good order a common mind would be sought. This has been, and is being done by an increasing number of churches, though it is difficult for an outsider to discern the theological grounds on which (though I have been given pragmatic reasons why) the Church of England, having determined to ordain women, could then introduce flying bishops to serve the needs of those who would neither accept the mind of the Church nor leave it. As for homosexuality, in the mainline churches with which I am familiar, the majority of members are content that all church offices be open in principle to all church members, and such unhappy secessions as there have been have generally been fuelled by differing understanding of the authority of the Bible, which has sometimes been wielded as a weapon in debate—by both sides.[56]

For a final example of intolerance in the Church which, in my judgement, derives from a theological failure and a sectarian spirit, I would mention the continuing division of Christians one from another at the Lord's table. We have Christian conservatives who say "Until we can all agree on biblical authority and doctrine we cannot have any truck with ecumenism, because unity must be unity in the truth" (by which they can only mean their interpretations of the truth); and we have Roman Catholics who say "Until other Christians are in communion with the Bishop of Rome there can be no inter-communion with them" (which seems to be a position more Roman than catholic). The positions are thus mirror images of one another. In both cases the protagonists are resting upon their little interpretations of what the mighty God has done; in both cases they are withholding themselves from those whom God has already made one in Christ with them. The only way out of this impasse that I can see would be a return to the tolerant, non-sectarian (or truly catholic) position that those whom God has called by the Spirit to himself and given to one another as branches united to Christ the Vine are one Church; and that what God has done (whether we like it or not) should take precedence over our feeble grasp of the truth and our imperfect understanding and practice of polity.[57]

---

56. I have offered some reflections on homosexuality in the context of a wider discussion of inclusiveness and exclusiveness in *Enlightenment, Ecumenism, Evangel*, ch. 12.

57. See further on the Holy Spirit and ecumenism, ibid. ch. 11; *The Great Ejectment*

VIII

In this paper I have sought to show that from the Reformation onwards, the seedbed of the liberal values of toleration and tolerance was the struggle for religious freedom. I traced the way in which these ideas developed in epistemological and Christian ways in the mind of John Locke, a major proponent of them, and I showed how natural rights were so influential in the thinking of the Rational Dissenter, Joseph Priestley. With John Stuart Mill any Christian justifications of toleration and tolerance were strictly unneccesary for the appeal was to utility, and we were in the secular world. Nevertheless Mill extracted from Christian teaching—especially its moral teaching—what was serviceable to his cause, whilst at the same time hoping that the demise of Christianity and its replacement by the Religion of Humanity would eventually come about.

Against this historical background I offered reflections upon the ways in which, in popular culture selective intolerance is sometimes the order of the day, while in academic and ecclesiastical circles, questions regarding tolerance and intolerance arise in relation to methodological, socio-political and ecumenical issues. I pointed out that on occasion we encounter the paradoxical situation that those who profess liberal values can be strangely prone to illiberal attitudes.

On more than one occasion I have hinted that the determination of which actions and attitudes are tolerant and intolerant turns upon a constellation of underlying values to which allegiance is paid. Far from being an original insight, this is simply a statement of the obvious, and Locke said it long ago with respect to the "private person": "we must not content ourselves with the narrow measures of bare justice: charity, bounty, and liberality must be added to it."[58] It is not possible to pursue all the relevant values now, but I trust that after all that I have written about tolerance, my readers will be minded to receive a concluding dogmatic postscript.

The first and final recourse of the church is to God's free grace, supremely active at the cross. Christian liberty is not licence, it is freedom under the Spirit; it is a characteristic of that new life which the Father bestows on the ground of the Son's saving work, which both redeems sinners and satisfies God's holiness. Because God is love, Christians are challenged to love all people, not excluding their enemies. Because

---

of 1662, ch. 4. For general discussions of ecclesiastical sectarianism see Sell, *Aspects of Christian Integrity*, 93–97; Sell, *Commemorations*, 46–59.

58. Locke, *A Letter Concerning Toleration*, 400.

God is holy, the prophetic voice of the Church must be heard against all injustice. In the course of facing up to these challenges and making the necessary decisions concerning attitudes to be adopted and actions to be taken, all the questions of toleration, tolerance and its limits, and intolerance will arise. But the first thing and the compelling thing is for the church to realise within its own borders the values it professes to uphold. Because the saints are sinners it is unlikely that we shall ever get the tolerance/intolerance balance exactly right. Because the saints are under judgement of holy love, we should do well to seek God's help as we strive to witness to his kingdom of love, righteousness and peace in this fractured world. As we make this attempt, confronted as we shall be by John Bunyan's "hobgoblins and foul fiends" (so sadly excised from some modern hymn books), we shall increasingly realize that it is only when they are under the authority of grace that people are truly free. As the hymn writer, George Matheson (1842–1906), put it:

Make me a captive, Lord,
And then I shall be free.

Now that is a paradox I can tolerate.

BIBLIOGRAPHY

Anon. Report in *The Christian Century*, 4 October 2005, 7.
———. Report in *The Observer*, 16 October 2005, 6.
Baillie, John. *Natural Science and the Spiritual Life*. London: Oxford University Press, 1951.
Bonaventure. *The Works of Bonaventure. V. Collocations on the Six Days*. Translated by J. de Vinck. Peterson: NJ: St. Anthony Guild, 1970.
Burrough, Edward. *A Visitation of Love and Presentation unto the King, and Those call'd Royalists*. London: Wilson, 1660.
De Beer, E. S. *The Correspondence of John Locke*. 8 vols. Oxford: Clarendon, 1976–89.
De Burgh, W. G. *From Morality to Religion*. London: Macdonald and Evans, 1938.
Forsyth, P. T. *The Principle of Authority*. 1913. Reprint. London: Independent, 1952.
———. "Revelation and the Person of Christ." In *Faith and Criticism: Essays by Congregationalists*, 95–144. 2nd ed. London: Sampson Low Marston, 1893.
Garvie, A. E. "The Limits of Doctrinal Restatement." In *Proceedings of the Third International Congregational Council*, edited by John Brown, 90–98. London: Congregational Union of England and Wales, 1908.
Gouldstone, Timothy Maxwell. *The Rise and Decline of Anglican Idealism in the Nineteenth Century*. Basingstoke, UK: Palgrave Macmillan, 2005.
Haac, Oscar A. *The Correspondence of John Stuart Mill and Auguste Comte*. New Brunswick, NJ: Transaction, 1995.
Helwys, Thomas. *A Short Declaration of the Mistery of Iniquity*. Amsterdam, 1612.
Locke, John. "A Letter from a Person of Quality to his Friend in the Country." In *Works* vol. 9, 200–246. London: n.p., 1675.
———. *Two Tracts on Government*. Edited by Philip Abrams. Cambridge: Cambridge University Press, 1967.
Lumpkin, William L. *Baptist Confessions of Faith*. Valley Forge, PA: Judson, 1969.
Marshall, John. *John Locke: Toleration and Early Enlightenment Culture*. Cambridge: Cambridge University Press, 2006.
Matthews, A. G. *The Savoy Declaration of Faith and Order 1658*. London: Independent, 1959.
Maugham, W. Somerset. *A Writer's Notebook* (1949). London: Pan, 1978.
McGrath, Alister. *Dawkins' God: Genes, Memes, and the Meaning of Life*. Oxford: Blackwell, 2005.
———. "God is Not Dead Yet." *The Times Higher Education Supplement*, 22 October 2004, 16.
McKie, Robin. "Doctor Zoo." *The Observer*, 25 July 2004, 25.
Mill, John Stuart. *Autobiography and Literary Essays*. Edited by John M. Robson and Jack Stillinger. Toronto: University of Toronto Press, 1981
———. *Collected Works of John Stuart Mill*. 33 vols. Toronto: University of Toronto Press, 1963–88.
Monck, Thomas, et al. *Sion's Groans for her Distressed*, 1661. In *Tracts on Liberty of Conscience and Persecution 1614–1661*, edited by E. B. Underhill, 349–82. London: Haddon, 1846.
Patai, Daphne. "You Say Social Justice, I Say Political Censorship." *The Times Higher Education Supplement*, 28 October 2005, 12.

Paul, Robert S. *The Assembly of the Lord: Politics and Religion in the Westminster Assembly and the "Grand Debate."* Edinburgh: T. & T. Clark, 1985.

Priestley, Joseph. *The Theological and Miscellaneous Works of Joseph Priestley (1817–1831).* Edited by J. T. Rutt. Bristol: Thoemmes, 1999.

Ross, F. Review of David Hackett, *Liberty and Freedom: A Visual History of America's Founding Ideas.* In *The Times Educational Supplement,* 17 June 2005, 26.

Sell, Alan P. F. *Aspects of Christian Integrity.* 1990. Reprint. Eugene, OR: Wipf & Stock, 1998.

———. *Commemorations: Studies in Christian Thought and History.* 1993. Reprint. Eugene, OR: Wipf & Stock, 1998.

———. *Confessing and Commending the Faith: Historic Witness and Apologetic Method.* 2002. Reprint. Eugene, OR: Wipf & Stock, 2006.

———. *Dissenting Thought and the Life of the Churches: Studies in an English Tradition.* Lewiston, NY: Mellen, 1990.

———. *Enlightenment, Ecumenism, Evangel: Theological Themes and Thinkers 1550–2000.* Milton Keynes, UK: Paternoster, 2005.

———. *Four Philosophical Anglicans: W. G. De Burgh, W. R. Matthews, O. C. Quick, H. A. Hodges.* Farnham, UK: Ashgate, 2010.

———. *The Great Ejectment of 1662: Its Antecedents, Aftermath, and Ecumenical Significance.* Eugene, OR: Pickwick, 2012.

———. *John Locke and the Eighteenth-Century Divines.* 1997. Reprint. Eugene, OR: Wipf & Stock, 2006.

———. *Mill on God: The Pervasiveness and Elusiveness of Mill's Religious Thought.* Aldershot, UK: Ashgate, 2004.

———. *Testimony and Tradition: Studies in Reformed and Dissenting Thought.* Aldershot, UK: Ashgate, 2005.

———. *Theology in Turmoil: The Roots, Course and Significance of the Conservative-Liberal Debate in Modern Theology.* 1986. Reprint. Eugene, OR: Wipf & Stock, 1998.

Smith, Thorne. *The Jovial Ghosts.* 1933. Reprint. London: May Fair, 1961.

Stenmark, Mikael. *Scientism: Science, Ethics and Religion.* Aldershot, UK: Ashgate, 2001.

Ward, Mrs. Humphrey. *Robert Elsmere.* London: Smith Elder, 1888.

Ward, Keith. *God, Chance and Necessity.* Oxford: One World, 1996.

Watts, Michael R. *The Dissenters from the Reformation to the French Revolution.* Oxford: Clarendon, 1978.

Wootton, David. *John Locke: Political Writings.* Harmondsworth, UK: Penguin, 1992.

Wykes, David L. "'A Finished Monster of the True Birmingham Breed': Birmingham, Unitarians and the 1791 Priestley Riots." In *Protestant Nonconformists and the West Midlands of England,* edited by Alan P. F. Sell, 43–69. Keele, UK: Keele University Press, 1996.

CHAPTER FIVE

The Use, Abuse, and Relevance of Religion

Some Reflections on Professor Abraham van de Beek's Proposal

It is fashionable to speak about the relevance of Christian faith nowadays. It should be relevant for society, of interest for politics, helping people in their personal development, and so on. This article discusses the question whether religion should be relevant at all, and what the consequences will be of a denial of it.

THUS THE PREAMBLE TO a paper by Professor Van de Beek entitled, "Religion Without Ulterior Motive."[1] This paper is compatible with that on "Christian Identity is Identity in Christ,"[2] which he delivered at the sixth conference of the International Reformed Theological Institute in Seoul, Korea, in July 2005. I shall refer to both papers in what follows.

The possibility that religion is irrelevant may confirm atheists, agnostics, and secularists in their opinion; it may comfort the "armchair

---

1. Since I am working from a typescript, and therefore have no final pagination, I shall refer to this paper as RWUM.

2. I shall refer to this paper as CI.

Christian"; and it may appear to activist Christians as a huge step towards heresy. It might therefore seem that the first task is to analyze the term "relevance," recognizing that to determine that something is relevant is to make a judgment for which there are good grounds (not simply good reasons). But I shall work my way towards such a discussion by commenting on Van de Beek's papers as they stand. I shall suggest that it makes sense to speak of both the "use"/abuse of religion as well as of the usefulness of it, and that the gospel of Jesus Christ is relevant in all times and all places. I wonder whether Van de Beek's disjunctive mode of expression (for I do not think it is a question of his beliefs) tends to obscure this fact. But let us proceed step by step.

Disjunction or Conjunction?

Van de Beek sets out from a remark by Samuel Hirsch, a Jewish author who, writing in 1854, declared that "The subordination of religion to any other factor means the denial of religion."[3] The context of Hirsch's remark was the mid-nineteenth-century concern with progress, which turned some minds in an instrumentalist direction: those things are useful which contribute to human progress; those things which do not, are to be left on one side. Over against this, Hirsch protests that religion exclusively concerns our standing under God's law; it is not a means to any other end. Religion is not to be judged according to its ability to blend with the prevailing climate of thought; it is not relevant only in so far as it does this. Van de Beek concurs: "You cannot use faith as an instrument in order to gain something. If you do so religion is soon delivered up to the whim of the day of any person who can use it for his or her own interest" (RWUM). He recognizes, of course, that the godly life is a blessed life, but godliness is not to be sought in order to obtain the blessings.

Similarly, Van de Beek observes that faith has ethical consequences, but the desirable consequences may not be deployed as arguments to justify faith, for "The aim of faith is only God Himself—and nothing besides Him. He won't give his glory to something else . . . not even to ethics" (RWUM). Hence his disquiet at what he perceives as the instrumentalism of both liberation theology and the programme of the World Council of Churches entitled, *Justice, Peace and the Integrity of Creation*, and his adverse criticism of the view that "the main task of Christians" is "to strive

---

3. He quotes Frank et al., *The Jewish Philosophy Reader*, 393.

The Use, Abuse, and Relevance of Religion

for the items that [the latter] program indicates" (CI). Over against this Van de Beek sets the injunction of Irenaeus that "It is the main task for Christians to think about their death"[4] (CI). He construes this to mean that we are not to strive for righteousness, for we cannot change things for the better. God alone can effect the desired changes, and the cross is the supreme testimony to this fact (CI).

Thus far Van de Beek appears to be committed to a disjunctive approach: we are to love God for his own sake; we are not to strive for righteousness. But later he writes, "We can call for justice to a corrupted regime, for we are not afraid even if they threaten us with death. . . . [Christians] do not try to change the world, because the world will not change for the better. They themselves have a different style of life" (CI). Is there not an ambivalence here? Why should we challenge a corrupt regime regarding justice if we have no hope that through our witness *God* may bring about change? We may agree that only by God's enabling grace will change be effected. But to rest in the conviction that we should not try to change the world because it will not change for the better would be to descend into a pessimism regarding God's ability which would cripple witness and foster the false comfort of quietism; or else it would land us in the unrealistic position of those evangelists who declare that when we (yes, they frequently speak as if they do it) have got everybody saved, all socio-political matters will be set to rights. If the former stance appears to deny the Christian obligation to be salt and light in the world, the latter seems to overlook the fact that the Bible has more to say about the faithful remnant, than about "packing all the sinners in."

The ambivalence emerges again in relation to liberation theology. Van de Beek writes, "Liberation theology is a clear example of religion with a goal. That goal is not God and his service, but political and economic liberation" (RWUM). Here again, *prima facie*, is the disjunction: we are to serve God; we are not to seek political and economic liberation. It is undoubtedly true that some of the earlier liberation theologians, under the dire circumstances of their socio-political contexts, did not always maintain their balance; but I should argue, and have indeed argued,[5] that the most insightful among them understood very well that since God uses means, our service and witness may be used by him in liberating ways. The ambivalence enters when Van de Beek, concurring

---

4. Irenaeus, fragment XI, *MPG* VII: 1233.
5. See Sell, *Enlightenment, Ecumenism, Evangel*, 306–25.

PART ONE: Confessing the Faith in Context

with Hirsch, qualifies the disjunction by saying that "True religion . . . is interested in material and social issues, but never in such a way that it makes a core issue of it [*sic*]. It must be clear that they are relative, second or even third level questions" (RWUM). But at least, now, they are legitimate questions: there would have been no Good Samaritan if the Samaritan, on seeing the wounded man, had said, "So sorry I cannot help you, I'm thinking about my death."

A further query concerns Van de Beek's declaration that "We cannot use arguments for our religion. . . . For at the very moment when we use an argument—for instance that it creates the most just society . . . then a just society is put above faith. . . . We are Christians only because we are Christians, and not because there is a good argument to be Christians" (RWUM). A number of points need to be untangled here. First, if we cannot use arguments for our religion we shall not be able to respond to those who confront us with their doubts and difficulties about the Christian faith; and this will be more than an intellectual failure, it will be a failure in witnessing, and it will frequently be a pastoral failure too. Secondly, I do not see that to point to the beneficial effects of Christianity is to put the effects above faith. It is rather to show that desirable consequences flow from faith, which is what Van de Beek himself believes. Of course, not every product of religion is beneficial, for believers may be fanatical, and empirical Christianity displays a sufficiently large multitude of blemishes to keep it in repentant mood to the end of time. Nevertheless, the fruit of faith can be highly beneficial to individuals and societies. Thirdly, we do not stand where we do as Christians because we have argued our way to faith (though through argument we may have removed some of the obstacles to faith which previously lay in our path or the path of others). Least of all is it the case that we "review God's claims and then admit Him as we are satisfied."[6] We are Christians because we have been called by God's free and sovereign grace. It does not follow, however, that reasoned, orderly, testimony is redundant.[7]

Instrumentalism

The above qualifications notwithstanding, Professor Van de Beek does well to insist that to "use" religion for extraneous ends is to abuse it. God

6. Forsyth, *The Principle of Authority*, 146.
7. See further Sell, *Confessing and Commending the Faith*; and ch. 7 below.

The Use, Abuse, and Relevance of Religion

is the end of religion, and the primary task and privilege of the church is the worship of the God of all grace who, in Jesus Christ has visited and redeemed his people, and who, by the Holy Spirit, is ever present with them to guide, guard, challenge, reprove and forgive. Of the church P. T. Forsyth said,

> Her note is the supernatural note which distinguishes incarnation from immanence, redemption from evolution, the Kingdom of God from mere spiritual progress, and the Holy Spirit from mere spiritual process. She must never be opportunist at the cost of being evangelical, liberal at the cost of being positive, too broad for the Cross's narrow way. And she must produce that impression on the whole, that impression of detachment from the world and of descent upon it.[8]

These words have lost none of their pertinence during the hundred years since they were first uttered: and note carefully that Forsyth speaks of *both* detachment *and* descent.

Opportunist, instrumentalist—call it what you will, such attitudes have tempted the church through the ages, as a random selection of examples will amply demonstrate. Consider first, individuals. Since Shakespeare presents us with no evidence of their habitual piety, we may not unjustifiably conclude that when, in *The Tempest*, the storm-tossed sailors cry, "All lost! To prayers! To prayers! All lost!"[9] they are "using" (that is, abusing) religion in an instrumentalist way: when all else fails, religion may bail us out. When television evangelists preaching a "gospel of success" tell their listeners that if they "come to Christ" their bank balances, their career prospects, their health (and, for all I know, their racing pigeons) will prosper, they are "using"/abusing religion in a very crude way and, moreover, storing up disappointment for those who, having succumbed to their enticements, subsequently discover something of the way of the cross. If a Christian mission in an impoverished part of the world seeks to tempt individuals into the Christian faith by material benefits: "Come to our splendidly equipped hospital (much better than the Baptist one), lose your tonsils and find a Saviour!" it is likewise "using"/abusing religion. With regard to societies at large, if an Anglican church dignitary argues, as some in England have recently been doing, that because of the parlous moral condition of society we must build

---

8. Forsyth, *Positive Preaching and the Modern Mind*, 82–83.
9. Shakespeare, *The Tempest*, I.i.

more Church schools, he or she is "using"/abusing religion, for religion becomes a tool of social engineering and, if a pupil's registration turns upon parental church attendance, an inducement to hypocrisy is offered which, as is well known, some will accept.

As far as groups are concerned: whenever nations or parties have justified war in the name of religion they have "used"/abused religion and have sought to cover extraneous motives with a cloak of respectability. When an allegedly Christian state, as in sixteenth- and seventeenth-century England, sought to enforce religious conformity in order to bring about national cohesion in face of foreign enemies (something against which the English Separatists and Dissenters protested at the cost of threats, imprisonment, banishment and even their lives), it was "using"/abusing religion. When a secular state contributes towards the cost of particular pieces of the church's social work which it would otherwise have to fund itself, this seems acceptable as payment for services rendered; but if the secular state contributes towards the cost of ministerial training, or the stipends of those who preach a gospel it repudiates, in the expectation of a more morally upright, benign and easily-governable society, it is hypocritically "using"/abusing religion. All of this seems undeniable, and Professor Van de Beek has done well to draw our attention to it.

But the case can be overstated. Van de Beek writes, "A church member uttered: 'If I would not have my faith, I would not know how to overcome my sorrows and troubles.' The underlying idea is that faith serves to overcome your problems—forgetting that Christian faith often is the cause of many troubles and that it is easier to speak like those people who do not worry about God, as Psalm 73 says" (RWUM). There can be no question that in certain circumstances the Christian faith can heap troubles upon the saints—remember, for example, the Separatists and Dissenters. But may it not be that the Professor also has momentarily forgotten something which he elsewhere grants, namely, that God can work through the testimony of believers? Hence, if a sincere Christian, not an evangelistic charlatan, makes a humble and grateful testimony to the peace which he or she has found in Christ, is it wrong if an untutored hearer whose life is in turmoil thinks, "I should like to have that peace"? May not God the Holy Spirit be prompting the thought, and may not that thought be the starting-point of a religious quest? Surely it would be callous in the extreme to say to such a person, "You only want religion because of what you can get out of it: you are 'using'/abusing religion." There is a great gulf between testimony to the power and solace of faith and the mistaken view that faith provides an escape hatch from the troubles of life. Extending this line of thought to society at large, and to the church's role as yeast, may we not say that the church's task of nurturing those who uphold such values as honesty, integrity, industriousness, generosity, is of great significance to society, and that this nurturing work should not be stopped simply because some may be tempted to regard societal goods as acquisitions to be obtained instrumentally *via* religion? Societal goods can also be understood as fruits flowing from that honouring of God which is at the heart of true religion.[10]

At this point, I think it is pertinent to refer to church assemblies, for they provide opportunities for activists to "use"/abuse religion in the furtherance of their several agenda, and to the detriment of the Church's primary obligations of worshipping God and proclaiming his gospel. There seem to be so many "causes" at the present time, yet in a sense this is nothing new. In 1876 Joseph Parker, minister of the City Temple, London, addressed the Assembly of the Congregational Union of England and Wales thus:

> What an amazing amount of so-called "business" we have to do! We have to disestablish the Church [of England], modernize the Universities, rectify the policy of School Boards, clear the way to burial-grounds, subsidize magazines, sell hymn-books, play the hose upon [the Anglican] Convocation, and generally give everybody to understand that if we have not yet assailed them or defended them, it is not for want of will, but merely for want of time.[11]

What is different nowadays is the way in which highly politicized caucuses, well versed in managerial tactics, and sometimes well funded, can make the notion of a church assembly in which the saints, united by grace to Christ and therefore to one another, corporately seek his mind an unrealizable ideal. Instead of the earnest quest of unanimity in Christ we have pressure groups whose members have no expectation that their minds will be changed by anything that is said; who on occasion adopt a sectarian stance which is more than willing to "unchurch" those who disagree with them; who sometimes hijack the Bible so that it becomes a weapon in their hands with which they bludgeon their opponents; and

---

10. See further, Fergusson, *Church, State and Civil Society*, 123.
11. Quoted by Peel, *These Hundred Years*, 264.

whose sole objective is to drive their favoured motion through. When they succeed, we may well have the situation in which what is ostensibly "the mind of the church" as agreed at the assembly is in fact poles apart from that of the majority of the church's constituency. This is a recipe for friction, even in some cases for secession; and all because the organs of the church have been "used"/abused in order to score partisan points and achieve sectional goals.[12]

Motives, Divine and Human

In the concluding paragraphs of RWUM, Professor Van de Beek very properly reminds us that "users"/abusers of religion may well be disappointed. We may work and pray in the hope of a good harvest, but there may be a famine (cf. Hab 3:17). The way of suffering may be inescapable, as it was for Jesus. This thought leads him to God's saving act at the cross. Here we see the supreme example of the way in which "God loves us for nothing." That is, he acts towards us without ulterior motive. This is certainly the case; this is the abounding generosity of grace. But although, as Van de Beek rightly says, God does not call us because of our status or prowess (he cites Deut 7:7), we have good reason to think that God acts as he does because he desires a people for his praise and service. With such a people he enters into a covenant relationship. May we not say that these are consequences or ends desired by God? But God does not "use"/abuse grace in order to secure the desirable consequences; his motives are never mixed. The problem is that ours are. It seems to be part of the human condition that sinners are susceptible to ulterior motives in a way that God is not. Hence the analogy between God's actions towards us, and our human actions breaks down; for God is perfect, we are not. The doctrine of total depravity, while it does not mean that everything we do is absolutely reprehensible, does mean that nothing we do is wholly pure, for we are not God. This by no means releases us from the obligation to strive after perfection, it simply cautions us against supposing that we have already reached that happy state.

12. At an assembly held some years ago the theme for study concerned the Bible in relation to Christian witness. The theme was intended as a theological exploration that would result in more effective outreach on the ground. I was intrigued to note that some activists present did not feel that the occasion was successful because no denunciatory resolutions had issued from it. The idea of an assembly devoid of such "prophetic" utterances seemed anathema to them.

The Use, Abuse, and Relevance of Religion

To put it somewhat crudely: it is easier for God to act without ulterior motives than it is for us, for his motives are not mixed. Thus, when Van de Beek writes, "We serve the Lord for nothing, as the book of Job says," this can be only a counsel of perfection held before the imperfect. It is an unrealizable ideal and, from all that experience teaches us, a psychological impossibility. We might even say that a significant aspect of the Creator-creature distinction is that God can act absolutely without ulterior motives whereas we, being sinners, cannot. But all may not be lost. Suppose that, given who we are, we are sometimes tempted to "use"/abuse religion because of certain goods which we think may accrue from it: may not our relatively lower motive be a means whereby God brings us face to face with our need of reorientation towards himself? For, when we remember ourselves, we know that apart from him we can do nothing, and we learn afresh that to desire the reward of faith (construed as the consequence of faith, not as a recompense for faith) without the root of faith (trust in God for his own sake) is futile. It is hardly necessary to add that the fact that sinners cannot act absolutely without ulterior motives does not legitimate the "use"/abuse of religion against which Van de Beek quite rightly protests, but it does go some way towards explaining it.

It will by now be clear that I am in total agreement with Professor Van de Beek that those who adopt a purely instrumentalist view of religion are grievously mistaken. Religion is not to be valued simply because of what can be got out of it. To fall into this error is to "use"/abuse religion. But are we necessarily bound to go to the extreme of maintaining that religion is irrelevant? Is it utterly use*less*? I shall attempt an answer to these questions by means of an analysis of the term "relevance."

Relevance

We may set out from the dictionary definition of "relevance" as being that which bears upon, or is pertinent to, the matter in hand. Clearly, the determination that something is, or is not, relevant entails a judgment, and such judgments can be mistaken. Suppose that during a severe winter the water pipes in my house freeze and the supply of water stops. I call in my neighbour, whom I suspect is something of a handyman because I have often seen him lying underneath his car. He looks at the situation and asks, "Have you any tools?" "Oh yes," I reply, and I go to the garden shed and return with a brace and bit, a plasterer's trowel and a garden rake. My neighbour now wishes that he had asked for relevant tools. In this case the irrelevance of the tools to the matter in hand is obvious. But such judgments are not always so straightforward. In some cases we may not be sure whether something is relevant (will work) until we have experimented with it. Hence sophisticated scientific investigations; hence homely attempts to see whether porridge will really seal a leaking car radiator. Again, many judgments of relevance are time-bound. A person may sincerely have believed that a particular remedy was relevant to a particular medical condition, whereas—perhaps many years later—this is shown not to have been the case. (This is why even Reformed Christians would normally prefer to swallow John Wesley's theology than his medicinal potions.)

All of the judgments so far exemplified concern what may be labelled "relevance objectively conceived." That is to say, the judgments made refer to matters that are deemed to be the case, regardless of the feelings, dispositions or opinions of the judges. But sometimes people will say, "This is not relevant *to me*." Here a subjective emphasis is given to the judgment, and with it the implication that what is not relevant to me may be relevant to somebody else. There are cases in which this is perfectly understandable, though often qualifications may need to be entered. Thus (on the assumption that he or she is not a family lawyer, or a civil servant in a pensions office) a young person may say "The provisions of retirement law are not relevant to me." We should then need to supply the qualification "immediately relevant"; for if the young person lives long enough, the provisions will in due course be relevant to his or her situation. Again, I may say that the particular skills of an obstetrician are not relevant to male me; but if a member of my family required the attention of such a specialist, I should then need to qualify the claim by saying that such skills are not "directly relevant" to me: they would certainly be indirectly relevant to me in such a case. Consider the assertion, "Traditional church worship is not relevant to me." If a young person says this, what may be meant is that the church music is old fashioned, the sermon boring, too many people wear suits. . . . If an older person says the same thing it may be because of a considered atheist or secularist conviction, or simply because the person manages his or her life without perceiving any need to partake in church worship which may, in any case, be quite foreign to the individual concerned.

Coming more directly to Christianity as such: can we justifiably judge that it is never relevant; that is always is; or that it is for some people

The Use, Abuse, and Relevance of Religion

and not for others? It would, on the face of it, seem odd to say of any religion that it has no bearing whatsoever on anything to do with the world as it is. Such a religion would be other-worldly in an exclusive sense; though even then it would presumably have a certain relevance to its human devotees, for it would at least constitute part of their identity. By contrast, as traditionally construed, the Christian claim is that the gospel of God's free and saving grace is relevant to all people in all ages in all places. It concerns their standing before God in this life and their eternal state; and it calls them into a new life of fellowship with the saints, visible and invisible, with the former of whom they are to engage in witness and service. If this is the case, we cannot say that Christianity is relevant only to some people and not to others. Of course, millions of people make a contrary judgment. Adherents of other faiths, secularists and others will, with varying degrees of politeness, deny the Christian claim. But denial is not refutation. It may, however, signal the beginning of a discussion in which the Christian will be called to give a reason for his or her hope.

In claiming Christianity's relevance in the sense described we are necessarily implying its usefulness for certain purposes—fulness of life, for example. But we are not indulging in the instrumentalist "use"/abuse of religion by thinking and witnessing in this way. Properly conceived, the gospel call is not an invitation to people to avail themselves of the fruit of faith without having the root of faith. In the light of God's gracious approach in Christ, and of his love supremely active at the Cross, the call is to repent and believe. New life and the fruit of the Spirit are the consequences of the divinely-enabled response, not a payment or reward for an unaided human vote for God.

As we live this new life in the company of the gathered saints, the implications (relevance) of the gospel will be worked out in practice. They concern, *inter alia*, going on to perfection, seeking first the kingdom of God, heeding the prophetic challenges regarding justice and peace. Since Professor Van de Beek would not deny any of this, I conclude that he overstates his anti-instrumentalist case in a disjunctive manner, and that a careful analysis of "use," "abuse," and "relevance" yields a more nuanced account in which the "either . . . or" is balanced by the "both . . . and." If the peril of the former is the godly ghetto, the peril of the latter is an activism ungrounded in the gospel: "We must, of course, go some way to meet the world, but when we do meet we must do more than greet. . . . Refinement is not reform; and amelioration is not regeneration."[13]

13. Forsyth, *Positive Preaching and the Modern Mind*, 89–90.

PART ONE: Confessing the Faith in Context

From the peril of the ghetto and the peril of ungrounded activism, good Lord deliver us. Rather, may we, by God's grace, know the joy and the challenge of that true piety before God that first honours him, and then inevitably becomes salt and light in the world—which is just another way of honouring him.

BIBLIOGRAPHY

Anon. *Justice, Peace and the Integrity of Creation.* Geneva: World Council of Churches, 1989.

Fergusson, David. *Church, State and Civil Society.* Cambridge: Cambridge University Press, 2004.

Forsyth, P. T. *The Principle of Authority.* 1913. Reprint. London: Independent, 1952.

———. *Positive Preaching and the Modern Mind.* 1907. Reprint. London: Independent, 1964.

Frank, D. H., O. Leaman, and C. H. Manekin. *The Jewish Philosophy Reader.* London: Routledge, 2000.

Irenaeus. Fragment XI. In *Patrologia Graeca*, vol. VII, edited J.-P. Migne, 1233. Paris: Migne 1857.

Peel, Albert. *These Hundred Years: A History of the Congregational Union of England and Wales.* London: Congregational Union of England and Wales, 1931.

Sell, Alan P. F. *Confessing and Commending the Faith: Historic Witness and Apologetic Method.* 2002. Reprint. Eugene, OR: Wipf & Stock, 2006.

———. *Enlightenment, Ecumenism, Evangel: Theological Themes and Thinkers 1550–2000.* Milton Keynes, UK: Paternoster, 2005.

CHAPTER SIX

Confessing the Faith in the Intellectual Context

THOSE WHO SERVE ON frontiers take a considerable risk. They are the target of opponents on the other side of the border, and they are in danger of "friendly fire" from their own side. So it is with those who brave the frontier between theology and philosophy. Despite the hazards, this frontier is one which I have felt called to occupy for half a century. The stimulus was provided by the contrast between the rigorous training I received in the heyday of analytical philosophy during my Arts degree, in which I specialized in moral philosophy, and the equally demanding but in some ways attitudinally different approach I experienced in the Faculty of Theology. It was out of the perceived difference between what went on in Arts ethics and Divinity Christian Ethics that I devised my MA thesis, "Christian Ethics in the Light of British Moral Philosophy since G. E. Moore"; and the broader question of the relations between Christian and secular philosophy in Britain in the twentieth century became the theme of the thesis I submitted for my first doctorate.[1] The underlying motivation in these pursuits was more than purely academic. From the outset I was concerned with the need to commend the faith to those who have intellectual difficulties with it, and with the most appropriate and effective way of setting about this task.

---

1. Extracts from the former have been published, though I should now wish to develop them further. The historical section of the latter appeared in expanded form as *The Philosophy of Religion 1875–1980*. I have drawn upon other sections of it in various places.

Confessing the Faith in the Intellectual Context

From one point of view I was faced with a very old question indeed. For as soon as Christianity began to find its way into contexts committed to other world views, the questions of communication, content, and method arose. At some periods apologetic concerns were to the fore, notably in the age of the apologists, and in the second half of the nineteenth century when naturalism, materialism, positivism, and the like were among the foes to be vanquished by the faithful, and when it was necessary to come to terms with modern biblical criticism, historical method, and evolutionary thought. Within Britain, the Scots were particularly active in developing the apologetics industry, with such names as those of Robert Flint, A. B. Bruce, and James Orr being prominent.[2]

From about 1920 onwards, however, apologetic zeal waned. Of course, one can still find books of apologetics which proceed as if in a nineteenth-century time-warp, but surely "*passé*-apologetics" is a contradiction in terms. I have even seen books in a Canadian Christian bookshop on a shelf labelled "Apologetics," written by authors zealously engaged in wanton cult-bashing. But as regards serious attempts to engage with the broader intellectual context, the post-1920 decline in such activity is there for all to see. One indication of it can be seen in the *Proceedings* of the World Presbyterian Alliance and the International Congregational Council, both of which, until the end of the First World War had published papers reflecting upon Christianity in relation to current thought. Such activity quite quickly dried up.[3] Why? Partly, I think, because of the increasing sense that the classical theistic arguments, which many older apologists had quite happily regarded as having cumulative force even if there were particular problems with each of them, could no longer bear the weight put on them; partly because of growing sophistication on the part of the Christian faith's intellectual opponents; and partly because the Barthian response to liberal theology seemed to many to rule out the apologetic enterprise from the start.

While I did not think that the classical theistic arguments constituted copper-bottomed demonstrations that only an idiot could repudiate; while I did not suppose that they ever yielded the "worshipable" God of Christianity (something with which I am sure that Anselm, Aquinas, and others fully agreed), I nevertheless felt that efforts should be made to commend the faith *vis à vis* the intellectual challenges to it, and that,

---

2. See further, Sell, *Defending and Declaring the Faith*. For apologetics in English Nonconformity see Sell, *Philosophy, Dissent and Nonconformity 1689–1920*, ch. 5.

3. See further Sell, *A Reformed, Evangelical, Catholic Theology*, ch. 5.

for all Barth's insight into the starting point of Christian faith and reflection as residing in the Word of God which addresses us clamantly by the Spirit, a *quasi*-Barthian ghetto protectively encircled by revelation and thereby insulated from such challenges was to be avoided.[4]

After some years of ruminating on this issue I embarked upon what turned out to be a fifteen-year project which resulted in a trilogy on Christian apologetic method. My plan was first to see what steps had been taken in the modern period to commend the Faith intellectually. I took two historical soundings which yielded the first two books of the trilogy: *John Locke and the Eighteenth-Century Divines*, and *Philosophical Idealism and Christian Belief*.[5] In the third volume, *Confessing and Commending the Faith. Historic Witness and Apologetic Method*, I worked my way towards an apologetic method which would, I hoped, make good some deficiencies in the older approaches, whilst at the same time meeting the challenges of those within and without the Christian fold who regard apologetics as a doomed enterprise.

I

John Locke has, with some justification, been called "the father of the English Enlightenment," and the eighteenth century has been called, with rather less justification, the Age of Reason: it was also the age of "enthusiasm", whether evangelical or mystical. Nevertheless, in the wake of the Toleration Act of 1689, which legalized the worship and churchly activities of trinitarian Protestant Nonconformists, there was a growing feeling in many quarters that the right of private judgment should be honoured; that the mechanism of Hobbes should be met by a reasoned Christian response; and that Baconian scientific method afforded clues to the establishment of sound philosophico-theological method. Not surprisingly, the eighteenth century was also the age of the cosmological argument.

Not, indeed, that the pursuit of a reasonable faith took the same form in every writer. Far from it. We have, for example, the deductive-rationalist approach of the high Calvinist Baptist, John Gill; the more

---

4. Clearly, the attempt to address the queries of the honest doubter or the perplexed believer is a pastoral, as well as an intellectual, matter.

5. The chronologically later topic appeared first because the earlier material took considerably longer to gather, based as I then was in Canada. I here deal with the first two volumes in chronological order of theme, not of publication.

sensationalist method of John Wesley, the rationalism of such a Presbyterian "Arian" as John Taylor of Norwich, the libertarianism of Richard Price, and the determinism of his friend and fellow-Presbyterian-turned-Unitarian, Joseph Priestley.[6]

In one way or another the presence of Locke hovered over all of these and many more. Some he influenced positively, others negatively. Indeed, the detection of "influence" is not the least of the problems in writing about eighteenth-century thought. For once they become current, ideas know no boundaries of space or time, and "Locke-like" ideas were sooner or later advanced by some who had hardly read him: they became part of the prevailing climate of thought. For this reason, as I pointed out three times in the course of my book, I was careful to discuss only those who at least mentioned Locke by name in their writings, and preferably discussed his texts in some detail.[7]

As is well known, it was in the winter of 1670–71 that Locke and five or six friends met to determine the principles of morality and revealed religion.[8] Their quest was prompted not by a fear that religion and morality might fail, but by a reluctance to claim more than could be known by the human understanding. Locke was thus led to enquire into the limits of human knowledge, to raise the epistemological question, What can we know? But with this he sometimes conflated the psychological question, How do we come to know? Repudiating innate ideas,[9] he answered that we acquire knowledge by sensation and reflection.

I proceeded to discuss the reception by eighteenth-century divines of Locke's epistemology, as well as his views on reason, revelation, faith, Scripture, morality, liberty, toleration and government, and Christian doctrine. I found that responses to him were varied not only because the starting points of some of his readers differed from his own, but also

6. See further Sell, *Enlightenment, Ecumenism,* Evangel, ch. 3.

7. A self-imposed ordinance which was overlooked by one reviewer, who complained that I had not discussed all those who had been "influenced" by Locke.

8. So a manuscript note of a copy of Locke's *Essay* which belonged to James Tyrrell, one of the friends who met with him. See Locke's *Essay concerning Human Understanding*, edited by Pringle-Pattison, 4 n. 1; cf. Bourne, *The Life of John Locke*, I, 248–49.

9. Some scholars have wondered if anyone, including Descartes, had advocated innate ideas in the sense in which Locke rejected them. See Sell. *John Locke*, 18. Others have rightly pointed out that Locke is not immune to Cartesian influence. For example, he is with Descartes in holding that the properties of mind differ from those of matter; but he denies that there is a corresponding dualism of substances such that the properties of mind could pass to matter, and *vice versa*.

because his writings could in places be construed in more than one way. I do not say that Locke set out to be elusive; but he was living through times of lively sectarian strife, he prized the notion of a tranquil civil society, he had himself lived in exile, and he was a diplomat. As far as Christian doctrine was concerned, he sought a highest common factor, believing that the affirmation, "Jesus is the Messiah"[10] would provide a platform upon which the majority of Christians could stand. In response to this precarious context, Locke did not disclose all of his hand in every place. More than is the case with most writers, with Locke it is necessary not only to hear what he is saying at a given time, but to remember what he has said on other occasions. I thus discovered that, taken as a whole, Locke is by no means only the empiricist epistemologist as portrayed by many and as enshrined in philosophy syllabi the world over. Certainly he was not a hard-line systematician. On the contrary, he was highly suspicious of the systems of the schools. We thus find that while he frequently appeals to reason, he also appeals to revelation, to the example of Jesus, and to the authority of Scripture. He is opposed to untoward authorities, whether ecclesiastical, civic or intellectual; but he is not opposed to all authority. However, these appeals are not neatly harmonized in a systematic methodological account. To put it crudely, we can see the joins.

I concluded that

> The way in which Locke reached out in the direction of divine authority, the teaching of Scripture and the example of Christ suggests that he himself felt the strain imposed upon his deepest convictions by his epistemological stance which, while properly acknowledging the limitations of human knowledge, imposed the restrictions of sensation and (ambiguously construed) reflection upon the human capacity to know, and was ignored by Locke himself at crucial points. If this is so, the problem bequeathed by Locke to modern thought is not so much that of the alleged illicit elevation of reason, as that of the illegitimate constriction of the sphere of human knowledge.[11]

As the "Age of Reason" drew to a close, Joseph Barber, the Independent (Congregational) tutor at the evangelical Hoxton Academy, London, lamented that "We live in shaking times, wherein many are departing from the faith; some professors [that is, professing Christians] running

---

10. See Locke, *The Reasonableness of Christianity*, 22–25; cf. Sell, *John Locke*, 186–201.

11. Sell, *John Locke*, 276.

into arminianism, some into arianism or socinianism, and others into antinomianism; yea, some have gone into very wild enthusiastic notions, and others into avowed infidelity."[12] From the opposite theological pole, Barber's contemporary, the Unitarian Thomas Belsham, was equally distressed. "Rational Christianity," he wrote, "is out of fashion with the learned and the great . . ."[13] Rationalist-*cum*-empiricist epistemology, it would appear, had not proved to be the panacea that its devotees had imagined it would be. Small wonder that already some were turning to a different starting-point.

II

By the third quarter of the nineteenth century Hegelianism was beginning to be discussed in English intellectual circles: J. H. Stirling's *The Secret of Hegel* (1857) being prominent in this connection. I think it true to say that none of the British idealists swallowed Hegel whole—in particular they queried his philosophy of history, and some of them, for example, T. H. Green and Edward Caird, tended to view him through Kantian spectacles. The philosophical soil in which they were rooted was also imbued with Humean scepticism, Scottish realism, naturalism, materialism, and agnosticism, and these impinged variously upon the British idealists. Nevertheless Hegel's immanentist thrust proved powerful and, to some, it seemed to accord with the increasingly important evolutionary thought which was swirling all around them. There was also the challenge of modern biblical criticism, and some idealists clearly felt that Christianity's teaching was at risk at the hands of those higher critics who were dissecting the biblical texts and in some cases pouring considerable scorn upon the notion that reliable history was to be found in the Bible. To these idealists the way to proceed was to dehistoricize the great themes, to separate the eternally valuable wheat from the problematic historical chaff.[14]

In *Philosophical Idealism and Christian Belief* I turned my attention to seven prominent British post-Hegelian idealists to see how far they managed to communicate Christian truth *via* the medium of idealism,

---

12. Barber. *A Sermon occasioned by the death of the Rev. Nathaniel Trotman*, 17. For Barber see *Evangelical Magazine*, 1811, 161.

13. Belsham, *Discourses, Doctrinal and Practical*, 478.

14. See further, Sell. *Theology in Turmoil*, chs. 1–3.

whether absolute or personal. It goes without saying that not all philosophical idealists were Christians: the prominent J. M. E. McTaggart, for example, was not. But to have focused upon such thinkers would have deflected me from my path, for atheists and agnostics had no interest in confessing and commending the faith. I therefore concentrated upon T. H. Green, Edward Caird, J. R. Illingworth, Henry Jones, A. S. Pringle-Pattison, A. E. Taylor, and C. C. J. Webb.

One of the mistakes which interpreters of Christian thought in relation to prevailing intellectual climates are liable to make is that of thinking that the Christian thought is in one box, and the secular thought is in the other, and that mutual communication is achieved when the contents of one box are mixed with those of the other. In fact, our understanding of Christianity is already to some degree processed by the intellectual environment into which we are born; and secular thought may be, to a greater degree than some of its exponents are happy to admit, influenced by religion, even if only negatively.

As I proceeded to investigate the thought of my chosen seven idealists it was increasingly borne in upon me that the labelling of thinkers is a hazardous undertaking indeed, for within this group there are significant differences of opinion.[15] In broad terms, Green was perhaps the most eclectic; Caird and Jones were absolute idealists: indeed, the latter was to a considerable degree an echo of the former, his teacher; Pringle-Pattison pioneered personal idealism in Britain; and Illingworth, Taylor and Webb, all Anglicans, were more alive to Christianity's doctrinal inheritance. More particularly,[16] whereas Green doubted that an universal philosophical synthesis could be constructed, Caird thought that it could; Taylor thought that Green's deity was "an only half-baptized Aristotelian God";[17] Pringle-Pattison found Caird's abstract principle of unity philosophically inadequate and religiously unsatisfying; Illingworth's incarnate, mediator-Christ was significantly different from Caird's exemplary Jesus; Webb, who lived through both World Wars, was more disturbed by evil than were Green and Caird, and both he and Taylor took history more seriously than either.

---

15. For further reflections on such labelling see ibid., chs. 5, 6; Sell, *Enlightenment, Ecumenism, Evangel*, ch. 12.

16. For the following, and additional, examples see Sell, *Philosophical Idealism*, 227–28.

17. Taylor, *William George De Burgh*, 22.

I paid particular attention to absolutism, ethics and society, and doctrine, and I came to the conclusion that the way in which Green jumped from epistemology to ontology was unsatisfactory; Jones's *decision* that the absolute must have the character of love was an unwarranted importation from Christian revelation; and that the tendency of the absolutists especially to use Christian language but in an attenuated way was unsatisfactory. Edward Caird's understanding of resurrection, for example, which amounts to the dying and rising motif discoverable in many literatures, seems far removed from God's saving act in history. Again, some of the idealists found it hard to maintain the Creator-creature distinction (not absolute disjunction—remember the *imago dei*), and to regard evil as anything other than a stage on the way to a greater good. As with Locke, albeit for different reasons, I came to feel that the Christian idealists believed more than they could accommodate within their philosophical parameters.[18] At times I even felt that there was something to be said for the atheist McTaggart's view that where theologians are concerned, Hegelianism is "an enemy in disguise—the least evident but the most dangerous."[19]

Taking my two historical soundings together, I concluded that Locke clamantly raised the question of starting-points in Christian apologetics, while the Christian idealists and, in his own way, Locke, raised the question of content, the nature of that which is to be commended. This left me with the task of asking whether there was a way of commending the Christian faith intellectually which would both mitigate the difficulties posed by Locke, his successors and the idealists, and also answer those twentieth-century writers, within and without the church, who have regarded the apologetic task as doomed from the start. I also realized that I was involved in a task of careful integration, for many of the positive insights thrown up by the historical enquiries were of importance. It seemed to me that "Since the terrain to be traversed by Christian testimony is wide, involving a texture of historical, existential, theological, metaphysical, ethical, aesthetic, liturgical assertions, its method must be correspondingly hospitable."[20] Accordingly, in my final volume, *Confessing and Commending the Faith. Historic Witness and Apologetic Method*, I went in quest of a way of commending the faith which would set out from

18. I had earlier reached this conclusion with regard to Edward Caird's brother, John. See *Defending and Declaring the Faith*, ch. 4.
19. McTaggart, *Studies in Hegelian Cosmology*, 250.
20. Sell, *Philosophical Idealism*, 235.

PART ONE: Confessing the Faith in Context

a commitment to the heart of the Christian confession, and which would take the form of a reasoned eclecticism, drawing upon relevant matters thrown up in the history of Christian thought and in Christian experience in such a way as to commend the faith and challenge those whose narrow starting-points would preclude the articulation of a Christian view of the world *ab initio*.

The title, *Confessing and Commending the Faith* was by no means haphazardly chosen. Rhythmically, it echoes my earlier title, *Defending and Declaring the Faith*—an account of some Scottish apologists who worked between 1860 and 1920. Of these, A. B. Bruce gave his major work, *Apologetics*, the subtitle, *Christianity Defensively Stated*. There are, of course, occasions on which it is appropriate to defend the faith against attack from within or without. But the word "defensive" has come to suggest the hesitant attitude of someone—perhaps a politician—who is unsure of his or her ground, or has something to hide. For this reason, but primarily because of my constructive objective, I place the emphasis positively upon *commending* the Faith, with any necessary work of defending being done *en passant* within that overall context.

III

As will by now be clear, my trilogy concerns the prolegomena to Christian apologetics. Two rather somnolent reviewers out of more than twenty that I have read regretted that I did not devote more attention to the religion and science debate. I could respond by saying that I did not devote much attention to theodicy or to the question of Christianity in relation to other world faiths either. I do not deny that these are questions to which in our time apologetic works might well devote attention. What I deny is that mine is in that sense an apologetic work. My entire project is a second-order study, and I thought I had made that very clear. I seek to take a step back from particular apologetic topics and ask, What are the matters which need to be clarified, and what are the presuppositions which need to be examined, before we embark upon the apologetic task? The first two volumes concerned ways of proceeding which were not entirely unproblematic; the task now was to see whether a more satisfactory approach could be made.

It occurred to me that the first thing was to ask what it is that Christians wish to confess. I felt that I had reviewed sufficient other starting-points to understand that if we begin somewhere else, we may very well be unable to work in at a later stage all that Christians wish to say. Moreover, only when we have addressed the question of confession can we attend to the question of commendation, for we need to know what we wish to commend before we embark upon the activity of commendation.

I divided the body of my third volume into three parts, each containing two chapters. The first part is entitled, "The Confession and the Confessors," and its first chapter is headed, "Confession and Church." I suggested that the heart of our testimony is both more and less than a systematic statement of doctrine. It is more in the sense that it concerns the whole of life: Christianity is a Way; it is less, because "a system may be so full, even complicated, and require such experience and sophistication both in it construction and its reception, that the majority of the childlike, for whom the Gospel is, would choke upon it."[21] As Erasmus consolingly put it long ago, "You will not be damned for not knowing whether the Spirit proceeds from one origin only, or from both the Father and the Son."[22] In questioning the centrality of systems as such, we should not, however, go to the opposite extreme and revel in the exclusively "inward," for that way lies an undifferentiated mysticism which, at its extreme, evacuates the gospel of those historical events, supremely the cross, which are its concrete and decisive expression. This led me to a consideration of the degree to which creeds and confessions of faith take us to the heart of the gospel. While endorsing the quest of clarity of testimony, and the desirability of churches setting down the things commonly agreed among them, I was cautious concerning undue cerebralism, and the untoward uses to which such documents may be put. Above all I was eager that their status as witnesses to the gospel and hence subordinate to it, should never be forgotten.[23]

But what is this gospel? I suggested that it will not do to say, with homiletic fervour, "Christ himself is the gospel," for while this is true, it is not very informative. We need to know who this Christ is; and I believe that we most surely come to see who he is through what he has done at the cross. I defended this view over against the incarnational thrust of a fair amount of Anglican theology, citing J. R. Illingworth, who declared

21. Sell, *Confessing and Commending the Faith*, 25.
22. Erasmus, Preface to the *Works of Hilary*.
23. See further, ch. 2 above.

that "[S]ecular civilization is . . . nothing less than the providential correlative and counterpart of the Incarnation."[24] I shall allow one of the wisest Anglican theologians of the twentieth century, A. M. Ramsey, to pronounce the verdict which I endorse:

> Bent upon the recovery of the incarnation as the central principle in theology, [Illingworth] wrote in deprecation of those who gave centrality to the Atonement. . . . This was incautious, inasmuch as the formulation of the doctrine of the Incarnation had sprung, alike in the apostolic age and in the patristic period, from out of the experience of Redemption: the saving act had been the key to the Church's faith in the divine Christ.[25]

Happily, the Church at large has never formulated an official doctrine of the atonement; but the witness to the grace and judgement of God's holy love at the cross has always been central to Christian proclamation and experience when the Church has been truest to itself.

Indeed, it is on the ground of the Son's finished work that the Father calls out the one holy, catholic, and apostolic church, and to this divinely-ordained body the task of confessing and commending the faith is committed. This task is discharged in a variety of ways, and I was very concerned to emphasise the fact that the commending of the faith in the intellectual context is but one aspect of the Church's overall calling. Whatever the Church does, however it organizes its worship and life, whatever ethical causes it embraces, it makes a witness, for good or ill. It follows that every Christian is a confessor, utilizing his or her gifts in the Lord's service. But within all of this there is a place for those who particular calling is to address the intellectual challenges which are posed to those who confess Christ.

This commending of the faith to those disinclined to embrace it, cannot but be influenced by the historical and cultural context in which it occurs. In my book I illustrated this point by reference to the first 250 years of the Church's life, and to the 250 years up to 1900. But we have not adequately defined those who commend the faith if we regard them as simply creatures of their time. More fundamental is the anthropological question: What is the nature of those who confess and commend the faith? I suggested that it is remarkable how many plunge into discussions

---

24. Illingworth, "The Incarnation in Relation to Development." In *Lux Mundi*, 155. See further Sell, *Philosophical Idealism*, 196–97.

25. Ramsey, *From Gore to Temple*, 4. Cf. Forsyth, *The Divine Self-Emptying*, bound with *The Taste of Death and the Life of Grace*, 116.

of religious language, reason, truth, faith, knowledge and experience, without raising this crucial question. I therefore argued that confessors are those made in the image of God, and that this both makes possible their relations with God, and provides the epistemological basis upon which they may relate and discuss with other human beings. I developed the point with reference to patristic authors and Reformers, querying some expressions of *theosis* doctrine, and I sought to face up to the concept of "total depravity." I concluded that the divine image is defaced but not obliterated—otherwise sin, the wilful flouting of God, would be an impossibility. In other words, I contended that "total" in "total depravity" signifies that none of our actions and motives is untainted, not that all of our actions and motives are utterly worthless.

But given the variety of Christian confessing through the ages, how far does it make sense to speak of the "same" faith from one period to another? Even if Vincent of Lérins's criterion of catholic truth, namely, that it comprises what is believed everywhere, always and by all, could be established—and this would entail the impossible task of discovering what was believed everywhere, always, and by all—any resulting doctrinal formulation would not necessarily be true. The fact remains that because of changing times, the explosion of knowledge and contemporary challenges, we could not today justifiably preach the sermons of Chrysostom or even Calvin just as they stand (though I can think of someone who is still preaching Spurgeon's sermons!). Similarly, we cannot sing some of the older hymns (or even some of the newer ones) with a clear conscience, not simply because of linguistic archaism, but because we do not believe in exactly that way. What, then, becomes of the "same" faith which we are supposed to hold in common with Christians of every generation? It seems to me that the answer lies in realizing that Christianity is first and foremost a way of life lived by those to whom new life has been granted; a life in which they praise and serve Christ, baptize people into his family and gather at his table to break bread and drink wine. In this one faith we are held by God the Holy Spirit, the bestower of both life and continuity of life. Above all, as the Quaker apologist Robert Barclay wrote, "the object of the saints' faith is the same in all ages, though held forth under divers administrations."[26] I therefore concluded this section by observing that "Because Christianity is a way, it involves a person's thought, practice, values, experiences—and all of these in relation to others. It will

26. Barclay, *An Apology for the True Christian Divinity*, 25.

PART ONE: Confessing the Faith in Context

not therefore be surprising if the intellectual commendation of Christian claims takes the form of a hospitable reasoned eclecticism in which reference is made to this range of considerations."[27]

IV

But when we have gained some idea of what is to be confessed, and who the confessors are, and in what sense they comprise a fellowship through the ages, we have not finished with the prolegomena to apologetics. For a number of presuppositions underlie the intellectual commending of the faith, and to these I turned in the second part of my book.

In the first place, it seemed important to me that Christians should be able to give reasons for thinking that religious language has meaning and legitimate use, and that it actually refers to God. This case, I felt, needed to be made out in face of logical positivists, some Wittgensteinians, and some postmodernists, all of whom have ways of denying that religious language is cognitive, that is, that it legitimately makes claims to knowledge.

Although in philosophical circles hard-line logical positivism has beaten a significant retreat over the past fifty years, its claims are still being advanced by some who embrace the religion of scientism, and others who stand, frequently with less wit, in the line of late nineteenth-century secularists. The high priest of English logical positivism was A. J. Ayer who, fresh from contacts with members of the Vienna Circle, published his manifesto, *Language, Truth and Logic* in 1936. According to the verification principle, those propositions alone are meaningful which are either analytic (that is, if we grasp the meaning of the terms we can attest their truth: $2 + 2 = 4$, for example) or empirically verifiable (at least in principle: until it became technologically possible we could not demonstrate empirically that the moon was not made of green cheese, but we knew what we should have to do to demonstrate the claim). Along this route Ayer branded metaphysical, ethical and religious assertions literally meaningless, for their meaningfulness could not be shown by what was deemed to be the only permissible method. They were reduced to emotive utterances so that in ethics, for example, "x is good" was equivalent to "I like x!" Thus to moralist and theist alike Ayer gave the "comfort" that "His

---

27. Sell, *Confessing and Commending the Faith*, 88.

Confessing the Faith in the Intellectual Context

assertions cannot possibly be valid, but they cannot be invalid either."[28] They were simply and literally non-sensical. Although Ayer modified his principle, it became no more hospitable to religious discourse.

The verification principle was criticized from many points of view, not least by the neo-Thomist philosopher, E. L. Mascall who, by a *tu quoque* argument showed that the proposition, "Only those propositions are meaningful which are either analytic or (in principle) empirically verifiable" was itself neither analytic nor empirically verifiable. I. M. Crombie argued that if we can specify the reference-range of religious assertions and show how they are used we can justifiably claim that they are meaningful;[29] while A. C. Ewing insisted that to regard religious claims as mere expressions of emotion was to falsify their character and, by extruding the factor of belief from them, to ensure that the emotion would not long survive.[30]

The next significant move in this discussion was the introduction by A. G. N. Flew of the principle of falsifiability. Flew was struck by the fact that religious believers will not allow anything to count against their fundamental claims. When pressed, they qualify their original statement. So, for example, if asked how they can believe in a God of love when unmerited suffering occurs, they may reply, "God's love is not exactly like ours," and so on. In the end, says Flew, their original assertion, "God is love," suffers "death by a thousand qualifications."[31] A number of responses were made to Flew, but their main thrust was encapsulated up by H. P. Owen, who argued that Flew "nowhere even attempts to prove (what cannot be proved) that empirical verifiability or falsifiability is a condition of either the meaningfulness or the validity of the truth-claims inherent in religious experience. Yet . . . he rests his case against theism on its empirical non-falsifiability."[32]

The general positivist stance may be further queried by saying that its exponents work with an untenable distinction between fact and

---

28. Ayer, *Language, Truth and Logic*, 116.
29. Crombie, "The Possibility of Theological Statements," 83.
30. Ewing, "Religious Assertions in the Light of Contemporary Philosophy," 207.
31. Flew in *New Essays in Philosophical Theology*, 97.
32. Owen, review of Flew, *God and Philosophy*, 282–85. For this too soon forgotten philosopher-theologian see Sell, *Convinced, Concise, and Christian*. I should in fairness point out that towards the end of 2004 Flew came out as holding that in view of recent scientific discoveries there may be sufficient warrant to think in terms, not of a God of a revealed system, but of an intelligent, organizing principle of the universe.

PART ONE: Confessing the Faith in Context

value. But what if evaluation, interpretation, enters into the designation of anything as a fact? Even if we let that pass, we can still contend that the positivists worked with an unduly narrow definition of "fact." There are facts of aesthetic, moral, and religious experience; from the Christian standpoint there are the facts of forgiveness, new life in Christ, and so on. The most telling argument against the positivists is that which shows that they have simply skewed the pitch so that only their side can win. Or, to use a culinary image, where Christian discourse is concerned they are like those who attempt to pick up soup with a fork: there is always some that falls through the prongs. More technically, their prescribed parameters of viable discourse illegitimately rule out Christian discourse *ab initio*, and we need not acquiesce in this.

My second illustration, Wittgenstein and his followers, led me towards a similar conclusion. I cannot here summarize my discussion of Wittgenstein, for to do so would risk falsifying the matter. But it will be recalled that Wittgenstein was initially concerned with meaning, but became more concerned with the use of discourse. But, along Wittgensteinian lines, when one has shown how language is being used, one has still not pronounced upon the truth or otherwise of what is asserted; nor, indeed, did Wittgenstein think that such pronouncements were possible, for philosophy does not make such judgements, it explores usage and then leaves things as they are.[33] That, at least, is his proclaimed procedure; but one frequently feels that he subtly introduces the idea of the *propriety* of using language in a certain way—at which points he has left usage description behind.

We see the same tendency in the writings of D. Z. Phillips, who has been influenced by Wittgenstein, but who stoutly denies that he is a Wittgensteinian fideist. Consider what Phillips says about prayer: "When deep religious believers pray *for* something, they are not so much asking God to bring this about, but in a way telling Him the strength of their desires."[34] Even if this were what believers thought they were doing (and I do not think it is a sufficient account of this) it seriously plays down the ontological reference, apart from which surely most Christians would deem prayer an unreal activity. Hence my further comment: "Time and again in Phillips's writings—when he is considering language concerning God as creator, Christ as Saviour, for example,—we meet doctrinal

---

33. Wittgenstein, *Philosophical Investigations*, I, 124.
34. Phillips, *The Concept of Prayer*, 121.

statements construed not as referring to facts or attitudes, but as pictures in which believers repose their confidence, and which sustain and regulate their lives."[35]

Having discussed the ways in which some have treated religious language, I then outlined some of my own thoughts on the matter, before turning to the third kind of critique of Christian language, that emanating from some postmodernists. I first expressed some sympathy with the writer who sighed, "When it is possible to call any number of heterogeneous items "postmodern"—from Madonna to Mark C. Taylor—we may reasonably ask how useful the term is."[36] I sketched the way in which the term had come into use, noting the influence of Bergson and Nietzsche and the roots in the artistic community, and I sought to show that the tendency towards relativism evinced by some who travel under this label (whether they accept it or not—and Derrida and Foucault did not) is disquieting; while their distress when we do not agree with them is illegitimate, since it implies an objective standard of truth of the kind which they have repudiated from the outset. While welcoming the reminder that we do not have a God's eye view, that we are neither fully self-conscious Cartesian ponderers nor "uncontaminated" Kantian moral agents, and that we inevitably bring a good deal of perspectival baggage with us when we seek to interpret the world and things in it, I felt bound in the end to take my stand with Donald MacKinnon on the fact that "however complex, diverse and rich the world of Christian language, that language in the end draws its point from the belief that some things [concerning Christ] are the case."[37]

At the heart of what, I take it, Christians wish to claim is that in Christ God has acted savingly on the stage of human history. I thus proceeded to discuss transcendence, immanence and history, outlining the history of the terms, and analysing them as carefully as I could. The death of God theologians, Bultmann, Barth and Tillich all came up for consideration as I worked my way towards my conclusion that

> The transcendent-yet-immanent holy God, who by a supernatural miracle of grace acts redemptively in the world, brings his truth home to us by the Holy Spirit and grants us new life.

35. Sell, *Confessing and Commending the Faith*, 115.

36. Rayment-Pickard, review of Terrence W. Tilley, *et al.*, *Postmodern Theologies*, 68.

37. MacKinnon, in George W. Roberts and Donovan E. Smucker, *Borderlands of Theology*, 74.

PART ONE: Confessing the Faith in Context

> Having once spoken, supremely in the Cross-resurrection event, he does not leave us. Rather, "By His Holy Spirit, he also assures me of eternal life, and makes me wholeheartedly willing and ready from now on to live for him."[38]

This conjunction of cognition and experience prompted me towards the final section of my book, "Alternative Apologetic Starting-Points."

V

While true to my conviction that the first thing to be done when commending the faith is to ask what is to be commended, who are the confessors, can we survive the challenges to religious discourse, and how may we best understand transcendence, immanence and history, I by no means ruled out the traditional apologetic starting-points of reason, faith and experience. It is simply that I believe that if we set out from any one of these we shall have difficulty in working into our account everything which Christians wish to confess. How far can human reason take us without a revelation from God himself? How reliable is faith, since people place their trust in all manner of things? Is not the appeal to experience merely psychologism which never gets us beyond the confines of our individual self? But, suitably qualified in the light of the matters already discussed, we can, I believe, introduce the insights of reason, faith and experience in appropriate ways. These help us to make our case that those who commend the Christian faith are not behaving irrationally; on the contrary, unless we fall for narrow, positivistic definitions of what counts as a fact, we can see that the facts of biblical witness and Christian experience being as they are, Christians are behaving reasonably when they adduce grounds for holding their position. We may therefore take heart from G. F. Woods's remark that, "No theory can be adequate which concludes that what happens cannot take place."[39]

With such thoughts in mind I explored the concepts of reason and revelation, endeavouring to heed advice flowing down from 1662 from (presumably) Simon Patrick: "he that will rightly make use of his Reason, must take all that is reasonable into consideration."[40] I discussed in turn

---

38. Sell, *Confessing and Commending the Faith*, 205, quoting the *Heidelberg Catechism*, Answer to Q. 1, in A. C. Cochrane, *Reformed Confessions*, 305.

39. Woods, "The Idea of the Transcendent," 52.

40. S[imon] P[atrick], *A Brief Account of the New Sect of Latitude-Men*, 10.

a selection of those from Calvin to Kuyper who regarded human reason as limited because wounded by sin; and that great variety of writers, from Descartes to evidentialists like B. B. Warfield and presuppositonalists like Cornelius Van Til, who have tended in the direction of rationalism. This prompted two digressions, the first concerning revelation as propositional and the role of analogy; the second concerning the *pros* and *cons* of foundationalism and the so-called Reformed epistemology of Plantinga, Wolterstorff, and others. I then returned to those from Origen onwards who had argued for a reason-revelation balance, and this led me into the debate over the viability of natural theology, and Barth's objections to it. I concluded that the noetic effects of sin are not uniform; that is, they are more disruptive in religious and moral questions where the will is concerned, than in scientific enquiry or formal logic and mathematics; I concurred with Clement Webb that "Rationalism is not really so much an excess of confidence in reason as a want of confidence in it; since it does not attempt to understand a great part of human experience";[41] and while welcoming Barth's insistence that if we would know God we must heed God, I nevertheless maintained, against him, that "on the ground of God's non-excludability from any part of his created order, and especially on the ground of the *imago dei* (defaced but not obliterated) and the *sensus divinitatis*, I side with those who construe the proofs of natural theology as building upon insights and intimations derivative from God's general revelation, which need to be taken into account in any attempt to commend the faith to unbelievers."[42] Unless such a position is adopted, I do not see how we can in the end avoid being trapped in a ghetto of revelation which would indeed render us impervious to rational assaults from without, but this security would be bought at the high price of our being unable to commend the faith to genuine enquirers, or to critics whether serious or flippant.

Under the chapter heading, "Faith, knowledge and experience," I discussed those key terms in some detail. If some appear to elevate reason above revelation, others appear to exalt experience above all else, sometimes to the point of driving a wedge between reason and faith—as Tertullian, on occasion, seems to do. I pursued the matter from the Fathers through the Reformation to Kierkegaard, noting in particular the semantic point that the denotation of the term "faith" came to be expanded

---

41. Webb, *Studies in the History of Natural Theology*, 358.
42. Sell, *Confessing and Commending the Faith*, 274.

from mere assent to existential commitment, with both understandings persisting down to our own time; and to these, following the Evangelical Revival, was added increasing reference to "saving faith". In this last connection I argued that such faith is a gift of God, it is justifying, and it is enabled by the Spirit. Built into it is assurance, which is not a matter of our subjective feelings, which fluctuate from time to time, but of confidence in the One of whom we are assured. But this implies that faith incorporates an intellectual element. As Calvin said, "Faith rests not on ignorance, but on knowledge."[43]

What, then, is the relation of religious experience to aesthetic and moral experience? I tiptoed into this hornet's nest of problems, concluding that for all the ambiguities of creation and artistic endeavour, God can address people through the beautiful, and through the moral obligations which are laid upon us. Robert Mackintosh summed it up thus: "In nature we find suggestions of God; in conscience the postulate of God; in Christ, the affirmation of God."[44] But language concerning an experience of God through Christ is not unproblematic and, once again, it requires us to protest against any reduction of the connotation of "experience" to "sense experience"—"a hostage to fortune let loose by Locke with consequences *via* Hume and the positivists that Locke did not foresee and would almost certainly have abominated."[45] Following a discussion of Schleiermacher's account of religious feeling, and of the encounter theology of such theologians as H. H. Farmer and John and Donald Baillie, I worked towards my conclusion that while one cannot produce a rational demonstration of the existence of God on the basis of personal experience—not least because of the difficulty of providing that one's addressee also acquires a sufficiently similar experience—something which hostile critics are not generally minded to do, Christians are not behaving irrationally if they claim that their experience of God through Christ is genuine, for this is not a matter of human subjectivity but of an enabled response to God who, in Christ, makes himself savingly known.

In my Conclusion I argued that on the basis of what God has done at the cross and in our experience we may develop a Christian view of the world. We shall always need to maintain "a reverent agnosticism before ultimate mystery, but we know enough, and a reasoned eclecticism need

43. Calvin, *Institutes*, III.2.6.7.

44. Mackintosh, *Essays Towards a New Theology*, 389.

45. Sell, *Confessing and Commending the Faith*, 333, referring to Sell, *John Locke*, ch. 2.

not be a haphazard muddle."[46] What is important in all of this is that, if we would make a serious attempt to commend the faith, we should not allow ourselves to be imprisoned by those methodological obstacles which some would place before us, whether from without the church (the positivists, for example) or from within it (Barth, for example). Any kind of ideological closing of doors can certainly prevent draughts, but it can also keep out fresh light and fresh air, and lead to a sectarianism of spirit which is not unknown either within Christianity or among its "cultured despisers."

Rather unusually in a work of this kind, I appended an Epilogue in the form of a short anthology of verse. The verses concern the approach of death, and I believe that they set my entire project in perspective. For unless our faculties are impaired or death comes instantaneously, the act of our dying affords our final opportunity of confessing and commending the faith.

On 18 September 1745 the "Arian" Presbyterian divine, Samuel Bourn, delivered the ordination charge to Job Orton at Shrewsbury. In the course of his remarks he said, "Be just to the Truths of God, and to the Gospel of Christ. Spare no Pains to be Master of the Evidences of Christianity and a Scripture Religion, in an Age wherein both serious and ludicrous Attacks are made upon it..."[47] No doubt our method cannot be exactly as his was; but the task is the same. Any who would prefer to be challenged not by an "Arian" but by the seventeenth-century's Reformed pastor *par excellence*, would do well to heed Richard Baxter: "What more can be done to the Disgrace and Ruin of Christianity than to make the world believe that we have no reason for it."[48]

I intended to finish with Baxter's challenge but, following the apostle Paul's example, I have one more "finally." I feel bound to express a concern that I have regarding the Church's ability in the future to undertake the task of commending the faith in face of intellectual challenges to it. I said at the outset that this is rather specialized work: it is not everyone's calling. It would be comforting to think that pastors at least would be acquainted with the philosophical background to the intellectual challenges, but what do we find? On the one hand, in the West philosophy of religion is frequently absent from seminary courses, crowded out by allegedly more

---

46. Sell, *Confessing and Commending the Faith*, 370.
47. Bourn, *A Charge Delivered at the Ordiantion of the Reverend Mr. Job Orton*, 44.
48. Baxter, *The Saint's Everlasting Rest*, II, Preface.

enticing, or more "practical" modules (as if the question of theodicy, for example, is not posed to pastors almost daily), and to a considerable degree restricted to a sometimes incestuous guild of university practitioners who write to one another through the pages of specialist journals. On the other hand in the South, I can perfectly well understand how the contextual challenges of poverty, AIDS, and the like can make apologetic reflection seem a luxury that cannot be afforded. Moreover, while in the South there is the welcome fact of rapid church growth in many parts this brings with it the concomitant challenge of nurturing sufficient Christian leaders for even the most basic pastoral tasks. But since ideas know no territorial boundaries, the intellectual challenges I have described cannot be confined to the West. I thus formulate my concern as a question: Will the churches take steps to rise to the challenge of apologetics—indeed, will they even see the point of attempting to do so? Before answering this question we might reflect upon the fact that our position as post-Constantinian Christians in some respects resembles more closely the pre-Constantinian context of the patristic writers than it does the period from Constantine through the Reformation to Schleiermacher, in which the claims of Christendom could more easily be taken for granted. Yet in the early Christian centuries the Church managed to nurture and retain some of the ablest minds of the age. If we believe that loving God with all our mind, though not the whole of Christian obedience, is an important element within it, what steps shall we take to encourage this disposition in those who need to be prepared so that they can think for Christ in the world of conflicting ideas?

BIBLIOGRAPHY

Anon., "Memoir of Joseph Barber." *The Evangelical Magazine* 19 (1811) 161–66.
Ayer, A. J. *Language, Truth and Logic*. 2nd ed. London: Gollancz, 1946.
Barber, Joseph. *A Sermon occasioned by the Death of the Rev. Nathaniel Trotman*. London, 1793.
Barclay, Robert. *An Apology for the True Christian Divinity*. 1678. Reprint. Glasgow: Murdoch, 1886.
Baxter, Richard. *The Saint's Everlasting Rest*. London: printed for Thomas Underhill and Francis Tyton, 1650.
Belsham, Thomas. *Discourses, Doctrinal and Practical; Delivered in Essex Street Chapel*. London: Hunter, 1826.
Bourn, Samuel. *A Charge Delivered at the Ordination of the Reverend Mr. Job Orton; at Shrewsbury, September* 18. 1745. Birmingham: Warren, 1745.
Bourne, H. R. Fox. *The Life of John Locke*. 2 vols, London: King, 1876.
Calvin, John. *Institutes*. Translated by Ford Lewis Battles and edited by J. T McNeil. 2 vols. Philadelphia: Westminster, 1961.
Cochrane, Arthur C. *Reformed Confessions of the 16th Century*. Philadelphia: Westminster, 1966.
Crombie, I. M. "The Possibility of Theological Statements." In *Faith and Logic*, edited by Basil Mitchell, 31–83. London: Allen and Unwin, 1957.
Erasmus, Desiderius. Preface to the *Works* of Hilary. *Hilarii opera*. 1523. Reprint. London, 1642.
Ewing, A. C. "Religious Assertions in the Light of Contemporary Philosophy." *Philosophy* 32 (1957) 206–18.
Flew, A. G. N. "Theology and Falsification." In *New Essays in Philosophical Theology*, edited by Flew and Alasdair MacIntyre, 96–130. London: SCM, 1955.
Forsyth, P. T. *The Divine Self-Emptying*. Bound with *The Taste of Death and the Life of Grace*. London: Clarke, 1901.
Illingworth, J. R. "The Incarnation in relation to Development." In *Lux Mundi*, edited by Charles Gore, 132–57. London: Murray, 1889.
Locke, John. *Essay concerning Human Understanding*. Edited by A. S. Pringle-Pattison. Oxford: Clarendon, 1924.
———. *The Reasonableness of Religion as Delivered in the Scriptures*. 1695. Reprint. Edited by John Higgins-Biddle. Oxford: Clarendon, 1999.
Mackintosh, Robert. *Essays Towards New Theology*. Glasgow: Maclehose, 1889.
McTaggart, J. M. E. *Studies in Hegelian Cosmology*. Cambridge: Cambridge University Press, 1901.
Owen, H. P. Review of A. G. N. Flew, *God and Philosophy* (1966). In *Religious Studies* 2 (1966–67) 282–85.
Patrick, Simon. *A Brief Account of the New Sect of Latitude-Men Together with some Reflections on the New Philosophy. By S.P: of Cambridge: In Answer to a Letter from his Friend at Oxford*. 1662. Reprint. Los Angeles: William Andrews Clark Memorial Library, University of California, 1963.
Phillips, D. Z. *The Concept of Prayer*. London: Macmillan, 1965.
Ramsey, A. M. *From Gore to Temple*. London: Longmans, 1960.
Rayment-Pickard, Hugh. Review of Terrence W. Tilley *et al.*, *Postmodern Theologies*. *Modern Believing New Series* 37 (1996) 67–69.

PART ONE: Confessing the Faith in Context

Roberts, George W., and Donovan E. Smucker. *The Borderlands of Theology and Other Essays*. London: Lutterworth, 1968.
Sell, Alan P. F. *Convinced, Concise, and Christian: The Thought of Huw Parri Owen*. Eugene, OR: Pickwick, 2012.
———. *Defending and Declaring the Faith: Some Scottish Examples 1860–1920*. 1986. Reprint. Eugene, OR: Wipf and Stock, 2012.
———. *Enlightenment, Ecumenism, Evangel: Theological Themes and Thinkers 1550–2000*. Milton Keynes, UK: Paternoster, 2005.
———. *John Locke and the Eighteenth-Century Divines*. 1997. Reprint. Eugene, OR: Wipf & Stock, 2006.
———. *Philosophical Idealism and Christian Belief*. 1995. Reprint. Eugene, OR: Wipf & Stock, 2006.
———. *Philosophy, Dissent and Nonconformity 1689–1920*. 2004. Reprint. Eugene, OR: Wipf & Stock, 2009.
———. *The Philosophy of Religion 1875–1980*. 1987, 1996. Reprint. Eugene, OR: Wipf & Stock, forthcoming.
———. *A Reformed, Evangelical, Catholic Theology: The Contribution of the World Alliance of Reformed Churches 1875–1982*. 1991. Reprint. Eugene, OR: Wipf & Stock, 1998.
———. *Theology in Turmoil: The Roots, Course and Significance of the Conservative-Liberal Debate in Modern Theology*. 1986. Reprint. Eugene, OR: Wipf & Stock, 1998.
Stirling, J. H. *The Secret of Hegel*. 1865. Reprint. Edinburgh: Oliver & Boyd, 1898.
Taylor, A. E. "William George De Burgh, 1866–1943." *Proceedings of the British Academy* 29 (1943) 371–91.
Webb, C. C. J. *Studies in the History of Natural Theology*. Oxford: Clarendon, 1915.
Wittgenstien, Ludwig. *Philosophical Investigations*. 2nd ed. Oxford: Blackwell, 1958.
Woods, G. F. "The Idea of the Transcendent." In *Soundings: Essays concerning Christian Understanding*, edited by A. R. Vidler, 43–65. Cambridge: Cambridge University Press, 1962.

PART TWO

Confessing the Faith Ecclesially and Hopefully

> Let saints below in concert sing
> With those to glory gone:
> For all the servants of our King
> In earth and heaven are one.
>
> CHARLES WESLEY (1707–88)

Introduction to Part Two

CHRISTIAN CONFESSING IS BY no means a concern of the individual Christian alone. For those who are by grace engrafted into Christ by the Spirit as branches of the Vine are necessarily and inescapably united with all the other branches. Christian confessing is thus both a matter of personal and ecclesial testifying to the Gospel of God's grace and mercy. Nor are we in our time the first confessors. We stand in a line of those who in diverse times and places, and often in contexts far removed from our own, have confessed the faith and commended the Gospel to others—sometimes at the cost of their lives. This common testimony to Christ as Saviour and Lord has been passed down to us, and this, above all, is the message to be conserved and communicated, no matter in which other directions our theological explorations may take us.[1]

Since Christianity places us within a communion of confessing saints, it is not surprising that the heritage of faithful testimony can inform and strengthen our confessing today. Not, indeed, that we can speak exactly as our forebears did, for times and circumstances change, and we cannot with integrity look through their eyes on all points of doctrine and practice. When we ponder the witness of the ages with respect to our own confessing we are inevitably involved in an act of distillation.[2] Chapter 7 exemplifies the fact, as I return to Calvin to see what he may have to say to the twenty-first century Church. Chapter 8 also exemplifies the fact, for my argument here is that the twenty-first century Church needs to hear some things that Calvin did not, in his context, find it necessary or possible to say: the process of distillation can both yield positive insights and reveal lacunae.

Calvin, building on the New Testament, reminds us that there can be but one church, for there is one Head of the church, Jesus Christ, and he cannot be divided. Empirically, as everybody knows, current ecclesial

---

1. See further, Sell, *Testimony and Tradition*, ch. 1.
2. See further, Sell, *The Great Ejectment of 1662*, 214–22.

confessing is undertaken by one church which is found in many forms around the world. Equally well known—and tragic—is the fact that its fellowship is marred by division at the Lord's table—a product of the sectarian spirit. Not the least important result of the modern ecumenical movement is the increasing respect and affection that has been generated among Christians of various stripes as they have learned from one another and mutually shared their insights. In chapter 9 I offer some personal reflections upon this activity, and suggest a way of further deepening the discussion by probing the question of the "matter" of the church.

Eschatology is the subject of chapter 10, and here we are reminded that Christian confessing is hopeful confessing; it is undertaken by those who live in the "atmosphere of heaven," joining in spirit with the saints of the ages who see God as he is and worship him as he deserves.

The descent from this elevated thought to current systematic theology may constitute a shock to the system. But chapter 11, my Epilogue, though written in genial style, has the serious intention of underlining much of what has gone before. In particular, that systematic and constructive theology are best understood as the product of a conversation between the Bible, the Christian confession of the ages, and the contemporary intellectual environment,[3] with all of which systematic theologians should be more than slightly acquainted;[4] and that the objective is both confession and commendation. Because of the former, all our theological thinking should be judged in the light of God's authoritative, saving act at the cross; because of the latter the apologetic task may not be eschewed lest the church become a ghetto basking in a revelation that it cannot or will not communicate to others. As for the ethical implications of the gospel: they may not reduced to a crippling new legalism, or be permitted to degenerate into a bland humanism amenable to the prevailing culture—this at the cost of the church's calling to testify to the things most surely believed and, on occasion, to make a counter-cultural witness.[5]

---

3. This is the thesis of my book, *Hinterland Theology*.

4. If they also have a background in analytical philosophy as a preservative against possible nonsense, so much the better. I do not, of course imply either that in the absence of such background the writing of nonsensical theology is inevitable, nor that those who have been thus exposed are entirely incapable of the perpetration of nonsense—hence "possible" in the previous sentence.

5. See Sell, *Confessing and Commending the Faith*, and ch. 7 above.

BIBLIOGRAPHY

Sell, Alan P. F. *Confessing and Commending the Faith: Historic Witness and Apologetic Method* (2002). Eugene, OR: Wipf & Stock, 2006.

———. *The Great Ejectment of 1662: Its Antecedents, Aftermath, and Ecumenical Significance.* Eugene, OR: Pickwick, 2012.

———. *Hinterland Theology: A Stimulus to Theological Construction.* Milton Keynes: Paternoster, 2008 and Eugene, OR: Wipf & Stock, 2009.

———. *Testimony and Tradition: Studies in Reformed and Dissenting Thought.* Aldershot: Ashgate, 2005.

CHAPTER SEVEN

Calvin's Challenges to the Twenty-First-Century Church

Reflections of the 500th Anniversary of Calvin's Birth

ONE HUNDRED YEARS AGO the Alliance of Reformed Churches holding the Presbyterian System held its ninth General Council in New York. The programme included ten lectures marking the 400th anniversary of Calvin's birth. It fell to Mr. J. H. Stevenson of Edinburgh to adumbrate "The salient features of Calvin's life." No other speaker was so enveloped by the celebratory haze as Mr. Stevenson. Calvin, said he, was "destined in the providence of God to save the Christian world from its downward course into paganism, and restore it to its vision of God's sovereignty and man's duty."[1] This begs the questions, Did he really do that? Did he do it all by himself? But I must not be too hard on Mr. Stevenson, for, one hundred years on, my title also begs a large question: How can a person born five hundred years ago challenge today's Church? After all, Calvin lived before the challenges of the Enlightenment, before the modern missionary movement, before the rise of modern biblical criticism, before the industrial revolution and the explosion of modern science,

---

1. Matthews, *Proceedings of the Ninth General Council*, 50. Mark Pattison had earlier, and somewhat more modestly, asserted that "Calvin*ism* saved *Europe*." See *Essays by the Late Mark Pattison*, II, 31 (my italics).

before atheism, agnosticism and secularism became acceptable belief systems, before the modern ecumenical movement, and before globalization embraced the whole world for good and ill. Moreover, Calvin could assume Christendom in a way which is now quite impossible for us (it was always undesirable); his implication in the death of Servetus, though understandable perhaps in one who could only be a child of his time, is not something we should wish to emulate; and his strident anti-Roman Catholic polemic, though characteristic of those who need psychologically to distance themselves from much of what has gone before, would today be deemed ecumenically unhelpful, grains of truth in it notwithstanding.

Before we begin to plunder Calvin's writings for challenges to ourselves we need to address another question which my title begs: How far is Calvin's confession the same as ours?[2] Indeed, more generally, what do we mean when we say that Christians keep the same faith through the ages—what is the analysis of "same" in this proposition? This is an especially acute question in the Reformed context, for the Reformed claim to be *semper reformanda*—which means not that as a matter of fact they are always being Reformed, but that they are always in the position of needing to be Reformed (it is a gerundive); and the distinction between a body which is always needing to be reformed and one which is in a constant state of *quasi*-Heraclitean flux is not always immediately apparent to our partners in ecumenical dialogue.[3] Why is it that we sometimes feel uncomfortable when invited to sing hymns from a previous generation? It is not simply because we may encounter archaic language or have politically correct (if anachronistic) scruples concerning modes of linguistic expression; it is that we no longer believe quite the same things as our forbears. While I have it on good authority that the sermons of the great nineteenth-century Baptist preacher, C. H. Spurgeon, may still be heard to this day in some churches (and they are, no doubt, preferable to what may be dredged up from the internet at eleven o'clock on a Saturday evening), most of us should not find it easy to preach the sermons of yesteryear—even Calvin's, still less John Chrysostom's—just as they stand. Because of changing contexts, and the global spread of the Reformed family it is not surprising—indeed it is a statement of the obvious—to

---

2. See further on this intriguing question Sell, *Confessing and Commending the Faith*, 79–89.

3. See further ch. 1 above.

say that "Over time Calvinists have developed some aspects of Calvin's teaching, neglected others, and reinterpreted still more."[4]

Hence the importance of the reminder that Christianity is a Way before it is any particular person's or group's tradition or system. Christians through the ages are those who confess Christ as Saviour and Lord; they have been called by the Father's sovereign grace, united with the Son as branches of the Vine, and they have received the gift of the fruit-bearing Spirit. They gather to worship, pray, hear the Word of God, receive the sacraments which testify to that Word, and ponder their mission and service. They are in the succession of all who proclaim the apostles' doctrine. As Calvin remarked on John 10:16, although Christ's "flock appears to be divided into different folds, yet they are kept within enclosures which are common to all believers who are scattered throughout the whole world; because the same word is preached to all, they use the same sacraments, they have the same order of prayer, and every thing that belongs to the profession of faith."[5] For this reason, although we cannot simply regurgitate the statements of our forebears in the faith, we can learn much from them and still be challenged by them.

How should we go about this task? I shall answer this question with direct reference to Calvin. In the first place we should read his texts with due heed to their context, and beware of uprooting arguments and phrases from their context. To give a simple example: some writers who have not been sympathetic to Calvin have wished to portray him as no more than a Stoic in ethics. But as John Hesselink has properly pointed out, while Cicero and Calvin speak in a similar way about natural law, Calvin's "concept of depravity makes an all-important difference."[6] My way of putting it is to say that if we uproot propositions from their intellectual contexts we are in danger of committing the logical howler of supposing that because Cicero and Calvin use the same words they mean the same things.

A further temptation is to consider the Church's current preoccupations or fads and then plunder Calvin's writings for anything of relevance he may have had to say about them. This would be to cast Calvin in the role of solver of our puzzles, or to annex him as the supporter of our agenda; we might even be inclined to read back into Calvin's writings

---

4. Various. "The Economic and Social Witness of Calvin," 4.

5. Calvin, *Commentary on the Gospel according to John* (Pringle) I, 408; (Parker) I, 267–68.

6. Hesselink, *Calvin's Concept of the Law*, 69.

what we wished to find; and in the process we might overlook many things he had to say that we should prefer not to hear. In this connection it is interesting to see what the representative body of the international Reformed family thought worthy of reflection in 1909 and 2009. In 1909 the World Presbyterian Alliance heard, in addition to Stevenson's biographical paper on Calvin, addresses on Calvin and the Reformation in Western Europe, in Eastern Europe, and in the British Isles; on Calvin's biblical expositions, his doctrinal system, and his views on Church government and the Christian ministry; on his ethics, on Servetus, on his theology; as well as on Calvinism and liberty, Calvinism's influence in the contemporary world, and its world-wide mission. In 2009 the World Alliance of Reformed Churches invited us to consider various interpretations of Calvin, his humanism, his view of the Bible as God's Word, his ecclesiology and his ethics;[7] and Calvin on the unity of the Church, on social justice, respect for God's creation, the environment, and war.[8] As we compare these two lists of addresses it seems clear that the 1909 list is more traditional and concerned with historical and systematic theology[9] whereas the 2009 list is more moved by the current situation which it conceives as being in urgent need of a theologically-grounded ethical response. Moreover, it is strikingly clear that the latter list has been greatly

---

7. See the papers under the general title, *John Calvin: What is His Legacy?* in *Reformed World* LVII.4 (2007).

8. See Nyomi, *The Legacy of John Calvin*. This book follows in the wake of the Alliance's Accra Confession of 2004, for which, with follow-up papers, see *Reformed World* 55.3 (2005). The Confession has commanded widespread interest, though some have found its approach to economic questions unduly simplistic.

9. So, too, was the series of articles published during 1909 in the *Princeton Theological Review*: Émile Doumergoue, "Calvin: Epigone or Creator?" August Lang, "The Reformation and Natural Law"; Herman Bavinck, "Calvin and Common Grace"; and B. B. Warfield, "Calvin's Doctrine of the Knowledge of God." The articles are reprinted in Armstrong, *Calvin and the Reformation*. Also in 1909 there appeared a collection of *Calvin Memorial Addresses*. These papers were somewhat broader in scope: Richard C. Reed, "Calvin's Contribution to the Reformation"; Henry Collin Minton, "Calvin the Theologian"; Thomas Cary Johnson, "Calvin's Contributions to Church Polity"; James Orr, "Calvin's Attitude towards and Exegesis of the Scriptures"; R. A. Webb, "Calvin's Doctrine of Infant Salvation"; S. L. Morris, "The Relation of Calvin and Calvinism to Missions"; George H. Denny, "Calvin's Influence on Educational Progress"; Frank T. Glasgow, "Calvin's Influence upon the Political Development of the World"; Samuel A. King, "How Far has Original Calvinism Been Modified by Time?"; Benjamin B. Warfield, "Present Day Attitude to Calvinism"; A. M. Fraser, "How may the Principles of Calvinism be Rendered Most Effective under Modern Conditions?"; Charles Merle D'Aubigne, "John Calvin—The Man and His Times."

influenced by the concerns of the global South, an area that it seemed possible to overlook in the commemorative papers of 1909.

Bearing all of these things in mind, my method in what follows is to watch what Calvin does, and well as to hear what he says. In particular, I wish to argue that Calvin challenges today's Church by the way in which he holds together things which ought to be held together, and too frequently are not.

I

First, Calvin holds together the gospel and the Church. John Hesselink quotes Calvin to the effect that "Christ did not first begin to be manifested in the gospel," adding in explanation, "As the eternal Son of God, one of the holy Trinity, he was continually present and at work in redemptive history."[10] In the Christian dispensation, however, the theme of union with Christ is central to Calvin's gospel. Who is this Christ? As Calvin remarked, he is the eternal Son of God and he is the second person of the Trinity; but it was in connection with Christ's work that Calvin set in motion a fresh train of thought concerning Christ's threefold office. Christ is prophet, priest and king;[11] he only is God's Word made flesh, he is the one only self-sacrificing Saviour, he is our only King and Lord. The doctrine of Christ's threefold office is, said Robert Franks, "the really characteristic Protestant doctrine of the work of Christ."[12] It is on the ground of Christ's mediatorial work that believers are called into union with him. Furthermore, says Calvin,

> that joining together of Head and members, that indwelling of Christ in our hearts—in short, that mystical union—are accorded by us the highest degree of importance, so that Christ, having been made ours, makes us sharers with him in the gifts with which he has been endowed. We do not, therefore, contemplate him outside ourselves from afar in order that his righteousness

---

10. Hesselink, *Calvin's Concept of the Law*, 163, quoting Calvin's *Commentary* John 5:29.

11. See Calvin, *Institutes*, II.xv.

12. Franks, *A History of the Doctrine of the Work of Christ*, II, 441. Reprinted in one volume, London: Nelson, 1962. For Franks, English Nonconformity's greatest twentieth-century theological scholar, see Sell. *Hinterland Theology*, ch. 10 and *passim*. For a stimulating account of the threefold office see Edmondson, *Calvin's Christology*, chs. 3–5.

may be imputed to us but because we put on Christ and are engrafted into his body—in short, because he deigns to make us one with him.[13]

In the opinion of Thomas Torrance, "It is around this doctrine of *union with* Christ . . . that Calvin builds his doctrine of faith, of the church as the living Body of Christ, and his doctrines of the Christian life, Baptism, and the Lord's Supper."[14] For our present purposes, we see clearly that in Calvin's view, to be united with Christ is to be united with all who are his; it is to be of his body, the Church. Gospel and Church are integrally related to one another. On the one hand, believers cannot be united to Christ the Vine and separate from one another; on the other hand, "Christ will not and cannot be torn from his church with which he is joined in an indissoluble knot, as the head to the body. Hence unless we cultivate unity with the faithful, we see that we are cut off from Christ."[15] By holding gospel and Church together in this way Calvin implicitly rebuts any who, under the influence of latter-day individualism, say that they can be a Christian in isolation from the church, or that Christianity is a private matter. It is personal, certainly, but private? Never. It is life in union with Christ and in fellowship with those who have heard, and have been enabled by grace to answer, his call. Still less would Calvin agree with those who claim to have received the gospel, but who regard the Church as a voluntary association which they may, or may not, join as they feel inclined. He would not understand those who have been baptized as infants who do not go on to profess their faith but who still claim the Christian name; nor would he understand those who are baptized as believers and then decline to join the church's roll of members. Nor is it difficult to guess what Calvin's reaction would have been to Professor Patricia Killen's characterization of the current state of religion in the Pacific Northwest of the United States. She explains that "From 1648 to 1970, we had essentially one idea of what it means to be religious in the Western world. To be religious was to be engaged with a religious institution. Now, and especially in the Pacific Northwest, people are seeking different, more individualistic and more fluid ways of being religious."[16]

---

13. Calvin, *Institutes*, III.xi.10.
14. Torrance, "Our Witness through Doctrine," 134 (author's italics).
15. Calvin, *Commentary* on Ezekiel 13:9, I, 18.
16. Quoted by Amy Frykholm, "In the None Zone," 22.

To Calvin the Church is a divine institution comprising those who, on the ground of Christ's mediatorial work, are saints by calling. You do not have the gospel and afterwards tack the Church onto it. The gospel is not simply about my soul. It is about that union with Christ as Saviour and Lord which is at the same time union with all who are his. Into the bosom of the church, Calvin declares, "God is pleased to gather his sons, not only that they may be nourished by her help and ministry as long as they are infants and children, but also that they may be guided by her motherly care until they mature and at last reach the goal of faith.... [F]or [here echoing Cyprian, Augustine and others] those to whom [God] is Father the church may also be Mother."[17]

Precisely because there is one Head of the Church there is but one Church:

> The church is called "catholic," or "universal," because there could not be two or three churches unless Christ be torn asunder—which cannot happen! But all the elect are so united in Christ that as they are dependent on one Head, they also grow together in one body, being joined and knit together as are the limbs of a body. They are made truly one since they live together in one faith, hope, and love, and in the same Spirit of God.[18]

The point is reiterated in Calvin's Geneva Catechism of 1541: the term "catholic" means that "as there is only one Head of the faithful, so they must all be united in one body, so that there are not several churches but one only, which is extended throughout the whole world (Eph 4:15; 1 Cor 12:12 and 27)."[19]

Calvin was deeply distressed by the reality that "the members of the church are being severed, the body lies bleeding." Indeed, he continued in a letter to Archbishop Cranmer, "So much does it concern me, that, if I could be of any service, I would not grudge to cross even ten seas, if need be, on account of it."[20] Few devoted as much energy to the quest of ecclesial healing as Calvin. He visited, he corresponded, he published; he sought to keep lines of communication open with Roman Catholics, Lutherans and Anglicans, and throughout it all his motive was that "as Christ has made known the glory of his Father in receiving us into favour

---

17. Calvin, *Institutes*. IV.i.1
18. Ibid., IV.i.2; cf. *Commentary on Ephesians*, 4:5, (Pringle) 269; (Parker) 172–73.
19. *The Geneva Catechism*, answer to Q. 97, in Torrance, *The School of Faith*, 20.
20. *Calvin's Letters*, IV, 348.

PART TWO: Confessing the Faith Ecclesially and Hopefully

when we stood in need of mercy; so it behoves us, in order to make known the glory of the same God, to establish and confirm this union which we have in Christ."[21]

It would be wrong to suggest that Calvin was for visible Church unity at any price. On the contrary, in his view there can be no unity unless the church is obedient to, and guided by, the Word of God;[22] but his earnest reaching out to others demonstrates that the two questions begged in that proposition, namely, What is it to be obedient to the Word of God? and What is it to be guided by it?, were regarded by him as stimuli to conversation, not dogmatic buffers against it. I therefore think that Calvin would not be able to understand a present-day Christian who claimed to be in possession of the evangel but who was hostile to the present-day ecumenical movement, the objective of which is, not to engineer, but to strive towards the manifestation of, the unity God has already given to the church in Christ, and this as an earnest of the coming unity of the whole inhabited earth. After all, said Calvin,

> We call on one God the Father, trusting to the same Mediator; the same Spirit of adoption is the earnest of our future inheritance. Christ has reconciled us all by the same sacrifice. In that righteousness which he has purchased for us, our minds are at peace, and we glory in the same head. It is strange if Christ, whom we preach as our peace, and who, removing the ground of disagreement, appeased to us our Father in heaven, do not also cause us mutually to cultivate brotherly peace on earth.[23]

Calvin reiterated the point, perhaps most tellingly of all in view of his searing attacks on Roman Catholic teaching and practice, in his reply to Cardinal Sadoleto of 1 September 1589. Against Sadoleto's view that to separate from fellowship with the Roman Church was to be in revolt against the Church, Calvin argued that the Protestant objective was the reform and restoration of the one Church. His concluding prayer was: "The Lord grant, Sadoleto, that you and all your party may at length perceive that the only true bond of ecclesiastical unity consists in this, that Christ the Lord, who has reconciled us to God the Father, gather us out

---

21. Calvin, *Commentary on Romans*, 15:9. See further Kromminga "Calvin and Ecumenicity"; Hesselink, "Calvinus oecumenicus."

22. See *Institutes*, IV.ii.5; *Calvin's Tracts and Treatises*, I, 60.

23. *Calvin's Tracts and Treatises*, II, 251.

of our present dispersion into the fellowship of his body, that so, through his one Word and Spirit, we may join together with one heart and soul."[24]

It is clear throughout that although Calvin has an understanding of the invisible Church comprising the great cloud of witnesses, this Church is not in his view a refuge from churchly fellowship with saints on earth who are also sinners. The gospel is addressed to people here below; the church is called out in response to the gospel; and all thus called comprise the one church of Christ, our prophet, priest and king. Gospel and Church cannot be sundered.

II

Secondly, Calvin holds together the Holy Spirit and the Word. The mutual relations of Spirit and Word are nowhere more clearly expressed than when Calvin declares that "For as God alone is a fit witness of himself in his Word, so also the Word will not find acceptance in men's hearts before it is sealed by the inward testimony of the Spirit. The same Spirit, therefore, who has spoken through the mouths of the prophets must penetrate into our hearts to persuade us that they faithfully proclaimed what had been divinely commanded."[25] Implicit here is what Calvin makes explicit elsewhere, namely, that he is fighting on two fronts. Against Rome with its authoritarian claim he pits God's Word as the supreme authority for faith and practice. He protests against "a most pernicious error [which] widely prevails that Scripture has only so much weight as is conceded to it by the consent of the Church. As if the eternal and inviolable truth of God depended upon the decision of men!"[26] Against the fanatics with their claim to be in receipt of extra-biblical, often eccentric, revelations he is no less severe. "Those," he thunders, "who, having forsaken Scripture, imagine some way or other of reaching God, ought to be thought of as not so much gripped by error as carried away with frenzy.... What devilish madness it is to pretend that the use of Scripture, which leads the children of God even to the final goal, is fleeting or temporal?"[27] Calvin insists that the Spirit confirms and brings home the Word, he does not contradict it or supplement it: "the Spirit, promised to us, has not the task

---

24. *Theological Treatises of John Calvin*, 256.
25. Calvin, *Institutes*, I.vii.4.
26. Ibid., I.vii.1.
27. Ibid., I.ix.1.

of inventing new and unheard-of revelations, or of forging a new kind of doctrine, to lead us away from the received doctrine of the gospel, but of sealing our minds with that very doctrine which is commended by the gospel."[28] As B. B. Warfield rightly saw, Calvin's doctrine of the testimony of the Holy Spirit "centres in the great doctrine of Regeneration—the term is broad enough in Calvin to cover the whole process of the subjective recovery of man to God—in which he teaches that the only power which can ever awaken in a sinful heart the emotions of a living faith is the power of this same Spirit of God . . ."[29] It is because of the Spirit's testimony both as accrediting Scripture and as applying it to human hearts that Calvin can say, in one of his most pastoral observations on the subject, that the Bible is the only pasture for our souls; it nourishes them to eternal life ("*C'est la pasture unique de nos ames, pour les nourrir à la vie eternelle*").[30] In one of his most concise utterances on the subject he states the fact and utters a warning: "We choke out the light of God's Spirit if we cut ourselves off from his Word."[31] No doubt; but let us be careful to draw an important distinction to which James Orr adverted in his *Calvin Memorial Address* of 1909: we may not rest "the authority of Scripture *exclusively* on the internal witness of the Spirit," because "it can apply only to Scripture taken as a whole, or in its general teaching, and can hardly be employed for the settlement of critical and exegetical questions, or the determination even of the canonicity of disputed books . . . and Calvin himself does not so employ it. He brings his full exegetical power to bear on every passage, and freely uses what critical or historical aids he possesses to determine points of difficulty."[32]

---

28. Ibid., Cf. I.ix.3.

29. Warfield, "John Calvin the theologian," *Proceedings of the Ninth General Council*, 141. For a fuller account see his paper in Armstrong, *Calvin and the Reformation*.

30. See Baum, Cunitz and Reuss, *Corpus Reformatorum*, IX, 823.

31. *Treatises against the Anabaptists and Against the Libertines*, 224–25. My focus here on Calvin and the Bible should not be taken as indicating that I regard him as simply a narrow theologian of the Word. On the contrary, I concur in Paul Helm's judgment that Calvin presents us with "a distinctive blend of scriptural appeal, rational argument, and reverential agnosticism"—not to mention, one might add, a rather heavy dose of swashbuckling polemics. See Helm, *John Calvin's Ideas*. 80.

32. Orr, "Calvin's attitude towards and exegesis of the Scriptures." In *Calvin Memorial Addresses*, 104. See further Frew, "Calvin as an expositor of Scripture." *Proceedings of the Ninth General Council*, 77–84; Gamble, "Calvin as theologian and exegete," 178–94.

Calvin's Challenges to the Twenty-First-Century Church

For all his emphasis upon the Scriptures, it would be foolish to suppose that Calvin knew nothing outside the scope of the Bible, and he certainly did not think that the Bible comprised a compendium of all available knowledge. He knew classical authors; he had historical awareness; he had a natural theology. But the Bible was where the gospel was to be found, for in its pages the Word made flesh was made known. Although Calvin lived before the rise of modern biblical criticism and felt able to draw on portions of the Bible without regard to context or to modern considerations of authorship[33] (though he was no biblical literalist), I contend that his holding together of Word and Spirit challenges today's church. The place of the Bible in the Church is of crucial importance. I well remember going to preach at a particular church during my student days. I was provided with an Order of Worship, one item of which was: "Reading from the Bible or other suitable literature." I thought then, and I continue to think, that if Christian worship is a primary context for the proclamation of the gospel then there is no "suitable literature" which is an alternative to Scripture, for the heart of the gospel is to be distilled from the Bible. But the heart of the gospel concerns Christ's saving act, and it is the gospel of God's sovereign grace and mercy in redemption which both called out the church and gave us the New Testament. Our supreme authority is the gospel, witnessed to in Scripture and brought home to us by the Spirit. On the other side, we witness today a considerable eruption of spirituality, some of it self-serving; some of it amorphous, some of it confessedly, even pugnaciously, non-doctrinal.[34] It is not unknown for Christians to claim new revelations of alleged truths which are not only quite unknown to Scripture, but are in opposition to it. It would therefore seem that from the side of both the Bible and the Spirit, Calvin's challenge to today's Church to hold Spirit and Word together is a pressing one.[35]

---

33. He thought that Moses wrote the Pentateuch, but he denied the Pauline authorship of Hebrews.

34. For further reflections on spirituality see Sell. *Enlightenment, Ecumenism, Evangel*, ch. 8.

35. In the heyday of theological liberalism Forsyth warned of a pitfall in another direction: "Detached from the Word, the supernatural action of the Holy Spirit becomes gradually the natural evolution of the human spirit." See his *Faith, Freedom, and the Future*, 95.

PART TWO: Confessing the Faith Ecclesially and Hopefully

III

Thirdly, Calvin held together the Word and the Church. On the one hand, Calvin the preacher had a degree of confidence in the infallibility of his biblical interpretation that I do not think we should nowadays wish to claim. In connection with the doctrine of predestination, as John Leith reminds us,[36] he told the Genevan Council in 1659 that "I am assured in my conscience that what I have taught and written did not arise out of my own head, but that I received it from God, and I must stand firmly by it, if I am not to be a traitor to the truth."[37] Indeed, he thought that his possession of "infallible truth" justified his punishment of heretics, whereas the Roman Church had no right to punish heretics because it did not have the truth and might therefore punish the innocent.[38] By the same token, Calvin did not expect adverse criticism of his sermons by members of his congregation, and he insisted that church members be obedient to their pastors. On the other hand, he wished to return to the people the Bible, that "greatest treasure," of which he believed they had been robbed by the "great men" who kept it in their own libraries.[39] Indeed, his primary objective in writing his *Institutes* was to encourage those who were competent "to help simple folk . . . and as it were to lend them a hand, in order to guide them and help them to find the sum of what God meant to teach us in his Word."[40] Nor are church members to be passive recipients of instruction only: "Every member of the church is charged with the responsibility of public edification according to the measure of his grace, provided he perform it decently and in order."[41] Furthermore, according to the Genevan Catechism, church members need to be able to distinguish between faithful pastors and "seductive and false prophets, who abandon the purity of the gospel and deviate to their own inventions"; these, "like ravening wolves, ought to be hunted and ejected from the people of God."[42] Although it was by no means a complete description of Geneva in Calvin's day (and some recipients of Calvin's discipline would

---

36. Leith, "Calvin's Theological Method." In Littell, *Reformation* Studies, 113. The two following quotations are drawn from Leith.
37. *Corpus Reformatorum*. XIV, 382.
38. Ibid., XXVII, 253.
39. Ibid., IX, 831.
40. Calvin, *Institutes*, 6.
41. Ibid., IV.i.12.
42. *The Geneva Confession* (1537), in *Theological Treatises of John Calvin*, 32.

have demurred), John Knox was not entirely unjustified in claiming that "This place is the most perfect school of Christ that ever was in the earth since the days of the Apostles."[43]

In all of this there resides a challenge from Calvin to today's Church. In many mainline Western churches the twentieth century saw a considerable decline in the edification of the saints. Bible study meetings became fewer in number, volumes of sermons by princes of the pulpit decreased in number as their authors vanished from the scene, and the weekly and monthly papers read by the generality of Christians in many cases carried reduced biblical and theological content. All of this, notwithstanding more than a century of required religious education in Britain's state schools, has left us with a constituency which has imperfect grasp of the contents of the Bible, and which has received much less help than might have been expected as to the nature and composition of the Bible as such. We shall never know how many people have quietly drifted away from the churches because they received no help in moving from a pre-critical, even an infantile, understanding of certain Bible stories to a mature approach which did not jar against the knowledge they obtained in other fields of enquiry.[44] It even seems to have been the policy of some ministers to have maintained silence on this matter for fear of disturbing the faithful. I am sure, however, that this, though well meant, is a counterproductive approach which raises the question of pastoral integrity.

It is my conviction that, insofar as we succeed, we discover the Word of God and discern the mind of Christ by the Spirit through the Word within the fellowship—understanding by "fellowship" here not simply the Christians with whom we gather, or the wider family of the Church around us, but the witness of the saints through the ages.[45]

---

43. Knox, Letter to Anne Lok, 1556, in Susan M. Felch, "Deir Sister," 53.

44. See further Sell, *Nonconformist Theology in the Twentieth Century*, 164–65. When in pastoral charge I found that what some might have thought of as the most unlikely people became enthused by the detective work involved in Pentateuchal criticism and the synoptic problem. It is never wise to patronize the saints, and in terms of spiritual insight in relation to biblical texts, many a church member can leave the minister standing. The ideal of every local church as a nursery of theologians is one to be striven after. See further Sell, *Testimony and Tradition*, 10–12; *Nonconformist Theology in the Twentieth Century*, 165, 189.

45. See further Sell, "By the Spirit, through the Word, within the fellowship," 41; and Holder's study, "*Ecclesia, legenda atque intelligenda Scriptura.*"

PART TWO: Confessing the Faith Ecclesially and Hopefully

IV

In the fourth place, Calvin held together the Word and the sacraments. Indeed, according to the *Geneva Confession*, Word and sacraments comprise the marks whereby we recognize the Church: "we believe that the proper mark by which properly to discern the Church of Jesus Christ is that his holy gospel be purely and faithfully preached, proclaimed, heard, and kept, that his sacraments be properly administered . . ."[46] The reason is that "the sacraments have the same office as the Word of God: to offer and set forth Christ to us, and in him the treasures of heavenly grace."[47] Furthermore, the sacraments require the accompaniment of "a full explanation of the ordinance and clear statement of the promises."[48] Thus "the right administration of the Sacrament cannot stand apart from the Word. For whatever benefit may come to us from the Supper requires the Word: whether we are to be confirmed in faith, or exercised in confession, or aroused to duty, there is need of preaching."[49] Three hundred years later the first President of Lancashire Independent College, Robert Vaughan, put it concisely: "Separate from preaching the meaning of external observances, even when of Divine origin, is soon obscured and lost."[50] One of Calvin's most stern charges against the Church of Rome was that the Lord's Supper had been "turned into a silent action . . . under the pope's tyranny."[51]

Calvin further thinks that the Lord's Supper is to be observed regularly.[52] It is well-known that his preference that the Word and sacrament be present together in worship every Sunday was denied by the Genevan magistrates, and that he settled at first for observing the Supper monthly, and after 1541, for holding it at Christmas, Easter, Pentecost, and on the first Sunday of September.[53] To him the Supper was "a spiritual banquet, wherein Christ attests himself to be the life-giving bread, upon which our

---

46. *The Geneva Confession* (1537), para. 18.
47. *Institutes*, IV.xiv.17.
48. Calvin, *Short Treatise on the Holy Supper of Our Lord*, para. 48.
49. *Institutes*. IV.xvii.39.
50. Vaughan, in an address to the subscribers to the College. See Thompson, *Lancashire Independent College*, 78. With this note I gratefully salute my *alma mater*.
51. Ibid.
52. See *Institutes*, IV.xvii.44.
53. For a full account of the subject see Wallace. *Calvin's Doctrine of Word and Sacrament*.

Calvin's Challenges to the Twenty-First-Century Church

souls feed unto true and blessed immortality."[54] It "consists in two things: physical signs, which ... represent to us ... things invisible; and spiritual truth, which is at the same time represented and displayed through the symbols themselves."[55]

As regards both baptism and the Lord's Supper, Calvin viewed them as sacraments of the Church and hence the former was for children of the covenant, the latter for professed believers. While Calvin could not readily understand a Christian who would avoid the sacraments, he nevertheless stopped short of affirming their necessity to an individual's salvation: "the grace of God is not so bound to [the sacraments] but that we may obtain it by faith from the Word of the Lord."[56] Again, "by neglecting baptism, we are excluded from salvation; and in this sense I acknowledge that it is necessary; but it is absurd to speak of the hope of salvation as being confined to the sign."[57]

Baptism, Calvin contends, "first points to the cleansing of our sins, which we obtain from Christ's blood; then to the mortification of our flesh, which rests upon participation in his death and through which believers are reborn into newness of life and into the fellowship of Christ. . . . [B]aptism is also a symbol for bearing witness to our religion before men."[58] He elsewhere expands upon this, remarking that baptism signifies our unmerited adoption by the Father into his Church; our restoration to the Father by Christ's blood; and our re-creation by the Spirit.[59] Or again, "baptism . . . is an entrance and a sort of initiation into the church, through which we are numbered among God's people: a sign of our spiritual regeneration . . ."[60] Baptized infants receive "some part of that grace which in a little while they shall enjoy to the full."[61] With this assertion Calvin seems to allow that the Spirit may bestow a blessing on an infant at baptism, whilst not wishing to assert that baptism is always and necessarily the occasion of regeneration. While believing that some

---

54. *Institutes*, IV.xvii.1.
55. Ibid., IV.xvii.11.
56. Ibid., IV.xv.22.
57. *Commentary on John*, 3: 5, (Pringle) 110; (Parker) 64, who gives, "it is absurd to confine assurance of salvation to the sign."
58. *Institutes*, IV.vi.2.
59. See *Commentary on I Cor.* 1: 13, (Pringle) 69–70; (Fraser), 29–30.
60. *Institutes*, IV.xvi.30.
61. Ibid., IV.xvi.19.

infants "are surely saved from that early age,"[62] more generally the *seed of future repentance and faith* "lies hidden within them by the secret working of the Spirit."[63] To those who argue that when Jesus called little children to him the context was not baptism, Calvin replies that those whom Christ receives are not to be shut out.[64] But the apparent openness of this statement is qualified by another: "those infants who derive their origin from Christians, as they have been born directly into the inheritance of the covenant, and are expected by God, are thus to be received into baptism."[65] Here is the covenant idea once more, and it is consistent with Calvin's view that the baptized, buried with Christ and dead to the world, live for God.[66] In other words, there is a separatist flavour both to Calvin's teaching on baptism and the Lord's Supper. In the latter case this flavour becomes especially discernible in relation to communion discipline. The sacrament is not to be violated, and soul-searching preparation is required on the part of those who approach the Lord's table.

Calvin's summary, in which he adverts to the eschatological note, is as follows:

> [B]aptism should be . . . an entry into the church, and an initiation into faith; but the Supper should be a sort of continual food on which Christ spiritually feeds the household of his believers. . . . [S]acraments have been appointed by God to instruct us concerning some promise of his, and attest to us his good will toward us. . . . It is for us to hunger for, seek, look to, learn, and study Christ alone, until that great day dawns when the Lord will fully manifest the glory of his Kingdom.[67]

In all of this I find the following challenges to today's Church. First, we should do well to strive for a fresh grasp of the meaning of the Church as God's covenant people. The sacraments are sacraments of the Church; infant baptism is for children of the covenant, and if parents are not themselves members of the Church then the Church's evangelical and educative mission should be purposefully undertaken. Equally, the Lord's Supper requires a disciplined approach, for it is a covenant meal

---

62. Ibid., IV.xvi.17.
63. Ibid., IV.xvi.20.
64. Ibid., IV.xvi.7.
65. Ibid., IV.xvi.24.
66. *Commentary on I Peter*, 3:21, (Owen) 117; (Johnston) 295.
67. *Institutes*, IV.xviii.19,20.

requiring preparation on the part of those who attend it. Calvin would welcome the emphasis on the liturgical movement of the past century on the desirability of keeping Word and sacrament in close relation in the Church's liturgy, since both proclaim the gospel, the one audibly, the other visibly, though only when in connection to the Word. But those whose tradition it is to invite to the table all those confess Christ as Lord and Saviour and are in good standing with his Church, should remember that those who in the past, and still in some places today, regard the Lord's Supper as a "second service" for members following the Service of the Word were endeavouring to uphold the truth that the sacrament is a sacrament of the Church, understanding by "Church" the "twice-born," visible saints. Some would say that the idea of the sacraments as sacraments of the Church is further eroded when the Lord's Supper is opened to catechumens—that is to say, to baptized persons (whether children or not) who have yet to make their profession of faith. They are within the covenant family of the Church, but they do not have the full responsibility of Church members; they are not yet enrolled saints. For his part, Calvin stoutly opposed the taking of communion by children. In all of this there is much to be pondered in ecumenical circles.[68]

Again, it may be argued that the widespread ecumenical conviction that baptism is the ground of the Church's unity is not only unrealistic in that so many Christian initiations are never completed; it can also marginalize the idea of God's gracious call in the gospel as being that which constitutes the Church, and it can even appear to sanction the sacerdotal apparatus introduced in the middle ages which was designed to provide for the situation in which those baptized and thereby deemed regenerate, continued thereafter to sin. Among the underlying themes in all of this, and one which clamours for further attention, is that concerning the balance to be struck between the church's being called out of the world (the separatist thrust) and its being sent into the world in mission and service. This is no new challenge, but it is a particularly clamant one in the Western world wherein the Church has in some places become so identified with the surrounding society as to be almost indistinguishable from it, and this to the detriment of the counter-cultural witness that the church on occasion is called upon to make.

---

68. See further Sell, *The Great Ejectment of 1662*, 257–59.

PART TWO: Confessing the Faith Ecclesially and Hopefully

V

Fifthly, in his understanding of ministry Calvin held together preaching and pastoral care. In Calvin's view there was nothing more noble or more humbling than the call to the Church's ministry. He concurs with Paul that "this human ministry which God uses to govern the Church is the chief sinew by which believers are held together in one body."[69] Ministers must he holy, they must be steeped in the Scriptures, and, in succession to the apostles, their primary duty is the preaching of the Word. But this Word is the Word of God, from which they may not deviate; and they are guided by the Spirit of truth, which Spirit also conveys the truth preached to those who receive it.[70] He goes so far as to say that God wishes to be heard only through the voice of his ministers.[71] The preacher's authority is Christ himself, and it is his voice that must be heard.[72]

To Calvin there is no distinction between preaching and pastoral work. Preaching *is* pastoral work. It is designed to move, instruct, encourage, console, and rebuke those who hear it. The gospel, he declares, is not simply something to be heard, it is a seed of eternal life designed to reform us and give us joy, peace, and the certainty of salvation.[73] Calvin would have regarded his prolific writing no less than his sermons as all part of his pastoral work of building up the Church. The pastoral work extends to the cure of individual souls in contexts of private confession and discipline.[74] It is equally clear that for Calvin judgment, albeit by the Word not the pastor, no less than consolation, were ingredients in genuine pastoral care. Thus he says that the minds of the weak must not be crushed by "excessive severity"; that evil must not be encouraged by "smooth language"; and that those who boldly and obstinately resist must be "broken and crushed" by the Word.[75] Calvin's teaching on the "third use" of the law in of relevance here. To the believer the law of God is not longer simply a schoolmaster to lead us to Christ, or a rule for political

---

69. *Institutes*, IV.iii.2.

70. Ibid., IV.viii.9.

71. See *Commentary on Isaiah*, 50:10, (Pringle), 61; cf. *Commentary on John*, 10:4, (Pringle), 396–97; (Parker) I, 260.

72. *Institutes*, IV.viii.7.

73. See *Commentary on I Peter*, 1:23, (Owen) 56–57; (Johnston) 252–53; and *Commentary on John*, 15: 11, (Pringle), II, 114–15; (Parker)II, 98–99.

74. See *Institutes*, III.iv.12.

75. See *Commentary on Isaiah*, 42:3, 289.

order, but a guide for the Christian life. Hence, as John Hesselink puts it, "To the seeking soul who cries in anguish: How can I know the will of God? How shall I respond to that God? Where can I find and true and certain guide in life? Calvin answers: in the law, because in it we have a direct, unmistakable revelation of God's character and will for us."[76] In a word, the law returns the regenerate to Christ, and by the Holy Spirit they are enabled to obey it.[77]

Negligent pastors who shun pastoral work earn a stern rebuke from Calvin. The negligence of those is inexcusable "who, having made one sermon, as if they had done their task, live for all the rest of their time idly, as if their voices were shut up within the church walls, seeing that so soon as they be departed thence, they be dumb."[78] Such behaviour was not merely an abnegation of pastoral responsibility, it was an affront to the discipline of the Genevan church, for prior to each of the four celebrations per annum of the Lord's Supper all church members were to be visited in their homes by elders and pastors, particular concern being expressed for the young.

How does all of this challenge today's Church? In the first place it reminds us that the call to ministry is a high and holy calling than which there is no higher. There is no adverse elitism in this; rather the call is to humility and submission to the Word, and to self-sacrificing service of those for whose souls one has a responsibility. This would seem to run counter to those managerial notions of ministry which prevail in some quarters today, and which facilitate the understanding of ministry as a job, as having a career pattern, as having specified terms of reference and hours of duty.

As to preaching: in Calvin's view, and in mine, there is no higher privilege than to proclaim the gospel of Christ. I do not say that preaching can only be undertaken from a pulpit, though I think there is something to be said for having, in the full liturgy, a particular place from which it is done, because this indicates the fact that something special is going on: this is precisely not an individual offloading his or her latest thoughts on this and that. This is where one stands who has been much in prayer, who has studied the Scriptures, who (normally) knows the people, and who proclaims, however unworthily, God's Word to them. I think that

---

76. Hesselink, *Calvin's Concept of the Law*, 33.

77. In addition to John Hesselink's ground-breaking study of the law in Calvin, see also Byung-Ho Moon, *Christ the Mediator of the Law.*.

78. *Commentary on Acts*, 20:20.

those who vacate the pulpit because they do not wish to be "six feet above criticism", or because they wish, in a feel-good, matey kind of way, to get close to the people, to whom they offer a casual word or two from the back of an envelope, may need to reflect further on what they are about.[79] I much prefer the attitude of the Bible Christian [Methodist] preacher, F. W. Bourne:

> My brethren, it is our business, not to conquer a world, not to amass a fortune, nor simply to become adepts in learning, but to save souls from death, to make not a few but many rich, to conquer and win a thousand hearts for Christ.... [W]e do want to be able in the last great day to go boldly up to the eternal throne, and say to Him who sitteth thereon, who gave us our commission, and who has often cheered us by His presence, "Here we are, and the children Thou hast given us." May it be so.[80]

From the outset the tradition to which Bourne belonged elevated preaching by both men and women, as this verse which appears in their *Minutes* of 1820 makes clear:

> Ye heralds of truth, Sent forth by the Lord,
> Both antient and youth, Who publish His Word;
> Ye sons and ye Daughters, Selected by grace,
> Be strong and courageous, And each fill his place.[81]

As to pastoral care: I gain the distinct impression that in some quarters this has degenerated in quality in two ways. First, its more serious disciplinary and catechetical aspects suffer neglect; secondly, ministers claim that with changing social patterns—both husbands and wives out at work every day, for example—and because of the pressure on their own time, they simply cannot fit pastoral visitation into their schedule. Such visitation can even be at the mercy of ministerial specialisms in those churches large and rich enough to have a team of pastors. An

---

79. I am, of course, aware of the incongruity of standing in a very high pulpit in a church with two galleries built to seat 2,000 people when the congregation comprises ten or a dozen people scattered around the ground floor. The preacher need not thus be physically elevated above the congregation. But even when preacher and people are on the same flat floor, there can be a particular, distinct, site from which the gospel is proclaimed and Scripture expounded and applied.

80. Luke, *Memorials of Frederick William Bourne*, 82. Bourne (1830–1905) was a minister of the Bible Christian Church.

81. Quoted by Shaw, *The Bible Christians*, 32. See further Sell, *Testimony and Tradition*, ch. 3.

advertisement for a "Minister for preaching and administration" left me strangely disquieted, and conjured up a vision of a person tied to an office all the week who emerges on Sundays to preach to those he has never met, catechized, or visited. It is hard to believe that any minister today could be busier than Calvin, and the dedicated can find ways of surmounting changing social patterns—and even of turning off the television during a pastoral visit. At the very least they ought to have a concern for the housebound, the hospitalized and the dying. Listen to another Methodist, Gordon Rupp:

> I have stuck my neck out as far as the next man's to get young men set aside for experimental and new ministries. . . . But I sometimes wonder whether some of them are not anxious to be involved in everything except chores, like learning N.T. Greek, or visiting the flock in hospital, or sweating away at sermons. . . . [T]here is in the end no substitution for this one essential ministry of the Church, the shepherding of souls, in the time of their wealth and of their tribulation, at moments of birth and marriage and in the article of death.[82]

VI

Finally, Calvin held doctrine and ethics, together. This is a very large subject, and it will suffice to illustrate the doctrine-ethics link in Calvin's mind if I refer only to altruism, the economic order and ecology.[83] The gospel, Calvin declares, "is a doctrine not of the tongue but of life. . . . [I]t must enter our heart and pass into our daily living, and so transform us into itself that it may not be unfruitful for us."[84] This comes out clearly, for example, in his discussion of the Lord's Supper. Among other things, he says, the Supper was ordained in order that participants might "nourish mutual love, and among themselves give witness to this love." But lest this seem a love restricted to the household of faith he commends the early Church, in which the "unvarying rule" was that "no meeting

---

82. Rupp, *The Old Reformation and the New*, 55. With this quotation I salute the late Professor Rupp, whose BD paper on the Continental Reformation (with texts in Latin, French and German) I managed to pass fifty years ago. (There are anniversaries other than Calvin's). For further reflections on pastoral care see Sell, *Aspects of Christian Integrity*, ch. 6.

83. I shall not, therefore, discuss culture in general or the political order.

84. *Institutes*, III.vi.4.

PART TWO: Confessing the Faith Ecclesially and Hopefully

of the church should take place without the Word, prayers, partaking of the Supper and almsgiving."[85] Elsie McKee is thus justified in claiming that Calvinist Reformed Christians understood "the parallel duties of worship (*pietas*) and love (*caritas*) as inseparable."[86] Calvin desired the Church not only to proclaim the truth, but to practise holy living. Christ "unites himself to us by the Spirit alone,"[87] and apart from this union Christian living and service would be impossible. The motivation of that life and service is gratitude to the Father for the salvation wrought by the Son, brought home to believers by the Spirit. Why, ask the authors of the *Heidelberg Catechism*, should we do good works? They answer, "Because since Christ has redeemed us by His blood, He renews us also by His Holy Spirit according to His own image, that with our whole life we may show ourselves thankful to God for His goodness, and that He may be glorified through us; and further, that we ourselves on our part may be assured of our faith by its fruits, and by our godly life may win our neighbours also to Christ."[88]

Among other motivations to godly living cited by Calvin are the believer's obligation to follow the example of Christ, "through whom we return to favor with God";[89] the desire on the believer's part to be "consecrated and dedicated to God in order that we may thereafter think, speak, meditate, and do, nothing except to his glory";[90] and the fulfilment of the duty to distribute our God-given possessions "for our neighbors' benefit."[91] There is, furthermore, the eschatological motivation: "We are God's: let all the parts of our life accordingly strive toward him as our only lawful goal."[92]

On this basis Calvin reviews many socio-political issues. "Where God then is known," he declares, "kindness to man also appears."[93] He rightly understands the parable of the Good Samaritan as teaching that

---

85. *Institutes*, IV.xvii.44. See further Templin, "The Individual and Society in the Thought of Calvin."

86. McKee. *Diakonia in the Classical Reformed Tradition and Today*, 41.

87. *Institutes*, III.i.3.

88. *The Heidelberg Catechism*, Q. and A. 86. In Torrance, *The School of Faith*, 86.

89. *Institutes*. III.vi.3; cf. *Commentary on I Corinthians*, 9: 21, (Pringle) I, 305; (Fraser) 195–96.

90. Ibid., III.vii.1.

91. Ibid., III.vii.5.

92. Ibid., III.vii.1.

93. *Commentary on Jeremiah*, 22:16, 104.

"we are not expected to limit the precept of love to those in close relationships"; indeed, "we ought to embrace the whole human race without exception in a single feeling of love; here there is no distinction between barbarian and Greek, worthy and unworthy, friend and enemy . . ." Why? because "all should be contemplated in God, not in themselves."[94] All of which is given added point when we recall that refugees were arriving in Geneva from many parts of Europe. He has a particular concern for the "poor and despised": "Let a Moor or a Barbarian come among us, and yet inasmuch as he is a man, he brings with him a looking glass wherein we may see that he is our brother and neighbour."[95] Calvin does not deny that "the great part of [humanity] are most unworthy if they be judged by their own merit." But that is not the point: the Scripture exhorts us "to look upon the image of God in all men, to whom we owe all honor and love."[96] Moreover, to give to the poor is to give to the Lord; so "if we believe heaven is our country, it is better to transmit our possessions thither than to keep them here where upon our sudden migration they would be lost to us."[97] Here, however quaint the language, is the eschatological motive once more. Driving still more deeply, Calvin declares that if we if we injure divine-image-bearing others, God is violated in them and suffers with them.[98]

Calvin had no objection to the private ownership of property.[99] He was by no means averse to the idea that we should enjoy this world's goods: "Did [God] not endow gold and silver, ivory and marble, with a loveliness that renders them more precious than other metals or stones? Did he not . . . render many things attractive to us, apart from their necessary use?"[100] Calvin answers his rhetorical question in the affirmative; but he immediately proceeds to distinguish this legitimate delight in things God has made or given, from the lust of the flesh. God's good gifts are not to be abused. Elsewhere he strongly opposed the economic exploitation of the poor by the rich.[101] The argument is extended to creation as a

---

94. *Institutes*, II.viii.55.
95. *Sermon* on Galatians 6:9-11.
96. *Institutes*, III.vii.6.
97. Ibid., III.viii.6.
98. *Commentary on Genesis*, 6:5-6, 247-49.
99. *Institutes*, III.xix.9.
100. *Institutes*, III,x.2.
101. *Commentary on Amos*, 8:6, 367.

whole. Human beings are to be good stewards of it and refrain from its wanton destruction.[102] If they are not, they forget the Maker and divert his good gifts towards unworthy ends.[103]

Enough has been said to show that and how Calvin holds together doctrine and ethics. In this connection I think that his challenge to today's church is that we do likewise. Just as some of our Christian contemporaries lament the increasing specialization which has in some cases led to the divorce of biblical from systematic theology, so there are not wanting signs that some Christian social ethicists are so quick to plunge into pressing issues that they leave doctrinal considerations behind, and their findings can sound like those of any right-minded humanist. But to Calvin the motivating force of his socio-political ethics was intensely doctrinal, rooted in the gospel. Nor was it simply an intellectual rooting in the sense of "If this is what you believe then this is what you should do." The doctrine was the articulation of lived experience, and thus it was a motivating force. Union with Christ by the Spirit on the ground of Christ's saving work prompted gratitude of a kind which led to seeing one's salvation, one's life, and all of one's possessions as gifts from God to be used for his glory, and in the service of others. To plunder Calvin's writings for ethical principles of use today without reference to their doctrinal-*cum*-experimental basis would be to miss Calvin's main point: "[W]e are God's: let us therefore live for him and die for him. We are God's: let his wisdom and will therefore rule all our actions. We are God's: let all the parts of our life accordingly strive toward him as our only lawful goal."[104]

---

102. *Commentary on Genesis*, 2:15, 125.

103. *Commentary on the Psalms*, 104:35, 171. This is not the place to address the familiar charge, flowing down from Max Weber, that Calvin or Calvinism instigated capitalism. My summary response to the charge is: 1. Capitalism was alive and well in fifteenth-century Roman Catholic business centres, sometimes in close relation to the Church. 2. It is true that Calvin sanctioned usury for the purposes of credit, but not as a means of avoiding work by living on interest. 3. He urged altruism to an unusual degree, and would not have countenanced antisocial economic individualism. 4. Critics of Calvin are inclined anachronistically to attribute to him a post-Enlightenment view of capitalism. His view that all of God's bounty, including wealth, is held in trust by us, and that we are accountable for the way we use, or abuse, it is at a far remove from modern notions of free enterprise. 5. The range of economic activity in Calvin's Geneva was circumscribed relative to our own—he knew the businessmen around him. He would have boggled at giant international business conglomerates, and still more at hedge funds.

104. *Institutes*, III.vii.1.

VII

As I said at the outset, Calvin cannot do all our work for us, and at particular points we may well disagree with him. We are not tied to his exegesis of Scripture, or to his view of the dating and authorship of the biblical books. We should do well to query the way in which he left his Church polity hanging with the elders and did not give due place to the priesthood of all the believers together—gathered under the sole Lordship of Christ in that credal assembly, the church meeting, where they seek his will for their witness and service, and to find unanimity in him (this is no democracy).[105] Again, while in principle Calvin sought to preserve the distinction between Church and state, in practice the lines became blurred in Geneva, where the officers of the state, having, according to the theory, been accorded their positions by God, were involved in the enforcement of doctrine deemed pure, the election of ministers and elders, and in the maintenance of good order.[106] It was left to such as the English and Welsh Puritan Separatists, who would not opt into the Church of England "by law established" to insist upon honouring the sole rights of the Redeemer in his Church—even at the cost of their lives.[107] While Calvin welcomed refugees and visitors from many lands, some of whom, like Knox, returned home revitalized;[108] and while he conducted a comprehensive mission to the immediate world around him, he was long dead before the Evangelical Revival laid the whole world upon the consciences of Christians in a clamant way;[109] and the not uncommon twenty-first century experience of societies which are religiously plural was beyond the purview of one who could still make the assumption of

---

105. See further ch. 10 below. In recent decades, and not least in the World Council of Churches convergence document, *Baptism, Eucharist and Ministry*, the "ministry of the people of God" is extolled. But in large tracts of the Church there is no provision for this in polity. Of course, for it to be practicable it is necessary to know who the enrolled saints are.

106. See *Institutes*, IV.xi.3; IV.20.2.

107. When Henry VIII was given "supreme power in all things" by "inconsiderate men," Calvin was grievously vexed: "they were guilty of blasphemy when they called him the chief Head of the Church under Christ." See his *Commentary on Amos*, 7:10–13, 338–52.

108. See Berg, "Calvin and missions." In Hoogstra, *John Calvin: Contemporary Prophet*, ch. 10; Hughes. "John Calvin: director of mission." In Bratt, *The Heritage of John Calvin*, ch. 3; Reid, "Calvin's Geneva: a missionary centr," 65–74.

109. Though see Beaver, "The Genevan Mission to Brazil." In Bratt, *The Heritage of John Calvin*, ch. 4.

PART TWO: Confessing the Faith Ecclesially and Hopefully

Christendom. Calvin was sharp enough in deploying a battery of inner-churchly arguments against Roman Catholics and others, but he did not have to face the apologetic challenges to the Christian faith flowing down from the Enlightenment that confront us (though I suspect that were he here he would tackle them head-on in a way that some of his quite well-known theological heirs have, on dogmatic grounds, dogmatically declined to do).

But for all that, I hope to have shown that in holding together the gospel and the Church, the Spirit and the Word, the Word and the Church, the Word and the sacraments, preaching and pastoral care, and doctrine and ethics, Calvin not only bequeathed us models for theological reflection and churchly life, but also set us a series of challenges which the one Church to which he devoted himself is far from fully meeting even after the passage of nearly five hundred years.

BIBLIOGRAPHY

Anon. *The Accra Confession*. In *Reformed World* 55 (2005) 185-90.
———. *Baptism, Eucharist and Ministry*. Geneva: World Council of Churches, 1982.
Armstrong, William Park. *Calvin and the Reformation*. Grand Rapids: Baker, 1980.
Baum, G., E. Cunitz, and E. Reuss. *Corpus Reformatorum: Joannis Calvini Opera Quae Supersunt Omnia*. 59 vols. Brunsvigae, Germany: Schwetschke, 1863-97.
Beaver, R. Pierce. "The Genevan Mission to Brazil." In *The Heritage of John Calvin*, edited by John H. Bratt, 55-73. Grand Rapids: Eerdmans, 1973.
Berg, J. Van den. "Calvin and Missions." In *John Calvin: Contemporary Prophet*, edited by Jacob T. Hoogstra, 167-83. Grand Rapids: Baker, 1959.
Calvin, John. *Commentary on the Acts of the Apostles*. Original translation revised by Henry Beveridge Edinburgh: Calvin Translation Society, 1844.
———. *Commentary on Amos* Translated by John Owen. Edinburgh: Calvin Translation Society, 1846.
———. *Commentary on I Corinthians* Translated by John Pringle. Edinburgh: Calvin Translation Society, 1848.
———. *Commentary on I Corinthians*. Translated by John W. Fraser. Grand Rapids: Eerdmans, 1960.
———. *Commentary on Ephesians*. Translated by William Pringle. Edinburgh: Calvin Translation Society, 1854.
———. *Commentary on Ephesians*. Translated by T. H. L. Parker. Grand Rapids: Eerdmans, 1965.
———. *Commentary on Ezekiel*. Translated by Thomas Myers. Edinburgh: Calvin Translation Society, 1850.
———. *Commentary on Genesis*. Translated by John King. Edinburgh: Calvin Translation Society, 1847.
———. *Commentary on Jeremiah*. Translated by John Owen. Edinburgh: Calvin Translation Society, 1852.
———. *Commentary on the Gospel according to John*. Translated by William Pringle. Edinburgh: Calvin Translation Society, 1847.
———. *Commentary on the Gospel according to John*. Translated by T. H. L. Parker. Grand Rapids: Eerdmans, 1961.
———. *Commentary on Isaiah*. Translated by W. Pringle. Edinburgh: Calvin Translation Society, 1853.
———. *Commentary on I Peter*. Translated by John Owen. Edinburgh: Calvin Translation Society, 1855.
———. *Commentary on I Peter*. Translated by William B. Johnston. Grand Rapids: Eerdmans, 1963.
———. *Commentary on the Psalms*. Translated by James Anderson. Edinburgh: Calvin Translation Society, 1847.
———. *Commentary on Romans*. Translated by John Owen. Edinburgh: Calvin Translation Society, 1849.
———. *Commentary on Romans*. Translated by Ross MacKenzie. Grand Rapids: Eerdmans, 1960.
———. *Institutes*. Translated by Ford Lewis Battles and edited by John T. McNeill. 2 vols, Philadelphia: Westminster, 1960.
———. *Letters of John Calvin*. Translated by Jules Bonnet. 4 vols, Philadelphia: Presbyterian Board of Publication, 1858.

PART TWO: Confessing the Faith Ecclesially and Hopefully

———. *Sermons on Galatians*. Translated by Kathy Childress. Edinburgh: Banner of Truth, 1997.

———. *Short Treatise on the Holy Supper of Our Lord in which is shown its True Institution, Benefit, and Utility* (1540). In *Tracts on the Sacraments*, vol. 2, translated by Henry Beveridge, 163–98. Edinburgh: Calvin Translation Society, 1849.

———. *Theological Treatises of John Calvin*. Translated by J. K. S. Reid. London: SCM, 1954.

———. *Tracts and Treatises*. Translated by Henry Beveridge. 3 vols, Grand Rapids: Eerdmans, 1958.

———. *Treatises against the Anabaptists and Against the Libertines*. Edited by Benjamin W. Farley. Grand Rapids: Baker, 1982.

Edmondson, Stephen. *Calvin's Christology*. Cambridge: Cambridge University Press, 2004.

Felch, Susan M. "Deir Sister: The Letters of John Knox to Anne Vaughan Lok." *Renaissance and Reformation* 19 (1995) 47–68.

Forsyth, P. T. *Faith, Freedom and the Future*. 1912. Reprint. London: Independent, 1955.

Franks, Robert S. *A History of the Doctrine of the Work of Christ in its Historical Development*. 2 vols. London: Hodder and Stoughton, 1918.

Frew, David. "Calvin as an Expositor of Scripture." In *Proceedings of the Ninth General Council of the Alliance of Reformed Churches holding the Presbyterian System Held at New York, 1909*, edited by G. D. Matthews, 77–84. London: Office of the Alliance, 1909.

Frykholm, Amy. "In the None Zone." *The Christian Century*, 2 December 2008, 22.

Gamble, Richard C. "Calvin as Theologian and Exegete." *Calvin Theological Journal* 23 (1988) 178–94.

Helm, Paul. *John Calvin's Ideas*. Oxford: Oxford University Press, 2004.

Hesselink, I. John. *Calvin's Concept of the Law*. Allison Park, PA: Pickwick, 1992.

———. "Calvinus Oecumenicus: Calvin's Vision of the Unity and Catholicity of the Church." *Reformed Review* 44 (1990) 97–122.

Holder, R. Ward. "*Ecclesia, legenda atque intelligenda Scriptura*: The Church as a Discerning Community in Calvin's Hermeneutic." *Calvin Theological Journal* 36 (2001) 270–89.

Hughes, Philip E. "John Calvin: Director of Mission." In *The Heritage of John Calvin*, edited by John H. Bratt, 40–54. Grand Rapids: Eerdmans, 1973.

Kromminga, John H. "Calvin and Ecumenicity." In *John Calvin: Contemporary Prophet*, edited by Jacob T. Hoogstra, 149–65. Grand Rapids: Baker, 1959.

Leith, John. "Calvin's Theological Method." In *Reformation Studies: Sixteen Essays in Honor of Roland H. Bainton*, edited by Franklin H. Littell, 106–14. Richmond, VA: John Knox, 1962.

Luke, W. B. *Memorials of Frederick William Bourne*. London: Gregory, 1906.

McKie, Elsie A. *Diakonia in the Classical Reformed Tradition and Today*. Grand Rapids: Eerdmans, 1989.

Moon, Byung-Ho. *Christ the Mediator of the Law: Calvin's Christological Understanding of the Law and the Rule of Living and Life-Giving*. Milton Keynes, UK: Paternoster, 2006.

Nyomi, Setri. *The Legacy of John Calvin: Some Actions for the Church in the 21st Century*. Geneva: World Alliance of Reformed Churches and the John Knox International Reformed Centre, 2008.

Orr, James, "Calvin's Attitude towards Exegesis of the Scriptures." In *Calvin Memorial Addresses*, 89–105. Vestavia Hills, AL: Solid Ground Christian Books, 2007.

Pattison, Mark. *Essays by the Late Mark Pattison, sometime Rector of Lincoln College, Collected and Arranged by Henry Nettleship*. Oxford: Clarendon, 1889.

Reid, W. S. "Calvin's Geneva: A Missionary Centre." *The Reformed Theological Review* 42 (1983) 65–74.

Rupp, E. Gordon. *The Old Reformation and the New*. London: Epworth, 1967.

Sell, Alan P. F. *Aspects of Christian Integrity*. 1990. Reprint. Eugene, OR: Wipf and Stock, 1998.

———. "By the Spirit, through the Word, within the Fellowship." *Touchstone* 7 (1989) 32–41.

———. *Confessing and Commending the Faith: Historic Witness and Apologetic Method*. 2002. Reprint. Eugene, OR: Wipf & Stock, 2006.

———. *Enlightenment, Ecumenism, Evangel: Theological Themes and Thinkers 1550-2000*. Milton Keynes, UK: Paternoster, 2005.

———. *The Great Ejectment of 1662: Its Antecedents, Aftermath, and Ecumenical Significance*. Eugene, OR: Wipf & Stock, 2012.

———. *Hinterland Theology: A Stimulus to Theological Construction*. Milton Keynes, UK: Paternoster, 2008.

———. *Nonconformist Theology in the Twentieth Century*. Milton Keynes, UK: Paternoster, 2006.

———. *Testimony and Tradition: Studies in Reformed and Dissenting Thought*. Aldershot, UK: Ashgate, 2005.

Shaw, Thomas. *The Bible Christians 1815-1907*. London: Epworth, 1965.

Stevenson, J. H. "The Salient Features of Calvin's Life." In *Proceedings of the Ninth General Council of the Alliance of Reformed Churches Holding the Presbyterian System Held at New York, 1909*, edited by G. D. Matthews, 50–56. London: Office of the Alliance, 1909.

Templin, J. Alton. "The Individual and Society in the Thought of Calvin." *Calvin Theological Journal* 23 (1988) 161–77.

Torrance, Thomas F. "Our Witness through Doctrine." In *Proceedings of the 17th General Council of the Alliance of Reformed Churches throughout the World holding the Presbyterian Order*, 133–45. Geneva: Office of the Alliance, 1954.

———. *The School of Faith: The Catechisms of the Reformed Church*. London: Clarke, 1959.

Various. *Calvin Memorial Addresses, delivered before the General Assembly of the Presbyterian Church in the U.S. 1909*. Reprint. Vestavia Hills, AL: Solid Ground Christian Books, 2007.

———. The Economic and Social Witness of Calvin for Christian Life Today. *Reformed World* 55.4 (2005).

Vaughan, Robert. "Address to the College's Subscribers." In *Lancashire Independent College, 1843-1893*, edited by Joseph Thompson, 77–82. *Jubilee Memorial Volume*. Manchester: Cornish, 1893. For the full text see *The Congregational Magazine* (1844) 237–41.

Wallace, Ronald S. *Calvin's Doctrine of Word and Sacrament*. Edinburgh: Oliver & Boyd, 1953.

Warfield, B. B. "John Calvin the Theologian." *Proceedings of the Ninth General Council of the Alliance of Reformed Churches holding the Presbyterian System held at New York, 1909*, edited by G. D. Matthews, 136–42. London: Office of the Alliance, 1909.

CHAPTER EIGHT

Rectifying Calvin's Ecclesiology

The Doctrinal and Ecumenical Importance of Separatist-Congregational Catholicity

IT IS HARDLY SURPRISING that baptism, eucharist, and ministry have been among the topics most regularly discussed in local, national, regional and international inter-confessional dialogues over the past forty years, for these are widely perceived as being neuralgic issues that clamour for attention. I, however, have become increasingly convinced that to treat ecclesiological themes in isolation from other doctrines and from certain particular presuppositions is not the most constructive way of proceeding if we genuinely wish to break the sectarian log-jams that prohibit the gathering of the saints at the table of the Lord. Thus, for example, the presuppositions that are entertained regarding doctrinal development cannot but influence what is believed concerning the ministry; yet, in my experience, the doctrine of the development of doctrine is rarely subjected to detailed scrutiny by those engaged in ecumenical dialogues. I have elsewhere elaborated upon this point.[1] As for ecclesiology-attendant doctrines, the argument of this paper is (a) that unless due attention is paid to the doctrines of election, regeneration, adoption, union with Christ, and covenant, our progress towards genuine catholicity will be seriously

1. See further Sell, *Enlightenment, Ecumenism, Evangel*, ch. 6.

Rectifying Calvin's Ecclesiology

impeded; and (b) that in the providence of God, and in the particular political circumstances in which they were placed, it fell to the English and Welsh Separatists and their successors in the Congregational branch of the Reformed family to articulate the relationship between these doctrines and ecclesiology more clearly than was done by Calvin himself.[2]

It goes without saying that Calvin was well aware of, and committed to, the doctrines I have just named. I think it can be argued, however, that he did not fully work out their implications concerning the "matter" of the Church and Church polity. I state what I take to be the case, I do not blame; for while, as is nowadays widely recognized, the restorationist hope of finding a specific church polity (namely, one's own) in the New Testament is doomed to disappointment, the corollary is that Church order has unquestionably been influenced by biblical clues, the diverse socio-political circumstances in which Christians have found themselves, and even by sometimes idiosyncratic personalities. Thus when in 1883 Eustace Conder (1820–92) declared that in the seventeenth century the Congregational objective was "the restoration of the Apostolic Church Polity: Christ's Church reformed on Christ's model,"[3] he (a) overlooked the fact that Christ left no one model polity; and (b) gave the impression that the Congregational witness concerns church organization alone—as if to say "We believe more or less the same as every other churchly body, except that we think that our polity is more biblical." This does not strike deeply enough, for the distinctive contribution derives from convictions concerning what the other doctrines imply as regards polity. Since, however, we are all children of our time, we never "see" all that is to be seen, and a modicum of humility will encourage us to wonder in regard to which topics, in two centuries' time, our heirs and successors will be specifying our relative blindness. I am aware that the title of my paper will offend any who think that Calvin's ecclesiology is that last word on the subject; and I do not intend to suggest that the originators of Separatist catholicity sat down in the quiet of their studies with a view to writing papers in which they would put Calvin right on ecclesiology. Rather, their position was forged in the court room and, in a number of cases,

---

2. Even "by anyone else"—but Calvin is enough to handle in one paper! My judgment is made on the basis of careful analysis, not in a triumphalist spirit—as will become clear when I come to the pitfalls of the polity. We should do well to remember that when writers on ecclesiology proclaim that "the Church is x, y, z," they frequently mean, "ideally, the Church is . . ."

3. Conder, "Independency in the Days of the Commonwealth," 195.

witnessed to on the scaffold. My claim is that their speeches, writings, and actions had the effect of rectifying Calvin's ecclesiology at certain points. If I may upset some Calvinistic purists, I may also puzzle any who regard "Separatist-Congregational catholicity" as a contradiction in terms. It is not; nor is it a paradox: it is a straightforward description. Moreover, it is an inheritance which flowed down from the Separatists themselves to their Congregationalist and united church successors.

Behind those words there lies a long story. It is clear that the Congregationalists/Independents of the mid-seventeenth century objected strongly when they were nicknamed "Separatists" or "Brownists" after Robert Browne, of whom more shortly. But they were living in that brief, Cromwellian, period of English history when circumstances had never been more favourable towards those of their ecclesiological stance. Indeed, they could even, briefly, contemplate a national church constituted along Congregational lines—the kind of establishment that their friends in Massachusetts were pioneering. In those circumstances to have owned the term "separatist" would have been counter-productive, and would have played into the hands of those whom it suited to regard them on a par with the more radical sectaries of Commonwealth times. The fact remains, as Alexander Mackennal (1835–1904) observed with reference to the seventeenth-century Congregationalists:

> They were not true Separatists; had they been so, they would not have sat in the Westminster Assembly, nor entered into Cromwell's purpose of founding a comprehensive National Church. But Baillie and Baxter, and the Presbyterians generally, were not wrong in calling them so. All they knew of Congregational Independency, gathered Churches, discipline, the association of the members with the ministers in church government, the desire for toleration, had been formulated for them by [the Separatists] Browne and Barrowe, and John Robinson, and Henry Jacob, and Henry Ainsworth.[4]

The preliminary explanations given, let us brace ourselves and proceed.

I

There is a constellation of doctrines which bear directly upon ecclesiology. No doubt the all-embracing, and Trinitarian, way of putting the point

---

4. Mackennal, *Sketches in the Evolution of English Congregationalism*. 123.

is to say that on the ground of the Son's finished work at the cross, the Father, by the Holy Spirit, graciously calls out one people for his praise and service. Here we have the root of catholicity—a point to which I shall return. But I am immediately concerned with the matter of the Church, and in this connection the doctrines of election, regeneration, adoption, union with Christ, and covenant clamour for attention. They are so closely intertwined as to be almost inseparable; they are saying the same thing in different ways, rather than specifying a series of particular occurrences in a temporal sequence. It is important to emphasize that in what follows I have no interest in denying that those of other communions than the Separatist-Congregational have maintained these doctrines. My concern is with the way in which the Separatists and Congregationalists worked out the implications of these in relation to the matter and polity of the church.[5]

John Leith told nothing less than the truth when he wrote that "John Calvin gave more attention to polity than did any other major reformer."[6] If we looked no further than the *Institutes*, we should find that Book IV, on the Church, runs to more than five hundred pages, and that it would remain a bulky contribution even if the Church history and the contextually understandable anti-Roman polemic were omitted. Calvin strove for orderly Church life in Geneva and for well-taught Christians. As means towards these ends he instituted the offices of minister, elder and deacon, later adding doctor. Ministers and elders were to meet together in the consitory, and all four offices he declared—with more than a little exaggeration—rested on the authority of Christ.[7] Above all, he insisted that "Wherever we see the Word of God purely preached and heard, and the sacraments administered according to Christ's institution, there, it is not to be doubted, a church of God exists."[8]

But who comprise the church? According to Romans 1:7 Christian believers are "saints by calling." Some English translations declare that they are "called to be saints," but this might be taken as implying that sainthood is something to be striven for—even that it is not achieved until perfection of life is attained. However, the former reading is to be preferred, not least because when Paul wrote to the saints of the various

---

5. For a fuller account of a number of matters here briefly touched upon see Sell, *Saints: Visible, Orderly and Catholic. The Congregational Idea of the Church.*

6. Leith, *Introduction to the Reformed Tradition*, 152.

7. Calvin, *Institutes*, IV.iii.4.

8. Ibid., IV.i.9.

churches he knew quite well that he was not writing to companies of the perfect: indeed, very often the purpose of his writing was to rebuke them and encourage them along the path of sanctification. Moreover, he knew in his own experience that the saints were also sinners, and that the "old man" was every trying to drag the "new creature" down. The saints, then, are the Christians, the believers—all of them, not a special class within them; and they are saints because they have been called. Here is the doctrine of election to which Calvin adhered with considerable intensity. At the same time, it must be granted that there is ambivalence in his writings, as John Whale (1896–1997) pointed out. Here Calvin thinks of the elect as comprising the invisible church; there he thinks of them as visible saints; and yet again he thinks of them as representing but a portion of the empirical Church, with all that that entails regarding Church discipline and even excommunication. Whale says, "he is playing at one and the same time the three roles of Augustine, Cyprian, and Wesley: the successive editions of the *Institutio* with their increasingly articulate churchmanship are a tense synthesis of the predestinarian logic of the first, the explicit churchmanship of the second and the perfectionism of the third."[9] As to the third strand of thought *The Second Helvetic Confession* (1566) pulled no punches: "[N]ot all that are reckoned in the number of the Church are saints and true members of the Church. For there are many hypocrites . . ."[10] As we shall see, Calvin's ambivalence was called into question by the Separatists and Congregationalists, who urged that the church comprises the "twice-born."

Those are saints who have been called by God's gracious Spirit. We may also say that they are the regenerate. According to *The Geneva Confession* (1536), "[W]e acknowledge that by his Spirit we are regenerated into a new spiritual nature . . . the evil desires of our flesh are mortified by grace . . . our will is rendered conformable to God's will . . . we are delivered from the servitude of sin."[11] Calvin rightly emphasizes the role of the Spirit, "For it would be easier for us to create men than for us of our own power to put on a more excellent nature."[12] God's purpose in regeneration is "to restore in us the image of God that had been disfigured

---

9. Whale, *The Protestant Tradition*. 151–52.

10. *The Second Helvetic Confession*, XVII. In Cochrane, *Reformed Confessions*.

11. *The Geneva Confession*, VIII. In Cochrane, *Reformed Confessions*. Cf. *Institutes*, II.v.15.

12. *Institutes*, III.iii.21. Cf. ibid., II.xv.7.

and all but obliterated through Adam's transgression."[13] Regeneration is bestowed upon the ground of Christ's death and resurrection, and by the Spirit's sanctifying work.[14] Hence we cannot parade our "works" or our deserts.[15] A long line of Separatists and Congregationalists echo the general idea, albeit they balk at making baptism the invariable occasion of regeneration, and later writers queried, or flatly denied, the imputation to us of Adam's sin. Thus in the seventeenth century John Owen (1616–83) declared that "*regeneration* is expressly required in the gospel to give a right and privilege unto entrance into the church or kingdom of Christ." While baptism is the symbol of this, the granting of regeneration "cannot consist in any outward rite, easy to be observed by the worst and vilest of men." In fact, "God alone is judge concerning this regeneration, as unto its *internal, real principle and state* in the souls of men. . . . The church is judge of its evidences and fruits in their external demonstration, as unto a participation of *the outward privileges of a regenerate state*, and no farther, Acts viii.13."[16] In our own time H. F. Lovell Cocks (1894–1983) explained that "To be regenerated is to have "the mind of Christ." . . . Nowhere is there any confounding of Christ with the believer, or of the Holy Spirit with the human spirit. We do not become Christs, nor are we absorbed into the divine substance, but we are remade after the pattern of Him who is the image of God. . . . [W]e receive the right to become children of God."[17]

This last sentence leads us to the next way of speaking of the status of saints: they are God's sons and daughters by the adoption of grace. As if to prove my claim that in considering this constellation of doctrines we are not dealing with isolable events in a temporal series, Calvin can say that regeneration confirms "the adoption that [believers] have received as sons."[18] This confirmation of status has more than immediate significance. Calvin reminds his readers that Paul calls the Holy Spirit "both 'the Spirit of adoption' and the 'seal' and 'guarantee' of the inheritance

---

13. Ibid., III.iii.8.
14. Ibid., IV.xv.6.
15. Calvin makes his points crisply in his *Geneva Catechism* (1541), Q&A 126, 330. In Torrance, *The School of Faith*.
16. Owen, *The True Nature of a Gospel Church and its Government* (1689). In his *Works* XVI, 12, 13.
17. Cocks, *By Faith Alone*, 154, 155. Cf. 183.
18. *Institutes*, III.vi.1; Cf. III.ii.11.

to come."[19] Both the immediate and prospective benefits of adoption are encapsulated in chapter XII of the Congregational *Savoy Declaration of Faith and Order* (1658), which at this point reiterates chapter XII of the *Westminster Confession of Faith* (1647):

> All those that are justified, God vouchsafeth in and for his onely Son Jesus Christ to make partakers of the grace of Adoption, by which they are taken into the number, and enjoy the liberties and priviledges of the Children of God, have his Name put upon them, receive the Spirit of Adoption, have access to the Throne of Grace with boldness, are enabled to cry Abba Father, are pitied, protected, provided for, and chastened by him as by a father, yet never cast off, but sealed to the day of Redemption, and inherit the promises as heirs of everlasting Salvation.[20]

Since, as has often been truthfully said, Nonconformists in general learned their doctrine through their hymns (even on occasion through what connoisseurs of fine writing might dismiss as "godly doggerel"), it is not inappropriate to quote the first stanza of one of Joseph Hart's many offerings: it was sung by an estimated 20,000 people in 1768 at his burial in Bunhill Fields, London:

> Sons of God by blest adoption,
>   View the dead with steady eyes:
> What is shown thus in corruption
>   Shall in incorruption rise:
> What is sown in death's dishonour
>   Shall revive to glory's light:
> What is sown in this weak manner
>   Shall be raised in matchless might.[21]

A further way of summing up the saints' status is to say that they are, by grace, united to Christ by faith. There can be little question that the idea of union with Christ pervades the writings of Calvin. Indeed, Thomas Torrance (1913–2007) judged that "It is around this doctrine of *union with Christ* . . . that Calvin builds his doctrine of faith, of the

---

19. Ibid., III.xxiv.1; see Rom 8:15, Eph 1:13–15, 2 Cor 1:22; 5:5.

20. See the *Westminster Larger* Catechism, Q&A 74; Owen, *Works*, II, 186, 207, 211.

21. Hart (1712–68). *Hymns*, 189–90. For an account of the burial service see the "Memoir" prefixed to the *Hymns*, xxiv–xxvi; Wright, *Joseph Hart*, 91–93. I know of no modern hymnal in which these words appear.

Church as the living body of Christ, and his doctrines of the Christian life, Baptism, and the Lord's Supper. Apart from *union with Christ*, Calvin says, all that Christ did for us in His Incarnation, death and resurrection, would be unavailing."[22] Baptism, declares Calvin, testifies that "we are not only grafted into the death and life of Christ, but so united to Christ himself that we become sharers in all his blessings."[23] In particular, to quote the great nineteenth-century Congregationalist, R. W. Dale (1829–95), "When God calls us into the fellowship of His Son Jesus Christ our Lord, He calls us back to those Divine heights which are native to us, and restores us to our original place in the Divine household."[24]

The word "household" with its corporate overtones leads us to the next point. We should be untrue to the Bible and to the Separatist-Congregational tradition if we were to construe election, regeneration, adoption and union with Christ atomistically—as if the concern were simply with me and my soul. On the contrary, Christian faith, though personal, is not private. It is life in fellowship with Christ; but life in fellowship with Christ necessarily entails life in fellowship with all who are his. To put it Johannine terms, those who by grace are grafted as branches into Christ the Vine are *ipso facto* related to all the other branches. This is the consequence of election, regeneration, adoption and union with Christ. In one word, saints are initiated into the covenant. In the words of the Separatist, Robert Browne (1550?–1633?), Christians are those who "by a willing covenant with our God . . . are under the government of God and Christ, and thereby do lead a godly and Christian life."[25] As the *Savoy Declaration of the Institution of Churches, and the Order Appointed in them by Jesus Christ* declares,

> [T]he Lord Jesus calleth out of the World unto Communion with himself, those that are given to him by his Father, that they may walk before him in all the ways of Obedience, which he prescribeth to them in his Word.
>
> Those thus called (through the Ministry of the Word by his Spirit) he commandeth to walk together in particular Societies or Churches, for their mutual edification, and the due performance of that publique Worship, which he requireth of them in this world.

22. Torrance, "Our witness through doctrine," 134. Author's italics.
23. *Institutes*, IV.xv.6.
24. Dale, *Fellowship with Christ*, 11.
25. Browne, *Writings*, 226.

PART TWO: Confessing the Faith Ecclesially and Hopefully

> The Members of these Churches are Saints by Calling, visibly manifesting and evidencing (in and by their profession and walking) their obedience unto that Call of Chris . . . [they] do willingly consent to walk together according to the appointment of Christ, giving up themselves to the Lord, and to one another by the will of God in professed subjection to the Ordinances of the Gospel.[26]

As John Owen, the principal architect of the document, elsewhere explained that a covenant between God and man requires "(1.) That it be of *God's appointment* and institution; (2.) That upon a prescription of duties there be a *solemn engagement* unto their performance on the part of men; (3.) That there be *especial promises of God* annexed thereunto, whereof mutual express restipulation is the form."[27]

It remains only to add that election, regeneration, adoption, union with Christ and membership of the covenant family implies a distinction of eternal significance between those who are in Christ and those who are not. This conviction was of great importance to the Separatists and Congregationalists: their entire polity turned upon it; and from the fact that it is seldom mentioned by their current heirs and successors we should not conclude that it is redundant. To Isaac Watts (1674–1748) it was crucial, and he addressed preachers thus: "Let your hearers know that there is a vast and unspeakable difference betwixt a saint and a sinner, one in Christ, and one out of Christ. . . . [The change results from] the operations of the word and Spirit of God on the hearts of men, and by their diligent attendance on all the appointed means and methods of converting grace. It is a most real change, and of infinite importance."[28] How does the change come about? Watts answers,

---

26. *Savoy Declaration of the Institution of Churches*, II, III, VIII. This document of thirty clauses is appended to the *Savoy Declaration of Faith and Order*. Paragraph VIII was reaffirmed in 1951 when Congregationalists were invited by the Faith and Order Department of the World Council of Churches to acquaint that body with their ecclesiological position. See Anon., *Congregationalism. A Statement*, 18.

27. Owen, *Works*, XVI, 27. Cf. ibid., 29. For an account of Congregational covenants, and other Congregationalist ways of confessing the faith, see Sell, *Dissenting Thought*, ch. 1.

28. Watts, *Works*, III, 18.

> The sovereign will of God alone
>   Creates us heirs of grace,
> Born in the image of his Son,
>   A new, peculiar, race.[29]

What could be more personal—or more corporate? As he looked back across the centuries to his early forebears in the Congregational Way, Dale remarked that "It was for the immense and immeasurable difference between those who are on Christ's side and those who are not that they were contending."[30]

Having now introduced some of the main doctrines on which the Separatist and Congregational polity was founded, I shall proceed to discuss their specifically ecclesiological principles from the point of view of their ecumenical importance.

II

From the Middle Ages there flowed down the idea of the divine right of kings, and the view that Church and state should be in intimate union. In the case of sixteenth-century England, newly Protestant and with Roman Catholic Spain its principal enemy, this led the authorities to conclude that in the interests of national unity there must be a comprehensive Church, and that in order to achieve this religious uniformity was essential and must be required. Compatibly with this it was held that to be a loyal English person was to be a Christian; that in England to be a Christian was to be a member of the Church of England; and that all born in one of that Church's parishes were such members. From the beginning of the English Reformation there were those who felt that the reform had not reached far enough. For them the break from Rome was but the beginning. They sought a pure church reformed according to the Word of God—hence their name, Puritan. Some of these hoped to achieve further reform from within the Church, others from the outset regarded that as an aspiration doomed to disappointment. Accordingly they did not *opt into* the Anglican establishment, and they became known as Separatists. This placed the in the position not of heretics, but of traitors, hence their shadowy underground religious practice.[31] It is

---

29. Watts, *The Psalms and Hymns*, Hymn 148.
30. Dale, *Essays and Addresses*, 194. Cf. his paper, "The Early Independents," I, 45.
31. I do not overlook the fact that the Roman Catholics were, and in England

important that their not opting into the established Church be clearly understood, for it has sometimes been suggested that English Dissent began with the Great Ejectment of 1662. By 24 August 1662, Black Bartholomew's Day in Dissenters' eyes, some 2,000 ministers had left their livings in the Church of England rather than give their "unfeigned assent and consent" to the *Book of Common Prayer,* and undertake to use it only in worship. It was not merely that they objected to some parts of the *Book of Common Prayer*—though they did; their principal objection was that it was not the prerogative of King or Parliament to order the worship of the Church. This act undoubtedly moved Dissent along, but the Separatist harbingers of Dissent of the previous century should not be passed over. As Congregationalism's distinguished historian, Bernard Lord Manning (1892–1941), pointedly remarked, "We of the Three Dissenting Bodies [that is the Congregationalist, Presbyterian and Baptist] never "left the Church." From the moment when, at the Reformation, the mediaeval Church began to split up, there were churchmen who stood in this country for a Church after the Calvinistic pattern, and hoped to make such a Church the Church of England. Of those men we are the descendants."[32]

I shall now specify the ways in which, in the light of the doctrines already mentioned, the Separatists and Congregationalists developed their ecclesiology in the politico-ecclesiastical context in which they found themselves. In the course of doing this their rectifications of Calvin's ecclesiology will become clear.

First, the Separatists and Congregationalists, like Calvin, understood that the Church invisible is prior to the Church visible. "We are not made members of Christ by being joined to the visible Church," wrote Lovell Cocks: "we are joined to the invisible Church, the company of true believers, by being joined to Christ in trust and love, and we unite ourselves to the visible Church because love of the brethren has been put into our hearts and we know we must share in the fellowship of their witness."[33] As to the visible Church, Calvin declares that

> Holy Scripture speaks of the church in two ways. Sometimes by the term "church" it means that which is actually in God's presence, into which no persons are received but those who are children of God by grace of adoption and true members of Christ

---

remain, technically Nonconformists, but in this paper I am concerned with Calvin's heirs only.

32. Manning, *Essays in Orthodox Dissent,* 132.
33. Cocks, *By Faith Alone,* 203–4.

> by sanctification of the Holy Spirit. Then, indeed, the church includes not only the saints presently living on earth, but all the elect from the beginning of the world. Often, however, the name "church" designates the whole multitude of men spread over the earth who profess to worship one God and Christ. . . . In this church are mingled many hypocrites who have nothing of Christ but the name and outward appearance.[34]

To the Separatists and Congregationalists, however, Calvin's first understanding of "Church" was the only one sanctioned by Scripture. They understood well enough that, as we might put it, sociologically, a church congregation might include unbaptized children and adults, hypocrites and visitors but, theologically, these were not the church, though the baptized children of professed members were within the covenant. In *The True Church and the False Church* (1588)—a work by Henry Barrow with possible contributions from John Greenwood (d. 1593)—we read, "The true planted and rightly established church of Christ is a company of faithful people; separated from the unbelievers and heathen of the land; gathered in the name of Christ, whom they truly worship, and readily obey as their only king, priest, and prophet; joined together as members of one body; ordered and governed by such officers and laws as Christ in his last will and testament hath thereunto ordained . . ."[35]

What is to be noticed here is that separation has primarily to do with separation from the "world" *qua* naughty, not *qua* geographical. As perceived by the Separatists, the problem was that the "world" had invaded the Church of England. This was, for example, a significant strand of the Cambridge-educated lawyer Barrow's testimony before the Lord Treasurer on 18 March 1588/9. When asked why he would not attend the parish churches he replied, "Because all the profane and wicked of the land are received into the body of your church."[36] He elsewhere denied that the established Church was a true Church of Christ because, among other things, the wicked and impenitent were permitted to receive the sacrament.[37] He shortly returned to the point in greater detail. The established Church's officers, he thundered, "justifie the most wicked, graceless, impenitent wretches, atheists, blasphemers, idolatours, papists,

---

34. *Institutes*, IV.i.7.
35. *The Writings of John Greenwood, together with the Joint Writings of Henry Barrow and John Greenwood*, 98.
36. *The Writings of Henry Barrow 1587-1590*, 179.
37. Ibid., 308.

PART TWO: Confessing the Faith Ecclesially and Hopefully

Anabaptists, heretickes, conjurers that dye in their sinnes, as though such could have anie benefite by the death of Christ."[38] Barrow levelled the identical charge against Calvin. Although Calvin had affirmed that one of the objectives of Church discipline was to ensure that "the good be not corrupted by the constant company of the wicked, as commonly happens,"[39] Barrow complained that Calvin "mad no scruple to receave al the whole state, even all the profane and ignorant people into the bozome of the church, to administer the sacraments unto them . . ."[40] He further objected to Calvin's restriction of the marks of the Church to right preaching and administration of the sacraments, for thus was omitted "obedience unto and practise of the word"—Church discipline.[41] With these Separatist sentiments the Congregationalist, John Owen, was in entire sympathy: "[I]t is so come to pass, that let men be never so notoriously and flagitiously wicked, until they become pests of the earth, yet they are esteemed to belong to the church of Christ; and not only so, but it is thought little less than schism to forbid them the communion of the church in all its sacred privileges."[42] The Church comprises gathered, disciplined saints. For maintaining these truths, in 1593 the names of Barrow and Greenwood were added to the list of those executed for their faith. In less dangerous times R. W. Dale thought that he was merely stating the obvious when he said that "The members of a Christian Church should be Christians." He added, "[T]his, I say, was the *fons et origo* of the whole Congregational movement."[43] There is a direct line from the Separatists, though Owen and Dale, to Geoffrey Nuttall (1911–2007): "[I]t would be difficult to deny that the Church is called out of the world: called out, it is true, that, back in the world, it may be the means of the world's redemption, but still called out first, to become, and in a sense perpetually to remain, different from the world, different from what the world, in its un-Christian state, can ever be."[44]

38. Barrow, *The Writings of Henry Barrow 1590–1591*, 83.

39. *Institutes*, IV.xii.5.

40. Barrow, *Writings 1587–1590*, 316.

41. Ibid., 295, 306. Discipline was added in the *Scottish Confession of Faith* of 1560, ch. XVIII, for which see Cochrane, *Reformed Confessions*.

42. Owen, *Works*, XVI, 11.

43. Dale, *Essays and Addresses*, 185. By contrast, the *fons et origo* of those comparative youngsters, the Methodists, was not ecclesiological, but evangelistic. From the outset the Separatists and their Congregationalists heirs were saying that the Church was something other than what the Church of England thought it was.

44. Nuttall, *Christian Pacifism in History*, 13.

Rectifying Calvin's Ecclesiology

Secondly, entry to the church is by the voluntary making of a credible profession of faith,[45] evidenced by a "godly walk." Barrow neatly put the two criteria together thus: "Ther may none be admitted into the church of Christ, but such as enter publicke profession of the true faith. None remayne there, but such as bring forth the fruites of faith."[46] Owen likewise ruled that "a man known to live in sin cannot regularly be received into any church."[47] As to profession of faith, not place of birth, as the requirement for reception into the Church, Browne wrote, in words which imply criticism of the Church of England: "the Kingdom of God Was not to be begun by whole parishes, but rather of the worthiest, Were they never so few."[48] "Then you hold that the parish do not make it a church?" the Lord Chief Justices asked John Greenwood on 25 March 1588/9. "No," Greenwood replied, "but the profession which the people

---

45. Classically, the profession of faith was made in person at church meeting, though with the passage of time a written statement from the candidate, or a sponsor, or a report by the minister, would suffice. The member would then be received as a member (i.e., not "made" a member—he or she was already within the covenant) and admitted to the full privileges and responsibilities of membership at the Lord's Supper. Attendance at church meeting would thereafter be expected. This assumed a confession of faith made at years of discretion. The increasing reception of children at the Lord's table on the ground that they are baptized obscures the logic of the classical order, and necessitates further instruction prior to the acceptance of the full responsibilities of membership. This change seems to have been influenced by the increasingly fashionable ecumenically-inspired view that infant baptism marks a person's entry to the Church (with which is frequently associated the untenable view that regeneration and baptism are necessarily contemporary events). Paedobaptism marks the beginning of a person's process of initiation and declares the gospel that when we can do nothing, God does everything: his grace is prevenient. In other words, the baptism of the children of members of the covenant places those children within the covenant as catechumens. The *first* thing to do in the case of the children of those who are not within the covenant is to evangelize their parents, for requests by such parents for baptism present evangelical opportunities which need to be taken. Edward White recalls the occasion on which a respected Congregational minister asked Archbishop A. C. Tait if joint evangelization of the people of England might be contemplated. "No," replied the Archbishop, "for you proceed upon the supposition that the non-church-going people require to be regenerated, man by man, but we proceed upon the belief that they are regenerated in baptism already." See White, "Broad Church Doctrine and Independency", II, 169. The truth would seem to be that all require to be regenerated, that this may or may not happen at baptism, that we cannot accurately specify the moment when it occurs, and, hence, that godly agnosticism is the most appropriate stance to adopt.

46. Barrow, *Writings 1587-1590*, 280.

47. Owen, *Works*, XVI, 11.

48. *The Writings of Robert Harrison and Robert Browne*, 404.

PART TWO: Confessing the Faith Ecclesially and Hopefully

make."[49] Furthermore, as Browne put it, "the Lord's people is of the willing sort."[50] Three hundred years later R. W. Dale put the Separatists' point thus:

> The English nation was not . . . a Church; for a man was not a Christian merely because he was born within the four seas and under the sovereignty of Queen Elizabeth. The population of an English diocese was not a Church. . . . The population of an English parish was not a Church. . . . To baptize the people of a parish did not make them Christians; to preach to them did not make them Christians; to give them access to the Lord's Supper did not make them Christians.[51]

In other words, "The constitution of the Anglican Church declined to recognize the awful contrast between those who are loyal to Christ and those who are in revolt against Him. The English nation constituted the English Church. This was the theory of Whitgift, as it was afterwards the theory of Hooker."[52]

It must be admitted that the Church of England's (and Calvin's) parish ideal poses ecumenical problems to this day. Because of its concern for whole parishes that Church is reluctant to speak of church membership in the sense of enrolled saints. The reality is, however, that in some parishes the majority population comprises those of other faiths, and even where that is not the case it cannot truthfully be said that the majority population of a parish is always baptized and hence deemed regenerate. Again, many Anglican churches are *de facto* gathered churches, drawing their congregations from across parish boundaries, and/or catering for one or other of the several traditions of churchmanship ranging from Forward in Faith to ultra-Protestantism that are to be found within that body. For all that, the gentle observation of a distinguished and gracious Methodist scholar, is indicative of a certain movement on the matter: "The establishment of the Parochial Roll is so far a recognition that the Church is not the nation, nor yet the baptized citizens."[53]

John Owen laid it down that those being received as members of the Church must "*make an open profession of the subjection of their*

49. *The Writings of John Greenwood*, 27.
50. Ibid., 162.
51. Dale, *Essays and Addresses*, 186.
52. Ibid., 181.
53. John T. Wilkinson, *1662 and After*, 198 n. 108.

souls and consciences unto the authority of Christ in the gospel, and their readiness to yield obedience unto all his commands"; they must have a "*competent knowledge*" of the gospel, "especially concerning *the person and offices of Christ*"; they must acknowledge "*the authority of Christ in the church,*" practise self-denial and cross-bearing, confess their sins, constantly perform "*all known duties of religion*", and abstain from sin.[54] Herein resides a challenge of *quasi*-monastic rigour, and at a time such as the present, when "spirituality" is rampant and sometimes amorphous, it is worthwhile recalling the doctrinal roots of the ecclesiology with which we are concerned. Of Congregationalism, Dale's contemporary, J. Guinness Rogers (1822–1911), wrote that its "ideal Church is a body of spiritual men converted by the grace of God, and living by faith in the Lord Jesus Christ. This is something radically different from a society of truth-seekers, resolved to live up to their light and wait in the hope that more light will come. Both societies manage their affairs on the same plan, but no agreement in method can get rid of the essential distinction in principle."[55]

To the Separatists and Congregationalists alike the fellowship of the Church was inescapable. To love Christ was to love the brothers and sisters:

> If we find a person that is orderly admitted into church society, he is as certain and evident an object of our love as if we saw him lying in the arms of Christ. . . . Let none, then pretend that they love the brethren in general, and love the people of God, and love the saints, while their love is not fervently exercised towards those who are in the same church Society with them. Christ hath given it you for a trial; He will try your love at the last day by your deportment in that church wherein you are.[56]

Owen's sentiments were delightfully updated by Bernard Lord Manning in an address to students at Cambridge:

> It is little use your feeling mystical sympathy with St. Francis who is dead, with St. Somebody Else who never existed, with men of good will all over the world whom you are quite safe from meeting. If you do not love your brothers whom you have

---

54. Owen, *Works*, XVI, 14–17.

55. Rogers, *The Church Systems of England*, 644. How seldom do those who, fashionably, make much of our "personal journeys" distinguish between the journey towards faith and the journey of faith.

56. Owen, Sermon XXI, "Gospel Charity," in *Works*, XI, 262.

PART TWO: Confessing the Faith Ecclesially and Hopefully

> seen . . . you cannot, in fact, love those brothers (whom you call the Church) whom you have not seen. Congregationalism makes us not flabby and sentimental about the Church, but tells us to get down to it in practice.[57]

As I have elsewhere put it, Congregationalism's "sainthood is a grounded sainthood."[58] More formally, Manning declared that "We Congregationalists and Baptists have never been able to conceive of a churchless Christianity, a private sect, a Christian experience that is not also an ecclesiastical experience. We have always associated the grace of our Lord Jesus Christ with the communion of saints."[59]

Thirdly, implicit in what has already been said is the conviction that what one is received into on profession of faith is the Church catholic comprising all the saints in heaven and on earth, of which the church local is an outcrop. Moreover, there is but one Lord of the Church and hence one Church. On this point the Separatists and Congregationalists were in entire accord with Calvin: "The church is called 'catholic,' or 'universal,' because there could not be two or three churches unless Christ be torn asunder—which cannot happen!"[60] Henry Allon (1818-92) put it bluntly, "Because we are Congregationalists we are of necessity Catholics. For more than this we do not care to contend."[61] Hence Owen's statement that "However . . . we plead for the rights of particular churches, yet our real controversy with most of the world is for the being, union, and communion of the church catholic; which are variously perverted by many, separating it into parties, and confining it to rules, measures, and

---

57. Manning, *Why Not Abandon the Church?* 37-38. This loving of one another is a sign of our regeneration (1 John 3:14). It also has implications for the size of local churches. John Robinson (c.1575-1625), the pastor to the Pilgrims, wrote, "No particular church under the New Testament, ought to consist of more members than can meet together in one place." See his *Works*, ed. R. Ashton, 1851, III, 13. John Owen thought in terms of pastoral care: "It is the duty of a shepherd to know the state of his flock; and unless he do so he will never feed them profitably." See his *Works*, IV, 511. Interestingly, present-day sociologists suggest that close working relations cannot be achieved where more than 200 people are involved. However that may be, one suspects that were Robinson or Owen *redivivus* to land in a megachurch they would have no difficulty in agreeing that was mega, but might well deny that it was a church. It is not easy to love (in the sense of know and care for) 20-40,000 individuals.

58. Sell, *Saints: Visible, Orderly and Catholic*, 3.

59. Manning, *Essays in Orthodox Dissent*, 99.

60. *Institutes*, IV.1.2.

61. Allon, "The History of Independence," 54.

canons, of their own finding out and establishment."[62] This amounts to a critique of that sectarianism which follows in the wake of the Galatian heresy by adding new circumcisions to the gospel. Whenever a group of Christians says to other Christians, "Unless and until you accept our truth in the way we declare and hold it, and/or bring your church polity and order into line with ours, we shall have no full fellowship with you and may even unchurch you" the sectarian spirit is at work. It was this attitude, for example, which prompted Manning to brand the Church of England "an Episcopalian sect,"[63] and this notwithstanding the fact that, officially, that Church teaches only that bishops are the *bene esse* of the Church, not its *esse*. Happily, since Manning wrote a good deal of water has flowed under the ecumenical bridge, yet still the full implementation of a recommendation in the international Anglican-Reformed dialogue report is awaited: "We recommend that where churches of our two communions are committed to going forward to seek visible unity, a measure of *reciprocal* communion should be made possible; for communion is not only a sign of unity achieved, but also a means by which God brings it about."[64] Despite this, there are still Anglicans who would not accept the Lord's invitation to communion in a Reformed church, and some who would deny that such churches have true sacraments at all.[65] This is a profound denial of catholicity. I do not believe that such persons affirm that the saints of my tradition are not called by grace, not regenerated, not adopted as God's sons and daughters, not united with Christ by the Spirit, not members of the covenant—in which case they ought to be at the Lord's table with us. What prevents them? It can only be that sectarian denominational small print is elevated above the gospel of God's grace. This is tragic.

Fourthly, it cannot be denied that while Calvin sought to preserve the distinction between Church and state, in practice the lines became blurred when the magistrates became involved in the enforcement of doctrine deemed pure, the election of ministers and elders, and the maintenance of good order. Thus "the magistrate ought by punishment and physical restraint to cleanse the church of offenses," and to "defend sound

---

62. Owen, *Works*, XVI, 186. Cf. ibid., XIII, 175 ff.
63. Manning, *Essays in Orthodox Dissent*, 136.
64. Anon., *God's Reign and Our Unity*, 82. Italics in the original.
65. See Sell, *Aspects of Christian Integrity*, ch. 4.

doctrine."[66] It was the magistrates who prevented Calvin from having the Lord's Supper as frequently as he would have wished.[67] The Separatists and Congregationalists would have none of this. Well aware of their obligations as citizens, frequently protesting their loyalty to the monarch, they nevertheless maintained that in spiritual matters the state was not above the Church. With reference to the Act of Uniformity of 1559, Henry Barrow was appalled that "All this people . . . were in one daye, with the blast of Queen Elizabeth's trumpet, of ignorant papists and grosse idolaters, made faithfull Christianes and true professors."[68] He grants that rulers may, by godly government, assist the church, comfort the faithful and advance the gospel,[69] but "no prince or mortal man can make any a member of the church."[70] As Dale later explained, "the complaint of the Congregationalists was not that the queen had trampled on the personal rights and violated the freedom of the English people, but that she had usurped the authority of Christ."[71] In Owen's day the issue was the legal imposition of the *Book of Common Prayer* with penalties specified for refusal to comply with its sole use. "Religious worship," declared Owen, "not divinely instituted and appointed is false worship, not accepted with God."[72] Throughout, the convictions were that Christ alone is head of the Church and hence the monarch cannot be the Church's temporal head; and that the Church is catholic, not national.[73]

It was left to P. T. Forsyth to make a further important point: "There is nothing in history that the State could not amend or annul in the great interest of the nation; but that is not so with the Church. No consideration of utility could justify the abolition of the historic gospel."[74] If one last observation may be made, it is this: it behoves the saints always to remember

---

66. *Institutes*, IV.xi.3; IV.xx.2.

67. On frequency see *Institutes*, IV.xvii.44.

68. *The Writings of Henry Barrow 1587–1590*, 283.

69. It must be granted that there were shades of opinion among the Separatists. Browne posited a judicial rule of the magistrates over the church, Barrow did not.

70. *The Writings of Henry Barrow 1587–1590*, 288.

71. Dale, *Essays and Addresses*, 217.

72. Owen, *Works*, XVI, 249.

73. A number of Congregationalists observed that at the Reformation the Church of England had isolated itself not only from the Dissenters but also from the Reformed churches of continental Europe. See, for example, J. Guinness Rogers, "Clericalism and Congregationalism," 217.

74. Forsyth, *Faith, Freedom and the Future*, 227.

that they are sinners. It must be admitted that those Congregationalists who sought religious freedom in the New World were not always so eager to accord it to others. Hence the banishment of Roger Williams to Rhode Island on his adoption of Baptist views; hence also the execution 1659 the Quakers, William Robinson and Marmaduke Stevenson, who had been banished from Massachusetts but had been sufficiently ill-advised to return. Assuredly the rule of the saints can be a terrible thing, and a theocracy can become a mirror image of those totalitarian states that do not have the excuse that they are acting as God's agents. The remedy is proper Church-state relations, always with the proviso which flows down to the United Reformed Church[75] from its Separatist and Congregational forebears:

> The United Reformed Church declares that the Lord Jesus Christ, the only king and head of the Church, has therein appointed a government distinct from civil government and *in things spiritual not subordinate thereto*, and that civil authorities, being always subject to the rule of God, ought to respect the rights of conscience and of religious belief and to serve God's will of justice and peace for all men.[76]

Fifthly, the most significant rectification of Calvin's ecclesiology made by the Separatists and Congregationalists was the institution of the church meeting, or to make the point clearer, the *church* meeting. Calvin was more than ready to acknowledge the importance of the idea of the priesthood of all believers, and he did allow that ministers should be called to pastorates "by the consent and approval of the people";[77] but the participation of the professed membership as a whole was not a regulative principle of his Church order which, from the point of view of

---

75. This Church resulted from the union in 1972 of the Presbyterian Church of England with the majority of the Congregational Church in England and Wales. In 1981 the Re-formed Association of Churches of Christ joined the union, as did the majority of the Scottish Congregationalists in 2000.

76. "A statement concerning the Nature, Faith and Order of the United Reformed Church." In Thompson, *Stating the Gospel*, 263. My italics. Cf. the "Principles of church order and discipline" adopted by the Congregational Union of England and Wales in May 1833: "the power of a Christian church is purely spiritual and should in no way be corrupted by union with temporal or civil power." This document was printed in full in *The Congregational Year Book* from 1846 to 1917. See further on historic Dissent vis à vis the Church of England, Sell. *Dissenting Thought*, ch. 22; Sell, *Testimony and Tradition*, ch. 11; *The Great Ejectment*, ch. 4.

77. *Institutes*, IV.iii.15.

PART TWO: Confessing the Faith Ecclesially and Hopefully

Congregationalism, was left hanging with elders and deacons. In his defence it might be suggested that with Anabaptists, some of them unduly excitable, and sundry other enthusiasts milling around, and all claiming inspiration by the Spirit, the possibility, never mind the rightness, of according a place in Church government to all the Church members was one of the things which, in his context, he did not "see." Frequently misunderstood by others, Congregationalists have not always been the best exponents of their polity. The scholarly R. F. Horton (1855–1934), who ministered at the fashionable Lyndhurst Road Congregational Church, Hampstead, London, from 1880 to 1930 lamented of his saints that "They do not know what a Church Meeting is. In fifty years I have failed to teach them."[78] At their best Congregationalists and their united heirs understand Church Meeting as closely related—indeed, as an extension of, public worship; for it is a credal assembly in which, under the guidance of the Holy Spirit, the mind of Christ is sought regarding the worship, service and mission of the church.[79] It is not a business meeting as such; it is not a democratic assembly of the "one-person-one-vote" variety where the objective is majority rule. After all, "*The democracy will recognise no authority but what it creates, the Church none but what creates it.*"[80] Rather, the objective is unanimity in Christ, and this is achieved analogously with the Quaker "sense of the meeting," rather than by voting. Moreover, the Church Meeting is chaired by the minister (not, for example, by someone with a lot of experience of business meetings) on the ground that the one called to lead the church to the throne of grace, and preach the Word, is the one to lead the church in reflecting upon the question, How are we to commend the gospel we have received? It is a prominent example of the Congregationalists' desire to honour "the crown rights of the Redeemer" in his Church.

To Henry Barrow, "It is manifest, that all the members of the church have a like interest in Christ, in his word, in the faith; that they altogether make one bodie unto him; that all the affairs of the church belong to that bodie together."[81] Later, having referred to formally called Church officers, he explains that "I never thought that the practise of Christ's government belonged only to these officers; I rather thought it had been

---

78. Peel and Marriott, *Robert Forman Horton*, 186.
79. Cf. Micklem, *Congregationalism and the Church Catholic*, 30.
80. Forsyth, *Faith, Freedom and the Future*, 192. Cf. ibid., 209.
81. *The Writings of Henry Barrow 1587–1590*, 319.

their duty and office to have seen this government faithfully and orderly practised by all the members of the church."[82] John Robinson went so far as to say,

> So far are the officers from being the formal cause of the church ... they are, in truth, no absolutely necessary appurtenance unto it.... And the reason is, because the church is essentially in the saints, as the matter, subject, formed by the covenant, unto which the officers are but adjuncts, not making for the being, but for the well-being of the church.... The Lord Jesus is the king of his church alone.... [He] doth communicate [his power] with his church, as the husband with the wife.... And in this holy fellowship, by virtue of this plenteous anointment, every one is made a king, priest, and prophet.... There is not the meanest member of the body but hath received his drop or dram of this anointing.[83]

To Dale, "The Church—the whole Church—is responsible for the persons who are received into membership and retained in membership; for the order of worship; for the substance, at least, of the teaching which is given to the Church itself, and which is given in the name of the Church to people outside."[84] To this I would add that the whole church is responsible also for those who are baptized in its midst; they are charged with surrounding the baptized individual and his or her family with Christian love and care. Again, it is the whole church that celebrates the sacrament of the Lord's Supper; it is not each member individualistically "making *my* communion," still less is it the saints having religion "done to" them by a priestly caste.

No doubt not every church meeting attains the heights, but many of them do. Probably most of them fall between the commendation of the meeting I once overheard a member give to an enquirer: "You come along to church meeting: it's where we can all stick our oar in!" (clearly thinking in terms of "an aggregate of 'saved' individuals" rather than of a living fellowship[85] or of the priesthood of all the believers *together*), and Dale's panegyric which used to be recited in church membership classes:

---

82. Ibid., 608–9.
83. Robinson, *Works*, II, 110 and extracts to 141.
84. Dale, *Essays and Addresses*, 203.
85. Lovell Cocks, "The Gospel and the Church," 37.

PART TWO: Confessing the Faith Ecclesially and Hopefully

> [T]o be at a church meeting—apart from any prayer that is offered—any hymn that is sung, any words that are spoken, is for me one of the chief means of grace. To know that I am surrounded by men and women who dwell in God, who have received the Holy Ghost, with whom I am to share the eternal righteousness, and eternal rapture of the great life to come, this is blessedness. I breathe a Divine air. I am in the new Jerusalem which has come down out of Heaven from God, and the nations of the saved are walking its streets of gold. I rejoice in the joy of Christ over those whom He has delivered from eternal death and lifted into the light and glory of God. The Kingdom of God is there.[86]

In the light of what has now been said, it may be clear why I was disappointed by the chapter on "Ministry" in the convergence document, *Baptism, Eucharist and Ministry*. The chapter begins well, with a section on the ministry of the whole people of God, and proceeds to say that "The word *ministry* in its broadest sense denotes the service to which the whole people of God is called . . ."[87] But then it almost immediately lapses into a discussion of the ordained ministry. There is no reflection upon how the ministry of the whole people of God might be given its due place in church polity.[88] No doubt this would have been an almost impossible task given that many churches, even if they adhere to the foundational doctrines of election, regeneration, adoption, union with Christ and covenant, do not draw out their ecclesiological implications. That is to say, they have no concept of saints enrolled on profession of faith. Far from simply rectifying one aspect of Calvin's ecclesiology, church meeting challenges all church orders as to the matter of the Church and the most appropriate way of honouring an important complex of Christian doctrines. With reference to the gathered company of believers J. Guinness Rogers wrote, "The power it possesses no prince or prelate can confer, and none can take away. It is a power which does not accrue from some natural right belonging to its members separately, or in their corporate capacity, but comes directly from the presence of Christ Himself in accordance with His own promise. Christ is wherever His saints meet in

---

86. Dale, "The evangelizing power of a spiritual fellowship," 136.
87. Anon., *Baptism, Eucharist and Ministry*, 21.
88. See further Sell, "Some Reformed Responses to *Baptism, Eucharist and Ministry*."

His name, and the presence of Christ makes the Church, and gives its decision validity and force."[89]

Lastly, charges of "granular independency" and isolationism notwithstanding (and there is no smoke without fire), the Separatist-Congregational tradition is well able to accommodate Church fellowship wider than that of the local church. It would be distinctly odd if this were not the case, given the acknowledgement that the one Church is found in many locations. Robert Browne endorsed the idea that "A Synod is a Joining or partaking of the authority of many Churches met together in peace, for redress, and deciding of matters, which cannot well be otherwise taken up."[90] Throughout the history, however, there was sounded the caution that the deliverances of wider churchly bodies should have moral, not legal authority only. We are not here in the realm of an hierarchy of church courts. The reasoning was that there could be no higher authority than that of the guidance of the Holy Spirit addressed to the gathered saints. Hence, "Besides these particular Churches, there is not instituted by Christ any Church more extensive or Catholique entrusted with power for the administration of his ordinances, or the execution of any authority in his name."[91] Nevertheless, advisory synods or councils were envisaged with the proviso that they "are not entrusted with any Church-Power properly so called, or with any Jurisdiction over the Churches themselves, to exercise any Censures, either over any Churches or Persons, or to impose their determinations on the Churches or Officers. . . . [N]or are there any Synods appointed by Christ in a way of Subordination to one another."[92]

With the passage of time the "particular churches" found themselves cooperating with one another in ever more ways: for example, in county mission societies, then in overseas mission, until at last in the nineteenth century, the age of the creation of denominations as we have come to know them, the Congregational Union of England and Wales was constituted in 1832. Some felt nervous at this departure, so the traditional refrain was reiterated in the Constitution: "[T]he Union shall not, in any case, assume legislative authority, or become a court of appeal."[93] In the

---

89. J. G. Rogers, "Clericalism and Congregationalism," 235.
90. *The Writings of Robert Harrison and Robert Browne*, 271.
91. *Savoy Declaration of the Institution of Churches*, VI.
92. Ibid., XXVI, XXVII. Cf. Owen, *Works*, XVI, 183–208.
93. *The Congregational Year Book*, 1846, xii.

PART TWO: Confessing the Faith Ecclesially and Hopefully

twentieth century the question arose whether the Union should transform itself into a Church. Among the reasons given for this were that the ever-increasing co-operation among the churches, and the mutual support offered by local churches to other churches through the Union's maintenance of the ministry scheme, for example; and the fact that the guidance of the Holy Spirit was sought in assemblies no less than in local church meetings—all of this, it was said, argued for the rightness, and not simply the usefulness, of the wider churchly body. This view was opposed by those who argued that the Bible knew of no "church" between the local church and the catholic Church; that wider churchly bodies ought to have no authority over local churches; and that to become a "Church" might harden the denomination into a bloc, thereby threatening the understanding of catholicity. The biblical point was granted, and the fears of many, though not all, were assuaged when it was made clear that an hierarchy of Church courts was not envisaged, and that mutuality of *episcope* would be practised as between the several *foci* of churchly life.[94] The crucial question, "Which body has the final authority—the Assembly or the local Church Meeting?" was answered thus:

> Neither. The final authority is in Christ. The local Church has the responsibility of seeking to learn the will of Christ on matters relevant to its own life, and the Assembly has the responsibility of seeking to learn the will of Christ for the whole fellowship of churches. Each in matters belonging to its proper sphere rightly claims the authority of Christ for decisions sincerely made in obedience to Him. Each should be prepared to learn from the other, and may have to admit that it as mistaken. Church Meetings, County Executives, and national Church Assemblies are all liable to err, and have erred.[95]

As for the suspected threat to catholicity, it was agreed that to use the term "Church" of the denomination was a temporary, irregular expedient, given the present divided state of the visible Church.

The decision to change from "Union" to "Church" was taken on 19 May 1965, and a Service of Thanksgiving and Dedication was held in London on 22 May 1966.[96] Six years later, some forty years after talks had

---

94. The tradition much prefers to think in terms of "farther and nearer" than of "higher and lower."

95. *Oversight and Covenant*, Q&A 6.

96. For a full and partly autobiographical account of this episode see Sell, *Testimony and Tradition*, ch. 12. See also Sell, *Saints: Visible, Orderly and Catholic*, 112–15.

begun between them, the Presbyterian Church of England united with the Congregational Church in England and Wales to form The United Reformed Church.

III

Since, humanly speaking, Church order is in the hands of saints who are also sinners, it is not surprising that every known polity is susceptible to error. If their can be argumentative Congregational church meetings, there can also be wayward episcopal bishops and recalcitrant Presbyterian assemblies. It cannot be denied that some in the Separatist-Congregational tradition have so construed autonomy as to transform the local church into their personal fiefdom; or that church discipline has on occasion degenerated into petty point-scoring by the insufferably pious. But, perhaps remarkably, for the most part it has not been so.

It is also the case that every Church order faces particular challenges. In traditional Congregationalism, for example, attendance at the Lord's Supper followed an individual's profession of faith. Moreover in the service of reception of members the duties of membership were specified in some detail, including that of faithful attendance at Church Meeting. Thus in a 1959 service for "The reception of members on profession of faith" the candidate is, *inter alia*, asked, "Do you resolve to fulfil the duties of membership in the Church, joining regularly in public worship, in the Communion of the Lord's Supper, and in the Church Meeting . . . ?"[97] By 1980, in the United Reformed Church's *Book of Services*, the question is more general, the importance of church meeting in the united Church notwithstanding: "Do you promise, in dependence on God's grace, to be faithful in private and public worship, to live in the fellowship of the Church and to share in its work . . . ?"[98] But in many churches today, as indicated earlier, children participate in the Lord's Supper at an early age, yet we do not, for example, expect five-year-olds to share in the discussions concerning the calling of ministers. This suggests the need of a reaffirmation of faith when a person accepts the full responsibilities of membership. Yet again, it was frequently the case that the Lord's Supper was held as a separate service following the ministry of the Word. This bore witness to the fact that the sacrament is the sacrament

---

97. *A Book of Services and Prayers*, 53.
98. *A Book of Services*, 58.

of the Church, and that those who receive it are professed believers (a class wider than enrolled Congregational saints). But the liturgical movement of the twentieth century has taught many that Word and Sacrament belong together—as, indeed, Calvin believed—and thus an integrated service is nowadays the norm. This sharpens, perhaps a little uncomfortably, the distinction between the Church, which takes communion, and other members of the congregation who are present, but do not partake. A witness is nevertheless made, and those who regularly attend but are not enrolled ought to receive pastoral care and, if they wish it, instruction with a view to making their profession of faith.

Sufficient has been said to indicate the some of the challenges faced by the Separatist-Congregational ecclesiology. The fact remains, however, that, properly conceived the Separatist-Congregational tradition was able to rectify Calvin's Church order at certain important points. Influenced both by the Bible and by the political circumstances in which they were set the Separatist-Congregationalists pursued the logic of the doctrines of election, regeneration, adoption, union with Christ, and covenant further into ecclesiology than did Calvin. They brought the eternal distinction between those who are in Christ and those who are not into the day-to-day ordering of the Church. They fastened upon the matter of the Church: the baptized, professed saints, believing that the Church comprises Christians, and that one cannot be a Christian "in general," for union by grace with Christ entails union with all who are his. Furthermore, all who are Christ's are to be loved for his sake—hence their opposition to any brand of sectarianism that would divide those whom God has made one in Christ, and their staunch commitment to, and leadership within, the modern ecumenical movement.[99] They committed the ordering of the church's life to *all* the saints gathered in church meeting where, under the guidance of the Holy Spirit, they sought the mind of Christ in relation to their church life, witness and service; and (albeit with certain fluctuations at particular times) they sought to honour the claims of the state whilst keeping it more at arms length that Calvin was able to do where the worship and governance of the Church were concerned, and insisting that the Church's catholicity was not to be compromised by national borders. In a word, they held that "The Church's *one* foundation

---

99. The names of A. E. Garvie (1861–1945), Norman Goodall (1896–1985), Leslie E. Cooke (1908–67), and W. John F. Huxtable (1912–90) spring at once to mind. I believe it remains the case that that Congregationalists have entered into more transdenominational united churches than any other confessional family.

is Jesus Christ her Lord." What they have never been able to understand is how some Christian bodies can, with such apparent ease, refuse to enjoy full communion with all whom the Holy Spirit has made saints by calling. Their catholicity challenges such sectarianism whether it arises from sacerdotalism on the one hand or conservative biblicism on the other, and they manifest it whenever, in the Lord's name, they welcome all who are his to his table.[100] As C. J. Cadoux (1883–1947) wrote some eighty years ago, "the key problem of reunion is, primarily, not agreement regarding ministerial orders or essential doctrines, but the mutual recognition of Christians by Christians as being really fellow-members of that One Church to which they severally claim to belong."[101]

In seeking thus to honour Christ as the only Lord of the Church those of the Separatist-Congregational Way developed what can only be described as a doctrine of the Church than which there is no higher. In the Victorian era they were not slow to employ the adjective in a cheekily polemical manner against those Anglo-Catholics who thought that they were high Church. The fact remains, however, that as P. T. Forsyth roundly declared, "Congregationalism . . . is High Church or nothing."[102] "On the one hand," wrote Bernard Lord Manning, "Congregationalists have outdone all other Christians in the emphasis that they have laid on the visible church and on the supreme importance of continuous personal exercise in it by every individual. On the other hand Congregationalists have clearly understood, frankly confessed, and effectually lived by the truth that this all-important visible church is a divine spiritual society, that it depends wholly on grace, not at all on law."[103] In both respects they rectified Calvin's ecclesiology—and all on the ground of the Father's electing, regenerating, adopting, uniting, covenantal grace, the Son's living presence in the midst of the saints, and the witness and guidance of God the Holy Spirit.

---

100. See further Sell, *Enlightenment, Ecumenism, Evangel*, ch. 11; and ch. 11 below.

101. Cadoux, "The true Catholicism," 58.

102. Forsyth, *Faith, Freedom and the Future*, 215.

103. Manning, *Essays in Orthodox Dissent*, 164. In this chapter are stated, all too briefly, the catholic principles that I have been privileged to introduce into ecumenical discussion from the local to the international over the past half century.

PART TWO: Confessing the Faith Ecclesially and Hopefully

BIBLIOGRAPHY

Allon, Henry. "The History of Independence." *The Congregational Year Book 1882*, 52–81. London: Jackson and Walford, 1882.

Anon. *A Book of Services and Prayers*. London: Independent, 1959.

———. *A Book of Services*. Edinburgh: Saint Andrew, 1980.

———. *Congregationalism. A Statement by Representatives of the Congregational Union of England and Wales to the Faith and Order Department of the World Council of Churches*. Geneva: World Council of Churches, 1951.

———. *Constitution* of The Congregational Union of England and Wales, prefixed to *The Congregational Year Book*, 1846.

———. *God's Reign and Our Unity. The Report of the Anglican-Reformed International Commission, 1981–1984*. London: SPCK/ Edinburgh: Saint Andrew, 1984.

———. *Oversight and Covenant. Interim Report of Commission no. I. Some Question and Answers*. London: Congregational Union of England and Wales, n.d. (but early 1960s).

———. *Principles of Church Order and Discipline*. London: Congregational Union of England and Wales, 1833.

———. *The Subordinate Standards and Other Authoritative Documents of the Free Church of Scotland*. Edinburgh: Free Church of Scotland, 1933.

Barrow, Henry. *The Writings of Henry Barrow 1587–1590*. Edited by Leland H. Carlson. London: Allen & Unwin, 1962.

———. *The Writings of Henry Barrow 1590–1591*. Edited by Leland H. Carlson. London: Allen & Unwin, 1966.

Browne, Robert. *The Writings of Robert Harrison and Robert Browne*. Edited by Albert Peel and Leland H. Carlson. London: Allen & Unwin, 1953.

Cadoux, C. J. "The True Catholicism." In *Essays Congregational and Catholic Issued in Commemoration of the Centenary of the Congregational Union of England and Wales*, edited by Albert Peel, 53–77. London: Congregational Union of England and Wales, 1931.

Calvin, John. *Institutes*. Translated by Ford Lewis Battles and edited by John T. McNeil. Philadelphia: Westminster, 1961.

Cochrane, Arthur C. *Reformed Confessions of the 16th Century*. Philadelphia: Westminster, 1966.

Cocks, H. F. Lovell. *By Faith Alone*. London: Clarke, 1943.

———. "The Gospel and the Church." In *Congregationalism Today*, edited by John Marsh, 30–44. London: Independent, 1943.

Conder, E. R. "Independents in the Days of the Commonwealth." In *Jubilee Lectures: A Historical Series Delivered on the Occasion of the Jubilee of the Congregational Union of England and Wales*, I, 173–219. 2 vols in one. London: Hodder & Stoughton, 1882.

Dale, R. W. "The Early Independents." In *Jubilee Lectures: A Historical Series Delivered on the Occasion of the Jubilee of the Congregational Union of England and Wales*, I, 1–56. 2 vols in one. London: Hodder and Stoughton, 1882.

———. *Essays and Addresses*. London: Hodder & Stoughton, 1899.

———. "The Evangelising Power of a Spiritual Fellowship." In *Constructive Congregational Ideals*, edited by Dugald Macfadyen, 129–44. London: Allenson, 1902.

———. *Fellowship with Christ and Other Discourses*. London: Hodder & Stoughton, 1900.
Forsyth, P. T. *Faith, Freedom and the Future*. 1912. Reprint. London: Independent, 1955.
Greenwood, John. *The Writings of John Greenwood, together with the Joint Writings of Henry Barrow and John Greenwood*. Edited by Leland H. Carlson. London: Allen & Unwin, 1962.
Harrison, Robert. *The Writings of Robert Harrison and Robert Browne*. Edited by Albert Peel and Leland H. Carlson. London: Allen & Unwin, 1953.
Hart, Joseph. *Hymns Composed on Various Subjects*. Cranbrook, Kent: Dennett, 1871.
Leith, John H. *Introduction to the Reformed Tradition*. Atlanta: John Knox, 1981.
Mackennal, Alexander. *Sketches in the Evolution of English Congregationalism*. London: Nisbet, 1901.
Manning, Bernard Lord. *Essays in Orthodox Dissent*. 1939. Reprint. London: Independent, 1953.
———. *Why Not Abandon the Church?* 1939. Reprint. London: Independent, 1958.
Matthews, A. G. *The Savoy Declaration of Faith and Order*. 1658. London: Independent, 1959.
Micklem, Nathaniel. *Congregationalism and the Church Catholic*. London: Independent, 1943.
Nuttall, Geoffrey F. *Christian Pacifism in History*. Oxford: Blackwell, 1958.
Owen, John. *Works (1850-53)*. Edited by William H. Goold. London: Banner of Truth, 1968.
Peel, Albert, and J. A. R. Marriott. *Robert Forman Horton*. London: Allen & Unwin, 1937.
Robinson, John. *Works*. Edited by R. Ashton. 3 vols. London: n.p., 1851.
Rogers, J. Guinness. *The Church Systems of England in the Nineteenth Century*. London: Hodder & Stoughton, 1881.
———. "Clericalism and Congregationalism." In *Jubilee Lectures: A Historical Series Delivered on the Occasion of the Jubilee of the Congregational Union of England and Wales*, II, 175–241. 2 vols in one. London: Hodder & Stoughton, 1882.
Sell, Alan P. F. *Aspects of Christian Integrity*. 1990. Reprint. Eugene, OR: Wipf & Stock, 1998.
———. *Dissenting Thought and the Life of the Churches: Studies in an English Tradition*. Lewiston, NY: Mellen, 1990.
———. *Enlightenment, Ecumenism, Evangel: Theological Themes and Thinkers 1550-2000*. Milton Keynes, UK: Paternoster, 2005.
———. *The Great Ejectment: Its Antecedents, Aftermath, and Ecumenical Significance*. Eugene, OR: Wipf & Stock, 2012.
———. *Saints: Visible, Orderly and Catholic: The Congregational Idea of the Church*. Allison Park, PA: Pickwick, 1986.
———. "Some Reformed Responses to *Baptism, Eucharist and Ministry*." *Reformed World* 39 (1986) 549–65.
———. *Testimony and Tradition: Studies in Reformed and Dissenting Thought*. Aldershot, UK: Ashgate, 2005.
Thompson, David M. *Stating the Gospel: Formulations and Declarations of Faith from the Heritage of The United Reformed Church*. Edinburgh: T. & T. Clark, 1990.

PART TWO: Confessing the Faith Ecclesially and Hopefully

Torrance, Thomas F. "Our Witness through Doctrine." In *Proceedings of the 17th General Council of the Alliance of the Reformed Churches throughout the World holding the Presbyterian Order*, 133-45. Geneva: Office of the Alliance, 1954.

———. *The School of Faith: The Catechisms of the Reformed Church*. London: Clarke, 1959.

Watts, Isaac. *The Psalms and Hymns of the Rev. Isaac Watts, D.D.* London: Caxton, 1718.

———. *Works*. 6 vols. London: Barfield, 1810.

Whale, John S. *The Protestant Tradition: An Essay in Interpretation*. Cambridge: Cambridge University Press, 1960.

White, Edward. "Broad Church Doctrine and Independency." In *Jubilee Lectures: A Historical Series Delivered on the Occasion of the Jubilee of the Congregational Union of England and Wales*, II, 137-74. 2 vols in one. London: Hodder & Stoughton, 1882.

Wilkinson, John T. *1662 and After: Three Centuries of English Nonconformity*. London: Epworth, 1962.

Wright, Thomas. *Joseph Hart*. London: Farncombe, 1910.

CHAPTER NINE

Receiving from Other Christian Communions and Overcoming the Hindrances Thereto

Some Reformed Reflections

As RECENTLY AS 1983 Thomas Ryan could characterize the term "reception" as the ecumenical movement's new "holy word."[1] Since that time the term has been publicized in publications, discussed in dialogues, and touted as a technical term. Thus, for example, Emmanuel Sullivan advises us that "there is a classical view of reception, viz., the acceptance of a doctrinal statement or a conciliar decision by either the local or universal church, and an ecumenical usage that takes into account the historic division of the churches in their commitment to the ecumenical movement..."[2]

Without wishing to deny this, I should like to point out that what might be called the ordinary language view of reception should not be overlooked. It is stating the obvious to say that all Christians receive things from other Christian traditions long before they study conciliar decisions or partake in ecumenical activities designed to surmount "the historic divisions of the churches," and even if they never do either of these things. Moreover, what is received in this ordinary way can become

---

1. Ryan, "Reception: Unpacking the New Holy Word."
2. Sullivan, "Reception: Factor and Moment in Ecumenism," 105.

variously a spur or an hindrance to reception in the more technical senses of the term. It is also clear that the manner, nature and extent of what is received will vary from time to time and from place to place. That is to say, what is available to be received will be conditioned by historical, psychological, and socio-political factors as well as theological ones. As examples of historical factors I might mention that in the area of England in which I was raised you would have looked in vain for an Orthodox church; and I did not meet a Mennonite until I was in my forties. Psychology enters especially when churches have originated in secessions or, as in the case of my own tradition, that of English Dissent, have refused to opt into ecclesiastical-*cum*-governmental arrangements. This leads to the definition of oneself over against the other, and also sometimes to a loss of confidence when, after perhaps a few centuries, the other rather suddenly becomes friendly. It can also lead to charges of treachery within one's own fold. On more than one occasion during the early years of my ministry I heard the complaint, "I think he *read* some of his prayers." This practice was deemed inappropriate because the reading of prayers was what the Church of England required of its clergy, and we thanked God that we were not like them. (The remedy, of course, was to learn to pray *ex tempore* in collect form.) As to socio-political factors, these also may be illustrated from the English context, by reference to the dawn of the English Reformation, and the experience of the early Separatists and those later Dissenters who, in the interests of upholding the "crown rights of the Redeemer in his Church" remained outside of, or subsequently departed from, the Church of England "by law established." While the Toleration Act of 1689 sanctioned the worship of orthodox Protestant Dissenters, the latter were still barred from the universities, from holding civic office, and the like; and so we have the entrenchment of the Church-chapel divide, manifestations of which can still be seen to this day. All through the eighteenth century sporadic attempts, some of them involving the burning of meeting houses, were made to turn back the clock of toleration.

Adverse socio-political factors notwithstanding, many Dissenters assumed the role of proto-ecumenists, and of these one of the greatest was Richard Baxter.[3] He abominated the sectarian spirit, thought "Presbyterian" an "odious Name,"[4] and declared that "I am a Christian, a meer

---

3. See Sell, *Commemorations*, ch. 2.
4. Baxter, *Reliquiae Baxterianae*, II, 373; cf. I, 55–56.

Christian. . . . If the name Christian be not enough, call me a Catholick Christian."[5] In explanation of this I quote his *Key for Catholicks*: "We still profess before men and angels that we own no religion but the Christian religion, nor any church but the Christian church, not dream of any Catholic Church but one, containing all the true Christians in the world, united in Jesus Christ as the head."[6] It was his decided opinion that "The contentions between the Greek Church and the Roman, the Papists and the Protestants, the Lutherans and the Calvinists, have woefully hindered the kingdom of Christ."[7]

I need only add that among early advocates of the toleration of Roman Catholics in England was the Unitarian Joseph Priestley,[8] whose own tradition was not legalized until 1813; and that Catholic Emancipation was largely secured in 1829, remaining anomalies being removed as recently as 1926.

No doubt it takes much more than enacted legislation to heal inner-Christian divisions, and in many places old animosities linger. One of my best friends at school was turned out of the house and cursed at the altar by his ardent Roman Catholic mother because he went to the cinema with a Protestant girl. He came to live with us for a number of days, until my father sallied forth to negotiate with the relevant priest, as a consequence of which my friend was restored to his family. From the Protestant side ill-informed anti-Roman tracts continue to be produced, and I know where there is a Christian bookshop in which one shelf is labelled, "Apologetics: Roman Catholicism and other False Religions." Of this kind of thing the Congregational historian, Bernard Lord Manning, wrote, "I yield to no one in my dislike of, and contempt for, a certain type of so-called Protestant propaganda. It is so stupid, so ignorant, so uncharitable, so unfair; its misrepresentations do Rome so much good that it is hard to think it is not financed directly by the Vatican."[9] More seriously, a reconciliation of memories as between the Church of England and the heirs of Old Dissent is still awaited, and I suspect that the delay is not unrelated, at least in part, to historical amnesia on all sides.[10]

---

5. Baxter, *Church-History of the Government of* Bishops, Preface, fol. b1.
6. Baxter, *Key for Catholicks*, 1659, Preface, 6.
7. Baxter, *Reliquiae Baxterianae*, II, 278.
8. See Priestley, *The Conduct to be observed by Dissenters*, 402–4.
9. Manning, *Essays in Orthodox Dissent*, 129.
10. As noted earlier in this collection, a *Service of Reconciliation, Healing of Memories, and Mutual Commitment for the Church of England and The United Reformed Church* was held in Westminster Abbey on 7 February 2012.

PART TWO: Confessing the Faith Ecclesially and Hopefully

I trust it has become clear from this extended illustration, that answers to questions of reception in the technical senses of the term cannot satisfactorily be provided unless due account is taken of what has already been received in the ordinary language sense at the grass roots. When one further considers that every region of the world has its own catalogue of impressions received, for good and ill, from a variety of Christian traditions, realism in relation to the ease and speed at which reception in the technical sense may be achieved is at once engendered.

I

All of which makes the increase of understanding and friendship between many members of the several traditions during the past seventy years all the more remarkable. It is probably the case that we have not as yet fully appreciated the significant change of attitude that has crept upon us during the span of one lifetime. What have Reformed Christians of the past seventy years received from traditions other than their own? I shall first briefly indicate some of the blessings that I have received from other Christian traditions during my earthly sojourn, while recognizing that the lists of others may be significantly different according to their starting-points and their context in the world. (Lest any should at this point wish to label me as a woolly-minded sentimentalist I caution that the dissuasives to reception will follow shortly).

Time would fail me to list all the theologians who have stimulated me. I have learned much from Origen, Athanasius, and the Cappadocian Fathers (though I suspect that the last named would be somewhat perplexed by the rather one-sided way in which they have been embraced by some contemporary exponents of the social Trinity). I find what might be called the evangelical portions of Augustine congenial, his sacerdotal portions disturbing; the meditations of Anselm of permanent interest, and the narrowing down of what Abelard taught about the atonement unfortunate. I have always had a liking for heretics—I think, for example, of Arius and Pelagius—not least because of the deep sincerity of most of them, and for the way in which they caused others furiously to think, and in the end contributed to a more balanced articulation of Christian doctrine. To Reformed ears—and even more to Reformed eyes—John of Damascus's elevation of God's good created order over against those who suspected makers and users of images as idolaters gives pause for thought:

"Is not the ink in the Most Holy Gospel Book matter?" he challengingly enquired.[11] I return time and again to Alexander of Hales and Bonaventure, and I marvel as much at Aquinas's intellectual synthesis as I do at the way in which he managed to keep most of his deep Christian experience clear of it. I think that Luther had the pearl of price in terms of the gospel; I learn much from the recorded religious experience of Quakers like George Fox, Isaac Penington and Francis Howgill, and from the ways in which Quaker understandings of the light implicitly challenge those of the Cambridge Platonists—an intriguing group of Anglicans indeed. The erstwhile Congregationalist turned Baptist, John Bunyan, can never be overlooked when the Christian way is under consideration; and where the Church's global mission is concerned, the theological and practical labours of the Baptist Andrew Fuller are of the first importance. As for contributions to worship, the Baptists Benjamin Beddome and John Fawcett have left us all in their debt, as have many Anglicans—Newton and Cowper among them, and the Methodist Charles Wesley—notwithstanding the desirability of balancing his personal pronouns with the objectivity of an Isaac Watts. I can rejoice to sing John Henry Newman's great hymn, "Praise to the holiest in the height", provided that I am permitted to omit the verse which speaks of "a higher gift than grace"—of which I know no such thing; and, incidentally, I even think that Newman has a word for those university vice-chancellors who seem to think that the first duty of universities is to be "business-facing". From Newman's contemporary, Kierkegaard, I have learned something of the nature of faith in its relation to rationalism and empiricism. Then there is the Baptist Charles Haddon Spurgeon's pithy advice to preachers: "Nonsense does not improve by being bellowed";[12] and the memory of fine preaching by the Methodists (not least by some of the local preachers) among whom, for residential reasons, I fell during part of my childhood and youth. In myriad ways, through literature (the Anglican metaphysical poets are particular favourites of mine), music (from Bach to Vaughan Williams) and architecture (meeting houses as much as cathedrals) I have been drawn into the presence of God. So much for a severely truncated list of benefits received by myself from those of other traditions. Other Christians, differently situated and with different interests would make different lists; but I should be surprised if there were no overlaps at all between mine and theirs, and

---

11. John of Damascus, *On the Divine Images*, 23.
12. Spurgeon, *An All-Round Ministry*, 42.

PART TWO: Confessing the Faith Ecclesially and Hopefully

I should hope that the non-Reformed among them might find a place for Calvin, Thomas Goodwin, John Owen, Isaac Watts, Philip Doddridge, Jonathan Edwards, Schleiermacher, and P. T. Forsyth.

More generally, it is encouraging to be able to say that during the past seventy years significant mutual receivings have occurred. On the intellectual front there have been convergences and common endeavours of considerable significance. For example, from about 1930 onwards Roman Catholic philosophy began to come out of the seminary and onto the stage of wider philosophical discussion.[13] In the field of biblical studies the co-operation of scholars from many Christian traditions on such translation projects as *The New English Bible* constituted a prominent example of ecumenical endeavour. Again, where the writing of biblical commentaries is concerned, if ever there was a Particular Baptist or Roman Catholic way of approaching the matter, there is so no longer. Such Roman Catholic scholars as Raymond Brown and Joseph Fitzmyer are as likely to be cited by the best Protestant commentators as any of their own "tribe"; and scholars of many traditions have been grateful for those Welsh and English Baptists who well nigh cornered the market in Old Testament studies during the middle decades of the twentieth century. Nor can Roman Catholic scholars neglect Protestant systematicians with impunity and *vice versa*; and as for church history and Christian intellectual history, Methodists have contributed fine studies of Luther, and Roman Catholics of Calvin, while the burgeoning field of eighteenth-century thought commands the attention of people of many Christian traditions and of none.

If we look at spheres wider than the intellectual we see that while there are still to be found Protestants who write pamphlets damning the practice of praying with Roman Catholics, across wide swathes of Christian life common prayer no longer raises an eyebrow, any more than does the presence on one and the same educational or ethical consultation of Orthodox, Anglican and Pentecostal representatives.

Individually, and in these more general ways, the Reformed and others have received much from traditions other than their own. But, turning now to the more technical sense of "reception" which relates specifically to ecumenical dialogue, it may also be said that the Reformed have gained much from the dialogues that have taken place during the past forty years (I refer here to official international bilateral dialogues

---

13. See further Sell, *The Philosophy of Religion*, 84–92, 242.

to which the Reformed family has been party).[14] The gains have been in mutual friendship, doctrinal convergence and, in some cases, recommendations that anathemas be repudiated, and that practical steps be taken towards and the manifestation of that unity which God has already given in Christ.

Thus, for example, the Lutheran-Reformed dialogue participants recommended that full pulpit and altar/table communion be established around the world;[15] among the recommendations in the Anglican-Reformed dialogue report is one to the effect that "where churches of our two communions are committed to going forward to seek visibly unity, a measure of *reciprocal* communion should be made possible";[16] following the repudiation of historic anathemas formally pronounced by the Reformed against the Anabaptists, an initial mutually-introductory consultation between the World Alliance of Reformed Churches and the Mennonite World Council (1986) led to a detailed study of baptism, peace and the state: the major neuralgic issues between the two traditions;[17] the primary recommendation in the Baptist-Reformed dialogue report is that consideration be given to a church order in which both paedobaptism and believer baptism might be accommodated, Christian initiation being regarded as a process comprising several moments;[18] with both the Methodist World Council and the Disciples Ecumenical Consultative Council the conclusion was that remaining differing doctrinal emphases (notably Arminianism/Calvinism and baptism, respectively) should no longer be regarded as church-dividing;[19] from the Roman Catholic-Reformed dialogue comes the affirmation (*prima facie* encouraging to one from the Congregational branch of the Reformed family) that "the Church catholic is really represented and exists in the local Church . . . It

---

14. See further, Sell, *Enlightenment, Ecumenism, Evangel,* ch. 10.

15. Anon., *Towards Closer Fellowship,* 28.

16. Anon., *God's Reign and Our Unity,* 82; see further Sell, *A Reformed, Evangelical, Catholic* Theology, 137–42.

17. See Bender and Sell, *Baptism, Peace and the State in the Reformed and Mennonite Traditions.*

18. See *Baptists and Reformed in Dialogue,* 19–20. See further Sell, *A Reformed, Evangelical, Catholic Theology,* 142–45. This was the practice of John Bunyan and of other churches in Bedfordshire; and it was the position which enabled the union of The United Reformed Church with the Re-formed Association of Churches of Christ in 1981. See further Sell, *Nonconformist Theology,* 125–27.

19. See Anon., *Reformed and Methodists in Dialogue,* 14; Anon., *Towards Closer Fellowship,* 14.

is only by participating in the local community that we share in the life of the universal Church"[20] (though there may be different understandings of "local"), and the declaration that in the eucharist the once-for-all-ness of Christ's sacrifice is proclaimed;[21] a significant degree of convergence on the Trinity became evident in the Orthodox-Reformed dialogue, albeit the Orthodox set out from the mystery of the incarnation while the Reformed begin from the biblical witness to the life, death and resurrection of Jesus;[22] the Reformed and the Oriental Orthodox agreed on "the normative function of Holy Scripture for the life of the Church," and that "The ultimate form of the Church's mission is to carry the whole creation in all its brokenness and misery before the transforming presence of the Triune God in a perpetual act of praise and thanksgiving."[23]

Many more instances of the encouragement received by the Reformed through dialogue with those of other Christian traditions could be given, but perhaps the general situation may be summed up by saying that underpinning all the ecumenical progress that has been made is the conviction that unity is God's gift; it is not of human manufacture. As Thomas Torrance put it, "Unity belongs to the very essence of the Church as the community of people who have been reconciled to God, and to one another, through the life and passion of the Incarnate Son."[24] If we pass over Philip Henry's exegesis according to which Jesus, in his high priestly prayer had church divisions in mind when he prayed that his disciples might be one (John 17:21), we can find the seventeenth-century Presbyterian divine in harmony with, and more specific than, his distinguished twentieth-century successor. He declares that Jesus showed

> That notwithstanding the many sad divisions that are in the church, yet all the saints, as far as they are sanctified, are one; one in relation, one flock, one family, one building, one body, one bread; one by representations, one in image and likeness, of one inclination and disposition; one in their aims, one in their askings, one in amity and friendship, one in interest, and one in their inheritance; nay, they are one in judgment and opinion; though in some things they differ, yet those thinks in which they

---

20. Anon., *The Presence of Christ*, 18, 19. See further Sell, *A Reformed, Evangelical, Catholic Theology*, 132–37.

21. Anon., *The Presence of Christ*, 27.

22. Vischer, *Agreed Statements*, 21.

23. Anon., *Oriental Orthodox-Reformed* Dialogue, 54, 55.

24. Torrance, *Theology in Reconciliation*, 20.

are agreed are many more, and much more considerable than those things wherein they differ. They are all of a mind concerning sin, that it is the worst thing in the world; concerning Christ, that he is All in all; concerning the favour of God, that it is better than life . . .[25]

But if Christians cannot create the unity of the Church, they can certainly mar it. Having considered what the Reformed have received from others, what do I hope they may yet receive? I answer: an affirmative response to the invitation, issued in the Reformed family in Christ's name, to all who by grace are one in Christ to join them at the table of the Lord; and secondly, a warm welcome to the same table on the part of those, whether Orthodox, Roman Catholic, Anglo Catholic, or Strict Baptist, who currently exclude multitudes of Christians from the Lord's table. With which we come to the hindrances to further reception.

II

Just as we receive many things from others in the ordinary language sense of "reception," so in the same sense of the term there are religious dissuasives which discourage some of the Reformed from receiving what others have to offer. It is a bran tub of items which vary from person to person and have as much to do with temperament and taste as they do with theology. Thus, to speak once again for myself: I profess to be a lover of many types of music, but after two hours of solid plainsong I am almost tempted to reach for the antidote of "Shine Jesus, shine"—a temptation I have thus far managed to resist. Again, there is the Roman cult of the saints, and the elaborate and time-consuming method by which saints are designated in that fold. It is not simply that I think of saints in a quite different way (as will shortly become clear); it is that I find such things as an advertisement in a responsible journal for intelligence concerning miracles which have occurred in consequence of prayers to G. K. Chesterton, in order that the cause of his elevation to sainthood may be advanced, to be strangely unhelpful to the ecumenical cause. I am disquieted by pastoral problems which continue to be raised in connection with mixed marriages, and by what appears to be heavy-handed discipline exercised against theologians and ethicists who are deemed to have spoken or written "off message."[26]

---

25. Henry, *The Life of the Rev. Philip Henry, A.M.*, 241.
26. For the latest example of which I am aware see the case of the Polish theologian,

PART TWO: Confessing the Faith Ecclesially and Hopefully

On the other hand, I do not find it easy to endorse some of the marketing techniques employed by enthusiastic church growth evangelicals, nor the feel-good religion purveyed in some quarters, nor the gospel of prosperity which is peddled through so many television channels, nor the more extreme expressions of charismatic expression (I think I would know if I had ever been slain by the Spirit). But, lest I appear as a fuddy-duddy who likes a quiet religious life, let me regret with P. T. Forsyth that "The freaks ascribed to the Spirit arrest far more attention than the frost which settles on the Word."[27]

But the matters just itemized do not, in my opinion, rank as being of sufficient importance to be church-dividing. As Philip Henry wrote, "In those things wherein all the people of God are agreed, I will spend my zeal; and wherein they differ I will walk according to the light that God hath given me, and charitably believe that others do so too."[28] I further recall that what Wesley branded the "gross superstition" of the Roman Catholics was relativized by his discovery of holiness among many of them; Forsyth rather cheekily declared of the Anglo-Catholic ecclesiastic, Charles Gore, that "Were there no alternative, Bishop Gore's gospel would make me put up, for the time being at least, with his view of the ministry";[29] and the remarkable William Jay (1769–1853), who ministered at Argyle Congregational Church, Bath, for sixty-two years, wrote that "I could never regard the differences of the truly godly as essential; and though I have had my convictions and preferences, they were never anathematizing and exclusive. And I could have communed with any of their churches, and should not have been sorry if circumstances had enabled me to say that I had done so."[30]

The hindrances to reception—now understood not as an ordinary language term, but in the technical sense of the disposition formally to receive what Christian partners of other traditions have to offer, may be classified under the headings: practical matters,[31] and doctrinal considerations.

Waclaw Hryniewicz, reported in *The Christian Century*, 18 November 2008, 18.

27. Forsyth, *Faith, Freedom, and the Future*, 41.
28. P. Henry in his *Life*, 127.
29. Forsyth, *The Principle of Authority*, 224.
30. Redford and James. *The Autobiography of William Jay*, 165.
31. See further Sell, *Enlightenment, Ecumenism, Evangel*, 276–78; Sell, "The Role of Bilateral Dialogues within the One Ecumenical Movement," 453–60.

Practical matters. First, I have already remarked upon the fact that not every Christian world communion is found in every part of the world. Accordingly it is not surprising if some members of a particular communion feel little connection to the report of a dialogue between their global family and a tradition with which they have never had any contact. Secondly, from the South, where in some regions the number of Christians is increasing exponentially, the charge is sometimes levelled that ecumenical dialoguing is a Western hobby, concerned with histories and disputes which are of no concern to them. But if we go back far enough we can readily see that all Western Christians have received the faith from aliens; and as for the ecumenical issues being of no concern, one of many possible retorts is, "Are we then to assume that in your country Roman Catholics, Orthodox Christians and Protestants practice reciprocal intercommunion?" The question is not whence came the divisiveness in their midst, but what is to be done about it. It is, of course, perfectly understandable that those Christians who serve in countries beset by war, famine and disease will find plenty of things to do before sitting down to ponder dialogue reports. Thirdly, in some quarters the claim is made that to focus upon those ecclesiological issues which are the concern of so many ecumenical dialogues is to fiddle while Rome burns. Instead, it is argued, the churches should devote themselves to alleviating poverty, promoting justice, striving for peace, safeguarding the planet. But why the ecumenical-social disjunction—especially if ecumenism concerns the whole inhabited earth? The pattern of the Decalogue, the gist of much of Jesus's teaching, and the arrangement of some of Paul's letters imply the injunction, "If this is what you believe, then this is what you should do." Fourthly, there is the fact that some churches, especially in the West, are currently facing internal disputes which consume so much energy that they hardly have any left for broader ecumenical concerns. Many of these disputes concern socio-ethical issues, and some of them are promoted by highly politicized pressure groups which "pack the Assembly" to such an extent that the primary objective of church assemblies, namely, that of seeking the mind of Christ and unanimity in him, becomes and ever-receding possibility. A serious discussion—indeed, an ecumenical discussion—of the question, "On what grounds ought we to determine that some ethical issues may properly be church-dividing whilst others are not?" would not come amiss.[32] Finally, I suggest that much good would accrue to the ecumenical cause if the findings of dialogue reports were

32. See further Sell, *Aspects of Christian Integrity*, ch. 3.

more regularly introduced into classes on systematic theology, and not confined to specialist modules as if the subject matter were the preserve of ecumenical enthusiasts only.[33] This would contribute to the formation of the rising generation of ministers and theologians, and might even discourage that re-inventing of the wheel which is not unknown in ecumenical writings and proposals.

Doctrinal considerations. That there are significant doctrinal matters which inhibit—even preclude—full fellowship with some other Christians would, I think be agreed by many within the Reformed family. In every case the neuralgic issues result in the sundering of the unity which God has already given to the Church in Christ by the Spirit. They are all forms of the Galatian heresy: new circumcisions. They all concern matters on which human interpretations are elevated above God's action in Christ and they amount to the claim that "We cannot have full fellowship with you until we agree on certain points of doctrinal interpretation, or read the Bible in our particular way, or toe the line with us on church order." ("If polity is the condition of unity, did not Christ die in vain?" Forsyth rhetorically asked[34]). In these ways denominational small print is rendered normative, and the sigh of the seventeenth-century Puritan, John Howe, echoes down the years: "Without all controversy, the main inlet of all the distractions, confusions, and divisions of the Christian world hath been by adding other conditions of Church communion than Christ hath done."[35]

Because the matters to which I shall now allude are so familiar as to be boring, I shall be brief. First there is the question of the Apostolic succession as held in the Roman and Anglo-Catholic churches. A Protestant who chortles over the fact that the presumed historic line is confused at certain points fails to understand that responsible Roman Catholic and Anglican scholars have said no less. Nor is it simply a matter of having personal representative leadership within the Church: many Protestant churches have that, and some of those thus elevated could give Anglicans and Romans lessons in autocratic behaviour. No, everything turns upon what bishops are supposed to be able to do; and this depends upon what is believed about the handing on of authority to the apostles in the Gospels. The case, *pro* and *con*, has been argued for years, but, for reasons

---

33. Similarly with feminist, liberation and other theological insights. These are too important to be the preserve of committed coteries.

34. Forsyth, *Congregationalism and Reunion*, 25.

35. Howe, *Works*, V, 226. See further Sell, *Aspects of Christian Integrity*, ch. 4.

which are too complicated to expand upon here, I side with those who hold that the apostles held an unique role as primary witnesses to God's grace in Christ, but that they did not pass on to successors their own commission, still less did they communicate to their heirs in the faith any special power to forgive post-baptismal sins or to render the Mass spiritually efficient:[36] things which cannot fail to foster the impression that the sacraments are somehow "done to" the people by the priests, whereas it is my firm conviction that it is the Church, the gathered companies of saints, who celebrate the sacraments; they are, strictly, churchly occasions, and Christ, not the ministers, is the host.[37] It further seems plain to me that those stand in the succession of the apostles who proclaim the apostolic gospel—something in which neither all bishops, nor, to state the obvious, all Reformed ministers, have excelled. The problem is that those who espouse apostolic succession as widely understood (with or without a pipe-line theory of grace) cannot but think that ministries other than their own are deficient; that what pass as sacraments in many Christian circles may not really be sacraments at all; and so you have the bandying about of the bogyman words, "invalidity" and "irregularity." The terminus is, as Roman Catholic documents from Vatican II to the present day have made plain, that other churches, not being in communion with the Bishop of Rome, are not truly churches in the fullest sense of the term.[38] This, to me, is undoubtedly a Roman sentiment, but I cannot see that it is a truly catholic one. I am probably missing something of great importance, but it appears that I am being asked to place my neck into a sectarian noose so that I may become more Roman, whereas I should be delighted if my Roman friends could see their way to becoming more catholic. For the Church catholic comprises all those in heaven and on

---

36. See further Forsyth, *The Charter of the Church*, 52; Forsyth, *The Principle of Authority*, 127; Forsyth, *The Church and the Sacraments*, 46, 139; T. W. Manson, *The Church's Ministry*.

37. See further Forsyth, *The Church and the Sacraments*, 237.

38. For an example of this Roman Catholic position see *Unitatis Redintegratio*, II para. 22; for further reflections on the matter with reference to more recent troublesome documents see Sell, *Testimony and Tradition*, 339–40; Sell, *Enlightenment, Ecumenism, Evangel*, 293–94; Sell, *Hinterland Theology*, 618–23. For some gracious Roman Catholic reflections see Jared Wicks, "Not-so-fully church," 9–11. Since writing this sentence I have learned that the Vatican is consulting with the Leadership Conference of Women Religious in the United States with a view to ensuring, *inter alia*, that the sisters are promoting the idea of "the primacy of the Catholic Church over other Christian denominations." See Anon., "Vatican to Investigate Nuns' Doctrinal Fidelity," 16.

earth who, on the ground of Christ's saving work, have been called to Christ by the Spirit and live in him and he in them, and they confess him as Lord and Saviour.

This is the very nub of the ecumenical problem. When Paul tells the fractured fellowship in Corinth that "the eye cannot say to the hand, 'I do not need you,'" his "cannot" is a logical cannot; and to his remark Christians have all too often responded in accordance with the rituals of the English pantomime season, "O yes it can!"; and they have hurled sectarian custard pies at one another throughout the course of that not unremittingly cheerful pantomime that we call church history. Hence the vocation of committed ecumenists who come along with their mops and buckets to clear up the mess so that the already given unity of the Church may clearly be seen.

If those called by grace to be united with Christ gather visibly at the Lord's table and invoke the presence of the Spirit (you will note that I am not referring to a non-specifiable invisible Church unity), are we really to believe that God would disappoint them? If so, are we not slighting what God in Christ has done by the Spirit? If not, how could we justifiably attach the labels of invalidity or irregularity to what is taking place, as some persist in doing? As the Congregational lay historian, Bernard Lord Manning wrote long ago,

> The entire conception of *validity* and *regularity*, *invalidity* and *irregularity*, applied to the means of grace and the action of the Body of Christ, is both ludicrous and blasphemous. If God acts at all He cannot act invalidly or irregularly; and if God is not acting in the Church there is no action; for the Church has no meaning whatever as a human society apart from God's action. . . . We simply do not know what an irregular or an invalid celebration is. We do not deal in percentages with the grace of God.[39]

Clearly related to the foregoing is the large question of papal primacy, a matter on which John Paul II expressed the hope that his Church and others would join in seeking the way forward.[40] I wish only to say here that this is far more than a matter of a useful figure-head for an international body (the Church differs in many important respects from Barclays or Shell), though I have heard some ecumenists talk in

---

39. Manning, *Essays in Orthodox Dissent*, 75, 116; cf. ibid., 133, 166. Cf. Forsyth, *The Charter of the Church*, 56–57.

40. See John Paul II, *Ut Unum Sint*, 107.

this strangely pragmatic way.[41] On the contrary, since 1870 dogmas that the Pope has promulgated *ex cathedra* are required to be believed by the faithful, and are deemed to be infallible. It is not simply that the dogmas spelled out may be thought problematic by many; much more serious is the fact that dogmas deemed infallible logically cannot be revised or rescinded even under the guidance of the Holy Spirit. No doubt the reply will be that the dogmas were themselves deliverances of the Spirit, who may, therefore, be deemed to be in favour of them. But our grasp of the will and purposes of God is always inadequate, God being who he is and we being who we are; and on more than one occasion in Christian history believers who have been utterly convinced that the Spirit was on their side have subsequently been shown to have been tragically mistaken. It therefore seems ill-advised on the part of any Church to put itself in a position in which its teaching on particular points, being deemed infallible, is not open to revision and even perhaps to repudiation in the light of an increase of knowledge or faith, or both. As the wise Scottish apologist, Robert Flint, wrote,

> I acknowledge that we may happily come to know the evil of that whereof we knew no evil before, or the good of that in which we knew no good before. . . . I acknowledge that there is ofttimes a great mistake, misunderstanding, error, and unsoundness in the judgment of Christian persons or Churches, so that godly men and true Churches may come to know that to be evil which they sometime thought good, and that to be false which sometime they thought true, or contrariwise; which experience hath taught, and may teach again. . . . I confess it is no shame for an Augustine to write a book of Retractions.[42]

An infallibilist stance which precludes any of this is, as it seems to me, ill advised; it precludes ecumenical advance, and it is conceivable that persistence in it would exclude the possibility of further illumination by the Holy Spirit.

I suggest that the underlying issue concerns the doctrine of doctrinal development, a matter on which there has been a profound silence

---

41. I suspect that the late J. M. R. Tillard was being over-optimistic in his judgement that "justification by faith, the eucharistic presence of Christ, the primacy of the Bishop of Rome, the eucharistic epiclesis, now appear as essential facets of the Christian truth as such." Still, three out of four is not a disastrous score. See his "The Ecclesiological Implications of Bilateral Dialogues," 415.

42. Flint, *On Theological, Biblical, and Other Subjects*. 77.

in the international dialogues with which I have been associated. I have elsewhere sought to analyze the concept of doctrinal development, not least because I think that differing assumptions concerning the meaning of the term, and the grounds on which some developments are deemed legitimate whilst others are not, account for a good deal of the "talking past" one another that can occur in dialogues.[43] Here I simply note the topic as an item which ought to be among the agenda of ecumenical consultations.

Inextricably linked to the idea of development[44] is that of authority: in particular, the locus of authority. In this connection the two familiar candidates are Scripture and Tradition. Much could be said at this point, but my shorthand thesis is that neither of these, severally or together, will yield an adequate foundation for Christian faith, life and witness. It is manifestly the case that so long as there are Christians both the Bible and Tradition will be construed, honoured, and side-stepped in diverse ways. Moreover the divergent interpretations offered are detectable not only between various Christian communions, but within them. All of this is so obvious as to need no argument. But one illustration may be appropriate. In my account of hindrances to reception I have concentrated upon the Roman Catholic Church because the hindrances there are of paramount importance from the point of view of the withholding of full fellowship from millions of those who are already one in Christ. But it is also the case, as I hinted earlier, that there are Protestant forms of the Galatian heresy no less than Roman and Anglo-Catholic ones. In particular there is the elevation of an allegedly inerrant Bible (though proponents differ over whether the Bible is inerrant throughout and therefore reliable as science and history, or whether is inerrant only where it speaks of doctrinal matters, which are then often ranked differently by different advocates). Either way, the Bible is construed legalistically, as if grace required the protection of law, and faith is reduced to assent to propositions supernaturally revealed. There frequently follows the further declaration—the mirror image of the Roman one—that only when you interpret the Scriptures as we do will be have full fellowship with you. To this is sometimes added the pious promise, "Meanwhile we'll pray that you may

---

43. See Sell, *Enlightenment, Ecumenism, Evangel*, ch. 6.

44. I prefer to speak of doctrinal change, since to many ears "development" connotes improvement. But developments may be adverse. Similarly, when many hear the term "criticism" they think of adverse criticism and rebuke; but criticism may be positive.

see the light." It is another sectarian stance which divides those whom Christ has made one. I deeply regret that this type of fundamentalism is being propagated at the present time by some enthusiastic Reformed missionaries, and I recall Forsyth's searing judgment of almost a century ago: "it is possible for a movement or a church to be very evangelical on the extensive scale but not evangelical at all on the intensive. . . . It spreads its gospel over the face of the earth, but not into the thought and temper of the age. It covers, but it does not leaven. . . . [Some missions] spread the Word rapidly—but so thin that it cracks."[45]

All of this underlines my contention that to hope for absolute uniformity of belief and practice is, in this vale of tears, to chase a will o' the wisp. We need to take seriously the oft-repeated mantra that unity does not imply uniformity. But to that we need to add the thought that it does not imply religious free-wheeling either. What it genuinely implies is that our given unity in Christ is of more importance than our interpretations of doctrine and polity. Our final authority is the risen and exalted Christ to whom the Bible, and the Church when in faithful mode, bear witness. Or as Forsyth put it, "Our final authority is our new Creator. The authority cannot, therefore, be either a Church or a Book—both of which are historically the products of such communion with God. They did not exist till it did, and therefore could not be the cause of its existence."[46] The seventeenth-century Congregationalist Thomas Goodwin said it well: "If a Christian's judgments be well and thoroughly grounded in the doctrine of God's free grace and eternal love, and of redemption through Jesus Christ alone, and in the most spiritual inward operations of God's Spirit, experimentally communicated, that will fence them against all errors, and from taking in of any falsehood of great moment."[47] No doubt; but realism and humility prompt the acknowledgement that this is something to be aspired to, not brandished as a trophy. Nevertheless Goodwin's ref-

---

45. Forsyth, *Faith, Freedom, and the Future*, 93-94.

46. Forsyth, *The Principle of Authority*, 53.

47. Goodwin, *Exposition of Ephesians*, Premise. In Wilson, *The Attributes of God*, 231. It is interesting to compare Goodwin's remarks with those of the Cambridge Platonist, John Smith, in the introduction to *A Discourse concerning the true Way or Method of attaining to Divine Knowledge*, in his *Select Discourses*, 4. Goodwin would have endorsed Smith's words, "It is but a thin, airy knowledge that is got by mere speculation which is ushered in by syllogisms and demonstrations," but whereas Goodwin drives directly to grace, redemption by Christ and illumination by the Spirit, Smith appeals for the reunion of truth and goodness: "The reason why . . . truth prevails no more in the world, is, we so often disjoin truth and true goodness . . ."

erence to free grace, eternal love and redemption does prompt us towards that lateral thinking apart from which I cannot conceive how the divided Christian communions will ever be able to manifest that unity in Christ which God has already given to us.

III

In saying that the great ecumenical need is of lateral thinking, what I have in mind is that Christians of all traditions should make a strenuous effort to think, not in terms of what we stand for, how we compute the *ordo salutis*, how we understand the Bible or the ministry and sacraments, or even what we have to offer to all the other Christians. We need to think in terms of a radical realism which asks, bluntly, "What has God done, and for whom has he done it?" Seriously to address this question will, I believe, direct us to the gospel, to a neglected aspect of ecclesiology, and thence to the implications for revitalized inter-communion fellowship.[48] I shall offer a few remarks upon each of these.

If I am asked, "What has God done?" I cannot answer without going straight to the cross. I am an unrepentant theologian of the cross.[49] I know very well that the incarnation is both temporally and logically prior to the cross, since Bethlehem preceded Calvary and Christ can do what he does on the cross only because he is who he is; I further understand that what Calvin called "the whole course of his obedience"[50] is integral to his work; and I think of the term "cross" as denoting not only the crucifixion but also the resurrection and ascension which confirm the Good Friday victory. Nevertheless, against those incarnationalisms that can so easily be transmogrified into idealistic immanentisms which have the final effect of uprooting the gospel from history,[51] I insist that at the cross, in the one, full, perfect, and sufficient sacrifice of Christ, something was done, not merely shown, to vanquish sin and all that could keep us from God. It is on the ground of this act that the church is called into being. The good news comes first: "The Church," said Bernard Manning, "is the

---

48. For a fuller development of this theme, with special reference to the work of the Holy Spirit, see Sell, *The Great Ejectment of 1662*, ch. 4.

49. See, for example, Sell, *Enlightenment, Ecumenism, Evangel*, ch. 13.

50. Calvin, *Institutes*, II.xvi.5.

51. I seem to have been harping on this theme for years. See, for example, *Theology in Turmoil*, ch. 1; Sell, *Philosophical Idealism*, 194–202; Sell, *Enlightenment, Ecumenism, Evangel*, 392–95.

creation, not the proprietor of the Good News. The gospel is not what the Church proclaims: the Church is that which proclaims the Gospel."[52] All of which is to say that at the deepest level the church's unity is in the gospel of God's grace. The negative implication of this is that our unity is, as Forsyth said, "not in the traditional polity, creed, or cultus we inherit. If unity is in polity, Christ died in vain."[53] Positively, as he elsewhere put it, "The prime duty of the Church is not to impress, not even to save, men, but to confess the Saviour. . . . The Church is there as the great confessor, in thought, word, and deed, of its Creator."[54]

On the ground of the Son's saving work, as I said, saints are called to the Father by the Spirit through the proclamation of the gospel. Whereas Jesus is Son of God by right, the saints are those who by grace are adopted as God's sons and daughters. They stand where they do not because of any merit of their own, but only because they have become "saints by calling" (Rom 1:7). They are regenerate, "twice-born", whether or (more usually) not they can date a conversion experience. They have experienced God's grace, and they know it in fellowship with all who have likewise been called. Their response to God's gracious call is their enabled repentance and faith.[55] Once again there is realism here: we are not concerned with a spiritual fellowship conceived in terms of the invisible church—a posture which can be world-denying and escapist.[56] On the contrary, by the grace of the Lord Jesus Christ we are drawn into the communion of visible saints—surrounded indeed by the cloud of witnesses who have preceded us; but a communion into which we are engrafted now with a view to praise and service. It is impossible to be a Christian "in general."

52. Manning, *Essays in Orthodox Dissent*, 73. Cf. Forsyth, *The Cruciality of the Cross*, 50 n. 1.

53. Forsyth, *Congregationalism and Reunion*, 21.

54. Forsyth, *Faith, Freedom, and the Future*, 220.

55. In an article entitled, "The Institutional Unity We Must Reject," 9, the Methodist Old Testament scholar, Norman Snaith, declares that "There is one way and one way only into the Christian Church, and this way is repentance and faith. There is no other condition. To impose any other condition is false and is against the Gospel." But this is too anthropocentric, and might even suggest that repentance and faith are "works." Hence my use of the word "enabled." Faith is always a gift, so that none may boast (Eph 2:8–9), and repentance and answering love are prompted as the gospel is received. At the same time, the faithful response is genuinely ours, but the Father's act of eliciting logically precedes it, so that we testify, "I, yet not I but Christ." In salvation the initiative is always divine.

56. For a concise rebuttal of the notion that "spiritual unity" will suffice, see Boyd, *Ecumenism*, 11–12.

PART TWO: Confessing the Faith Ecclesially and Hopefully

To be a Christian is to be engrafted into Christ the Vine, and hence to be in living relation with all the other branches. To be a Christian is to be a saint in fellowship with other saints here and now and hereafter. It follows that "What the Gospel created was not a crowd of Churches but the one Church in various places,"[57] and the only way of being a member of the church catholic is to gather with, and be anchored among, the saints locally.

However all of this may strike others, to me it is as plain as the nose on my face. I therefore find it astonishing that in the international and other bi- and multilateral dialogues of which I am aware so little attention has been paid to what the old divines called the matter of the Church. We hear much of the nature of the Church, its ministry, sacraments, and order; but the question "*Who* are the Church?" has not, I think, received the attention it deserves. Yet there is a real need of careful investigation of this issue, not least because the position I have outlined—and I believe it to be biblically grounded and, indeed, unanswerable, is threatened by a variety of views which are commonly held in certain quarters. For example, it is threatened by popular establishment views which suppose that one is somehow made a Christian by virtue of being born in a particular county which has a national Church. It is threatened by views which contend that one becomes a Christian simply by the fact of having been baptized. I am well aware that in saying this I am setting my face against the doctrine that regeneration is necessarily temporally related to baptism, and I certainly think that the baptized infants of the saints are themselves within the covenant community, but they are so as catechumens, and their initiation is as yet incomplete. Bernard Manning once more: "We do not baptise [infants] in order to make them children of God. That is the false and hideous doctrine of Romanists and Anglo-Catholics. We baptise them because they are already God's. They are not outside His Kingdom until it occurs to them to enter it or until it occurs to us to push them into it. The water of baptism declares that they are already entitled to all God's mercies to men in the passion of Christ."[58] Empirically, the large number of the incompletely initiated who inhabit the earth suggests that not all who have been baptized actually become saints by calling, or "twice-born". For this reason I think that the emphasis in ecumenical circles upon baptism as the focus of Christian unity is over-optimistic

---

57. Forsyth, *The Church and the Sacraments*, 68.
58. Manning, *Why Not Abandon the Church?* 46–48.

and, more seriously, that it glosses over the fact that in the early Middle Ages the question, "How are we to deal with the problem of the post-baptismal sins of those deemed to be regenerate?" was a major stimulus to the introduction of that sacerdotal apparatus which has so sundered the Church's catholicity.[59] Be that as it may, in my understanding a Christian is an enrolled saint,[60] and it may be that as this century proceeds it will become increasingly necessary that we know who are the church. Our tendency to value often inflated membership statistics should not cause us to forget that the Bible has more to say concerning the faithful remnant than in does about packing everyone in before it is too late.[61]

In the Church, which comprises those who are saints by calling, a particular kind of fellowship is experienced. It is the fellowship of adopted brothers and sisters, and at the heart of it is that love which first loves God and then those who are his—a love which is denied by those who say they love God and then withhold full fellowship from their brothers and sisters in Christ (1 John 4:7–21). Hear Richard Baxter:

> I apprehended it a matter of great necessity to imprint true Catholicism on the minds of Christians, it being a most lamentable thing to observe how few Christians in the world there be, that fall not into one sect or another, and wrong not the common interest of Christianity, for the promoting of the interest of their sect; and how lamentably love is thereby destroyed, so that most men think not that they are bound to love those, as the members of Christ, which are against their party, and the leaders of most sects do not stick to persecute those that differ from them, and think the blood of those who hinder their opinions, and parties, to be an acceptable sacrifice to God. And if they can but get to be a sect which they think the *holiest* (as the Anabaptists and

---

59. See further Sell, *Hinterland Theology*, 615–17.

60. In holding this view I am not thereby committed to affirming the contrary, namely, that those who are not enrolled are not Christians. (The practice of drawing negative implications from legitimate positive affirmations has had a disastrous effect on the articulation of Christian doctrine through the centuries—*double* predestination being a prime example. See further Sell, *Enlightenment, Ecumenism, Evangel*, 325–38.) I make no judgments concerning their present state of the non-enrolled, or their final destiny. I do, however, find it odd that a person should wish to claim the name of Christ whilst refusing the fellowship of his body, the Church. To the extent that this refusal is a consequence of the fact that the saints, being also sinners, have failed in witness or have been unwelcoming, may God forgive us.

61. I have made a much fuller case for the position hinted at in this paragraph in Sell, *The Great Ejectment of 1662*, ch. 4.

Separatists), or which is the *largest* (as the Greeks and Papists), they think then that they are sufficiently warranted, to deny others to be God's Church, or at least to deny them Christian love and communion.[62]

Lying behind this challenging utterance is Baxter's view, which I share, that Christianity is a Way before it is a doctrinal system. Said he, "I knew how ticklish a business the enumeration of fundamentals was."[63] Entrance to the church is not by outward assent to particular doctrinal formulae, or by the endorsement of particular polities, both of which appear to be *quasi*-mechanistic attempts to engineer fellowship. To repeat, the church comprises those who are saints by calling, who by grace have made the enabled response of repentance and faith. One of the remarkable features of the fellowship of saints is the ready way in which the saints recognise one another. Earlier in this paper I listed a number of those of Christian traditions other than my own from who I have received much. That list could have been much longer. But my point now is that when thinking of them I do not think of them in the first place as Baptists, Roman Catholics, or whatever they may be. I think of them first as brothers and sisters in Christ. And those who are such ought to be together at the table of the Lord; and anything ecclesiastical which prevents this, whether it emanate from Roman or Anglo-Catholic circles, or from those Strict Baptists who, with inexorable logic reason that those only are the true church who have been baptized by immersion on profession of faith and hence they alone may partake of the Lord's Supper since it is a sacrament or ordinance of the Church—anything of this sort is the sectarian "leaven of the scribes and pharisees."[64] Is it not a tragic breach of fellowship; indeed, is it not an act of gross disobedience to a Saviour who invites us all to keep his Supper, to bar a fellow Christian from the Lord's table, or to refuse an invitation to communion issued in the Lord's name? "Love as I have loved you," he said (John 15:12). This is not only the quintessence of Christian ethics, it is the pattern for, and the stimulus towards, Christian fellowship; it is also the model for good liturgical behaviour. We have been accepted by Christ just as we are; and he has

---

62. Baxter, *Reliquiae Baxterianae*, I, 112.

63. Ibid., 138.

64. The words are Robert Mackintosh's; see the epigraph to this book. I have pursued this theme in greater detail in *Enlightenment, Ecumenism, Evangel*, ch. 11.

accepted all of us; why, then, can we not accept one another completely and joyfully?

Mine is not a plea for sloppiness, as if doctrines and Church order do not matter. I am not an advocate of the free-wheeling, undisciplined Church; but there is a great gulf between disciplinary judgments made by churches and individuals in relation to particular expressions of churchly life with a view to honouring God and in the hope of restoring offenders, and the *a priori* refusal of full communion to large swathes of the Church with whom one is already by grace united. Mine is a plea for putting first things first; for reckoning seriously with the gospel of God's saving grace on the basis of which the saints are gathered into a fellowship which knows no bounds of time or space, and for adjusting our attitudes and practices accordingly. Shall we succeed in this? Shall we even embark upon necessary reformation? Or shall we continue as we are, elevating our received traditions and favoured opinions above the good news of God's saving act in Christ, whilst all the time vainly looking forward to "the coming great Church?" But it is already here. Can we not see it? Can we not manifest its life more faithfully? Or shall we, in Thessalonian mode, sit around waiting for the heavenly banquet? That *shall* be a truly ecumenical occasion, where we shall all gather around the one table in the presence of the one Host as one family in Christ—whether we like it or not. In which connection, hear Richard Baxter once more:

> We shall then rest from all our sad divisions and unchristian quarrels with one another. How lovingly do thousands live together in heaven, who lived at variance upon earth! . . . O happy day of the saints' rest in glory, when, as there is one God, one Christ, one Spirit, so we shall have one heart, one church, one employment for ever.[65]

---

65. Baxter, *The Saints' Everlasting Rest*, 54, 55.

PART TWO: Confessing the Faith Ecclesially and Hopefully

BIBLIOGRAPHY

Anon. *Baptists and Reformed in Dialogue.* Geneva: World Alliance of Reformed Churches, 1984.
———. *God's Reign and Our Unity.* London: SPCK/ Edinburgh: Saint Andrew, 1984.
———. *Oriental-Orthodox-Reformed Dialogue: The First Four Sessions.* Geneva: World Alliance of Reformed Churches, 1998.
———. *The Presence of Christ in Church and World.* The Vatican: Secretariat for Promoting Christian Unity, and Geneva: World Alliance of Reformed Churches, 1977.
———. *Reformed and Methodists In Dialogue.* Geneva: World Alliance of Reformed Churches, 1988.
———. Report on Waclaw Hryniewicz. *The Christian Century,* 18 November 2008, 18.
———. "Vatican to Investigate Nuns' Doctrinal Fidelity." *The Christian Century,* 18 May 2009, 16.
———. *Towards Closer Fellowship.* Geneva: Lutheran World Federation and World Alliance of Reformed Churches, 1989.
———. *Unitatis Redintegration, (Decree on Ecumenism).* The Vatican, 21 November 1864.
Baxter, Richard. *Church-History of the Government of Bishops and their Councils Abbreviated.* London: Simmons, 1681.
———. *A Key for Catholicks, to open the juggling of the Jesuits, and satisfie all that are but truly willing to understand, whether the cause of the Roman or Reformed Churches be of God.* London: R. W. for Nevil Simmons, 1659.
———. *Reliquiae Baxterianae.* Edited by M. Sylvester. London: Parkhurst et al., 1696.
———. *The Saints' Everlasting Rest: or, a Treatise of the Blessed State of the Saints in their Enjoyment of God in Heaven.* London: The Religious tract Society, n.d.
Bender, Ross T., and Alan P. F. Sell. *Baptism, Peace and the State in the Reformed and Mennonite Traditions.* Waterloo, ON: Wilfrid Laurier University Press, 1991.
Boyd, Robin. *Ecumenism: Threat or Promise?* Dublin: Irish School of Ecumenics, 1981.
Calvin, John. *Institutes* Translated by F. Lewis Battles and edited by John T. McNeil. 2 vols. Philadelphia: Westminster, 1961.
Flint, Robert. *On Theological, Biblical, and Other Subjects.* Edinburgh: Blackwood, 1905.
Forsyth, P. T. *The Charter of the Church: Six Lectures on the Spiritual Principle of Nonconformity.* London: Alexander and Shepheard, 1896.
———. *The Church and the Sacraments.* 1917. Reprint. London: Independent, 1953.
———. *Congregationalism and Reunion.* London: Independent, 1952.
———. *The Cruciality of the Cross.* 1909. Reprint. London: Independent, 1957.
———. *Faith, Freedom and the Future.* 1912. Reprint. London: Independent, 1955.
———. *The Principle of Authority.* 1915. Reprint. London: Independent, 1952.
Goodwin, Thomas. *Exposition of Ephesians.* Premise. In *The Attributes of God as they may be Contemplated by the Christian for Edification, Peace, and Consolation, Selected from Charnock, Goodwin, Bates, and Wishart,* edited by W. Wilson. London: Seeley and Burnside, 1835.
Henry, Matthew. *The Life of Philip Henry, A.M.* (1688). Corrected and enlarged by J. B. Williams. 1825. Reprint. Edinburgh: Banner of Truth, 1974.
Howe, John. *Works.* Edited by Henry Rogers. 5 vols. London: n.p., 1862–63.

John of Damascus. *On the Divine Images: Three Apologies against Those Who Attack the Divine Images*. Translated by David Anderson. Crestwood, NY: St. Vladimir's Seminary Press, 1980.

John Paul II. *Ut Unum Sint: Encyclical Letter of the Holy Father . . . on Commitment to Ecumenism*. London: Catholic Truth Society, 1995.

Manning, Bernard Lord. *Essays in Orthodox Dissent*. 1939. Reprint. London: Independent, 1952.

———. *Why Not Abandon the Church?* 1939. Reprint. London: Independent, 1958.

Manson, T. W. *The Church's Ministry*. London: Hodder and Stoughton, 1948.

Priestley, Joseph. *The Conduct to be Observed by Dissenters, in order to procure the Repeal of the Corporation and Test Acts, 1789*. In *The Theological and Miscellaneous Works of Joseph Priestley*, Vol. 15, edited by J. T. Rutt, 389-404. 1817-32. Reprint. Bristol: Thoemmes, 1999.

Redford, George, and John Angell James. *The Autobiography of William Jay*. 1854. Reprint. Edinburgh: Banner of Truth, 1974.

Ryan, Thomas. "Reception: Unpacking the New Holy Word." *Ecumenism* 82 (1983) 27-34.

Sell, Alan P. F. *Aspects of Christian Integrity*. 1990. Reprint. Eugene, OR: Wipf and Stock, 1998.

———. *Commemorations: Studies in Christian Thought and History*. 1993. Reprint. Eugene, OR: Wipf & Stock, 1998.

———. *Enlightenment, Ecumenism, Evangel: Theological Themes and Thinkers 1550-2000*. Milton Keynes, UK: Paternoster, 2005.

———. *The Great Ejectment of 1662: Its Antecedents, Aftermath, and Ecumenical Significance*. Eugene, OR: Wipf & Stock, 2012.

———. *Hinterland Theology: A Stimulus to Theological Construction*. Milton Keynes, UK: Paternoster, 2008.

———. *Nonconformist Theology in the Twentieth Century*. Milton Keynes, UK: Paternoster, 2006.

———. *The Philosophy of Religion 1875-1980*. 1988, 1996. Reprint. Eugene, OR: Wipf & Stock, forthcoming.

———. *A Reformed, Evangelical, Catholic Theology: The Contribution of the World Alliance of Reformed Churches 1875-1982*. 1991. Reprint. Eugene, OR: Wipf & Stock, 1998.

———. "The Role of Bilateral Dialogues within the One Ecumenical Movement." *The Ecumenical Review* 46 (1994), 453-60.

———. *Testimony and Tradition: Studies in Reformed and Dissenting Thought*. Aldershot, UK: Ashgate, 2005.

———. *Theology in Turmoil. The Roots, Course and Significance of the Conservative-Liberal Debate in Modern Theology*. 1986. Reprint. Eugene, OR: Wipf & Stock, 1998.

Smith, John. *A Discourse concerning the True Way or Method of attaining to Divine Knowledge*. In *Select Discourses*, 1-21. London: Flesher, 1660.

Snaith, Norman H. "The Institutional Unity We Must Reject." *The British Weekly*, 21 March 1963, 9.

Spurgeon, C. H. *An All-Round Ministry: Addresses to Ministers and Students*. 1900. Reprint. London: Banner of Truth, 1960.

PART TWO: Confessing the Faith Ecclesially and Hopefully

> Sullivan, E. "Reception: A Factor and Moment in Ecumenism." *Ecumenical Trends* 15 (1986) 105–10.
> Tillard, J. M. R. "The Ecclesiological Implications of Bilateral Dialogues." *Journal of Ecumenical Studies* 23 (1986) 412–23.
> Torrance, Thomas F. *Theology in Reconciliation: Essays towards Evangelical and Catholic Unity in East and est*. London: Chapman, 1975.
> Vischer, Lukas. *Agreed Statements from the Orthodox-Reformed Dialogue*. Geneva: World Alliance of Reformed Churches, 1998.
> Wicks, Jared. "Not-So-Fully-Church." *The Christian Century*, 21 August 2007, 9–11.

CHAPTER TEN

Eschatology

Historical Fluctuations and Perennial Practical Importance

One of my most regularly intoned mantras is to the effect that the most satisfactory theology derives from what God has been pleased to reveal, and not from what he has not. This cautionary word is nowhere more appropriate than when eschatology is under discussion. As is well known, throughout the Christian ages eschatology has been a happy hunting-ground for apocalyptically-minded persons—a class that, allegedly, includes at least one former President of a world power. People have ransacked the biblical books of Daniel and Revelation for information concerning Armageddon; the date of the end of the world (notwithstanding that Jesus said that this is not ours to know); the identity of the Beast (Luther/sundry Popes/Napoleon/Hitler—or anyone else who does not take the searcher's fancy); the mechanics of Christ's return, and much more besides. Indeed, three days before I began to type this paper Britain's oldest and most highly regarded Sunday newspaper carried the headline, "Americans stock up to be ready for end of the world."[1] The theme of the news item is that in response to terrorism and the economic recession a legion of "preppers" has been spawned—people who are determined to be prepared for whatever disaster may strike. "Preppers," apparently, are not all of one kind. At one end of the spectrum are those

1. Harris, "Americans Stock Up," 48.

PART TWO: Confessing the Faith Ecclesially and Hopefully

seeking a more self-sufficient lifestyle; at the other are those who are stocking up for Armageddon (though one might be tempted to think it imprudent to stockpile millions of tins of baked beans in readiness for a great conflagration). As if all this were not enough, I have it on good authority that there are "people who have bumperstickers on their cars that say, 'Warning: In case of the rapture, the driver of this car will disappear.' Lately I have been seeing some others that say, 'When the rapture comes, can I have your car?'"[2]

Whether we regard such eschatological activity and responses as amusing or disturbing, they do at least underline the point that reflections of an eschatological kind (whether bizarre or sober) are more readily prompted by particular events than is reflection on most other Christian doctrines. The fall of Jerusalem, the collapse of the Roman empire, the rise of Islam, the Reformation, the inauguration of the slave trade, the Lisbon earthquake of 1755, the French Revolution, the First World War, the advent of the atom bomb, and now the threat of terrorism and the global warming: all of these and many others have caused the thought of many to turn to the last things. It is as if eschatological reflection is existentially engendered to a degree that reflection on the Trinity or the Virgin Birth, for example, is not. It is this fact, I think, that helps to explain both the growth of interest in eschatology at particular times, and also the recycling, modification, and supplementation of eschatological doctrines through time.

I grant at the outset that not all eschatological speculation is of the extreme kind. On the contrary, the Society for Psychical Research, for example, has numbered some eminent scholars among its members, the philosopher Henry Sidgwick and W. R. Matthews, sometime Dean of St. Paul's among them.[3] I here bypass such enquiries into human survival after death on the ground that even if this were proved beyond doubt, we should be far from the Christian belief in, and experience of, a life of fellowship with God which begins now, is unimpeded by death, and is characterized by unsullied joy hereafter.

Rather, I shall first illustrate some of the fluctuations through which Christian eschatological doctrines have passed on their way to us. I shall then suggest that despite all the historical fluctuations, and after a due measure of agnosticism has enabled us to pick our way through wilder

2. Taylor, "Expecting the Second Coming," 35.

3. For Sidgwick (1838–1900) and Matthews (1881–1973) see ONDB; for the latter see also Sell, *Four Philosophical Anglicans.*.

accounts of the doctrines, there remains a cluster of ideas of perennial importance not only for theological enquiry, but also for Christian experience, worship and pastoral work. I shall further suggest that these ideas pose questions of apologetic interest, not least those concerning the nature and status of Christianity as a supernatural religion, and the credibility of Christian testimony.

It will suffice if I briefly, and necessarily selectively, illustrate eschatological fluctuations by reference to two aspects of the complex of doctrines that travel under the umbrella "eschatology": the millennium and the Second Coming, and judgment and the afterlife.

Eschatological Fluctuations: The Millennium and the Second Coming

In the *Didache* (c.AD 60) we find a post-communion prayer that includes the following words: "Let grace come and let this world pass away. . . . Maranatha. Amen." Not, indeed, that progress towards this end will be without tribulation. We are warned that "in the last days the false prophets and the corrupters shall be multiplied", that the "world-deceiver" will appear as the Son of God and perform wicked acts; then will come the trial of fire and many will perish in it,

> But they that endure in their faith shall be saved from this curse. And then shall appear the signs of the truth; first the sign of an opening in heaven, then the sign of the trumpet's sound, and thirdly, the resurrection of the dead; yet not of all, but as it has been said, The Lord will come and all the saints with him. Then shall the world see the Lord coming upon the clouds of heaven.[4]

As compared with some later eschatological ruminations the Twelve Apostles strike a restrained note. So, too, does the *Epistle of Barnabas* (70–150): "Let us give heed unto the last times. For all the time past of our life and our faith will profit us nothing, unless we continue to hate what is evil, and to withstand the future temptations."[5] There follows a calculation based upon the biblical assertion that with God a thousand years is as one day, and that since God finished making the world on the sixth day, the world would come to an end in six thousand years.[6]

---

4. *Didache*, X, XVI.
5. *Ep.Barn.*, IV.
6. Ibid., XV.

Justin Martyr (c.100–c.165) is more specific regarding the millennium. In dialogue with Trypho he affirms that "I and others, who are right-minded Christians on all points, are assured that there will be a resurrection of the dead, and a thousand years in Jerusalem which will then be built, adorned, and enlarged, [as] the prophets Ezekiel and Isaiah and others declare."[7] For his part, Irenaeus (c.130–c.200) envisages the coming of the Antichrist. He refers to Daniel and 2 Thessalonians, and finds their sentiments confirmed by Jesus's reference to the "abomination of desolation" (Matt 24:15).[8] Later, Irenaeus argues that John (that is, the author of Revelation) and Daniel have predicted the fall of the Roman empire, following which the end of the world will come and Christ's eternal kingdom will be inaugurated. In making his case he trounces Marcion, Valentinus, and all the Gnostics "falsely so called" who are, in reality, "emissaries of Satan."[9]

Meanwhile in the West, Tertullian (c.160–c.225) was also, at some considerable length, repudiating the views of Marcion. He declares that the heavenly Jerusalem will exist on earth for a thousand years, that believers will be caught up in the clouds to meet the Lord, and that following the resurrection of the saints the destruction of all things will take place at the judgment.[10] It is noteworthy that in his younger days Tertullian himself had been influenced by the apocalyptic-*cum*-charismatic movement inspired by Montanus of Phrygia, who thought that the heavenly Jerusalem would descend near Pepuza in his homeland.[11] Hippolytus of Rome (c.170–c.236) wrote of the first and second advents, and of the judgment of the good and the evil,[12] while Lactantius (c.250–c.325) discoursed upon Christ's descent from heaven, the destruction of the wicked, and the judgment of the living and the dead. Following the judgment, the righteous dead will be raised to eternal life and the King will reign with them on the earth for a thousand years, during which time the holy city will be built. Then the prince of the demons will be released and the city of the saints will be stormed. The saints themselves will be hidden from persecution, and then will come the last judgment and the

---

7. *Dial.*, V.lxxx.
8. Irenaeus, *Adv. Haer.*, V.xxv.5.
9. Ibid., XIV.
10. Tertullian, *Adv. Marcion*, III.xxv.
11. See Eusebius, *HE*, V.xvi.7ff.
12. Hippolytus, *De Christo et Antichristo*,

Eschatology

second resurrection—of the good to eternal life, and of the wicked to eternal punishment.[13]

From the East there came some strong protests, similar to those of Irenaeus, against this-worldly understandings of post-resurrection life as promulgated in Gnostic circles. Clement of Alexandria (c.150–c.215) drew a strong contrast between those Gnostics whose lives are centred in worldly goods and the true Gnostic—the Christian believer—who "Tastes not the good things that are in the world, entertaining a noble contempt for all things here; ... having a clear conscience with reference to his departure, and being always ready, as "a stranger and pilgrim," with regard to the inheritances here; mindful only of those that are his own, and regarding all things here as not his own; ... he does and thinks what is holy."[14]

Similarly, Origen (c.185–254) stoutly opposes those Gnostics who contend

> That after the resurrection there will be marriages, and the begetting of children, imagining to themselves that the earthly city of Jerusalem is to be rebuilt ... [that] the natives of other countries are to be given them as the ministers of their pleasures, ... and [that] they are to receive the wealth of the nations to live on.... And to speak shortly, according to the manner of things in this, life in all similar matters, do they desire the fulfilment of all things looked for in the promises, viz. that what not is should exist again. Such are the views of those who, while believing in Christ, understand the divine Scriptures in a sort of Jewish sense, drawing from them nothing worthy of the divine promises.[15]

In the following century Basil of Caesarea (330–379) wrote letters against Apollinarius, who envisaged a post-resurrection return of believers as Jews maintaining Jewish rites and customs.[16] Indeed, declared Basil, "So meanly and poorly has he dared to explain the blessed hope laid up for all who live according to the Gospel of Christ, as to reduce it to mere old wives' fables and doctrines of the Jews."[17]

---

13. Lactantius, *Divinae Institutiones*, LXXII.
14. Clement of Alexandria, *Stromateis*, VII.xii.
15. Origen, *De Princ.*, II.xi.2.
16. Basil, *Ep.*, CCLXIII.iv.
17. Ibid., *Ep.*, CCLV.ii.

PART TWO: Confessing the Faith Ecclesially and Hopefully

The most significant protest against a this-worldly, even in some cases a *quasi*-Baccanalian, understanding of post-resurrection life came from Augustine (354–430). He admits that he himself had once held such a view, but now he strongly advocates a spiritual understanding of the relevant biblical texts. Moreover,

> Seeing the avouchers [of the false doctrine] affirm that the saints after this resurrection shall do nothing but revel in fleshly banquets, where the sheer shall exceed both modesty and measure, this is gross, and fit for none but carnal men to believe. But they that are really and truly spiritual do call those of this opinion Chiliasts. The word is Greek, and may be interpreted, Millenarians, or Thousand-year-ists.[18]

As for the saints, Christ will reign with them for a thousand years from the date of his first coming, and then will come the end of the world and the commencement of Christ's eternal reign.[19] This assumes that the first resurrection is that of the soul in baptism, the second is that of the body at the end of time.[20]

The combined forces of prominent Eastern and Western theologians did much to quell the wilder and more materialistic understandings of the millennium and the Second Coming, and centuries were to pass before a significant fresh outburst of apocalyptic zeal occurred. Among the harbingers of later thought on the subject was Joachim of Fiore (c.1130–1202). In his *Liber concordie Novi ac Veteris Testamenti*, he sought to drive to the spirit behind the letter of Scripture, and presented a philosophy of history along Trinitarian lines. According to his scheme history falls into three ages: that of the Father (the Old Testament dispensation), that of the Son (the New Testament dispensation, due to last for forty-two generations each of thirty years), and that of the Spirit. He further holds that the first age was characterized by polygamy, the second by matrimony, and that the third will be the age of celibacy. Not surprisingly, therefore, contemplatives will take precedence during the last age, and Joachim helpfully supplies a diagram of the New Jerusalem which shows the several grades of monks gathered around the throne of God, with secular clergy and lay brothers relegated to less auspicious positions. Joachim builds on this work in his *Exposito in Apocalypsim*, which

---

18. Augustine, *De Civ. Dei.*, XX.vii.
19. Ibid., XX.ix.
20. Ibid., XX.vi.

Eschatology

concerns the ages of the Son and the Spirit. It is a story of several stages of struggle: between the apostles and the synagogue; the martyrs and their persecutors; the Church's doctors and the heretics; the monastic orders and Islam; and Rome and the Empire. The final struggle is that between spiritual men and a dragon, and two beasts which stand for Saladin and "Maximus Antichrist"—the propagator of all heresies. Then will follow the age of the Spirit.

The ideas of Joachim were adopted or, perhaps better, adapted, by a variety of Christians who followed him. Some Franciscans turned his account of spiritual warfare in a revolutionary direction; Thomas Müntzer (c.1489–1525) expressed indebtedness to Joachim in his *Von dem gedichteten Glauben* (1524), albeit it was a pseudo-Joachimite commentary on Jeremiah that persuaded him that he was a chosen instrument of God.[21] Moreover his expectation was that the apocalypse was imminent, and with revolutionary fervour he did his best to bring it on. Melchior Hoffman (c.1500–c.1543) likewise expected the immanent apocalypse: indeed, he expected it in 1533, but himself outlived his predicted time by ten years. As was customary, apocalypticism was fuelled by what we would nowadays regard as the manhandling of Revelation. The contemporary problem for the magisterial Reformers was that on the one hand Roman Catholics were saying that Protestants repudiated the book (and Zwingli had pronounced it non-canonical, while Luther had originally viewed it askance), and that on the other hand the Anabaptists were drawing attention of the wrong kind to it. Thus in his *Commentary on 2 Thessalonians 2* (1540), in which Paul advocates circumspection regarding the last day, Calvin had the Hoffmanites in mind when referring to "overcurious individuals" who "seized this inappropriate moment to begin a discussion concerning the time of this day."[22]

England was by no means immune to apocalyptic writings and even fervour. Joseph Mede (1586–1638) published *Clavis Apocalyptica* in 1627. This is an exposition of, or at least a rumination upon, Revelation that is not immune to seasoning from astrological speculations. Mede held that Christ would return prior to the millennium, and construed the day of judgment as a millennium of peace for the church on earth. He also knew precisely who the Antichrist was, namely, the Pope. But it was during the Commonwealth, in the wake of the socio-political

---

21. See Williams, *The Radical Reformation*, 45.
22. Calvin, *Commentaries . . . Romans*, 396.

upheaval following the Thirty Years' War, the Civil War, and the execution of Charles I in 1649, that a number of sects, some secular, some religious to the point of revolutionary grew up. Of particular interest to us here are the Fifth Monarchy Men. A number of Baptists, some Independents (Congregationalists) and the erstwhile Presbyterian minister, John Rogers, travelled under this banner. Inspired by Daniel 2:44, it was believed that the first four monarchies—the Assyrian, Persian, Macedonian, and Roman—being no more, the fifth monarchy—Christ's rule of the world with his saints—was imminent. Whereas some orthodox Puritans, John Owen among them, entertained millennial ideas in a spiritual sense, the Fifth Monarchy Men took up arms by way of hastening the day. Thomas Venner led an uprising in 1657, but was spared, and the millennium was delayed. In 1661 he and some fifty comrades launched a three-day assault on London. Again the millennium was delayed, and this time Venner and thirteen members of his army lost their heads.

During the nineteenth century there was a further flurry of millennial speculation. This was the age of fear of revolution, and of wars on the European continent; of rapid industrialization; of the movement of people from the country to the towns; of the shaking of the foundations of belief (however vaguely held), partly as a result of the moral critique of modes of doctrinal expression which was engendered by the Enlightenment, partly because of the advent of modern biblical criticism and evolutionary thought, and partly because of some increasingly vocal agnostics and secularists. This turbulence fostered the millennial hope in those susceptible to it, and some of these found a leader in Edward Irving (1792–1834). In 1827 Irving, a minister of the Church of Scotland, published his translation of a work by the Spanish Jesuit, Lacunza: *The Coming of the Messiah in Glory and Majesty*. This caught the attention of another Scot, Henry Drummond (1786–1860), an ardent enquirer into things eschatological. In 1830 Irving was excommunicated by his Church on the ground of heresy concerning the humanity of Christ, but he disregarded the judgment and continued to preach at Regent Square Scottish Church, London. The London Presbytery finally deposed him in 1832, whereupon, together with Drummond and other likeminded souls he founded the Catholic Apostolic Church. This body majored on the Second Coming; its worship was of the "high" sort; its liturgy was eclectic, with items drawn from Eastern and Western Christian sources; and its church order was restorationist to the extent of appointing twelve "Apostles" of the Church. Therein lay its downfall; for it was believed that

Eschatology

the Second Coming would take place before the last Apostle died. He, however, died in 1901, it was swiftly observed that the Parousia had not occurred, and with that the confidence and the numbers of the membership dwindled.

More durable are the Plymouth Brethren (frequently called Christian Brethren nowadays—except for that branch known as Exclusive). Whereas in calamitous times Thomas Venner and his Fifth Monarchy men had taken up arms in the interests of the millennium, the societal uncertainties of the nineteenth century prompted some to resort to an eschatologically-inspired other-worldliness—something for which they were teased by the socially conscious Baptist preacher, C. H. Spurgeon who, alluding to Acts 1:11 said, "Ye men of Plymouth, why stand ye here gazing up into Heaven?"[23] The leader of the Plymouth Brethren was the erstwhile Church of England cleric, J. N. Darby (1800–1882). He and his followers paid great heed to dispensationalism, and the Scofield Reference Bible (1909) was widely used by later generations of them. Darby expected the immanent return of Christ which would be concurrent with the secret rapture of the saints, all of whom would later return to reign for a thousand years. B. W. Newton (1807–99), on the other hand, expected that the great tribulation would pre-date the return of Christ. It should not be supposed that thoughts concerning the rapture were entertained only by those belonging to the new religious movements of the nineteenth century. Of William Cunningham (c. 1776–1849), who had published works on Daniel and Revelation, and who was the founder and first minister of Stewarton Congregational Church, Ayrshire, it was said (admittedly by an unfriendly witness) that he was given "to curious speculations upon the Last Trump. A thunderstorm at midnight, or the glare of a farmer's haystacks burning, threw him into a fever of expectation.... Every night he dressed himself in a newly laundered white nightgown and night cap in preparation for the Advent, but as he expected it to be somewhat cold flying through the clouds he always put on plenty of woolens [sic] beneath."[24]

To J. H. Philpot (1802–69), who left his Church of England living and became a leader among the Gospel Standard Baptists, much of the prevailing eschatological speculation was idle, and in its place he advocated the reading of the Bible in relation to the signs of the times. He

23. Spurgeon, *An All-Round* Ministry, 54.
24. McNaughton, *Early Congregational Independency in Lowland Scotland*, II, 251, quoting Thomas Cassels, *History of John Knox Church*, 20–21.

found no difficulty in using Revelation to weigh and measure nineteenth-century England, and he worked up a particular enthusiasm for the evil spirits likened to frogs (Rev 16: 3). He equated the first frog with infidelity as seen in the writings of Voltaire and Rousseau; the second with republicanism, and the third with Roman Catholicism. Concerning the last, in a masterpiece of elegant invective, he declared that "Popery is the bullfrog, croaking and spitting in the Roman marshes; the Puseyite priest, and the Methodist minister, and the great independent D.D. are but tadpoles, which would grow into frogs did the English climate permit. But the chilling breeze of popular opinion keeps them at present wriggling in their little pools, without power to crawl to land and swell out into a frog."[25]

Millenarian and dispensational thought began to be represented by some speakers at the annual Keswick Convention (1875),[26] and when in 1917, during World War I, the Advent Testimony and Preparation League was constituted and drew the support of the prominent Baptist F. B. Meyer, the learned Congregationalist, P. T. Forsyth, snorted that none of those associated with the League's "obsolete" views "ever did the New Testament the honour of being a recognised scholar in it."[27] I need hardly add that North America has given birth to Seventh Day Adventism, or that millenarianism has been one of a number of significant strands within American fundamentalism.[28] Both of these are indebted to the ideas of William Miller (1782–1849). The publication of Hal Lindsay's book, *The Great Planet Earth* in 1970, and the phenomenal success of the *Left Behind* series of novels by Tim LaHaye and Jerry Jenkins demonstrates that speculation upon the millennial hope, the rapture and related notions is, from one point of view, big business and, from another, more than a little disturbing.

---

25. Philpot, *Mr. J. C. Philpot's Review*, 23.

26. The Convention continues to be held annually under the slogan, "All one in Christ Jesus."

27. Forsyth in *The Christian World*, 15 November 1917, 7. For this reference I am indebted to the excellent paper by Randall, "'The things which shall be hereafter' . . ."

28. See Sandeen, *The Roots of Fundamentalism*; Sell, *Theology in Turmoil*, ch. 5.

Eschatological Fluctuations: Judgment and the Afterlife

There can be no question that the New Testament witnesses to a divine judgment that is both present and to come. It is a prominent theme of John's Gospel that those who hear and respond to Jesus receive the gift of life eternal, while those who refuse are adversely judged already (John 3:17–21). This in no way precludes the final judgment, when God's final verdict upon persons and the world will be pronounced (John 5:28–29). Throughout, the criterion of judgment will be the relationship, or lack of it, with Christ. In Revelation a new heaven and a new earth are predicted, while the idea of judgment by fire is found in Matthew 3:12, 1 Corinthians 3:13, 2 Thessalonians 1:8, and Hebrews 10:27.

The theme of the destruction of the world by fire is taken up by a number of early writers. Some think in terms of a destructive fire, others of a purificatory one. Thus, for example, Justin Martyr argues that were it not for "the seed of Christians . . . the fire of judgment would descend and devour all things."[29] By contrast, Irenaeus holds against Valentinus that "neither is the substance nor the essence of the creation annihilated," but rather that when the present order passes away humanity will be renewed and flourish "in an incorruptible state," and the new heaven and new earth will be inaugurated.[30] Similarly, Origen contends that "if the fashion of the world passes away, it is by no means an annihilation or destruction of [the heavens'] material substance that is shown to take place, but a kind of change of quality and transformation of appearance."[31] Elsewhere, however, when opposing Celsus he denounces those Greeks who ridicule "the doctrine of a conflagration of the world," but construes the fire as a refiner's purifying fire which "burns, indeed, but does not consume."[32] Augustine, with reference to Revelation 20 and 21, states that those whose names are "not in the book of life being judged, and cast into eternal fire (what, or where it is [he prudently adds] I hold is unknown to all but those unto whom it pleases the Spirit to reveal it); then shall this world lose its form by worldly fire," whereupon the new heaven and earth will appear.[33]

---

29. Justin Martyr, *Apol.*, II.vii.
30. Irenaeus, *Adv. Haer.*, V.xxxvi.1.
31. Origen *De Princ.*, I.vii.4; cf. II.i.3.
32. Idem, *Contra Cels.*, V.xv.
33. Augustine, *De Civ. Dei*, XX.xvi.

PART TWO: Confessing the Faith Ecclesially and Hopefully

The question of the final destination of human beings exercised the minds of Christians through all the succeeding centuries. There was little disagreement that the righteous would arrive in heaven and live in eternal fellowship with God—albeit the New Testament's indication of realized eschatology was frequently swamped by heaven construed as the future reward of godly living; but the question of the wicked gave rise to intense and mutually contradictory speculation. Without question there has been a long tradition of belief in the eternal punishment of the wicked. If in his Reformed *Catechism* of 1581 John Craig was matter-of-fact in writing:

Q. With whom and where will the wicked be?

A. With Satan in hell, oppressed with infinite miseries;[34]

and if the Quaker William Dewsbury was sufficiently straightforward in saying that "the mighty day of the Lord is coming that shall burn as an oven . . . and all you that do wickedly shall be stubble, and the day that cometh shall burn you up, saith the Lord of hosts, and it shall leave you neither root nor branch,"[35] their forebear in the faith, Hippolytus, has a graphic description of the sufferings of the wicked.[36] As is well known, throughout the medieval period popular piety combined with great art to depict the pains of hell. Not a little of this flowed down into post-Reformation times, where the fear of hell became a prominent psychological tool in the hands of many preachers. Even Jonathan Edwards (1703–58) could declare that "The God that holds you over the pit of hell, much as one holds a spider, or some loathsome insect, over the fire, abhors you, and is dreadfully provoked . . . it is nothing but his hand that holds you from falling into the fire every moment. It is to be ascribed to nothing else that you did not go to hell the last night . . ."[37] Nor can it be denied that there has been a long strand of godly gloating over the fate of the wicked. Tertullinan was but one of many who indulged in this: "Which sight gives me joy? Which arouses me to exultation?—as I see so many illustrious monarchs . . . groaning in the lowest darkness . . . and those . . . too, who persecuted the Christian name, in fires more fierce than

34. Craig's *Catechism*. In Torrance, *The School of Faith*, 164.

35. Dewsbury *A True Prophecy of the Mighty Day of the Lord*. In Barbour and Roberts, *Early Quaker Writings*, 564.

36. Hippolytus, *De Christo et Antichristo*, LXV.

37. Edwards, "Sinners in the hands of an angry God." In *Works*, II, 10.

Eschatology

those with which in the days of their pride they raged against the followers of Christ."[38] Thomas Aquinas thought that among the blessings that the saved would enjoy in heaven was that of witnessing the sufferings of the damned—only, however, because these sufferings vindicated God's justice.[39] "How good God is!" declared a twentieth-century Calvinist woman to her minister: "He has damned all my friends, but he has saved me!"[40]

One of the important benefits of the English Enlightenment was the contribution of more liberal divines to the moral critique of more grotesque expressions of Christian doctrine.[41] Not surprisingly some of these challenges concerned the eschatological implications of predestinarian doctrine. The Presbyterian divine, Henry Grove (1683–1738) may illustrate the point:

> The love of God [so it is said] . . . is his making choice of some to be the objects of his munificence, while others, and they the vastly greater number, are left destitute of all power to emerge out of that miserable condition into which they are fallen through no fault of their own. Is there not too much reason to say, that this notion of the *love* of God to man is utterly unworthy of him? What does the Deity discover by such a *love* (if it must be called by that name) but *uncontrollable power* . . . ?[42]

But what Grove would have regarded as unacceptable eschatology was precisely one of the principal motivating factors of the modern missionary movement that arose from the Evangelical Revival of the eighteenth century (in the first instance from its Calvinistic wing). The conviction that thousands were doomed to hell if they did not hear the gospel, and that they themselves would be blameworthy if they did not risk all to communicate it, inspired many missionaries who faced uncertainty, disease and even death for Christ's sake. But as the nineteenth century progressed increasing numbers of these began to take what liberal theologians would have regarded as a more ethical view of God and hence a more hopeful view of the unchurched.

38. Tertullian, *De Spec.*, XXX.
39. Aquinas, *Summa Theologica*, VIII, Suppl., Q. 94.3.
40. Quoted by Poole-Connor, *Evangelicalism in England*, 116 n. I fear that many a TV religious channel will supply further examples of this grotesque sort.
41. See further Sell, *Enlightenment, Ecumenism,* Evangel, ch. 3.
42. Grove, *Ethical and Theological Writings*, IV, 101. For Grove see ODNB; Sell, *Dissenting Thought*, ch. 6; Sell, *Testimony and* Tradition, ch. 5.

PART TWO: Confessing the Faith Ecclesially and Hopefully

At issue was the question of the eternity of punishment, not least that of those who through no fault of their own had never heard the gospel. To meet this perceived difficulty two main options were proposed. Some found it appropriate to revive the doctrine of the annihilation, rather than the eternal punishment, of the wicked. This view, also known as conditional immortality, had been advanced in the third/fourth century by Arnobius, who warned his readers that "unless you give yourselves to know the Supreme God, a cruel death awaits you when freed from the body, not bringing sudden annihilation, but destroying by the bitterness of its long-protracted punishment."[43] Although this doctrine was formally condemned at the Fifth Lateran Council of 1513, it was not entirely obliterated. On the contrary, it surfaced in the thought of the Socinians, among them John Biddle, who denied the eternity of punishment in his *Twofold Catechism* (1654), as did Samuel Richardson in his discussion *Of the Torments of Hell* (1658). Anglicans as different in churchmanship and theology as Jeremy Taylor and the Latitudinarian John Tillotson saw no discrepancy between conditional immortality and the historic faith of the Church. In the nineteenth century the doctrine was revived by the Congregational minister, Edward White, whose book, *Life in Christ*, appeared in 1846 and was enlarged and re-written in 1875. White followed Paul in contending that the wages of sin is death, but unlike many others, he did not construe "death" to mean "spiritual death", but rather the extinction of the soul—not immediately, but after a shorter or longer period of punishment. At its first appearance his view was deemed heretical by many, but in 1887 White was called to the Chair of the Congregational Union of England and Wales—a significant indication of speed with which a traditionally Calvinist body had (according to taste) gone astray or loosened up.[44] R. W. Dale, the prominent minister of Carrs Lane Congregational Church, Birmingham, espoused the doctrine, and some newer groups, the Christadelphians among them, made commitment to annihilationism a distinguishing feature of their teaching. It is important to note that in Dale's view the doctrine of annihilation "is not simply a theory on the future destiny of the impenitent. It is a restatement of the relation of the human race to the Lord Jesus Christ. It is a reassertion in a more definite and emphatic form of the ancient doctrine of the Church concerning the nature and necessity of regeneration."[45] It also, of course, squared with

43. Arnobius, *Adv. Gentes*, II.lxi.
44. See further Sell, *Enlightenment, Ecumenism, Evangel*, ch. 5.
45. Quoted by A. W. W. Dale (son), in *The Life of R. W. Dale*, 313

Eschatology

Dale's Congregational ecclesiology according to which there is a distinction of eternal significance between those who are "in Christ" and those who are not.

The alternative option espoused by those who could no longer stomach eternal punishment was universal restoration. Earlier suggestions of the doctrine notwithstanding, there is general agreement that Origen was the first major theologian to advance this view. It should, however, be noted that in his earlier writings he so emphasized human freedom that he could envisage the redeemed in eternity as continuing to fall into, and out of, sin; and he did not altogether forswear the doctrine of eternal punishment. Thus, having said that matters concerning the consummation are to be "treated by us with great solicitude and caution, in the manner rather of an investigation and discussion, than in that of fixed and certain decision," he declares that

> The end of the world . . . and the final consummation, will take place when every one shall be subjected to punishment for his sins; a time which God alone knows, when He will bestow on each what he deserves. . . . [S]uch is the end, when all enemies will be subdued to Christ, when death—the last enemy—shall be destroyed, and when the kingdom shall be delivered up by Christ (to whom all things are subject) to the Father . . .[46]

Gregory of Nyssa (c.335–c.395) followed Origen's lead. He thinks in terms of a refining fire that will prepare all souls for their destined conformity with the divine image, and he envisages a time when "a harmony of thanksgiving will arise from all creatures, as well from those who in the process of the purgation have suffered chastisement as from those who have needed no purgation at all."[47] In the ninth century John Scotus Eriugena (c.810–c.877), deeply concerned to harmonize the biblical idea of creation with the Neoplatonist doctrine of emanation, sought to show that all things begin and end in God. This being so, he expressed surprise: "I wonder on what principle you deliberate and hesitate, thinking that evil and the death of evil torments can remain for ever in that humanity the whole of which the Word of God took into Himself and redeemed; whereas true reason teaches that nothing contrary to the divine goodness

---

46. Origen, *De Princ.*, I.vi.1, 2.
47. Gregory of Nyssa, *The Great Catechism*, XXVI.

PART TWO: Confessing the Faith Ecclesially and Hopefully

and life and blessedness can be co-eternal with them. For the divine goodness will consume evil, eternal life will absorb death and misery."[48]

Just as there was a revival of annihilationist thought during the nineteenth century, so it was with universalism. The Anglican divine, F. D. Maurice (1805–72) caused consternation in some circles when his *Theological Essays* appeared in 1853. His views in opposition to the doctrine of eternal punishment, namely, that time and eternity were generically different, and that eternal life was the perception of God's love and eternal punishment the loss of that capacity, prompted his deposition from his Chair at King's College, London.[49] It is also noticeable that just as the medieval Church of Rome posited purgatory as a halting-place between this world and the next, so many in the nineteenth century, whilst advocating what they called the "larger hope," nevertheless thought that the divine purpose would be advanced if there were an intermediate state of probation, so that those who had never heard the gospel, or had by the time of their decease spurned it, might be won for Christ. It was precisely this heresy, as he perceived it, that prompted C. H. Spurgeon's crusade against what he called the Down-Grade in the Baptist Union, and eventually led to his resignation from that body. Spurgeon was not alone in countering the doctrine of post-mortem probation. "The glory of the authentic Gospel," declared the Scottish theologian, H. R. Mackintosh, "is that the love of God does not wait upon our fitness. . . . 'Fitness' is a thought born of morality, not religion; and neither in this life nor the next can the believer accept it as indicating or controlling the relation of the Father's mercy to human need."[50]

It would be wrong to leave the impression that as the nineteenth century progressed all Christian theologians and ministers opted for the eschatological party of their choice. On the contrary, many ministers pursued their pastoral duties whilst paying little heed to eschatology, while others were variously perplexed, or prudently silent. Thomas Binney's position, as described by Henry Allon, is probably representative of that of a number of his Victorian contemporaries:

> He was one of the earliest of his generation to maintain the broad universal purpose of the divine Father's love, and of the salvation

---

48. Eriugena, *De Divisione Naturae*, V.

49. See Maurice, *Theological Essays*, 437. As early as the seventeenth century some had repudiated the idea of eternal punishment. See Walker, *The Decline of Hell*.

50. Mackintosh. *Immortality and the Future*, 154.

> which is proffered through Christ. . . . [F]or the same reasons he rejected the doctrine of eternal punishment. . . . While Mr. Binney shrank from propounding any alternative theory of the destiny of the wicked, he distinctly refused to believe in eternal torments. He felt that conclusions from which . . . in their best and holiest feelings, good men instinctively recoiled, could not be possible to the holy and loving God.[51]

Reflections on the Fluctuations

I may now claim to have shown, all too briefly, that approaches to eschatological doctrine have fluctuated considerably through the Christian ages. Theories sober and fantastic have jostled for the minds of Christians, interpretations realistic or spiritual have been promulgated. There can be little question that in some cases the mantra with which I began this paper was justified; and if my authority does not suffice, Arnobius will support me. To those inclined to probe beyond the capacities of the human mind he said, "Your reason is not permitted to involve you in such questions, and to be busied to no purpose about things out of reach."[52] What is my response to the eschatological positions as now recorded?

First, I must confess to an almost complete inability to work up interest concerning the millennium. For this reason I did not delay over the excitements which some have found in pre-, post-, or a-millennial theorizing. Origen hinted that the source of millennial expectation was in Jewish speculation during the centuries surrounding the birth of Christ and, given the evidence of the messianic expectation in the first century book, 2 Enoch (the Slavonic Enoch), I think that he was right to do so. The subject is not mentioned by Jesus, nor does it appear in any of the classical creeds or the Reformed confessions of faith and catechisms known to me. The explanation for this, surely, is that with Christ the kingdom is already present; at Pentecost the Spirit of Christ returns, and in the ascension Christ's universal sway is confirmed; accordingly, there is no room for a millennial reign.

This is not to say that in God's good time there will not be a winding up of history, a consummation—the event witnessed to by the doctrine of the Second Coming: "Salvation covers more than individual destiny,"

---

51. Allon, *Sermons Preached in the Kings Weigh-House Chapel*, liv.
52. Arnobius, *Adv. Gentes*, II.lxi.

wrote H. R. Mackintosh, "it is perfected only in the perfecting of the Kingdom, and Christ's perfecting of the Kingdom, coinciding with the end of this world, is His Advent."[53] But here again we need to be circumspect. Notwithstanding numerous of our disappointed forebears whose calendrical calculations came to nought, we do not know the time when this will occur, and we should be ill advised to think of it in too literalistic terms. Some theologians and preachers still make much of the fact that Christ will come visibly on the clouds. The twentieth-century New Testament scholar J. J. Müller said this, though he declined to speculate whether television would be the means whereby the event would be universally witnessed.[54] The advice of the Puritan William Gurnall (1616–79) is more to the point: "The servant that looks for his master will be loath to be found in bed when he comes; no, he sits up to open the door for him when he knocks. Christ hath told us he 'will come'; but not *when*, that we might never put off our clothes or put out the candle."[55]

"Take Christ now as you Saviour or meet Him later as your Judge."[56] Thus spoke the celebrated Methodist preacher, W. E. Sangster. I fear, however, that he propounded a false dichotomy, for Christ cannot be now judge, later saviour: he is always both judge and saviour, and according as our response to him is positive or negative, we are judged favourably or adversely. But to say that judgment is here and now is not to deny a final judgment. The latter idea is too prominent in the New Testament to be ignored. What I think may be said with confidence was said was said best by two most perceptive theologians of an earlier generation: Sydney Cave and H. R. Mackintosh:

> Amid all that is uncertain, this at least is sure. Our Judge will be the God whose glory we have seen in the face of Jesus Christ. In judgement as in redemption, Christ is the image of the Father, and so we know that judgement will not be arbitrary or purposeless. It will be the judgment of love like the love of Christ.[57]

> To be tried at last, in Christ's presence, may be truly designated as the last means of grace for the redeemed. . . . [O]ur sin will then be shown us, not to torture us, but in order that more and

---

53. Mackintosh, *Immortality and the Future*, 140.
54. Müller, *When Christ Comes Again*, 35.
55. Gurnall, *The Christian in Complete* Armour, II, 507.
56. Sangster, "The Probation of Life," 105.
57. S. Cave, *The Doctrines of the Christian Faith*, 301.

more we may understand the length and breadth and greatness
of His mercy who knows what is in man.[58]

But if judgment is here and now, and to come, so is heaven. It was a great step forward when C. H. Dodd (1884–1973), pre-eminently in Britain, drew renewed attention to what he called "realized eschatology"—the idea conveyed in the New Testament that the kingdom of heaven is here now, and to come in its fullness. Dodd developed this theme in relation to Acts, Paul's letters and, above all, to the parables of the kingdom. With the coming of Jesus God's kingly reign is inaugurated, and the whole of his life and ministry testifies to the fact. In somewhat different ways more recent theologians such as Moltmann and Pannenberg have developed this idea. Heaven is life in the presence of God now; it is not a location the passport to which is death. But, we believe, our fellowship with God will be more wonderful hereafter; and it is all of grace.

The questions of hell and the fate of the wicked cannot, however, be sidestepped. As has often been remarked, we cannot describe the furniture of heaven or take the temperature of hell. We are bound to have recourse to symbolism, but we should not be misled by it. There is much that we do not know. There is New Testament evidence to support the view that if heaven begins here and now, so too does hell; that hell is to be understood as the agony of separation from God. As Calvin wrote, "[W]e ought especially to fix our thoughts upon this: how wretched it is to be cut off from all fellowship with God."[59] But this holy God, in whose presence sin cannot stand, is also the God who does not desire the death of the wicked but rather that they repent and live. What are we to make of this? There are, in my opinion, sufficient warnings in the New Testament to preclude the dogmatic assertion of universalism (however much one might hope that it is true, and that God's relentless seeking will be rewarded with ultimate finding). Perhaps the parson-poet George Crabbe (1754–1832) put it most succinctly when—with reference to the Swedenborgian universalism, but it applies more widely—he wrote,

> The view is happy, we may think it just;
> It may be true—but who shall add, it must?[60]

---

58. Mackintosh, *Immortality and the Future*, 194.
59. Calvin, *Institutes*, III.xxv.12.
60. Crabbe, "The Borough, Letter IV."

PART TWO: Confessing the Faith Ecclesially and Hopefully

In H. R. Mackintosh's opinion, "No one certainly is in a position to affirm that there must be those who eternally remain unsaved. This would be much more than to admit the possibility of eternal sin; it would plant intrinsic moral dualism at the heart of things."[61] On the other hand, would God override his gift of freedom—even the freedom doggedly to refuse his love eternally? Or should we be swayed by Sydney Cave's suggestion that "if any be lost, it will be because they have so identified themselves with evil that they have lost the power of choice; they have ceased to be persons, and as things may pass into the void"? He immediately adds, "Such surmises deal with what lies beyond our knowledge."[62] Is there anything that we can say with some degree of certainty? What seems clear from the New Testament is that the religious will have some surprises when they see who are enjoying the afterlife in heaven—and who are conspicuous by their absence therefrom!

Precisely because of our limited knowledge and the numerous interpretations of eschatological matters that have been advanced, we should be ill advised to elevate assent to particular aspects of eschatological doctrine into terms of Christian fellowship or church membership. With reference to one particularly contentious issue the prominent Baptist, Robert Hall (1764–1831), saw the point in the early nineteenth century: "[I]n my humble opinion, the doctrine of the eternal duration of future misery, metaphysically considered, is not an essential article of faith, nor is the belief of it ever proposed as a term of salvation; . . . if we really flee from the wrath to come, by truly repenting of our sins, and laying hold of the mercy of God through Christ, by a lively faith, our salvation is perfectly secure, whichever hypothesis we embrace on this most mysterious subject."[63]

Apologetic Matters Arising

When we have done our best to wrestle with the Bible's eschatological pronouncements, and have cut a path through literalism and lurid and eccentric interpretations, we are still not out of the wood if we would commend the faith to others. The eschatological assertions we wish to

---

61. Mackintosh, *Immortality and the Future*, 211.

62. Cave, *The Doctrines of the Christian Faith*, 301.

63. Hall, *Works*, V, 528–29, from "Letter LXIV, "To a Gentleman at Trinity College, Cambridge," dated 30 April 1821.

Eschatology

make remain susceptible to challenge by sincere enquirers no less than by sceptical opponents. All that can be done here is to specify some of the issues that clamour for more attention than some theologians devote to them.

It is first of all necessary to show that Christianity is not committed to the doctrine of immortality understood as the human being's natural right. On the contrary, as John Baillie insisted, "It is time there was an end to the expectation that anything even remotely corresponding to the Christian hope may be extracted from premises of a purely humanistic kind."[64] Christianity is not concerned with the mere survival of an aspect of our selves deemed indestructible—the escape, in Platonic fashion, of the soul from its body-tomb; or with the *post-mortem* re-assembling of our body parts; or with the pantheistic absorption of our selves in the Absolute;[65] or with our "living on" in the memories of those who knew us (though we may hope that some may remember us—but for how long?). The One into whose fellowship we are called by grace is the God and Father of our Lord Jesus Christ, and that relationship means a new life which begins in the present and continues after death, and joy and peace that know no end; and all of this because Jesus Christ was raised, and those who are united to him are raised with him. Death has no power over them, for it was defeated once-for-all at the cross. As Geoffrey Nuttall wrote, "The New Testament begins and ends with Christ: He is the Alpha and the Omega. . . . And the Church begins and ends with the Resurrection."[66]

But already I have used a number of terms, and made some huge assumptions, which many find problematic. I have spoken of new life but not, of course, of absolutely novel life. There is continuity between what Paul thought of as the old life and the new—not least the continuity marked by the fact that those who are saints by calling are also sinners. The newness rather consists in the fact that the saint has a new outlook, new motives, new attitudes, new power, new friends in the church—God's adopted family, and a new song of praise and glory to God.[67] Hear P. T. Forsyth: "Eternal life is a new *gift* to us by a new act, a new creation. It is a second birth. It is not the development of a power or an ideal immanent

---

64. Baillie, *And the Life Everlasting*, 123.
65. See further Sell, *Philosophical Idealism*.
66. Nuttall, "The Heirs of Heaven," 9.
67. For a fuller exposition of these points see Sell, *The Spirit Our Life*, 24–25.

to the world or Humanity. It is a gift of God, through an act of God. To evade that act of God is to turn religion to a piece of aesthetic. In an ethical religion we are redeemed. We do not glide into heaven; we are taken, not to say plucked, into it."[68]

As if this were not enough, there is the biblical promise of a new heaven and a new earth. There is to be a redemption of the physical as well as of the spiritual. Hence Paul's use of the *prima facie* contradictory term "spiritual body" (1 Cor 15:4). Nothing that God has created is beyond the reach of his re-creative power. This returns us to the assertion that Christ's resurrection, confirmatory of his victory at the cross over all that is opposed to God, is of cosmic significance.[69] What is clear from this is that Christianity takes a linear view of history with teleology at its heart: a purpose is being worked out. This cannot but puzzle those who take a cyclic view of history and, to the best of my knowledge, this is marks a chasm between the Christian faith and some other faiths which thus far seems insurmountable.

I have said that the new life begins now and continues more wonderfully hereafter. Many Christians would endorse this claim, among them the blacksmith who, having heard Brownlow North (1810–75) preach, said, "Surely a believing sense of the presence and favour of God enjoyed is heaven begun on earth."[70] "The Christian's assurance of life after death," wrote Geoffrey Nuttall, "is . . . never a sheer *datum*, it is always consequent upon his faith, an inference from it, we might say, albeit a necessary inference."[71] No doubt; but the problem for some is that the alleged new, post-mortem, life is said to be the believer's life, but it does not involve the bodily and other features whereby others would recognize us in this present life, or by which we would recognize ourselves in a mirror or in accurate pictorial representations of ourselves. The question thus presses whether the believer's life now and the life hereafter is the life of the *same* person.[72] It is in the interests of Christian testimony to insist that it is, as F. H. Cleobury whimsically points out. He imagines a man who says to him, "You are immortal, but by this I mean that the Albert Memorial will be unaffected by your death." To those who ask whether anyone really

---

68. Forsyth, *This Life and the Next*, 86.
69. See further Beek, *Why? On Suffering, Guilt and God*, ch. 23.
70. Stewart, *Brownlow North*, 53.
71. Nuttall, "The Heirs of Heaven," 17.
72. For a fuller discussion of this point see Flew. "Death."

talks like this Cleobury replies, "There are people who tell me that I am immortal and then hasten to add that the 'I' which is immortal is not what *I* call 'I', but some other entity which, they assure me, is my real self. And when they try to explain this real self, it seems to me that even if it existed it could with as little reason be identified with me as can the Albert Memorial."[73]

Furthermore, the new life is said to involve a relationship with a God deemed to be personal. But God, being, according to Christian doctrine, omnipresent spirit, seems to be an odd entity with whom to have a personal relationship. Here we must refer at once to God's supreme revelation in Jesus Christ. From him we learn that God is our Father; in Jesus we see God's love—as holy and righteous as it is merciful and free. We can rest in this knowledge; any other thoughts about One who inhabits eternity conceived as an environment not conditioned by space and time are quite beyond our powers of comprehension.

Yet again, the new life is said to be a life of union with Christ and within the communion of saints which begins here and continues hereafter. How might such a claim be defended? We can without difficulty understand that Christians may associate in this life with other believers in the fellowship of the Church. An unbeliever might understand this fellowship as analogous to the fellowship others find in a darts club or a bee-keeping society. The Christian would then be tempted to complicate matters by explaining that the analogy in imperfect because Christian fellowship is vertically inaugurated whereas other human associations are horizontally inaugurated. That is to say, in the latter case enthusiasts band together, raise money, appoint committees, and promote their interest. In the former case the saints are called by God into his new family. But this does not settle the problem of communion with the saints hereafter. I do not see that we can say more than this: "If we are to assume any kind of continuity of personality (and apart from this assumption the resurrection of Jesus has no meaning either for Himself or for anyone else), it would seem unreal, as well and unnecessary, to rule out some kind of continuity in those personal relationships out of which the stuff of personality is shaped and nurtured, and which, as we grow older, seem to depend less rather than more on the use of our bodies as means and instruments."[74]

---

73. Cleobury, "Immortality and Purpose," 62.
74. Nuttall, *The Reality of Heaven*, 79–80.

PART TWO: Confessing the Faith Ecclesially and Hopefully

What, then, of union with Christ? The *Westminster Larger Catechism* (1648) affirms that "The union which the elect have with Christ is the work of God's grace, by which they are spiritually and mystically, yet really and inseparably, joined to Christ as their Head and Husband, which is done in their effectual calling."[75] Behind this claim lies, once more, the fact of Christ's resurrection: not so much the empty tomb, for no amount of empirical evidence of the most reliable kind would by itself convey the gospel. The disciples *experienced* the risen Christ and proclaimed their good news to all who would hear.

But I have just used the term "experience," and this leads us to the heart of the matter of commending the faith to others. For clearly a person's religious experience is properly a matter of testimony, but it is not a matter of demonstrative proof which could convince a sceptic. Moreover, we cannot bestow our faith on another. If we are charged, as we may well be, with being deluded, or at least with being liable to error (if we can be mistaken where relations with other humans are concerned—how much more where God is the subject of our experience), we can but take our stand. As Ronald Hepburn put it, "There seems no way, *at the experiential level*, of settling the really urgent questions, most of all the following: Do we have in theistic experience *mere* projection? Or do we have a projection matched by an objectively existing God?"[76]

What has become clear as this part of our discussion has progressed is that the idea of the supernatural runs throughout. I am not, of course, thinking in terms of Hollywood "spookery." Rather, if I may quote myself, "I understand the saving act to be supernatural in two respects: first, its provision is not from nature, least of all from human beings, but from the holy God of all grace. Secondly, it has to restore nature, especially ours."[77] The Christian's calling; our new life here and now and to come; our relations with God and the communion of saints here and now and to come: all of this turns on the action of God at the cross on the very stage of that history, human and material, which is in the process of being redeemed. If our honest enquirers and equally honest (however sceptical) opponents cannot see this (and apart from the approach of the Holy Spirit they will not), there is no more that we can do by way of testimony. We cannot, for example, convince them by showing how coherent our

75. Torrance, *The School of Faith*, 197.
76. Hepburn, "Religious experience," VII, 168.
77. Sell, *Confessing and Commending the Faith*, 180. The point is elaborated on pp. 177–84.

Eschatology

system of thought is (though we should strive for coherence), because they will simply retort that the Nazi and the *Alice in Wonderland* world views are coherent: the question is whether they are true.

The upshot is that what is at issue here is a clash of world views. To espouse one is to reject another; to move from one to another is to be converted, because what is at issue is the "total assertion" that a person makes about the world, and not simply a change of mind on one or more particular points of belief. Thus, for example, in the heyday of logical positivism, some maintained that those propositions only are meaningful which are either analytic or, at least in principle, empirically verifiable. They thereby ruled out aesthetic, moral and religious propositions as literally non-sensical, meaningless. So long as a person maintains this view, all Christian claims (amongst many others) are ruled out *ab initio*. Or if a Christian and a member of an eastern religion were discussing the philosophy of history, the Christian would presumably wish to assert a linear view of history, whereby there is a forward movement through time and a teleological objective in view, whereas the other person might advocate a cyclic view of history with all that that entails in terms of the transmigration of souls, reincarnation and the like. Clearly such stances differ significantly from straightforward differences of opinion among those who espouse the same world view on matters on which one might legitimately be persuaded to change one's mind (the date of the Second Coming, for example). All that can be done in such cases is to commend one's own stance, and to seek to show that, by adopting his or her world view, the other person is precluded from accommodating matters of importance. What cannot be done, I suggest, is to declare that, however it may be with other world views, the Christian world view derives from revelation and is *ipso facto* utterly divorced from metaphysical assumptions. The fact is that even those, whether philosophers or theologians, who have eschewed metaphysics are *ipso facto* indebted to it in that they are making claims to the effect that the world is, or is not, such and such. As has been well said, "Even the violently anti-metaphysical theology of Karl Barth and his neo-Calvinist followers finds itself involved in self-contradiction when it denies all validity to metaphysics. Such a denial is itself metaphysical and, ironically, an uncompromising revelational theology has implicit metaphysical foundations which are concealed only by a kind of theological sleight of hand."[78]

---

78. Root, "The logic of eschatology," 95.

PART TWO: Confessing the Faith Ecclesially and Hopefully

The Perennial, Practical, Importance of Eschatology

So much for Christian eschatological testimony *vis à vis* honest enquirers and sceptical opponents. What, finally, is the importance of eschatology for Christians themselves? I shall suggest that eschatology is important for theology, for Christian living, for pastoral work, and for worship.

It is a characteristic feature of Christian doctrine that with whichever doctrine one begins, if the enquiry is deep enough, all the other doctrines will eventually come under consideration. This is certainly the case with eschatology. The fact has been implicit in all that has gone before in this paper. We cannot think of re-creation without pondering creation; when we speak of eternal union with Christ and we cannot suppress the Christological and soteriological questions, Who is he? and What has he done? Our continuing sense of his presence cannot but lead us into pnematology, and when we think of the communion of saints we are clearly on the threshold of ecclesiology. Underlying all is God, our holy, merciful Father, in whose presence sin cannot stand—sin in which we are involved. It is the gospel of God's grace in Christ's saving work which shines the spotlight on ourselves, and our anthropological enquiries must take due account of this. It is our confidence in that same saving grace that gives us hope for the future even as we live the resurrection life now. Yet the theologian, Gordon Kaufman, can say that "I don't think there can be any future for heaven and hell."[79] While no theologian should be held to a soundbite spoken to a magazine reporter, my view is that if Kaufman were denying heaven and hell as *quasi*-material locations he was stating the obvious; but if he meant that the terms have no continuing significance he was profoundly mistaken.

My reference to our call to "live the resurrection life here and now" is of the greatest importance, for if eschatology were but a handmaid to those who wish to devise theological systems, most believers would be left high and dry. In fact eschatological themes are crucial to our Christian living. This may not always be readily apparent, and this is at least in part because eschatological themes are, in some quarters, seldom touched upon in churches except at funerals (by which time is it too late for the deceased). As long ago as 1915 H. R. Mackintosh felt able to declare that "Sermons on the joys of heaven or future retribution are tolerably rare."[80] It would be a gross exaggeration to say that there has

79. Quoted by Woodward in "Heaven," 54.
80. Mackintosh, *Immortality and the Future*, 100.

been any improvement in this regard in most of the churches with which I am acquainted. This is the more disturbing because at the present time death is prominently in the news. We hear much of euthanasia (not in Augustus Montague Toplady's sense of the "happy death" of Christians), and of "assisted suicide." Death regularly confronts us on television when we, as it were, visit war zones or scenes of devastating natural disaster. Christian applied ethicists do seem to be busy in the fields of abortion and euthanasia, and I have seen copies of the *Journal of Thanatology*. But systematicians and, especially perhaps, preachers, do not always give to eschatological themes the place that they deserve, and this is unfortunate for a number of reasons. Our pulpits ought to be places in which, over a period of time, the Bible is expounded in such a way as to cover the major issues of life, not excluding death. As Archbishop Vincent Nichols, the leader of the Roman Catholics of England and Wales said in a sermon on 13 February 2010, "We do not know how to deal with death. But fear cannot be our guide. . . . If we reduce death to a clinical event and manage it through a series of standard procedures, then we do not deal with death well, either clinically or humanly."[81] Nichols' remarks were addressed to society as a whole, but they apply *a fortiori* to the church, for Christian people should be those able to leaven society in general and the health services and voluntary agencies in particular with their witness not simply to the fact that persons are more than bundles of medical problems, but to the fact that there is a gospel word of hope and peace.

I can perfectly well understand why preachers may feel a certain reluctance to broach eschatological matters with their church members. The record of pulpit activity in this field has not been an unmixed blessing. For too long a "carrot and stick" approach was employed by some, the carrot being the joys of heaven, the stick the flames of hell. We recall that even Jonathan Edwards succumbed to this homiletic method. I, however, am convinced that preachers are well advised to eschew any attempt to play upon fears with a view to frightening people to Christ. If the gospel is not heard as good news it will not be heard at all, and people generally only begin to be aware of their needy condition as sinners when they begin grasp what God has done to rescue them.

It is interesting to note that a highly knowledgeable historian of English Dissent has published a paper entitled, "Why did the English stop going to Church?" He concludes as follows: "The Tractarian leader,

---

81. Quoted by Amelia Hill in her Report, 26.

PART TWO: Confessing the Faith Ecclesially and Hopefully

Edward Bouverie Pusey once commented that nothing keeps men from the pleasures of sin 'but the love of God and the fear of Hell', and that it is 'the fear of Hell' that 'drives people back to God.' The English churches by and large ignored his advice and as a result English men and women stopped attending church services."[82] This argument has, I fear, a flavour of the fallacy of incomplete enumeration about it, for there can be no question that societal change, with the alternative options of secularism, materialism, evolutionism and, perhaps above all, the massive dislocation of the First World War were significant factors in the drift of people from the churches. Watts does not, of course, advocate the rekindling the flames of hell in our pulpits.

It may be in part a reaction against ill-conceived applications of the doctrine of hell that there is, among many church members today, the conviction that the churches must be "inclusive" in the sense of being open and welcoming to all, regardless of race, sex, culture and the like. This is as it should be.[83] But the open door approach can have the effect of blunting the angularity of the gospel, so that people are not challenged to consider that there is a distinction of eternal significance between those who are regenerate and those who are not. Yet it is the former who comprise the "matter" of the Church. In the absence of this challenge local churches can so take the colour of the communities in which they are set that when a counter-cultural witness is called for, they are impotent.

Whatever may be the cause of the decline in presenting the eschatological challenge to our congregations (that is, not only to our churches), I believe it to be a pastoral failure not to expound the necessity of repentance and faith as leading to the eternal life of fellowship with Christ and his saints. Only if they are living in what one might call the atmosphere of heaven can our people be equipped to face death. As Thomas Doolittle (1630/33?–1707) insisted, "We live to learn to die. Our business is *not* to get riches, honours, or pleasures, but that we may depart in peace with God. Every corpse is a sermon; every tomb a teacher; every funeral an oration—to persuade you to learn to die."[84] Only if prepared will believers

82. Watts, *Why did the English Stop Going to Church?* 14. He quotes from Rowell, *Hell and the Victorians*, 120.

83. For further reflections on inclusivity and exclusivity see Sell, *Enlightenment, Ecumenism, Evangel*, 325–75.

84. Thomas Doolittle in a funeral sermon preached on 19 September 1690 on the occasion of the death of Matthew Henry's cousin, Robert Bosier. Quoted by Williams, *Memoirs of . . . Matthew* Henry, 12.

regard death (except where loss of faculties or sudden fatal accident intervene) as the last occasion of earthly witness to God's grace. Of that act of witness the Puritan John Flavel (bap. 1630, d. 1691) wrote, "At death the saints are engaged in the last and one of the most eminent works of faith, even the committing themselves into the hands of God when they are launching forth into that vast eternity and entering into that new state which will make so great a change to us in a moment. In this, Christ sets us a pattern: 'Father, into thy hands I commend my spirit.'"[85] Only as forgiven and redeemed can they experience the hopefulness to which Flavel's contemporary, Thomas Watson (d. 1686), testified: "He may look on Death with Joy, who can look on Forgiveness with Faith."[86] Only so can they adopt the matter of fact attitude of Richard Baxter (1615–91), of whom William Bates (1625–99) said that he "was conversant in the Invisible world."[87] Baxter famously drew up a list of sixty-two saints whom he was eager to meet in heaven. His list includes Abraham, Moses, Peter, Paul and John, Bernard of Clairvaux, Calvin (not Luther), and some of his contemporaries.[88] Of such he wrote,

> As for my friends, they are not lost;
> The several vessels of thy fleet,
> Though parted now by tempests tossed,
> Shall safely in the haven meet.[89]

Among others who were equally matter-of-fact about death were the somewhat eccentric preacher Rowland Hill (1744–1833) and the Methodist evangelist, Mark Guy Pearse (1842–1930). On meeting an equally elderly friend the former remarked, "If you and I don't march off soon, our friends yonder . . . will think we have lost our way."[90] On his deathbed the latter instructed those around him thus: "Please understand, no mourning, no grief, no gloom, no 'Dead March.' Start the service with 'Praise God from whom all blessings flow,' and let the stops be out on the organ, and ask the people to thunder it out when they ring it in

---

85. Flavel, *The Mystery of Providence*, 175. Cf. Owen, *Works*, I, 281.
86. Watson, *A Body of Practical Divinity*, 824.
87. Bates. "Epistle Dedicatory" to *A Funeral-Sermon*.
88. See *Reliquiae Baxterianae*, 71.ii.143.
89. Baxter's verse has come down to this day in a hymn the first line of which is, "He wants not friends that hath thy love."
90. Jay (who preached a funeral sermon for Hill) in Jay, *Autobiography*, 359.

PART TWO: Confessing the Faith Ecclesially and Hopefully

triumph. *Remember . . . I shall be with you and shall join in the singing.*"[91] Less rumbustiously, but no less sincerely, John Howe (1630–1705) wrote some *Consolations to my Wife and other Relations, supposing they hear of my Death*, among them this: "Let it be some satisfaction to you that I go willingly, under no dread, with no regret, but with some comfortable Knowledge of my Way and End."[92]

Only if ministers of religion live in what I have called the atmosphere of heaven will they be able to speak to the condition of their people in times of trial and at the approach of death. When William Jay's daughter, Statira, died at the age of nineteen, he wrote:

> As my ministry has always been very much of a consolatory kind, I began to dread the application of an address of Eliphaz to Job, "Behold thou hast instructed many, and thou hast strengthened the weak hands; thy words have upholden him that was falling, and thou hast strengthened the feeble knees. But now it is come upon thee, and thou faintest; it toucheth thee, and thou art weary." . . . As being not only her husband, but her pastor, I ought to have solaced and supported my wife under the loss, but she solaced and supported me.[93]

John Flavel was expert in encouraging saints under trial: "It is no small comfort to the saints that this world is the worst place that they shall ever be in. . . . If there are no candles in the house, we do not much trouble over it if we are sure it is almost break of day; for then there will be no use for them. This is the case with us; 'for now is our salvation nearer than when we believed'" (Rom 13:11).[94] "Death can do thee no harm," said John Bunyan, "It is only a passage out of a prison into a haven of rest, out of a crowd of enemies to an innumerable company of true, loving, and faithful friends."[95] As Abraham van de Beek put it, "Where the fear of death is gone, where anxiety over guilt is gone, where the ambivalence of choice is gone, there is freedom."[96] It is the minister's high calling to lead and encourage the saints towards that freedom. The ministers' qualification for doing this is the call of God and their own experience of that

---

91. Unwin and Telford, *Mark Guy Pearse*, 239–40.
92. Quoted by Edmund Calamy, *Memoirs of . . . John Howe*, 66.
93. Jay, *Autobiography*, 99–100.
94. Flavel, *The Mystery of Providence*, 138.
95. Quoted by Brown, *John Bunyan*, 119.
96. Beek, *Why?*, 347.

grace-given freedom. It need hardly be added that the same qualifications alone will enable ministers to comfort those who mourn the loss of loved ones. As Bernard Lord Manning drily remarked, "The mourner is not to be put off with descriptions of the architecture and climate of the new Jerusalem."[97]

Finally, only if the Church lives in the atmosphere of heaven will its worship be as fitting as it ought to be. We join our praise with the saints of the ages; we keep the Lord's Supper until he come; and we know that for all of us, what William Jay said to his people at Argyle Church, Bath, is true: "You will soon change your place, but not your employment; only you will worship without weariness, imperfection, or end."[98] In the meantime, to allude to the title of the celebratory volume in which an abbreviated version of this chapter first appeared, we are "Strangers and Pilgrims on Earth."[99] Why? Because as the old evangelical hymn has it:

> I'm but a stranger here,
> Heaven is my home.[100]

---

97. Manning, "The Burial of the Dead," 220.
98. Jay, *Autobiography*, 67.
99. Borght and Geest, *Strangers and Pilgrims on Earth*.
100. The author of this hymn, first published in 1836, was Thomas Rawson Taylor (1807–35), a Congregational minister. He served at Howard Street, Sheffield (1830–32), and then became classical tutor at Airedale College, Bradford, whose President, Walter Scott, preached the sermon at his young colleague's funeral service.

PART TWO: Confessing the Faith Ecclesially and Hopefully

BIBLIOGRAPHY

Allon, Henry. *Sermons Preached in the Kings Weigh-House Chapel, London, 1829-1869 . . . Second Series, edited with a Biographical and Critical Introduction by Henry Allon*. London: Macmillan, 1875.

Arnobius. *Adversus Gentes*. Ante Nicene Christian Library. Edinburgh: T. & T. Clark, 1871.

Augustine, *The City of God*. 2 vols. London: Dent, 1945.

Baillie, John. *And the Life Everlasting*. 1934. Reprint. London: Epworth, 1961.

Barber, Hugh, and Arthur O. Roberts. *Early Quaker Writings*. Grand Rapids: Eerdmans, 1973.

Barnabas. *Epistle of Barnabas*. In *The Apostolic Fathers*. The Ancient and Modern Library of Theological Literature, Part 1. London: Farran, n.d.

Basil of Caesarea. *Saint Basil: The Letters*. 4 vols. London: Heinemann, 1926-39.

Bates, William. *A Funeral-Sermon for the Reverend, Holy and Exellent Divine, Mr. Richard Baxter, who deceased Decemb. 8. 1691. With an Account of his Life*. London: printed for Brab. Aylmer, 1692.

Beek, Abraham van de. *Why? On Suffering, Guilt and God*. Grand Rapids: Eerdmans, 1990.

Biddle, John. *A Twofold Catechism: the one simply called A Scripture-catechism, the other, A Brief Scripture-catechism for children*. London: J. Cottrell for Ri. Moone, 1654.

Borght, Eduardus Van der, and P. van Geest. *Strangers and Pilgrims on Earth*. Leiden: Brill., 2012.

Brittain, F. *Bernard Lord Manning: A Memoir*. Cambridge: Heffer, n.d.

Brown, John. *John Bunyan: His Life, Times and Work*. London: Isbister, 1885.

Calamy, Edmund. *Memoirs of the Life of the late Revd. Mr. John Howe*. London: Chandler, 1724.

Calvin, John. *Commentary on The Epistles of Paul the Apostle to the Romans and to the Thessalonians*. Translated by F. Ross Mackenzie. Edinburgh: Saint Andrew, 1972.

Cassels, Thomas. *History of John Knox Church, Stewarton*. Kilmarnock: Irving, 1925.

Cave, Sydney. *The Doctrines of the Christian Faith*. 1931. London: Independent, 1952.

Clement of Alexandria. *Stromateis*. Ante Nicene Christian Library. Edinburgh: T. & T. Clark, 1869.

Cleobury, F. H. "Immortality and Purpose." *The Modern Churchman* (1959) 60-71.

Crabbe, George. "The Borough: A Poem in Twenty-four Letters." In *The Poetical Works of the Rev. George Crabbe*. London: Murray, 1853.

Dale, A. W. W. *The Life of R. W. Dale of Birmingham*. London: Hodder and Stoughton, 1899.

Dewsbury, William. *A True Prophecy of the Mighty Day of the Lord which is Coming, and is Appeared in the North of England, and is arising toward the South; and shall overspread this Nation, and all the Nations of the World* (1655). In *Early Quaker Writings*, edited by Hugh Barbour and Arthur O. Roberts, 93-102. Grand Rapids: Eerdmans, 1973.

Didache. In *The Apostolic Fathers*. The Ancient and Modern Library of Theological Literature, Part 2. London: Farran, n.d.

Edwards, Jonathan. *Works*. 2 vols. 1834. Reprint. Edinburgh: Banner of Truth, 1972.

Eriugena, John Scottus. *De Divisione Naturae*. Montréal: Bellarmin, 1987.

Eusebius of Caesarea. *Church History*. Oxford: Parker, 1905.

Flavel, John. *The Mystery of Providence*. 1678. London: Banner of Truth, 1963.
Flew, A. G. N. "Death." In *New Essays in Philosophical Theology*, edited by Flew and Alasdair MacIntyre, 267–72 London: SCM, 1955.
Forsyth, P. T. *This Life and the Next*. 1918. Reprint. London: Independent, 1953.
Gregory of Nyssa. *Dogmatic Treatises*. Nicene and Post-Nicene Fathers of the Christian Church. Second Series. Edinburgh: T. & T. Clark, 1893.
Grove, Henry. *Ethical and Theological Writings*. 1747. Reprint. Bristol: Thoemmes, 2000.
Gurnall, William. *The Christian in Complete Armour: A Treatise of the Saint's War against the Devil*. 1655–62. Reprint in one vol. London: Banner of Truth, 1964.
Hall, Robert. *Works*. 6 vols. London: Holdsworth and Ball, 1833.
Harris, Paul. "Americans Stock Up to be Ready for End of the World." *The Observer*, 14 February 2010, 48.
Hepburn, Ronald W. "Religious Experience. Argument for the Existence of God." In *The Encyclopedia of Philosophy*, vol. 7, edited by Paul Edwards, 163–68. New York: Macmillan, 1967.
Hill, Amelia. Report in *The Observer*, 14 February 2010, 26.
Hippolytus of Rome. *De Christo et Antichristo*. In *Patrologia Graeca*, vol. 10, edited and translated by J-P Migne. Paris: Migne, 1857.
Irenaeus. *Adversus Haereses*. 2 vols. Ante Nicene Christian Library. Edinburgh: T. & T. Clark, 1883–84.
Jay, William. *The Autobiography of William Jay*. Edited by George Redford and John Angell James. 1854. Reprint. Edinburgh: Banner of Truth, 1974.
Justin Martyr. *Apology*. Ante Nicene Christian Library. Edinburgh: T. & T. Clark, 1867.
———. *Dialogue with Trypho*. Ante Nicene Christian Library. Edinburgh: T. & T. Clark, 1867.
Lactantius. *Divinae Institutiones*. As *Divine Institutes*. Liverpool: Liverpool University Press, 2004.
Mackintosh, H. R. *Immortality and the Future: The Christian Doctrine of Eternal Life*. 2nd ed. London: Hodder and Stoughton, 1917.
McNaughton, William D. *Early Congregational Independency in Lowland Scotland*. 2 vols. Glasgow: The United Reformed Church and the Trustees of Ruaig Congregational Church, Tiree, 2007.
Manning, Bernard Lord. "The Burial of the Dead." *The Congregational Quarterly* 19 (1941) 213–22.
Maurice, F. D. *Theological Essays*. Cambridge: Macmillan, 1853.
Müller, J. J. *When Christ Comes Again*. London: Marshall, Morgan and Scott, 1956.
Nuttall, Geoffrey F. "The Heirs of Heaven." *The Congregational Quarterly* 35 (1957) 9–20.
———. *The Reality of Heaven*. London: Independent, 1951.
Origen. *Contra Celsum*. Ante Nicene Christian Library. Edinburgh: T. & T. Clark, 1872.
———. *De Principiis*. Ante Nicene Christian Library. Edinburgh: T. & T. Clark, 1869.
Owen, John. *Works*. Edited by William H. Goold. 1850–53. Reprint. London: Banner of Truth, 1965.
Philpot, J. C. *Mr. J. C. Philpot's Review of "Apocalyptic Sketches," "Signs of the Times," and "The Coming Struggle." Reprinted from "The Gospel Standard,"* 1854. Grand Rapids: Zion Baptist Church, 1913.
Poole-Connor, E. J. *Evangelicalism in England*. New ed. Worthing, UK: Walter, 1956.

PART TWO: Confessing the Faith Ecclesially and Hopefully

Randall, Ian, "'The Things that Shall be Hereafter': Strict Baptist Views of the Second Coming." *The Strict Baptist Historical Society Bulletin* 27 (2000) 1–24.

Richardson, Samuel. *Of the Torments of Hell: The Foundations and Pillars thereof Discovered, Shaken, and Removed.* London, 1658.

Root, H. E. "The Logic of Eschatology." *The Modern Churchman* 3 (1959) 85–98.

Rowell, Geoffrey. *Hell and the Victorians: A Study of Nineteenth-Century Theological Controversies concerning Eternal Punishment and the Future Life.* Oxford: Clarendon, 1974.

Sandeen, Ernest R. *The Roots of Fundamentalism: British and American Millenarianism 1800–1930.* Chicago: Chicago University Press, 1970.

Sangster, William E. "The Probation of Life." In *The Great Mystery of Life Hereafter,* edited by H. V. Hodson, 97–105. London: Hodder and Stoughton, 1957.

Sell, Alan P. F. *Confessing and Commending the Faith: Historic Witness and Apologetic Method.* 2002. Reprint. Eugene, OR: Wipf & Stock, 2006.

———. *Dissenting Thought and the Life of the Churches: Studies in an English Tradition.* Lewiston, NY: Mellen, 1990.

———. *Enlightenment, Ecumenism, Evangel: Theological Themes and Thinkers 1550–2000.* Milton Keynes, UK: Paternoster, 2005.

———. *Four Philosophical Anglicans: W. G. De Burgh, W. R. Matthews, O. C. Quick, H. A. Hodges.* Farnham, UK: Ashgate, 2010.

———. *Philosophical Idealism and Christian Belief.* 1995. Reprint. Eugene, OR: Wipf & Stock, 2006.

———. *The Spirit Our Life.* Shippensburg, PA: Ragged Edge, 2000.

———. *Theology in Turmoil: The Roots, Course and Significance of the Conservative-Liberal Debate in Modern Theology.* 1986. Reprint. Eugene, OR: Wipf and Stock, 1998.

Spurgeon, C. H. *An All-Round Ministry: Addresses to Ministers and Students.* 1900. Reprint. London: Banner of Truth, 1965.

Stewart, K. Moody. *Brownlow North: His Life and Work.* 1878. Reprint. London: Banner of Truth, 1971.

Taylor, Barbara Brown. "Expecting the Second Coming. Don't Say When." *The Christian Century,* 21 September 2004, 35.

Tertullian, Q. S. F. *Adversus Marcion.* Ante Nicene Christian Library. Edinburgh: T. & T. Clark, 1870.

———. *De Spectaculis.* Ante Nicene Christian Librasry. Edinburgh: T. & T. Clark, 1869.

Thomas Aquinas. *Summa Theologica.* 5 vols. New York: Benziger, 1948.

Torrance, Thomas F. *The School of Faith: The Catechisms of the Reformed Church.* London: Clarke, 1959.

Unwin, Mrs. George, and John Telford. *Mark Guy Pearse: Preacher, Author, Artist.* London: Epworth, 1930.

Watson, Thomas. *A Body of Practical Divinity, consisting of above one hundred and seventy-six Sermons on the Lesser Catechism composed by the Reverend Assembly of Divines at Westminster.* London: printed for Thomas Parkhurst, 1692.

Watts, Michael R. *The Dissenters from the Reformation to the French Revolution.* Oxford: Clarendon, 1978.

———. *Why did the English Stop Going to Church?* London: Dr. Williams's Trust, 1995.

Walker, D. P. *The Decline of Hell: Seventeenth-Century Discussions of Eternal Torment.* London: Routledge and Kegan Paul, 1964.

White, Edward. *Life in Christ: 4 Discourses upon the Scripture Doctrine that Immortality is the Peculiar Privilege of the Regenerate.* London: n.p., 1846.

Williams, George Huntston. *The Radical Reformation.* Philadelphia: Westminster, 1962.

Williams, J. B. *Memoirs of the Life, Character and Writings of the Rev. Matthew Henry.* 1828. Reprint. London: Banner of Truth, 1974.

Woodward, Kenneth L. "Heaven: This is the Season to Search for New Meanings in Old Familiar Places." *Newsweek*, 27 March 1989, 54.

CHAPTER ELEVEN

Confessing the Faith in Systematic Theology? The Locus and Authority of Revelation *vis à vis* Systematic Method

An Epilogue Cheerful in Style, Serious in Intent

I DO NOT SET myself up as a new Luther. Accordingly, I shall modestly content myself with advancing 9.5 theses only. Each thesis will be illustrated as appropriate from theology, philosophy, history, and churchly practice. I offer a bird's-eye-view of a large terrain and, of necessity, I write in shorthand, as it were. I shall do little more than state my theses: articles and even books would be required for their satisfactory exposition and defence. It is thus patently obvious to me that almost every claim I shall make demands fuller analysis and is open to objection. I persist, however, because it is sometimes helpful to gain perspective upon a sequence of topics that are clearly related but, for reasons good or ill are frequently treated in isolation from one another. To make the point in more homely language: what follows is an attempt to see the wood, not selected trees.

After the manner of an old-fashioned preacher, I shall hang my points on one letter of the alphabet, in this case, A. I shall propose that the locus of God's supreme revelation is the redemptive *act* accomplished at the cross of Christ (where "cross" is construed as an umbrella term). It is *astounding*, *authoritative*, *appropriated*, *accommodated*, and *acknowledged*. Its content is sometimes *abused* by Christians by *amplification*, *attenuation*, *avoidance*, and *amendment*. Its significance and implications are to be *articulated* by systematic theologians. The revelatory act *appropriates* all other Christian doctrines and *appertains* to such satellite disciplines as apologetics and ethics.

Thesis 1. The locus of God's supreme revelation is the redemptive *act* accomplished at the cross of Christ by the God of holy love.[1] If, on reading this assertion, you suspect that you are hearing an echo of Britain's most stimulating twentieth-century theologian, P. T. Forsyth, your suspicion is well founded. Indeed, one of the things I had in mind when first pondering my theme in 2010 is the fact that that year marked the centenary of the publication of Forsyth's lectures on *The Work of Christ*. I shall refer to this work and, indeed, to other parts of Forsyth's *corpus* as we proceed. I shall also refer in passing to W. G. de Burgh, W. R. Matthews, O. C. Quick and H. A. Hodges, whom I happen to have in mind because they are the subjects of my book, *Four Philosophical Anglicans* (Ashgate, 2010). None was more insistent than Forsyth that at the cross we are concerned not merely with a demonstration of the love of God and of the extent to which God goes to win sinful humanity back to himself—as if the cross were simply a divine visual aid which might prompt such aesthetic responses as "How moving!", "How utterly self-giving!" "How horrible!" Rather, at the cross something is *done*, not merely shown. The forces of evil are defeated in principle once and for all, hence the cosmic significance of the cross. Happily, these points have been made by theologians of many Christian traditions. The Anglican, O. C. Quick, for example, weighed Platonizing Christologies and found them wanting because they could not accommodate the fact that "God is not only truly revealed in Jesus, but that he has decisively and finally acted."[2]

I have already implied that the term "cross" connotes much more than "crucifixion". It encompasses the resurrection which confirms the Good Friday victory; it embraces also the ascension which signifies both

---

1. See Forsyth, *The Principle of Authority*, 7.
2. Quick, *Doctrines of the Creed*, 140.

the return of the Son to the Father and the Son's ministry of intercession on behalf of humanity. As young William Jay, who ministered at Bath for sixty-two years, declared in his ordination confession of faith of 30 January 1791, "The Gospel relates to what [Jesus] *did*. It contains his history from the throne to the cross, and from the cross back to the throne."[3] Furthermore, as I shall shortly suggest, the cross illuminates every other Christian doctrine.

To affirm that the cross is God's supreme revelation is not to say that it is his sole revelation to us, as if there were no revelation of God anywhere else. Least of all should we deny that what Calvin called "the whole course of [Christ's] obedience"[4] is revelatory of God. Again, we may properly hold that there is a general revelation of God in nature (albeit not a copper-bottomed natural theology demonstrative of his existence) which is sufficient to leave sinners "without excuse"[5]; though Hume and John Stuart Mill would forcefully remind us that nature's "red in tooth and claw-ness" is not the least obstacle in the path of those who seek too easily to believe; nor, when considering the unmerited pain and suffering inflicted upon human beings should we fasten too quickly upon an observation of the Puritan Thomas Watson, as if it were a complete answer to the problem of evil. Watson declared that "When God lays men upon their backs, then they look up to heaven."[6] We might, on the contrary, conclude that humanity's and nature's groaning and travailing is testimony to that cosmic "out-of-sorts-ness" which, together with human sin, can be dealt with only from God's side, so to speak.

But this reference to human sinfulness brings us to the idea that the supremely revelatory act is a reconciling act and, moreover, that it is an act which affects God as well as human beings. "This reconciliation," wrote Forsyth, "means change of relation between God and man—man, mind you, not two or three men, not several groups of men, but man, the human race as one whole. And it is a change of relation from alienation to communion..."[7] The reason why reconciliation affects both parties is that the love active at the cross is holy love. It is a love which both redeems us

---

3. Redford and James, *The Autobiography of William Jay*, 82.

4. Calvin, *Institutes of the Christian Religion*, II.xvi.5. Cf. Forsyth, *The Cruciality of the Cross*, 42.

5. Rom 1:20.

6. Watson, *A Divine Cordial*, 42.

7. Forsyth, *The Work of Christ*, 57; cf. 76–77; 99.

and vindicates the Father's holiness and righteousness.[8] "If in the cross we have but the greatest of love's renunciations," Forsyth declared, "instead of the one establishment of God's holy will, if we have but the divine Kenosis and not also the divine Plerosis, then the sense of God's presence in the cross, and in the Church, and in the world's moral war, is bound to fade."[9] Hence, to proclaim a doctrine of atonement which affects only ourselves is to proclaim less than half of the doctrine, and it is almost blasphemously self-serving, for the first thing to be done is "to hallow the holy name."[10]

Another way of saying that God's revelation at the cross is supreme is to say that it is final—not in the temporal sense that God has revealed nothing of himself since Calvary; but in the sense that the cross is that aspect of the divine revelation to which all else is to be referred. We shall never know more of God's holy love and merciful righteousness than we learn from the cross. Not, indeed, that we are always careful learners, and it is not inconceivable that somewhere there lurks a systematic theologian who has yet to assimilate the cautionary word of another Anglican, W. R. Matthews: "Revelation is always the self-disclosure of God and not the supernatural announcement of theology."[11]

Thesis 2. The dryness of some writing in systematic and constructive theology notwithstanding, God's supreme revelation is *astounding*. As I have elsewhere put the point: "The truly astonishing thing is that *God*, no less, justifies the *ungodly* (Rom 4:5; cf. Rom 3:19–24)! He proves his love to us in that 'while we were yet *sinners* Christ died for us'. This is the heart of the Christian gospel."[12] Thomas Wilcox came as close to jumping out of his socks in astonishment as ever a Puritan came when he contrasted this with the kind of gospel that human nature might have devised: "Let Nature but make a gospel, and it would make it quite contrary to Christ: it would be to the just, the innocent and the holy. Christ made the gospel for you; that is, for needy sinners. . . . Nature cannot endure to think the gospel is only for sinners: it will rather choose to despair than to go to Christ upon such terrible terms."[13]

8. See Forsyth, *The Cruciality of the Cross*, 67; Forsyth, *God the Holy Father*, 4.
9. Forsyth, *The Cruciality of the Cross*, 36.
10. Forsyth, *The Justification of God*, 165.
11. Matthews, *Signposts to God*, 91.
12. Sell, *The Spirit Our Life*, 28.
13. Wilcox, *Honey out of the Rock*, 9.

PART TWO: Confessing the Faith Ecclesially and Hopefully

If Wilcox thinks of the individual dimension of the redeeming act, P. T. Forsyth who, temperamentally, was always on the dour side of happy-clappy, nevertheless got quite worked up about the astounding cosmic implications of the gospel: "The evil world will not win at last, because it failed to win at the only time it ever could. It is a vanquished world where men play their devilries. Christ has overcome it. It can make tribulation, but desolation it can never make."[14] There is something peculiarly sad about a systematic or constructive theologian to whom the discipline's material has become so commonplace that the excitement has evaporated and the desire to worship has been snuffed out. (It is otherwise, of course, with philosophers of the Christian religion, who may or may not be Christians, as some of the most incisive of them are not.) Forsyth put it still more personally when, with reference to Christians in general (no doubt not excluding the sub-class of pedlars of what George Tyrrell called the gaseous, the liquid, the solid, namely, theological books), he lamented that "There has passed away from faith that moral amazement and awe which are inseperable from the mystery of grace. . . . [T]o-day there is only a minority of Christians whose piety takes the form of standing and overwhelming wonder that God should touch or save 'me'. . . . [W]hether or not it be from . . . stupidity or over-feeding, or from the trivializing of grace—we have lost the power to wonder at grace."[15]

<u>Thesis 3</u>. The supreme revelation is *authoritative*. To say that there are many claimants to authority, and to the power—whether physical or psychological—that it commands is to utter a truism. The authority with which we are concerned here is, to ally characteristically Pauline and Johannine terms, the authority of grace and truth. Nowhere is God's overwhelming love towards the undeserving more savingly active or more clearly seen than at the cross, where the truth concerning God and ourselves is placarded on the stage of human history.

This authoritative act of God relativizes the New Testament, the Church, and all "official theology" such as that proclaimed in creeds and confessions or declarations of faith. It does so precisely because it is the *fons et origo* of them all. With regard to Scripture, as Forsyth bluntly put it, "If revelation is, at the root of it, redemption, if it is God's redeeming Act on life, and not a mere reinterpretation of life, then it cannot be

---

14. Forsyth, *The Justification of God*, 223.
15. Forsyth, "Immanence and Incarnation," 54.

identical with a book."[16] In any case, as Calvin saw, "even if [Scripture] wins reverence for itself by its own majesty, it seriously affects us only when it is sealed upon our hearts by the Holy Spirit."[17] The Spirit directs us to the Christ of the Bible and, as Maurice Wiles declared, "It is the specialness of the events rather than the special way in which the divine action was understood to be operative in them that is most fundamental."[18] But if this is true as to the original witnesses, it is no less true of any who would discern the action of God in the saving events today. It is not that the Spirit misleads, but our interpretative skills are less than infallible, and our wills are recalcitrant; we may therefore mistake the message or even refuse it. Not for nothing did Richard Baxter write, "experience hath constrained me against my will to know that reverend learned men are imperfect, and know but little as well as I, especially those that think themselves the wisest."[19]

As to the Church, she is called to witness to God's supremely revelatory and authoritative act at the cross. It is to this that she owes her existence, since, to put it in Trinitarian language, it is on the ground of the Son's saving work that the Father calls out by the Spirit one people for his praise and service. The Church must never seek to usurp the cross. As Robert Paul said, "The fundamental criticism of placing all authority in the Church itself is that too often it has ruled out the possibility of repentance for the Church itself, and this has meant that whereas the Church is called to service, she has often presented an arrogant face to the world."[20] For an example of the way in which the Church may place itself above the gospel we may turn to the words of an Irish Jesuit Robert Nash who, even after Vatican II, with its clear declaration that the Spirit gives the Church the word it must proclaim, could still contend that the Church rather than the Spirit is the supreme teacher, and that "God promises that His Holy Spirit will be with her, endorsing her words."[21] This does seem to be the wrong way round: the Holy Spirit is the Church's electing creator, not its rubber stamp.

16. Forsyth, "Revelation and the Bible," 240.
17. Calvin, *Institutes*, I.vii.5.
18. Wiles, "Religious Authority and Divine Action," 11–12.
19. Baxter, *Autobiography*, 114.
20. Paul, *Ministry*, 168.
21. Nash, *The Sunday Press*, Dublin, 8 February 1981.

The same argument applies, *a fortiori*, to the creeds, confessions, and declarations of faith that have proliferated through the Christian ages.[22] Oliver Quick put it in a nutshell: "The real and permanent object of Christian faith is, not the Creeds, but Christ and his gospel."[23] In an article that addresses the question, "What is systematic theology?" Nicholas M. Healy has said, justifiably enough, that "The requirement of obedient conformity to official theology by the churches' members has often in the past been warranted by a sequence of commonly held beliefs: that my salvation is contingent upon my faith in the correct construal of Christianity; that this construal is to be found in, and determined by, official theology; that if I knowingly believe something that conflicts with official theology, I am in danger of damnation." But then he lamely adds, "The difficulty is that these beliefs are no longer commonly held."[24] Not so! The difficulty is that these beliefs are not, and never were, true; and that while "There are doctrines of salvation, [there are] no saving doctrines."[25] We are not saved by the work of intellectual assent but by grace though faith; and we are not saved by doctrines but by the Saviour. The upshot is, as Forsyth saw, that "That is over the Bible which is over the Church and the Creeds. It is the Gospel of Grace, which produced Bible, Creed and Church alike. And by the Gospel is meant primarily God's act of pure Grace for men, and only secondarily the act of men witnessing it for God in a Bible or a Church."[26]

It is more than likely W. R. Matthews had learned that lesson well from his senior colleague in the London University Faculty of Theology, for he put it concisely and well when he wrote, "it is the Gospel which invests both Church and Bible with their authority."[27] I should like to think that Matthews' forlorn quest of credal revision was inspired by a further remark of Forsyth: "There is far too much said . . . about the Creeds and their simplicity and the way they keep to the Christian facts. Yes, and all but ignore the one fact on which Christianity rests—the fact of

---

22. See further ch. 1 above. For an account of the variety of ways in which the faith was confessed in English Congregationalism see Sell, *Dissenting Thought*, ch. 1.

23. Quick, *Doctrines of the Creed*, 18.

24. Healy, "What is Systematic Theology?" 31.

25. Forsyth, "Authority and Theology," 69.

26. Forsyth, *The Church, the Gospel and Society*, 67; cf. ibid., 69; Forsyth, *The Principle of Authority*, 53.

27. Matthews, *The Gospel and the Modern Mind*, 46.

redemption by grace alone through faith."[28] Forsyth himself could never overlook the fact that "Everything else, Church, or Bible, is authoritative for us in the proportion in which it is sacramental of this final and absolute authority, of the Creator as Redeemer, the authority not merely of God but of a God of grace."[29]

Thesis 4. The supreme revelation is *appropriated* by enabled faith, and is a gift of the Holy Spirit. Knowledge of it is neither a reward of effort expended (so that none may boast, Eph 2:9), nor a personality-obliterating thunderbolt from a *deus ex machina*. This faith is enabled in the sense that "Christ's death was a death on behalf of people within whom the power of responding had to be created."[30] The characteristic feature of the human response is trust (*fiducia*), and it is the prelude to an experience-moulding relationship between the Christian and God. This faith is, moreover, a great leveller. It is not the possession of the scholar or of the religious professional only: indeed it is conceivable that it may not be theirs at all. It is what Forsyth called "layman's evidence," and in this connection he said that "The essential thing is not historic belief in the Resurrection of Jesus (which devils might believe and tremble), but moral faith in a risen Saviour."[31] It is the faith of those who have, by grace, been adopted as sons and daughters of the Father.

Thesis 5. The supreme revelation is *accommodated* to our intelligence and *acknowledged* by our conscience (to introduce a problematic term for the sake of brevity). Were it otherwise nothing could or would be revealed to us. The philosopher W. G. de Burgh stated the obvious when he declared that "a revelation which was not adjusted to human intelligence would fail to reveal."[32] In a paper entitled, "What is Systematic Theology?" A. N. Williams amplifies the point thus: "If the divine *ratio* stands so far above us or is of such a different kind that we cannot grasp it using our divinely-given rational capacities, then it is hard to see how we could grasp it in any respect."[33] So far this is well said, though we must allow for the Spirit's enabling lest we tumble headlong into a rationalistic version of

---

28. Forsyth, *The Church, the Gospel and Society*, 124.
29. Forsyth, *The Principle of Authority*, 299.
30. Forsyth, *The Work of Christ*, 15.
31. Forsyth, *The Church, the Gospel and Society*, 82.
32. Burgh, *The Life of Reason*, 225.
33. Williams, "What is Systematic Theology?" 54.

Arminianism. The divine adaptation of the revelation witnesses to God's accommodation to humanity's situation and needs. Donald McKim further explains: "Given the great gulf between God and humankind, by virtue of God's transcendence and human finiteness, God's holiness and human sinfulness, for God to communicate with humanity and God's revelation to occur God must condescend to communicate in ways humans can understand, according to the limits of human capacities. This method of revelation of God's speaking and acting in human forms is God's accommodation."[34]

As for our conscientious reception of the revelation: the latter must commend itself to what is best in us, but I am far from asserting the notion which has been mistaken for the Protestant principle, namely, that conscience is our supreme authority. Rather, conscience bows before, and acknowledges, the authority of grace active and revealed at the cross. If we make our conscience, or our inner light—call it what we will—ultimate, we usurp the authority of the gospel, and the result is an individualistic version of what the Church collectively does when it assumes the primary place.

<u>Thesis 6</u>. The supreme revelation is *angular*. It does not cry peace where there is no peace. On the contrary, it divides humanity into those who stand for God, or for the world, the flesh and the devil; into those who worship God and those who worship Mammon; into those who are sheep and those who are goats. To express the point in ecclesiological terms we might say that there is a distinction of eternal significance between the saints and the "worldlings," and that the Church comprises the former, the saints by calling (Rom 1:7). Clearly, this position poses recognition difficulties, and no Christian should be so sure of *another's* status before God as to exclude the possibility of error. After all, the New Testament makes it clear that the religious will be surprised when they discover who is in the heavenly home and who is not. Even so, sufficient has been revealed to place a question mark against the uncritical adoption of the popular notion of inclusiveness. On the one hand, the Church is called to be receptive to, and welcoming of, all sorts and conditions of people. On the other hand, the Church comprises Christians; the Church is not coterminous with the congregation (unless, of course, the reference is to the

---

34. McKim, *Encyclopedia*, 1; reprinted in McKim, *The Westminster Handbook*, 1. It is hard to think of a more accurate and lucid expositor of Reformed teaching than Donald McKim.

congregation of the saints). From the human side, decision and choice are demanded by the cross: are we for him or against him? And while that choice will always be an enabled one—"I, yet not I but Christ"—we are responsible for it; and to turn towards is also to turn away from. It is not, of course, the Christian way to despise intellectual opponents, or to trample upon those who adopt alternative standpoints, but the fact remains, as the philosopher H. A. Hodges put it, that "the acceptance of some standpoints brings with it automatically the rejection of others."[35] If we deny this we are on the way to holding that beliefs do not matter—perhaps even that sincerity is all; that one belief is as good as another; and that there is no satisfactory way of adjudicating between them. This is not the stance of those who are called to "test the spirits to see whether they are of God" (1 John 4:1).

The angularity of the revelation concerns not only the identity of the Christian and the matter (to use the old word) of the Church; it concerns the Church's mission. On this Forsyth, unusually, quoted from another—in this case, Kierkegaard: "For long the tactics have been: use every means to move as many as you can—to move everybody if possible—to enter Christianity. Do not be too curious whether what they enter *is* Christianity. My tactics have been, with God's help, to use every means to make it clear what the demand of Christianity is—if not one entered it."[36]

Forsyth at once admits that "The statement is extreme; but that way lies the Church's salvation. . . . It cannot live on a cross which is on easy terms with the world as the apotheosis of all its aesthetic religion, or the classic of all its ethical intuition. The work of Christ, rightly understood, is the final spiritual condition of all the work we may aspire to do in converting society to the kingdom of God."[37] And against any sentimentalized idea of the love of God, Forsyth thunders, "there is everything in the love of God to be afraid of. Love is not holy without judgment. It is the love of holy God that is the consuming fire."[38] His contemporary, Robert Mackintosh, Britain's most incisive theologian of the twentieth century, was even crisper: "Love is justice at white heat."[39] It may be that nothing would do more to revitalize Christian worship in such a way that joy and

---

35. Hodges, *Languages, Standpoints and Attitudes*, 44.
36. Forsyth, *The Work of Christ*, xxxii.
37. Ibid.
38. Ibid., 85.
39. R. Mackintosh, *Essays*, 378.

reverence were married together than sober reflection upon the angularity of grace, the holiness of God's love, leading to the conclusion that there is a significant difference between a heavenly Friend and a locker room buddy.

Thesis 7. The content of the supreme revelation is *abused* by Christians when its content is unwarrantably *amplified, attenuated, avoided,* or *amended* on ideological grounds. Let us look at each of these in turn.

The classic example of *amplification* is surely the Galatian heresy, according to which salvation is said to be by grace through faith plus certain Jewish rites, notably circumcision. Paul thunders that this is no gospel at all, and that salvation is by grace through faith plus nothing. Throughout Christian history amplifications have taken many forms, and very often they have become badges of sectarianism.[40] They can be doctrinal, as when the impression is conveyed that salvation is by grace through faith plus signing on the dotted line to our favoured doctrinal formulae. They can be ecclesiastical, as when the addition concerns our favoured polity; and it is a well known fact that modern ecumenical discussions have been bedevilled by encrustations of denominational small print that have been added to the gospel, and even in some cases elevated above it. Additions can also concern approved morality—often in a disturbingly hypocritical way, as when the saints devise lists of those sins to be avoided which they are not particularly inclined to commit themselves: "Believe on the Lord Jesus Christ and do not smoke or drink alcohol; if you're a racist in your heart nobody will know that—but don't be seen in such a sink of iniquity as a lap-dancing club!" Thus arise new, false, legalisms of the kind that prompted Robert Mackintosh's pertinent observation that in the case of the Calvinistic Puritan, "doctrinally and emotionally he was expected to live by grace; but his conduct was to be exactly the same *as if he expected to be justified by works.*"[41] For an extreme example of ecclesiastical-cum-ethical amplification consider the case of Joseph Jacob, whose followers built him a meeting house in Parish Street, Southwark, in 1698. Jacob was expert in devising terms of churchly fellowship which were quite unknown to the New Testament. Periwigs were banned; women's dress was regulated; male members were required to wear moustaches on their upper lips; worship elsewhere was strictly forbidden; intermarriage with those of other churches was forbidden, and all marriages had to be

---

40. See R. Mackintosh, *The Authority of the Church*, 10–11.
41. R. Mackintosh, *The Insufficiency of Revivalism as a Religious System*, 8.

performed by Mr. Jacob. Those who offended were excommunicated. It comes as no surprise to learn that four years later "his church dwindled away so far that he was obliged to quit his meeting house." [42]

P. T. Forsyth drew the general conclusion:

> We make [Christ] a legislator, as if He were a finer Moses. We are all ritualists by nature, and we think it grace. . . . We make the cardinal mistake of thinking that the Kingdom of God was set up in the ideal precepts of Jesus, instead of in His cross. But it is by the cross we are to read all the precepts, and, if necessary, revise them. . . . People treat the New Testament as a Christian code. But this is entirely foreign to the genius of Christianity. It is falling from grace with Galatian levity.[43]

Attenuations or dilutions of the content of the supremely authoritative revelation come in a great variety of forms. For example, of the General Baptist turned Independent, James Foster, who ministered at Pinners' Hall, London, from 1744 to 1753, it was said that "he understood the great design of Christ's mediation to be, the reconciling men to God, by promoting virtue, and advancing the interests of truth and goodness in the world."[44] Notwithstanding that in eighteenth century England life for many was dangerous, libertine and squalid, ministers of this kind readily became the targets of Christians whose hyper-sensitive doctrinal antennae twitched violently because of what was *not* being said. Thus in the 1790s, during the ministry of Abraham Webster at Broseley Baptist church, Shropshire, a member of the congregation clearly eager to uphold the Second London Confession of the Particular (Calvinist) Baptists, rose to his feet during a service and said,

> Friends, we have been served out with milk and water plentifully, with scarcely enough of the one to colour the other, but our minister effects no disguise now; he gives us water, out and out water, and that not of the purest kind. The Holy Ghost is not in his creed. Jehovah is only candidate, and man's will is the supreme arbiter in this world and the world to come. Can you follow such a leader? I cannot, and God helping me I will have no more of his trash.[45]

---

42. Wilson, *The History and Antiquities of Dissenting Churches*, I, 141
43. Forsyth, *The Church, the Gospel and Society*, 16, 17.
44. Wilson, *The History and Antiquities of Dissenting Churches*, II, 280.
45. Quoted by Collis, *An Account of the Baptist Churches of Shropshire*, 48.

PART TWO: Confessing the Faith Ecclesially and Hopefully

Not, indeed, that we should let the orthodox off the hook altogether, for the revelation can be attenuated by unbalanced *amplification*. There can be no question that the Calvinistic methodological reversion to scholasticism yielded in some cases grotesque distortions of Christian truth, such that God became an oriental despot who could not be gracious until his ever-obedient Son had suffered. One of the inestimable benefits of the English Enlightenment (when did you last read a sentence that began like that?) is that a critique of such theology on moral grounds was initiated, not least by the oft-despised so-called "Arian" divines, who were inclined to charge the confessionally orthodox Protestant with "Protestant Popery." Thus John Taylor of Norwich, in his well-known work, *The Scripture-doctrine of Original Sin* (1740) dealt with perceived abuses of that doctrine with sufficient skill to draw an adverse criticism from Jonathan Edwards. Taylor argues that the doctrine of original sin as proclaimed by the orthodox turns God into a monster. "Pray consider seriously," he asks, "what a God He must be who can be displeased with and curse His innocent creatures even before they are born. Is this thy God O Christian? . . . Imputed guilt is imaginary guilt."[46]

Nearer to our own time we find that the content of the supremely authoritative revelation was *attenuated* by those Liberal Protestants who emphasized the humanity of Christ, and were careful to name him Teacher, Friend, Elder Brother, Master, rather than Lord and Saviour. Here the attempt was to suppress the Christological question by dwelling upon the ministry and teaching of Jesus, the greatest man who ever lived. From the popular stall in this stable came the conviction that if only everybody lived in accordance with the Sermon on the Mount the world would be a better place. Not only does this overlook the fact that, as Paul discovered, the problem is not that one does not know what to do, it is the doing of it, and the avoiding of what is wrong; but it betokens a very cursory reading of the Sermon on the Mount, to which R. W. Dale strongly objected. With reference to the Sermon he asked, "Who can this be through whom the sins of the race are forgiven, through whose death we ourselves have received the forgiveness of sins. . . . Who is He? . . . If you shrink from calling Him God, what other title adequate to the greatness of His work

---

46. Taylor, *The Scripture-Doctrine of Original Sin*, 151, 244. For Forsyth on the fate of Protestant scholastic orthodoxy see his *Positive Preaching and the Modern Mind*, 84–85. See also Sell, *Enlightenment, Ecumenism,* Evangel, ch. 5; Sell, *Hinterland* Theology, 569–77 and *passim*.

will you attribute to Him?"[47] In view of all such attenuations Forsyth protested that "Too many are occupied in throwing over precious cargo; they are lightening the ship even of its fuel."[48]

From the conservative evangelical side come those attenuations that so emphasize the salvation of the individual as to neglect the necessity of the Christian community and the cosmic implications of the gospel. Again, there are those who peddle a Jesusology which amounts to a unitarianism of the second person, or a charismatic emphasis so pronounced as almost to suggest a unitarianism of the third person. I need not elaborate further upon this.[49]

For a more strongly intellectual attenuation we might turn to those among the post-Hegelian philosophical idealists who were not hostile to Christianity, but whose philosophical presuppositions led them to tend in the direction of transmuting the revelation into a set of inspiring ideas, thereby sitting loose to the anchorage of the revelation in history. Thus, for example, Edward Caird claimed that the cross of Christ symbolizes the religious principles of self-realization through sacrifice, and of "dying to live." He writes, "It is not, as St Paul represents it, that Christ dies to save us from death, as the penalty from sin: for he does *not* save us: it is that he makes death itself the greatest means of manifesting and realising the new principle of life, and enables us also to take death in the same way, and so overcome its power. . . . In this way the resurrection of Christ becomes the pledge and proof that all who have his spirit will rise again. . . ."[50] There is an evolutionary, "Onward, ever upward", cast to this way of thinking which seems to make it on the one hand easy to bypass the historic cross, and on the other hand to sanitize evil by making it a stage on the way to a greater good.[51] This is often accompanied by the idea that the human problem is that of finitude rather than that of sin—on which matter Forsyth was characteristically blunt: "Any theology that places us in a spiritual *process*, or native movement between the finite and the infinite, depreciates the value of spiritual *act*, and thus makes us independent of the grace of God. Its movement is processional spectacular,

---

47. Dale, *Christian Doctrine*, 114.

48. Forsyth, *The Principle of Authority*, 261.

49. For a fuller account of liberal and conservative attenuations see Sell, *Theology in Turmoil*, ch. 6.

50. E. Caird, "St. Paul and evolution," 13.

51. For a full treatment of such points see Sell, *Philosophical Idealism and Christian Belief*. Cf. Forsyth, *The Principle of Authority*, 179.

aesthetic, it is not historic, dramatic, tragic or ethical. If it speak of the grace of God it does not take it with moral seriousness."[52]

To some extent related to this trend of thought, but also in some writers the product of the revival of patristics in the middle of the nineteenth century, we find a strong emphasis upon the incarnation, to the point that the cross is well nigh neglected. It is claimed that salvation resides in the fact that by the incarnation Christ has united himself with humanity, and that in this fact lies our hope. Clearly, the incarnation is temporally prior to the Cross since Bethlehem comes before Calvary; and it is logically prior too, since Jesus can do what he does only because he is who he is. In my view, however, and for all the importance of Jesus's life and ministry, the predominant witness of the New Testament is summed up in James Denney's words, "The rationale of the incarnation is in the atonement."[53] The Anglican, Quick, is in entire accord: "The Atonement is the primary purpose of the Incarnation, since it was to save His people from their sins that Jesus was born."[54]

Since incarnationalism, sometimes blended with immanentism, has been a characteristic feature of much Roman Catholic and Anglican theology, we shall do well to observe that Reformed writers like Forsyth and Denney were not alone in querying it. The Anglo-Catholic philosopher, Hodges, wrote,

> We have been told that Christianity and in particular Catholicism is the religion of the Incarnation. By the mere fact of living among us, God has sanctified our race. By wearing a human body He has declared once and for all the sanctity of matter and put an end to the dreams of the Platonist and the Manichee.... These are the beginnings of his ways. The Catholic faith is more than this. The Apostles did not preach a religion of the Incarnation. They preached the Resurrection.[55]

Michael Ramsey, possibly the wisest and most scholarly Archbishop of Canterbury of the twentieth century concurred: "the formulation of the doctrine of the Incarnation had sprung, alike in the apostolic age and in the patristic period, from out of the experience of Redemption: the saving act had been the key to the Church's faith in the divine Christ."[56]

52. Forsyth. *Positive Preaching and the Modern Mind*, 146.
53. Denney, *The Christian Doctrine of Reconciliation*, 65.
54. Quick, *Essays in Orthodoxy*, 77.
55. Hodges, *The Pattern of Atonement*, 26.
56. Ramsey, *From Gore to Temple*, 4. Thus Ramsey against the *Lux Mundi* author,

Once again Forsyth may sum matters up: the incarnation, "central as many find it, has no such centrality as the principle of atoning forgiveness. The doctrine of the incarnation did not create the Church. It grew up (very quickly) in the Church out of the doctrine of the cross which did create it—in so far as that can be said of any doctrine, and not rather of the act and power which the doctrine tries to state."[57]

Concerning the *avoidance*, or side-stepping, of the supreme revelation I may be brief. I recently read a description of Gretta Vosper's book, *With or Without God: The Way We Live is More Important Than What We Believe*. The description is as follows: "God does not answer our prayers. Jesus is not the saviour who saved the world by dying for our sins. Simply put, Christianity is 'love one another.'" If this is an accurate description, and it appears to be confirmed by the extracts from the book that I have read, it would seem that God's supreme revelation is being skirted by this author, who belongs to a church which has the *Westminster Confession*, the *Savoy Declaration* and Wesley's *Sermons* in its heritage. It is possible that the backward glance is not favoured by such radicals as this author claims to be (albeit *radix* means "root"); indeed, she thinks it important to launch out into new directions; but I confess that as I read I was reminded of Bernard Lord Manning's reference to the Wayside Pulpit outside a church in Cambridge that placarded David Livingstone's slogan, "I will go anywhere if only it be forward." Manning writes, "On seeing it a satirical friend of mine said, 'I should like to write underneath *And so say all of us (signed) the Gadarene* Swine.'"[58] Oliver Quick's earlier caution against the theological *avant garde* likewise comes ringing down the years: "Modernism, where it is unorthodox, is not unorthodox because it restates Christianity, but because it states something which is not Christian."[59]

As for the *amendment* of the redemptive revelation on ideological grounds, this is sufficiently illustrated by reference to an Order of Worship I recently saw. It contains no Trinitarian blessing; the doxology, "Praise God from whom all blessings flow" is bowdlerised, presumably so that the saints will not be required to utter the threefold name containing the

---

J. R. Illingworth, whom he accuses of incautiously denigrating those who made the atonement central.

57. Forsyth, *The Cruciality of the Cross*, 50 n. Cf. Forsyth, *The Church, the Gospel and Society*, 119–20; Forsyth, *The Justification of God*, 89–91

58. Manning, *Essays in Orthodox Dissent*, 140.

59. Quick. *Liberalism, Modernism and Tradition*, vi.

PART TWO: Confessing the Faith Ecclesially and Hopefully

word "Father." It has always seemed to me that the first thing to say about God as Father is that he is the God and Father of our Lord Jesus Christ. Were this not the case the New Testament would have to be regarded as intentionally misleading, Christian experience would be fraudulent, and the systematic theology of the ages would be scuppered. Again, I do not think it is seriously doubted that Jesus invited his friends to call God "Father," and this, surely, is one of the greatest privileges of those who have by grace been adopted as his sons and daughters. Then on the order of worship we find that the hymn, "Forth in thy name O Lord I go" is amended so that the term "lord" will not pass the worshippers' lips, and there is an item on the order entitled "The prayer of Jesus," which would seem to refer to what most of us would call the Lord's Prayer. I assume that here the reasoning is—and I have heard this on more than one occasion—that to call Jesus "Lord" is to employ hierarchical language, and this is to be avoided. On this I have three comments. First, I believe in a Lord who takes a towel and does slaves work, washing his disciples' feet, than which nothing could be less hierarchical; and this is reinforced by the infancy narrative concerning a stable not a palace, by a crown not of gold but of thorns, and by the Christological hymn in Philippians 2. Secondly, I firmly believe that the Church is called at times to be counter-cultural, and that this sometimes means that far from rejecting our language we should retain it and use it to explain to the world that it has not understood it yet. I was preaching in the former Czechoslovakia during the communist period when congregations were infiltrated by informers and one had to be aware of this. At the end of the service an elderly woman shot out of her pew and almost ran towards me because she wanted to say something to me without being overheard by others. What she said was, "These Ceaușescus and Honeckers—they're not really lords are they?" I said, "Of course they're not"—and off she went! My case is that the Church is on occasion charged to proclaim Lordship of Christ in the face of the little tin-pot lords who strut the stage of history for a few years, and that if we sacrifice our language we shall have rendered ourselves dumb, and the witness will not be made. Thirdly, I think that what amounts to the censoring of worship on ideological grounds raises acute ethical and vocational questions. In public worship the minister is a public person who does not selfishly perform his or her private devotions, but leads the people's worship. It is a high calling. In a Trinitarian tradition the people have a right to Trinitarian worship. Thomas Belsham realized this. He was a tutor at the Dissenting academy at Daventry, and whilst there he became persuaded of the unitarian position. He resigned his post in 1789 and went to teach in the second Hackney College in London—a Unitarian foundation. I believe that he acted with an integrity that accommodated both his conscientious inability to continue to lead Trinitarian worship and the people's right to partake in worship of that kind.

What, then, of that amendment to the received revelation that consists in the advice from some systematic theologians that we may not put our trust in a God who is a child-batterer? This is the kind of accusatory representation of Christian doctrine that one might expect to emanate from the Richard Dawkins School of Theology; and, as a description of what the Christian faith teaches, one would not expect to read it in a first year student essay. But some theologians are representing this as if it were a Christian belief that needs to be countered, and I find this distinctly odd and not a little distressing. The general point is that unqualified anthropocentrism is not a firm foundation for the interpretation of revelation. More particularly, to view God's revelation through the lens of a particularly cruel and indefensible experience which some children sadly undergo leads to an amendment to the revealed Word which undercuts the faith altogether, for it drives a wedge between the Father and the Son, whereas at the heart of the gospel is the declaration that "*God* was *in Christ* reconciling the world to himself" (2 Cor 5:19). "It is God in Christ reconciling," said Forsyth, "it is not human nature offering its very best to God."[60] The Father is never against the beloved Son with whom he is well pleased;[61] and to the obnoxious view that God could not be gracious until Jesus had suffered on the cross, Calvin properly objected that "it was not after we were reconciled to him through the blood of his Son that [God] began to love us. Rather, he loved us before the world was created . . .";[62] and in what I have sometimes called the single most important sentence in the whole of British theological literature of the twentieth century, Forsyth declared that "The atonement did not procure grace, it flowed from grace."[63]

---

60. Forsyth, *The Work of Christ*, 24; cf. ibid., 92, 99; Forsyth, *The Cruciality of the Cross*, 17.

61. See Forsyth, *The Work of Christ*, 156–57; 181–82; Forsyth, *The Cruciality of the Cross*, 29–30.

62. Calvin, *Institutes*, II.xvi.4.

63. Forsyth, *The Cruciality of the Cross*, 41.

PART TWO: Confessing the Faith Ecclesially and Hopefully

Thesis 8. The significance and implications of the supreme revelation are to be *articulated* by systematic theologians. "Revelation," Forsyth reminds us, "did not come in a statement, but in a person; yet stated it must be . . . else it could not be spread; for it is not an ineffable, incommunicable mysticism."[64] While every member of the Church is a theologian in so far as they have thoughts of God, Christ, eternity, and more,[65] systematic and constructive theologians are privileged to have been called to reflect in depth upon, and to communicate to and through the Church, those things which lie at the heart of the Christian faith. This is an awesome challenge, not least because, as Hodges wrote, "forms of statement, as well as forms of worship, condition the apprehension of reality and mould the spiritual life."[66]

How, then, do systematic theologians occupy themselves? The most accurate answer is, "Variously." There are those who continue to take us on an orderly Cook's tour of the several departments of systematic theology, from creation to eschatology. On occasion the result is a cops and robbers variety of systematics, for strong disjunctions abound, and frequently prejudices are revealed, as we encounter Alexandrians *versus* Antiochenes, Augustinians *versus* Pelagians, Thomists *versus* Scotists, Calvinists *versus* Arminians, Trinitarians *versus* Unitarians, and Barthians *versus* everybody else! Tomes of this kind can be useful, but their very range can issue in unsubtlety at certain points; and when they become tools employed to straitjacket the minds of students within a doctrinal party line the temptation to hide them is overcome only by the realization that such censorship would violate the principles of higher education.

Other systematicians, and sometimes the same ones, dwell upon one theologian in particular, and Barth has become a primary candidate for treatment of this kind. We may even be forgiven for thinking that just as A. N. Whitehead thought that "The safest general characterization of the European philosophical tradition is that it consists of a series of footnotes to Plato,"[67] so some systematicians give the impression that their discipline is a series of footnotes to Barth, or even a series of footnotes to other scholars' footnotes to Barth. In that half-life between wakefulness and sleep I sometimes have a vision of systematicians puzzling over the

---

64. Forsyth, *The Person and Place of Jesus Christ*, 15.
65. See further Sell, *Testimony and Tradition*, 6–12.
66. Hodges, *The Christian in the Modern University*, 21.
67. Whitehead, *Process and Reality*, 63.

question, "With whom have I not yet compared or contrasted Barth?" Again, there are systematicians who follow an old tradition of seeking to accommodate Christian thought to the spirit of the age, and for these Forsyth composed a *quasi*-epitaph: "I am sure that, if we had a theology brought entirely up to date in regard to current thought, we should not then have the great condition for the Kingdom of God. It is the wills of men, and not their views, that are the great obstacle to the Gospel, and the things most intractable."[68] Yet again, there are systematicians who take out shares in the religion and science industry, and others who, in recent years, have been majoring on the doctrine of the Trinity. I very much welcome the renewed attention to the Trinity, though I am made to feel very inferior by those writers who know so much about the inner workings and relations of the persons of the Trinity that they can draw analogies as to how the empirical Church should be conducting itself. In this connection Calvinist divines who seemed to know a good deal about God's *inscrutable* will come, unbidden, to mind, followed by Herbert Spencer with his Unknowable. In hot pursuit comes Peter Dean (1849–1905), sometime Unitarian minister in Walsall. In 1883 the *Walsall Observer* reported a sermon by the town's Vicar on good and bad angels. In his publication, *The Religious Reformer* for November of the same year, Dean, a former journalist,ced wrote thus:

> In Walsall, one is constantly being reminded that it requires little mental capacity to be a Church of England vicar. . . . We should think [the Vicar] can even beat the yokel who said, "I made this wheelbarrow out of my own head and I've wood enough to make another one!" . . . From beginning to end the Vicar's statements . . . are pure fancy. The Walsall Vicar has no more KNOWLEDGE of angels, what took place in heaven and on earth before man was created &c., than has the Walsall Billsticker; and as the latter has the good sense to say nothing of things of which he knows nothing, the Vicar would do well to follow his good example.[69]

Where the mysteries of the faith are concerned a modicum of godly agnosticism never comes amiss, as the Presbyterian Samuel Chandler insisted in his reply to the high Calvinist Congregationalist, John Guyse. Chandler refused to speculate upon the precise personal distinctions within the Trinity "because 'tis incomprehensible and cannot be

68. Forsyth. *Positive Preaching and the Modern Mind*, 197.
69. For further entertainment of this kind see Sell, *Dissenting* Thought, 460–71.

understood and known by us. And I am more persuaded of this, because you gentlemen, who set up for the direct preachers of Christ, and to be the only sound men in the doctrine of the Trinity, differ greatly yourselves about it."[70]

I by no means deny that productive systematic and constructive work can be done, and is being done, in many ways. But I sometimes feel that the supremely revelatory *act* at the cross is not accorded its rightful place. It is scarcely mentioned by most of the writers who contributed to the January 2009 issue of the *International Journal of Systematic Theology* which was largely devoted to the nature and method of systematic theology. John Webster does, however, grant that "in the *ordo cognoscendi*, systematic theology ordinarily takes its rise in attention to God's temporal acts of creation, election and deliverance," but he cautions that "the order of knowing is not simply reduplicated in the order of being." Should this happen, he continues, "part of [systematic theology's] subject-matter may be pushed to the periphery, and the centre of gravity shift accordingly from *de Deo* to *de creaturis et de moribus hominum*," and "the real character of the *works* of God will remain obscure as the agent upon whom these works depend becomes increasingly elusive."[71] In saying that there *may* occur a shift from *de Deo* to *de creaturis et de moribus hominum* Professor Webster implies that this need not necessarily happen, and with this I agree. I further agree that, since God is apprehended but not fully comprehended by us, "the order of knowing is not simply reduplicated in the order of being." I nevertheless wish to reiterate my conviction that it is supremely through the temporal acts, above all through the cross, that we are given the best knowledge available to us of God's nature and purpose; that God is as he has revealed himself to be; and that were it otherwise we should not have a revelation of *God*.

While not, therefore, seeking to inhibit the flow of all the other activities that may take place under the umbrella of systematic theology, I propose that one way of being systematic is to set out from God's supremely authoritative revelation, and to find in it one's point of reference throughout. This was Forsyth's way of being a systematic theologian, and it explains why his thought on almost every theological topic spirals

---

70. Chandler, *A Letter to the Reverend Mr. John Guyse*, 28. For Chandler (1693–1766) see Sell, *Hinterland* Theology, ch. 4 and *passim*.

71. Webster, "Principles of Systematic Theology," 65.

out from the cross and sooner or later returns to its source.[72] With this thought I come to the next thesis.

Thesis 9. The supreme revelation *appropriates* all other Christian doctrines, and *appertains to* such satellite disciplines as apologetics and ethics.

One of the difficulties about systematic theology is that not everything can be said in one breath. Doctrine rolls into doctrine, and I suspect that if one were to expound any particular doctrine as fully as one could, all of the other doctrines would, sooner or later, need to be drawn in. But it seems me that this is nowhere more clearly demonstrated than in connection with the cross. For to speak of God's supreme revelation is to speak of him as he is; it is to ponder God's grace and humanity's state and need of redemption; it is to understand Jesus as the Son of God who, because he is human can save *us*, and because he is divine can *save* us; it is to view the whole of creation in the context of recreation with all its eschatological implications; and it is to consider the church as the saved community into which the regenerate are called by the Spirit with a view to worship, witness and service. Moreover it is because of the supremely revelatory saving act that we have a doctrine of the Trinity at all, grounded as it is in biblical clues, the experience of forgiveness and new life in Christ and the power of the Spirit, and honed through debate with those deemed heretical, whose intellectual objections have benefited us all. Precisely because of the way doctrine rolls into doctrine, I do not argue that all theological systems must set out from the cross. I am, however, puzzled by the way in which some who undertake the systematic task seem so easily able to bypass it.

I believe that systematic theology is a piece of orderly testimony to God's saving grace which takes the form of a conversation between the Bible, the heritage of Christian testimony and the current intellectual environment. It is in this last connection especially that God's supreme self-revelation at the cross can stimulate apologetic and ethical enquiries. For apologetics should not be regarded exclusively as a matter of defending the faith against alien philosophies and world views, but as confessing the faith and dealing with intellectual opponents *en passant*. But the analysis of what is to be commended, who the confessors are, how their presuppositions may be analyzed, and whether their language is genuinely referential—these are some of the issues to be teased out

---

72. See further Sell, *Testimony and Tradition*, ch. 7.

PART TWO: Confessing the Faith Ecclesially and Hopefully

when the prolegomena to apologetics are under review.[73] As for Christian morality, it is gratitude for God's gracious redemption that is its primary motive. But how does this bear upon Christian ethics considered as a discipline in which the logic of language and the probing of presuppositions ought to play a larger part than is frequently the case?[74] As if this were not enough, there is the huge task of probing the metaphysical and epistemological questions raised by Christian thought and experience, not to mention the viability of systematic claims *vis à vis* developments in the philosophy of history. Systematicians will never be at a loss for something to do. However they employ themselves, we may hope that they will have the humility to recognize with H. R. Mackintosh that "Theologies from the first have perished; they wax old as doth a garment; as a vesture Time folds them up, and lays them down. Nothing save the Gospel is abiding, and its years shall not fail."[75]

Thesis 9.5. The *absence* of the cross from systematic theology brings what H. G. C. Moule called "a long dreary falsetto into the whole music of theology."[76] Accordingly, it behoves us . . . Amen.

---

73. See my trilogy on Christian apologetic method: *John Locke*; *Philosophical Idealism*; *Confessing and Commending the Faith*. For my summary account of this project see ch. 6 above.

74. For some suggestions see Sell, *Testimony and Tradition*, ch. 9.

75. H. R. Mackintosh, *Some Aspects of Christian Belief*, 176.

76. Letter of 19 January 1898 to W. R. Nicoll, quoted in Darlow, *William Robertson Nicoll*, 160.

BIBLIOGRAPHY

Baxter, Richard. *Autobiography (Reliquiae Baxterianae* abridged). London: Dent, 1931.
Burgh, W. G. de. *The Life of Reason.* London: Macdonald and Evans, 1949.
Caird, Edward. "St. Paul and Evolution." *The Hibbert Journal* 2 (1903) 1–19.
Calvin, John. *Institutes.* Translated by Ford Lewis Battles and edited by John T. McNeil. Philadelphia: Westminster, 1960.
Chandler, Samuel. *A Letter to the Reverend Mr. John Guyse, Occasioned by his Two Lectures Preached at St. Helens, on Acts ix. 20. In which the Scripture-Notion of Preaching Christ is Stated and Defended: And Mr. Guyse's Charges against his Brethren are Considered and Proved Groundless.* London: Gray, 1728.
Collis, Michael J. *An Account of the Baptist Churches of Shropshire and the Surrounding Areas.* Newtown, UK: The Shropshire Group of Baptist Churches, 2008.
Dale, R. W. *Christian Doctrine.* 1894. Reprint. London: Hodder and Stoughton, 1903.
Darlow, T. H. *William Robertson Nicoll: Life and Letters.* London: Hodder & Stoughton, 1925.
Denney, James. *The Christian Doctrine of Reconciliation.* London: Hodder & Stoughton, 1917.
Forsyth, P. T. "Authority and Theology." *The Hibbert Journal* 4 (1905) 63–78.
———. *The Church, the Gospel and Society.* London: Independent, 1962.
———. *The Cruciality of the Cross.* 1909. Reprint. London: Independent, 1957.
———. *God the Holy Father.* London: Independent, 1957.
———. "Immanence and Incarnation." In *The Old Faith and the New Theology*, edited by C. H. vine, 47–61. London: Sampson Low, Marston, 1907.
———. *The Justification of God.* 1917. Reprint. London: Independent, 1957.
———. *The Person and Place of Jesus Christ.* 1909. Reprint. London: Independent, 1961.
———. *Positive Preaching and the Modern Mind.* 1907. Reprint. London: Independent, 1964.
———. *The Principle of Authority.* 1913. Reprint. London: Independent, 1952.
———. "Revelation and the Bible." *The Hibbert Journal* 10 (1911) 235–52.
———. *The Work of Christ.* 1910. Reprint. London: Independent, 1958.
Healy, Nicholas M. "What is Systematic Theology?" *International Journal of Systematic Theology* 11 (2009) 24–39.
Hodges, H. A. *The Christian in the Modern University.* London: SCM, 1961.
———. *Languages, Standpoints and Attitudes.* London: Oxford University Press, 1953.
———. *The Pattern of Atonement.* London: SCM, 1965.
McKim, Donald K. *Encyclopedia of the Reformed Faith.* Louisville: Westminster/John Knox, 1992.
———. *The Westminster Handbook to Reformed Theology.* Louisville: Westminster/John Knox, 2001.
Mackintosh, H. R. *Some Aspects of Christian Belief.* London: Hodder & Stoughton, 1923.
Mackintosh, Robert. *The Authority of the Church.* Edinburgh: Scott & Ferguson and Burness, 1893.
———. *The Insufficiency of Revivalism as a Religious System.* (Bound with the following item).
———. *Essays Towards a New Theology.* Glasgow: Maclehose, 1889.

PART TWO: Confessing the Faith Ecclesially and Hopefully

Manning, Bernard Lord. *Essays in Orthodox Dissent*. 1939. London: Independent, 1953.
Matthews, W. R. *The Gospel and the Modern Mind*. London: Macmillan, 1930.
———. *Signposts to God*. London: SPCK, 1938.
Nash, Robert. In *The Sunday Press*, Dublin, 8 February 1981.
Paul, Robert S. *Ministry*. Grand Rapids: Eerdmans, 1965.
Quick, O. C. *Doctrines of the Creed: Their Basis in Scripture and their Meaning Today*. 1938. Reprint. London: Collins Fontana, 1971.
———. *Essays in Orthodoxy*. London: Macmillan, 1916.
———. *Liberalism, Modernism and Tradition*. London: Longmans Green, 1922.
Ramsey, A. M. *From Gore to Temple: The Development of Anglican Theology between* Lux Mundi *and the Second World War 1889–1939*. London: Longmans, 1960.
Redford, George, and John Angell James, *The Autobiography of William Jay*. 1854. Reprint. Edinburgh: Banner of Truth, 1974.
Sell, Alan P. F. *Confessing and Commending the Faith: Historic Witness and Apologetic Method*. 2002. Reprint. Eugene, OR: Wipf and Stock, 2006.
———. *Dissenting Thought and the Life of the Churches: Studies in an English Tradition*. Lewiston, NY: Mellen, 1990.
———. *Enlightenment, Ecumenism, Evangel: Theological Themes and Thinkers 1550–2000*. Milton Keynes, UK: Paternoster, 2005.
———. *Hinterland Theology: A Stimulus to Theological Construction*. Milton Keynes, UK: Paternoster, 2008.
———. *John Locke and the Eighteenth-Century Divines*. 1997. Reprint. Eugene, OR: Wipf & Stock, 2006.
———. *Philosophical Idealism and Christian Belief*. 1995. Reprint. Eugene, OR: Wipf & Stock, 2006.
———. *The Spirit Our Life*. Shippensburg, PA: Ragged Edge, 2000.
———. *Theology in Turmoil: The Roots, Course and Significance of the Conservative-Liberal Debate in Modern Theology*. 1986. Reprint. Eugene, OR: Wipf and Stock, 1998.
———. *Testimony and Tradition: Studies in Reformed and Dissenting Thought*. Aldershot, UK: Ashgate, 2005.
Taylor, John. *The Scripture-Doctrine of Original Sin*. London: printed for the author by J. Wilson, 1740.
Vosper, Gretta. *With or Without God: The Way we Live is More Important Than What We Believe*. Toronto: Harper Collins, 2008.
Watson, Thomas. *A Divine Cordial*. Grand Rapids: Sovereign Grace, 1971.
Webster, John. "Principles of Systematic Theology." *International Journal of Systematic Theology* 11 (2009) 56–71.
Whitehead, A. N. *Process and Reality*. 1929. Reprint. New York: Harper Torchbooks, 1960.
Wilcox, Thomas. *Honey out of the Rock*. (Original title: *A Choice Drop of Honey out of the Rock Christ, or, A Short Word of Advice to all Saints and Sinners*, 1690). Sheffield: Zoar, c.1970.
Wiles, Maurice F. "Religious Authority and Divine Action." *Religious Studies* 7 (1971) 1–12.
Williams, A. N. "What is Systematic Theology?" *International Journal of Systematic Theology* 11 (2009) 40–55.
Wilson, Walter. *The History and Antiquities of Dissenting Churches and Meeting Houses in London, Westminster and Southwark*. 4 vols, London: Button, 1818–12.

Index of Persons

Abelard, 210
Acland, Thomas Dycke, 90
Ainsworth, Henry, 38, 178
Alexander of Hales, 211
Allon, Henry, 192, 248–49
Anselm, 119, 210
Arius, 210
Armstrong, William Park, 150, 156
Arnobius, 246, 249
Ashton, R., 192
Athanasius, 210
Augustine, 60, 153, 180, 210, 238, 243
Austin, J. L., 5
Ayer, A. J., 130–31

Bach, J. S., 211
Bagshaw, Edward, 85
Baillie, Donald, 136
Baillie, John, 97, 136, 253
Baillie, Robert, 178
Barber, Joseph, 122
Barbour, Hugh, 31, 244
Barclay, Robert, 44, 129
Barlow, William, 24
Barrow, Henry, 29–30, 33, 178, 187–89, 194, 196
Barth, Karl, 120, 133, 135, 137, 257, 286–87
Bartlet, William, 68, 69
Basil of Caesarea, 237
Bates, William, 261
Baum, G., 156
Bavinck, Herman, 150

Baxter, Richard, 31, 34, 38, 39, 40, 43, 44, 45, 46, 54, 69, 137, 178, 208–9, 227–28, 229, 261, 273
Bayle, Pierre, 94
Beaver, R. Pierce, 172
Beddome, Benjamin, 211
Beek, Abraham van de, ch. 5, 254, 262
Belsham, Thomas, 123, 284
Bender, Ross T., 213
Berg, J. Van den, 171
Bergson, H., 133
Bernard of Clairvaux, 161
Beza, Theodore, 67
Biddle, John, 246
Binney, Thomas, 248
Blount, Thomas Pope, 53
Boekholt, Johannes, 37
Bold, Samuel, 59
Bonaventure, 97, 211
Borght, Eduardus Van der, 263
Bosier, Robert, 260
Bourn, Samuel, 15, 137
Bourne, F. W., 166
Bourne, H. R. Fox, 121
Bouwsma, William J., 36
Boyd, Robin, 225
Boyle, Robert, 63
Bradberry, David, 7
Braithwaite, W. C., 35
Bratt, John, 171, 172
Bridge, William, 42, 69
Brown, John, 37, 262
Brown, Raymond, 212

Index of Persons

Browne, Robert, 29–30, 32, 178, 183, 189, 190, 199
Bruce, A. B., 119, 126
Bultmann, Rudolf, 133
Bunyan, John, 33–34, 35–37, 46, 102, 211, 262
Burgh, W. G. de, 91, 269, 275
Burke, Edmund, 88
Burnet, Gilbert, 59
Burrage, Champlin, 27, 41, 42
Burrough, Edward, 31, 72, 83
Burroughes, Jeremiah, 42, 69
Busher, Leonard, 67

Cadoux, C. J., 203
Caird, Edward, 123, 124, 125, 281
Caird, John, 125
Calamy, Edmund, 262
Calvin, John, 67, 129, 135, 136, 143, ch. 7, ch. 8, 212, 224, 239, 251, 261, 270, 273, 285
Canipe, Lee, 66
Carlson, Leland H., 32, 33, 41, 42
Cartwright, Thomas, 24, 42
Cassels, Thomas, 241
Castellio, S., 59
Cave, Sydney, 250, 252
Ceauşescu, N., 284
Celsus, 243
Charles I, 24
Charles II, 25, 35, 85
Chandler, Samuel, 287–88
Chatham, Earl of, 57
Chesterton, G. K., 51, 215
Chrysostom, John, 129, 148
Cicero, 149
Clark, Samuel, 38–39
Clement of Alexandria, 237
Cleobury, F. H., 254–55
Cochrane, Arthur C., 8, 14, 134, 180
Cocks, H. F. Lovell, 181, 186, 197
Cole, Thomas, 84
Collins, Anthony, 61
Collis, Michael J., 279

Comte, A., 90, 91, 92
Conder, Eustace, 177
Constantine, 43, 138
Cooke, Leslie E., 202
Cooper, Anthony Ashley, 63, 85
Corbet, John, 62
Cotton, John, 67–68
Cowper, William, 211
Crabbe, George, 251
Craig, John, 244
Crombie, I. M., 131
Cromwell, Oliver, 32, 44, 52
Cromwell, Richard, 71
Cudworth, Ralph, 53, 54
Cunitz, E., 156
Cunningham, William, 241
Cyprian, 153, 180

Dale, A. W. W., 246
Dale, R. W., 14, 183, 185, 188, 194, 197–98, 246–47, 280
Darby, J. N., 241
D'Aubigné, C. M., 150
Dawkins, Richard, 97, 285
Dean, Peter, 287
De Beer, E. S., 85
Denney, James, 17, 282
Denny, George H., 150
Derrida, J., 133
Descartes, R., 121
Deweese, Charles W., 29
Dewsbury, William, 244
Dickens, A. G., 60
Dionne, E. J., 93
Dixhoorn, Chad van, 42
Dixon, R. W., 7
Dodd, C. H., 251
Doddridge, Philip, 6, 212
Dodwell, Henry, 60
Doolittle, Thomas, 260
Doumergoue, Émile, 150
Drummond, Hay, 57
Drummond, Henry, 240
Du Moulin, Lewis, 84

Index of Persons

Edmondson, Stephen, 151
Edwards, Jonathan, 212, 244, 259, 280
Edwards, Thomas, 68–69
Elizabeth I, 30, 190, 194
Erasmus, D., 127
Eusebius, 236
Ewing, A. C., 131

Fairbairn, A. M., 55
Farmer, H. H., 136
Fawcett, John, 211
Felch, Susan M., 159
Fergusson, David, 111
Fisher, Samuel, 31
Fitz, Richard, 27
Fitzmyer, Joseph, 212
Flavel, John, 40–41, 261, 262
Flew, A. G. N., 131, 254
Flint, Robert, 119, 221
Forsyth, P. T., 6, 9, 11, 13–15, 17–20, 29, 76, 97, 108–9, 115, 128, 157, 194, 203, 212, 216, 218–20, 223, 225–26, 242, 253–54, 269, 270–72, 274–75, 277, 279–81, 283, 285–88
Foster, James, 279
Foucault, M., 133
Fox, George, 31, 45, 211
Foxe, John, 60
Frank, D. H., 106
Franks, Robert S., 151
Fraser, A. M., 150
Fraser, John W., 161, 168
Frew, David, 156
Frykholm, Amy, 152

Gamble, Richard C., 156
Garvie, A. E., 96, 202
Geest, P. van, 263
Gill, John, 120
Glanvill, Joseph, 54–55
Glasgow, Frank T., 150

Goldie, Mark, 63
Goodall, Norman, 202
Goodwin, John, 14
Goodwin, Thomas, 16, 42, 69, 212, 223
Goold, William H., 45
Gore, Charles, 216
Gouldstone, Timothy Maxwell, 96
Gratton, John, 35, 45
Greaves, Richard L., 37
Green, Ian, 24, 43
Green, T. H., 123–25
Greenwood, John, 29–30, 189, 190
Gregory of Nyssa, 247
Grove, Henry, 245
Gulston, William, 59
Gurnall, William, 250

Haac, Oscar A., 90, 91
Haley, K. H. D., 63
Hall, Robert, 252
Harris, Paul, 233
Harrison, Robert, 32
Hart, Joseph, 182
Hayden, Roger, 18
Haykin, Michael A. G., 46
Haymes, Brian, 66
Healy, Nicholas M., 274
Hegel, G. W. F., 123
Helm, Paul, 156
Helwys, Thomas, 30–31, 66–67, 72, 75, 82
Henry VIII, 171
Henry, Matthew, 260
Henry, Philip, 32, 214–16
Hepburn, Ronald W., 256
Herbert of Cherbury, 53, 84
Hesselink, I. John, 149, 151, 154, 165
Heywood, Oliver, 39, 46
Hick, John, 53, 54
Hill, Amelia, 259
Hill, Rowland, 261
Hippolytus of Rome, 236, 244

295

Index of Persons

Hirsch, Samuel, 106, 108
Hobbes, Thomas, 120
Hodges, H. A., 269, 277, 282, 286
Hoffman, Melchior, 239
Holder, R. Ward, 159
Honecker, E., 284
Hoogstra, Jacob T., 171
Hooker, Richard, 64
Horton, John, 56
Horton, R. F., 196
Howard, K. W. H., 28
Howe, John, 44, 52, 53, 61, 218, 262
Howgill, Francis, 211
Hryniewicz, W., 216
Hughes, Philip E., 171
Hume, David, 270
Hurd, Alan G., 7
Huxtable, W. John F., 202

Illingworth, J. R., 124, 127–28, 283
Irenaeus, 107, 236, 243
Irving, Edward, 240
Ivimey, Joseph, 28

Jacob, Henry, 42, 178
Jacob, Joseph, 278–79
James I, 24, 66
James, John Angell, 216, 270
Jay, Statira, 262
Jay, William, 216, 261–63, 270
Jenkins, Jerry, 242
Joachim of Fiore, 238–39
John of Damascus, 210, 211
John Paul II, 220
John Scotus Eriugena, 247, 248
Johnson, Thomas Cary, 150
Johnston, William B., 162
Jones, Henry, 124
Jordan, M. Dorothea, 66
Justin Martyr, 230, 243

Kaufman, Gordon D., 258
Keach, Benjamin, 46
Keeble, Neil H., 23, 24

Keillor, Garrison, 93
Kierkegaard, S., 135, 211, 277
Killen, Patricia, 152
King, Samuel A., 150
Klooster, Fred H., 12
Knollys, Hanserd, 46
Knox, John, 159, 171
Kromminga, John H., 154
Kuyper, A., 135

Lactantius, 236, 237
Lacunza, Manuel, 240
LaHaye, Tim, 242
Lang, August, 150
Lecky, W. E. H., 55
Leith, John, 158, 179
Limborch, Philippus von, 63, 85
Lindsay, Hal, 242
Littell, Franklin H., 158
Livingstone, David, 283
Locke, 55–56, 57–58, 59, 63–64,
   67, 84–86, 88, 91, 93, 94, 96,
   101, 120–22, 125
Lok, Anne, 159
Luke, W. B., 166
Lumpkin, William L., 5, 42, 66,
   67, 82
Lund, Roger, 62
Luther, Martin, 211, 212, 239, 261,
   268
Lynch, Beth, 36

McGrath, Alister, 96
McKee, Elsie, 168
Mackennal, Alexander, 178
McKie, Robin,
McKim, Donald K., 276
MacKinnon, Donald M., 133
Mackintosh, H. R., 248, 250–51,
   252, 258, 290
Mackintosh, Robert, 10, 136, 228,
   277, 278
McNaughton, William D., 241
McTaggart, J. M. E., 124, 125

Index of Persons

Madonna, 133
Manning, Bernard Lord, 26, 186,
    191–92, 193, 203, 209, 220,
    224–26, 263, 283
Manson, T. W., 219
Marcion, 236
Marriott, J. A. R., 196
Marshall, John, 63, 84
Martin, Hugh, 36
Mascall, E. L., 131
Matheson, George, 102
Matthews, A. G., 13, 42, 43, 70, 84
Matthews, G. D., 147
Matthews, W. R., 234, 269, 271, 274
Maugham, W. Somerset, 94
Maurice, F. D., 248
Mede, Joseph, 239
Mendus, Susan, 56
Mercer, Johnny, 81
Meyer, F. B., 242
Micklem, Nathaniel, 196
Mill, James, 89
Mill, John Stuart, 88–97, 101, 270
Miller, William, 242
Milton, John, 64, 68, 71
Minton, Henry Collin, 150
Moffatt, James, 14
Moltmann, J., 251
Monck, Thomas, 63, 64, 83
Montanus of Phrygia, 236
Moon, Byung-Ho, 165
Moore, G. E., 118
More, Henry, 56
Moule, H. G. C., 290
Müller, J. J., 250
Mullett, Michael, 37
Müntzer, Thomas, 239
Murton, John, 67

Nash, Robert, 273
Nayler, James, 31, 33
Newman, John Henry, 211
Newton, B. W., 241
Newton, John, 211

Nicholas of Cusa, 53
Nichols, Vincent, 259
Nietzsche, F., 133
Noake, John, 7, 28
North, Brownlow, 254
Nuttall, Geoffrey F., 14, 188, 253,
    254, 255
Nye, Philip, 42, 69
Nyomi, 150

Origen, 135, 210, 237, 247, 249
Orr, James, 119, 150, 156
Orton, Job, 137
Owen, H. P., 131
Owen, John, 13, 32, 38, 44–45,
    58–59, 63, 68, 71–74, 84,
    181–82, 184, 188–92, 194,
    199, 212, 240
Owen, John (nineteenth century),
    162

Parker, Samuel, 62
Pannenberg, W., 251
Parker, Joseph, 111
Parker, T. H. L., 149, 153, 161, 164
Patai, Daphne, 98
P[atrick], S[imon], 134
Pattison, Mark, 147
Paul, Robert S., 42, 69–70, 75, 82,
    273
Peach, Bernard, 57
Pearse, Mark Guy, 261
Peel, Albert, 30, 32, 111, 196
Pelagius, 210
Penington, Isaac, 25, 31, 72, 211
Penn, William, 31, 34, 82
Phillips, D. Z., 132
Philpot, J. H., 241, 242
Pitt, William, the Younger, 87
Plantinga, Alvin, 135
Plato, 286
Poole-Connor, E. J., 245
Porter, Cole, 94
Powell, Vavasor, 46

Index of Persons

Powicke, F. J., 14, 15, 16
Price, Richard, 57
Priestley, Joseph, 64, 72, 86–88, 91, 101, 209
Pringle, William, 149, 153, 161, 164, 168
Pringle-Pattison, A. S., 121, 124
Purkis, William, 86
Pusey, E. B., 90, 2

Quick, O. C., 269, 274, 282, 283

Ramsey, A. M., 128, 282
Randall, Ian, 242
Rayment-Pickard, Hugh, 133
Redford, George, 216, 270
Reid, W. S., 171
Reuss, E., 156
Richardson, Samuel, 60, 69, 246
Rigg, J. M., 44
Roberts, Arthur O., 31, 244
Roberts, George W., 133
Robinson, John, 16, 60, 65, 75, 178, 192, 197
Robinson, William, 195
Robinson, W. Gordon, 16
Rogers, J. Guinness, 191, 194, 199
Rogers, John, 240
Root, H. E., 257
Ross, Fiona, 93
Ross, Kenneth R., 12
Rousseau, J.-J., 242
Rowell, Geoffrey, 260
Rupp, E. Gordon, 167
Ryan, Thomas, 207

Sacheverell, Henry, 86
Sadoleto, J., 154
Sandeen, Ernest R., 242
Sangster, W. E., 250
Schleiermacher, F. D. E., 138, 212
Schochet, Gordon, 62
Scott, Walter, 263
Selbie, W. B., 65

Sell, Alan P. F., 6, 8, 12, 15, 17, 19, 20, 26, 35, 42–43, 64, 68, 83–84, 86, 89, 91, 95, 97, 100–101, 107, 108, ch. 6, 143–45, 151, 159, 163, 166, 167, 176, 179, 184, 192, 195–96, 198, 200, 203, ch. 9, 234, 245–46, 253, 256, 271, 274, 280–81, 286–90
Servetus, M., 150
Shaftesbury. *See* Cooper, Anthony Ashley
Shakespeare, William, 109
Sharrock, Roger, 37
Shaw, Thomas, 166
Sidgwick, Henry, 234
Sim, Stuart, 36
Simpson, Sidrach, 42
Smith, John, 223
Smith, Thorne, 94
Smith, William, 71
Smucker, Donovan E., 133
Smyth, John, 41, 65, 67, 82
Snaith, Norman H., 225
Socinus (Sozzini), Fausto Paolo, 81
Spencer, Herbert, 97, 287
Spurgeon, C. H., 129, 148, 211, 241, 248
Stachniewski, John, 36
Stenmark, Mikael, 96
Sterry, Peter, 53–54
Stevenson, J. H., 147, 150
Stevenson, Marmaduke, 195
Stevenson, Robert, 37
Stewart, K. Moody, 254
Stillingfleet, Edward, 58–59
Stirling, J. H., 123
Stoughton, John, 69
Stubbe, Henry, 85
Sullivan, Emmanuel, 207

Tait, A. C., 189
Taylor, A. E., 124
Taylor, Barbara Brown, 234

Index of Persons

Taylor, Jeremy, 62, 246
Taylor, John, 121, 280
Taylor, Mark C., 133
Taylor, Thomas Rawson, 263
Templin, J. Alton, 168
Telford, John, 262
Tertullian, 59, 236, 244, 245
Thomas Aquinas, 119, 211, 245
Thomas, D. O., 57
Thompson, David M., 195
Thompson, Joseph, 160
Tillard, J. M. R., 221
Tilley, Terrence W., 133
Tillich, Paul, 133
Tillotson, John, 84, 246
Toplady, A. M., 259
Torrance, J. B., 11
Tyrrell, James, 121, 182
Torrance, James B., 11
Torrance, Thomas F., 43, 152, 168, 181–83, 214, 244, 256
Tyrrell, George, 272

Underhill, Edward Bean, 64, 67, 83
Unwin, Mrs. George, 262
Urwick, William, 28

Valentinus, 236, 243
Van Til, Cornelius, 135
Vaughan, Robert, 160
Venner, Thomas, 25, 240, 241
Vincent of Lérins, 129
Vischer, Lukas, 5, 9, 214
Voltaire (Françoise-Marie Arouet), 242
Vosper, Greta, 283

Waldron, Jeremy, 55–56
Walker, D. P., 248
Walker, Williston, 6, 42
Wallace, Ronald S., 160
Ward, Mrs. Humphrey, 94, 97
Ward, Keith, 96
Warfield, B. B., 135, 150, 156

Watson, Thomas, 36, 43–44, 261, 270
Watts, George, 35
Watts, Isaac, 6, 46–47, 184–85, 211
Watts, M. R., 26, 260
Webb, C. C. J., 124, 135
Webb, R. A., 150
Weber, Max, 170
Webster, Abraham, 279
Webster, John, 288
Wesley, Charles, 141, 211
Wesley, John, 114, 121, 180, 283
Whale, John S., 180
Whichcote, Benjamin, 57
White, Edward, 189, 246
Whitefield, George, 7
Whitehead, A. N., 286
Whitehead, John, 25
Whitgift, John, 190
Wicks, Jared, 219
Wilcox, Thomas, 271–72
Wiles, Maurice F., 273
Wilkinson, John T., 190
William of Orange, 87
Williams, A. N., 275
Williams, George Hunston, 239
Williams, J. B., 33, 260
Williams, Ralph Vaughan, 211
Williams, Roger, 67, 75, 81, 195
Wilson, Walter, 279
Wilson, William, 223
Wittgenstein, Ludwig, 130, 132
Wolseley, Charles, 52
Woods, G. F., 134
Woodward, Kenneth L., 258
Wright, Thomas, 182
Wykes, David L., 86

Zwingli, Ulrich, 1, 18, 239

Index of Subjects

Acts of Uniformity, 25, 62, 83, 194
adoption, 154, 161, 176, 179, 181–84, 186, 198, 202, 276
Advent Testimony and Preparation League, 242
Anglicans, 30–31, 83, 86, 90, 109, 111, 124, 127–28, 153, 185, 190, 193, 211–13, 218, 246, 248, 269, 271, 282; *see also* Church of England
Anabaptists, 11, 31, 68, 188, 196, 213, 227, 239
Apologetics, 4, ch. 6, 144, 172, 209, 235, 252–57, 269, 289–90
Arianism, 6–7, 15, 29, 68, 121, 123, 137, 280
Arminianism, 6, 14, 45–46, 57, 81, 123, 276, 286
atheism, 63, 68, 91, 148
atonement, 17, 128, 210, 271, 282–83, 285; *see also* cross
authority, ch. 11; *see also* Bible, authority of
autobiography, 35–37

Baptists, 3, 5, 18, 25–26, 28–31, 33, 41–42, 46, 60, 63, 65–67, 69, 72, 75, 81–83, 120, 148, 186, 192, 195, 211–12, 215, 228, 240–42, 248, 252, 279
Baptist Union of Great Britain and Ireland, 18, 248
Bible, 8, 11, 14, 30–31, 58, 65, 67, 107, 111–12, 121, 137, 144, 155–58, 164–66, 171, 183, 186–87, 200, 202, 212, 214, 224, 227, 237–38, 241, 252, 259, 272–73, 289
    authority of, 9, 10, 15, 18, 45, 66, 75, 100, 122, 150, 169, 218, 222, 223, 274–75
    study of, 38–39, 159
bilateral dialogues, 213–14

Calvinism, 7, 10, 26, 36, 43, 46, 57, 120, 147, 149, 150, 168, 170, 178, 186, 209, 213, 245–46, 257, 278–80, 286–87
catechisms, 41–44, 70, 249
    Craig's, 244
    Geneva, 153, 158, 181
    Heidelberg, 168
    Quaker, 31
    Racovian, 14
    Twofold, 246
    Westminster Larger, 182, 256
    Westminster Shorter, 43
Catholic Apostolic Church, 240
catholicity, 176–79, 193, 200, 202–3, 227
Chalcedonian Formula, 6
church, 3, 10–12, 14, 18–20, 24, 30, 35, 42, 45, 47, 57–58, 60, 62, 66, 71, 83, 95, 102, 109, 111, 128, 137–38, 143–44, ch. 7, ch. 8, 208–9, 214–15, 218–21, 223–29, 246, 253, 263, 271–77, 282–83, 284
    church and state, 3, 25, 30–31, 52, 56–57, 65–75, 80–82, 110, 171, 185–86, 193–95, 202

Index of Subjects

church (*cont.*)
    church covenants, 7, 27–29, 184, 187, 197
    church discipline, 3, 52, 58, 70, 71, 74, 158, 162, 164–65, 178, 180, 188, 195, 201, 215, 229
    church meeting, 6, 7, 16, 34, 46, 171, 189, 195–98, 200–202
    church membership, 6, 13–14, 25, 27–28, 30–31, 33, 39, 42, 47, 56, 62, 64, 99–100, 151–3, 158–59, 162–63, 165, 178, 180, 184–90, 192–203, 210, 217, 226–27, 241, 252, 259–60, 274, 278, 286
  Church of England, 25–27, 30–32, 54–55, 57–61, 64, 66, 83–84, 100, 171, 185–90, 193–95, 201, 208–9, 241, 287; *see also* Anglicans
  Church of Scotland, 9, 11, 240
  colleges and universities
    Cambridge University, 187, 191
    Christ Church College Oxford, 73, 84
    Hackney (Congregational) College, London, 6
    Hackney (Unitarian) College, London, 285
    King's College London, 248
    Lancashire Independent College, Manchester, 160
    Oxford University, 32, 44, 45, 73, 84
    University of Massachusetts, 98
  confessions/declarations of faith, ch. 1, 41–42, 249
    Belgic, 8
    English Congregation in Geneva, 8
    First Basel, 8
    French, 8
    Geneva, 8, 160, 180
    London, 67, 69
    Savoy, 6, 12–13, 42, 70, 84, 182–84, 283
    Scots, 8, 14, 188
    Second Helvetic, 8, 11, 180
    Second London, 42, 279
    Smyth's, 92
    Standard, 42
    Twentieth-century, 9, 18, 150
    Westminster, 8, 10–12, 16, 70, 84, 182, 283
Congregationalism/ists, 3, 6–7, 9–10, 12, 14, 16, 25–29, 31–32, 40–42, 44–46, 52, 61, 65, 67–70, 72, 75, 81–82, 84, 111, 119, 122, ch. 8, 209, 211, 213, 216, 220, 223, 240–42, 246–47, 263, 274, 279, 287
cross, 6, 17–20, 27, 34, 41, 101, 107, 109, 112, 115, 127–28, 134, 136, 144, 179, 224, 253–56, 269–73, 276–79, 281–83, 285, 288–90
Cumberland Presbyterian Church, 9

dialogue, 5, 47, 148, 176, 193, 207, 212–14, 217, 222, 226
Disciples Ecumenical Consultative Council, 213
Dissenters, 3, ch. 2, ch. 3, 83, 93, 101, 110, 186, 194, 208
docetism, 6

ecclesiology, ch. 7, ch. 8
ecumenism, 17, 19, 47, 100–101, 144, 148, 154, 163, 176, 185, 189–90, 193, 202–3, ch. 9, 278
election, 11, 171, 176, 179–80, 183–84, 193, 198, 202, 288
epistemology, 53–57, 63, 67, 73, 84–86, 101, 121–23, 125, 129, 135, 290
eschatology, ch. 10, 286

Index of Subjects

eternity, 243–62
ethics. *See* morality
experience, 6, 17, 39, 126, 128–36, 170, 225, 234, 256, 261–62, 275, 282, 284, 289–90

Fifth Monarchy Men, 25, 240, 241
Free Church of Scotland, 10, 11

gospel, 1, 7, 15–18, 20, 24, 36, 40, 42, 44, 52, 56, 60–61, 70–71, 74, 85–86, 88, 92, 106, 109, 110–11, 115, 127, 137, 143–44, 151–58, 160, 163–67, 170, 172, 184, 189, 191, 193–94, 196, 211, 219, 223–26, 229, 245–46, 248, 256, 258–60, 271–74, 276, 278, 281, 285, 287, 290

Holy Spirit, 8, 12–14, 16, 18–19, 27, 38, 45, 72, 74, 100–101, 109–10, 115, 120, 127, 129, 133–34, 136, 143, 149, 153–57, 159, 161–62, 164–65, 168, 170, 172, 179–81, 183–84, 187, 193, 196, 199, 200, 202–3, 216, 218, 220–21, 223–25, 229, 238–39, 243, 249, 256, 273, 275
hymns, 6, 46–47, 102, 111, 129, 182, 198, 211, 261, 263, 284

idealism/ists, 95, 123–25, 224, 281
incarnation, 17, 19, 109, 127, 183, 214, 224, 282–83
International Congregational Council, 119
intolerance
 methodological, 95–8
 socio-political, 98–100

judgment, 243–52

Keswick Concention, 242
knowledge, 14, 27, 33, 53, 55, 61, 74, 84, 95, 97, 121–22, 129–30, 135–6, 159, 191, 221, 223, 252, 262, 275, 287–88

language, 20, 54, 125, 129–30, 132–33, 136, 148, 207, 210, 215–16, 184, 189–90
Latitudinarians, 84, 246
letters, 32–35
Lutherans, 153, 209, 213

Mennonite World Council, 213
Methodism/ists, 166–67, 188, 190, 211–12, 225, 242, 250, 261
Methodist World Council, 213
millenarianism, 235–42
ministry, 15, 39, 43, 150, 153, 164–65, 167, 171, 176, 183, 198, 200, 208, 216, 224, 226, 251, 270, 279, 280, 282
morality, 7, 11, 20, 55–56, 63, 73, 91, 94, 101, 106, 109–10, 118, 121, 125, 130, 132–33, 135–36, 149, 150, 167–72, 199, 228, 240, 245, 248, 252, 257, 269, 271, 275, 278, 280, 282, 289–90

natural law, 52, 56, 73–74, 149
natural theology, 135, 157, 270

Oriental Orthodox Church, 214
Orthodox Churches, 214

Platonists, 53, 247, 253, 269, 282
 Cambridge Platonists, 53–54, 56–57, 211, 223
Plymouth Brethren, 241
polemical tracts, 29–32
preaching, 7, 20, 27, 32, 40, 43, 58, 62, 74, 88, 109–10,

303

Index of Subjects

preaching (*cont.*)
129, 148–49, 154, 157–58, 164–67, 172, 179, 184, 188, 190, 196, 211, 240, 241, 244, 250, 254, 259–61, 263, 282, 284, 288
Presbyterian Church of Canada, 9
Presbyterian Church of England, 9, 195, 201
Presbyterians/ism, 7, 9–12, 15–16, 18, 24–26, 29–32, 40, 42, 44, 46, 61–62, 68–70, 75, 82, 119, 121, 137, 147, 150, 178, 186, 195, 201, 208, 214, 240, 245, 287
Puritans, 3, 14, 16, 24, 41, 43–44, 61, 71, 81, 171, 185, 218, 240, 250, 261, 270–71, 278

Quakers, 25, 31–35, 44, 62, 71–72, 75, 82–83, 129, 195–96, 211, 244

rationalism, 121, 135
reason, 55–56, 84–85, 89, 115, 120–22, 129, 134–35, 137, 247, 249
reception, 207, 208, 210, 212, 215–24
Re-formed Association of Churches of Christ, 213
regeneration, 115, 156, 161, 176, 179–81, 183–84, 189, 192, 198, 202, 226, 246
religion
relevance of, ch. 5
and instrumentalism, 108–12
religious experience, 131–32, 136, 211, 256
revelation, 6, 13, 14, 17, 97, 120–22, 125, 134–35, 144, 165, 255, 257, 269–72, 275–81, 283, 285–86, 288–89

Roman Catholics, 5, 10, 24, 26–27, 58–59, 61–64, 72, 75, 83, 85–88, 100, 148, 153–55, 160, 170, 172, 185, 209, 212–13, 215–19, 221–22, 238–39, 242, 248, 259, 282

sacraments, 149, 160–63, 172, 179, 188, 193, 219, 224, 226
baptism, 42, 152, 161–63, 176, 181, 183, 189, 213, 219, 226–27, 238
Lord's Supper, 46, 152, 160–63, 165, 167, 183, 189–90, 194, 197, 201 228, 263
saints, 3, 7, 18–20, 24–25, 27–29, 36, 40, 44, 61, 70–71, 74, 80, 102, 110–11, 115, 141, 143–44, 153, 155, 159, 163, 171, 176, 179–84, 187–88, 190–99, 201–3, 214–15, 219, 225–29, 235–36, 238, 240, 251, 253, 255–56, 258, 260–63, 276–78, 283
Scripture. *See* Bible
Second Cumberland Presbyterian Church, 9
sectarianism, 15, 19–20, 58, 85, 95–96, 99, 100–101, 111, 122, 137, 144, 176, 193, 202–3, 208, 219–20, 223, 228, 278
Separatists, 3, ch. 2, ch. 3, 110, 162, 171, ch. 8, 208, 228
sermons, 39–41, 58, 61–62, 87, 114, 129, 158–59, 164–65, 167, 258–61, 263, 287
Socinians, 64, 75, 81, 246
systematic, ch. 11

theism, 131
toleration, 3, 26, 30–31, ch. 3, ch. 4, 121, 178, 208–9

304

Toleration Act, 23, 25–26, 64, 69, 120, 208
Trinity, 7–9, 15, 18, 20, 29, 88, 120, 178, 238, 273, 283–84, 286

union with Christ, 151–53, 170, 176, 179, 182–84, 198, 202, 255–56, 258
Unitarians/ism, 9, 16, 26, 83, 121, 123, 209, 285–87
United Church of Canada, 9
United Church of Christ, 9
United Presbyterian Church of Scotland, 9, 11
United Presbyterian Church USA, 18
United Reformed Church, 83, 195, 201, 213
utilitarianism, 88, 91

verification principle, 130–31

Westminster Assembly, 12, 42, 67, 69–70, 75, 82, 178
World Alliance of Reformed Churches, 150, 213
World Council of Churches, 106, 171, 184
World Presbyterian Alliance, 119, 150
worship, 3, 16, 19, 23, 25–26, 30–31, 46, 47, 52–53, 57, 59, 70–75, 83–84, 90, 109, 111, 114, 119–20, 128, 144, 149, 157, 160, 168, 183, 186–87, 194, 196–97, 201–2, 208, 211, 235, 240, 258, 263, 272, 276–78, 283, 284–85, 289

www.ingramcontent.com/pod-product-compliance
Lightning Source LLC
Chambersburg PA
CBHW070059020526
44112CB00034B/1629